RISE OF THE BLACK SERIAL KILLER

Documenting a Startling Trend

SECOND EDITION

JUSTIN COTTRELL

2015

RISE OF THE BLACK SERIAL KILLER
Documenting a Startling Trend

Cover by my buddy Chad.
All photographs are from the Associated Press, unless otherwise noted.

Second Edition
June 2015

Printed in the United States of America

RISE OF THE BLACK SERIAL KILLER

"*The Rise of the Black Serial Killer* is thoroughly-researched and powerful refutation to a heinous lie against European Americans. This book is more than information; it is ammunition."

—James Edwards
Host of The Political Cesspool Radio Show

"My friend Justin Cottrell has daringly confronted America with a willfully-ignored truth - Negro serial killers exceed their Caucasian counterparts in both numbers and body count. He has laid waste to the White-hater's cherished myth that serial murder is a peculiarly White sociopathy. *The Rise of the Black Serial Killer* is a much-needed iconoclasm."

—Winston Smith
Co-Host of The Political Cesspool Radio Show

Dedicated to the thousands of victims of the serial killers listed in this book, and to their families for keeping their memory alive.

Table of Contents

List of Tables and Charts

Acknowledgements

When the thoughts of publishing my research began percolating in my head, I was fearful of how this information would be received. A thousand different questions popped into my head. Would I be written off as a racist kook before people had even read my book? Would people look at me, a non-degreed nobody, as the expert on the subject? How would my book be received by the victims' families and by the black community? Could this book possibly help prevent another serial killing?

At times, these questions and their implications would give me cold feet. But I was always encouraged to stay the course with every victim's life story I heard, by reading of the families who had been left without their loved one, and by many dear friends who told me that these stories must be told. Therefore, I owe a debt of gratitude to the few brave media channels and countless internet sites that were not afraid to carry these stories. I thank the families who shared their strength, grief, struggles, and triumphs due to these adverse situations.

I will never forget the day I first told my best buds the full depth of my research. They knew I had dabbled in the subject a little, but they did not know to what extent I had gone. That fateful night, they encouraged me not to horde the information any longer, but to let the world know without fearing the fallout that might occur. To Chad and Daniel, I lift my stein to you guys and am grateful for the many encouraging conversations we have had.

After telling my wife of the encouragement my friends had given me, she became my biggest supporter. Her assistance in making sure things ran smoothly while I wrote, as well as being my daily sounding board, was an enormous help. To my bride, I thank you, and I could not have made it this far without your kind heart and daily encouragement.

There are countless others along the way who have given me encouragement and who passed names or stories to me which I would not have found on my own. Your help has been warmly received, and the importance of it is not to be underestimated. I would list each of you and your contributions, but that would be a work in itself. For those unnamed friends and supporters, I thank you.

I owe my gratitude and thanks to Dr. Michael Aamodt for kindly allowing me to exchange our databases with one another. Your knowledge of killers prior to 1960 helped to fill many voids in my early research.

Every book needs someone to provide technical advice. Two dear friends, Robert and Michael, offered their advice and criticism without hesitation. Aside from this, their interest in the subject and gentle pushing were very much appreciated. A hearty thanks to you, gentlemen, and to your contributions.

I owe a big thanks to my friend Ben, known affectionately as the grammar Nazi. Whenever I dared make a misstep in my grammar or syntax, which can be quite frequent, he was there to bring order with his meticulous eye. Thanks for helping me clean up my act.

A researcher is nothing without a competent research staff that methodically helps in analyzing data and uncovering stories. For this, my oldest two children have been a godsend. When their studies were finished, they were always willing when asked to help with sorting data, looking for duplicate names, and finding new leads. Both of you are fine young researchers who have an eye for detail and a bright future.

Lastly, a man is nothing without his faith and convictions. I praise the God of my forefathers, the Lord Jesus, for giving me a compassionate heart, a methodic eye for detail, and a love for story-telling. Most importantly, I am thankful for the drive He has put in my heart to uphold the faith of my fathers and not to sway in my beliefs in this era of political correctness, when convictions have bent the knee to compromise.

Justin Cottrell

Introduction

It started off as a simple challenge by someone on an internet forum. Find a few dozen black serial killers, or admit that whites comprise the majority of serial killers, if not all of them. We had had a heated debate about crime in America, and he had consented that blacks are vastly overrepresented in violent crime in comparison to whites. But he insisted that only whites were capable of crimes as heinous as serial murder.

Up until that time, like my challenger, I thought that serial killers were most always white, middle-class citizens who charmed ladies with their charisma and witty one-liners. I had seen numerous serial killing movies, read a few novels, and even read a few books that detailed some of the horrific crimes. Despite feeling that I had above-average knowledge of serial killers, I could only muster up one black serial killer, Wayne Williams. Yet I could ramble off almost two dozen white killers.

This challenge sparked a two-year search, either to prove or to disprove that black serial killers existed. What I found enthralled me, and I burned midnight oil for the first few nights in search of information. Within days of my search, I had a list of sixty-seven possible black serial killers from an online crime forum. After I spent a few late nights verifying the stories of each one, I had whittled the list down to fifty-seven black serial killers, after having dismissed two white men, one Hispanic man, and seven mass-murderers.

Feeling fairly confident that there were almost five dozen black serial killers, I went back to my challenger. Impressed, but not moved, he pointed out that the small number I found did not even touch the demographics for the black population in the US. In addition, he showed me that the number of white serial killers in America, as best as he could tell, was in excess of 700. I conceded to his point, but acknowledged that there could be several black serial killers which the creator of the list I had found had missed. So I dug deeper, and I have never stopped since.

Often spending hours trying to verify whether a killer was in fact a black serial killer, I would get stuck sometimes for days on one suspect. Other times I was able to verify several in a short time, because of well-written local news stories on them or detailed online court documents. Regardless of the time each took to verify, the process has always been the same.

Whether I was simply looking on my own, or chasing a lead given to me, first, I would verify the basic information: name, race, and whether the killer had murdered at least two people on different oc-casions, with a cool-down period between kills. Numerous internet lists I found had killers listed who recently had been cleared of their accused crimes with DNA evidence, while others were nothing more than suspects in the investigation, never charged with the crime. Aside from this, the internet lists I found were plagued with errant information, white killers, spree-killers, and mass-murderers; and on one occasion an investigator who had been investigating a serial killer was himself listed as a killer! Therefore, from the onset, I vowed to use a scientific, systematic process, trying to find information to support a suspected killer, then trying to disprove it before including the person on my list.

After I had determined that a suspect met the qualifications of a black serial killer, in the correct location and timeframe, I next looked for a confession, DNA evidence, or a solid conviction. If none of these existed, the suspect was released from my list as a definite serial killer, even if he was the best possible police suspect in the case. There is no hearsay on my list, no people there simply because of rumors or public suspicion. To falsely list someone in my database, in my mind, is a crime in itself. Instead, suspects that fall into this category went one of two directions: if police are certain the suspect is the killer and are trying to build a case, then he is listed as a suspected killer until proven innocent or guilty. So far, only two fit that description. However, if police do not have a case against a suspect, and it is likely they never will, I drop his name from my list altogether.

Methodically going over every bit of data, while time-consuming, is the only possible way to insure the database is accurate. In doing so, I have removed at least four names from my list that often appear in online lists, men who have been released from prison and cleared of any such crime as a result of DNA evidence. In each of those cases, the DNA evidence did point to another killer, who was then either added to my list or already a member.

Following these stringent guidelines, my database steadily grew. No one was more surprised than I was when I hit 100 confirmed killers within a few weeks of starting my search. Three months later, I hit 200, and thought that was surely the limit. Another year later, after months without growth, the number climbed rapidly to 300, with no signs of slowing even as I eclipsed the 400 mark in July of 2011. About this time, I set a ceiling height of 600, thinking that was the theoretical limit. Now, in 2015, the database is nearing the 1,000 mark, and it will steadily grow in my continual search of old records and as new killers are added. As of this writing, there are three serial killers for whom police are searching in different parts of the country, who are each described as black males and who all began killing in 2011. Aside from this, cold cases across the nation are slowly being solved by advances in DNA technology. As names are released or new killers surface, their stories will be verified, and if they meet the qualifications, they will be added.

Unfortunately, my original challenger backed away soon after I presented the list of fifty-seven and let him know that I was still on the hunt. I do not know if he was afraid of what I might find, or if he simply lost interest. He would be pleased to know that not only does the data meet the demographics of blacks in the US, but it far surpasses it, and in fact shows that they are greatly overrepresented when compared to the portion of the population they represent.

After embarking on this journey, it did not take long before I started reading stories about the victims. This helped keep things in perspective. No longer was I just uncovering data that has been ignored or suppressed by academia and the media. I was helping tell the world about these killers' crimes while learning the tragic stories of thousands of lives that had been extinguished. No longer were they to be just a sad statistic; instead, their tragic deaths were my motivation to continue researching in my small attempt to curb the rising number of serial killers.

Occasionally it was the death of a young child that helped keep me going. Other times, it was a young woman who was forced for whatever reason into prostitution, lured to her last sale for a quick buck. More than once, it was someone's grandmother bludgeoned to death as she lay sleeping her last night, after having seen her family for the last time. Regardless of who it was, their stories kept me interested in this subject.

"Something has to be done; their stories have to be told," is what I kept telling myself. Therefore, this book's primary purpose is to slow this growing trend. I could not care less if, in the process of telling this story, the contents of this book step on the toes of the media or offend people because of what my research has uncovered. My intent is not to offend, but to bring awareness to this problem. I am simply a deliverer of facts, statistics, and stories.

If, throughout the course of this book, you feel that I am a bigot, racist, finger-pointer, or tattletale, take a moment to reflect. It could have been your loved one who was a victim of one of these killers. I was not the judge, jury, or even part of the investigation team. I am merely a documenter, picking up the facts and presenting them to the world. As my mother taught me, sometimes the truth hurts. While I am not meaning pain or stress on any person or group, the research found in this book will open eyes to trends, media bias, double standards, racism, and the grandiose scheme of wiping not-so-politically-correct stories under the rug.

Before diving in, I have got to answer one nagging question which is posed to me quite frequently. I have been asked numerous times, by both whites and blacks: "Why is a white guy interested in black serial killers?" Oftentimes they add, "Are you a racist?" or "Are you trying to hurt blacks?"

The truth is, quite simply, that I found the subject fascinating. It was as if I hit a goldmine of data that had never been mined. I am simply filling a void no one else has attempted to properly fill. If, in the beginning, I found someone had already done the footwork and presented the information, I would have been just as happy purchasing his book and learning from him. Likewise, if instead of this void in black serial killers, I had found a void in some crime involving whites, I would have dug in just as hard. As a lifelong researcher and story-teller, the thrill of finding information and retelling stories was my only interest.

As for the charge of racism, I often scratch my head and then laugh. Nowhere in the course of history has presenting factual data been considered racist, until our modern times. My motive is not to belittle the black race, nor to present them in a negative light. True, there have been members of the black race who have committed unimaginable crimes. Likewise, I will be the first to admit that my race has had its fair share of serial killers, mass-murderers, spree-killers, and other violent deviants of whom I am not proud. These are facts all people at some point have to admit: their people, tribe, or race has had both success as well as failure; it is not an example of racism. Serial killers of every stripe and color are the nadir of humanity, a low point which should be seen as a total failure; but that does not mean that this minority within humanity has to outweigh the accomplishments and successes each race has made.

In our politically correct society, everyone is too quick to pull the race card. On one hand, if I had chosen never to publish this data, and a group of black activists had stumbled onto my research via some internet site, I would have been labeled a racist for not feeling the subject was important enough to produce. On the other, I am a racist for presenting the data. All I can say is this: read the facts and stories I present, and then draw your own conclusions. If you do this with an open mind, I am positive you will realize something has to be done to help stop this problem.

While on the subject, one thing to note is the titles I have chosen to use concerning the different races. Just in the course of my lifetime, the terminology black people have been called has changed numerous times. In the not-too-distant past, the terms "Negro" and "Colored" were considered respectful, but by the time I was born, they were on the wane but still in use by the older generation of blacks. Soon after, "black" was the term of choice, but later fell to "Afro-American," which quickly gave way to "African-American," and is sure to change again someday. However, the modern term assumes too much and provides too little in return.

I have chosen to use the term "black" for a variety of reasons. Chief to me is fairness: for instance, I have used "white" for myself, instead of "European-American" or "Caucasian." But my using both "white" and "black" stemmed first as a matter of simplicity. With the frequency with which each term is used, it would make the text arduous for the reader to stumble over lengthy appellations, when a simple one-word solution is more efficient and still expresses the intended message. This precedent has already been established in other books on criminology, where their authors have had the same conviction; and because many prison and court records still use the simple one-word classification system, I have followed their stead.

Lastly on the subject, I once called a black man "African-American," only to have him correct me and tell me that he was Jamaican, as well as that some in his country would be insulted to be referred to as "African-American." He recommended that I use "black," because it covered all the bases, regardless of the country of origin from which a black person hails. I have asked numerous blacks from a variety of locations in this country, and the general consensus was that "black" was not a demeaning term but actually solved the problem of properly addressing black people of non-African descent. This helped tremendously, because there are a few of the serial killers in my database who are non-African in ancestry but still black, as well as a small handful who are from the Caribbean. While the latter do trace their ancestry to Africa, the former would be highly insulted to be called "African-American." Again, "black" is more than adequate, just as "white" is fine to represent anyone of European or Aryan descent, regardless of their ancestors' country of origin. Personally, it pains me to have to explain so lengthily a simple choice to make the reading of this book easier. But I am sure that, if I had not, then my e-mail inbox would be full of negative e-mails demanding that I apologize. Hopefully this will drastically reduce the number of hecklers, and people will instead focus on my work, not getting hung up on the designation I chose to use.

Before diving into the data, I must make one more mention. This book covers only black serial killers in the United States. There are numerous examples in South Africa, Liberia, Brazil, Europe, and other parts of Africa. I have researched a little into some of these countries and have thought of someday documenting some of these crimes. However, at this time, there is a large degree of difficulty in doing so. For instance, out of the continent of Africa, South Africa keeps the best documentation, but oftentimes murders go unreported (especially against the Boers), or the murderers are let off because of technicalities and they fall off the radar. The problem in Liberia and other African countries is even worse, where after years of civil wars their record-keeping is subpar at best. As for Europe, the problems presented are the result of having numerous countries which do not always have their records online; this would necessitate a lengthy and expensive trip for research. Trust me: even when restricting the database to America, this has been a daunting task in itself. I am perfectly happy to have kept my research confined to my country.

It is my hope that this work initiates others to dive into this subject, to help bring awareness to the masses. And as previously mentioned, it is also my hope that the number of serial killers, regardless of their race, will decline, and that the killing of innocent people at their hands will cease.

May your journey to better understand this topic be a joyful one, despite the painful stories you will read.

Enjoy.

Introduction 2015

After publishing the first edition of this book in 2012, I never imagined the response I'd have up to this point. While it had a few minor typos and formatting errors. Not to mention there were a few killers I'd missed in my research. The book has still been an underground success. While slow and steadily received, it's been quoted on the national news, in news blogs, newspapers, radio shows, and is even used as the chief reference for black serial killers in some universities.

But most importantly the stories have gotten out. I've had victim's families thank me, which made my efforts worth every hour spent in research. Law enforcement officers in two states have contacted me thanking me for bringing awareness to the subject, including one that arrested one of the killers in this book. Another retired officer thanked me after he realized I told the story of an inmate he'd watched as a jailer. A professor has highly recommended my book to his students. Other authors have quoted me in their books on crime. Talk show radio hosts have quoted it and recommended people get a copy. Random black people have contacted me, thanking me for bringing awareness to this oft ignored topic. All of these things are an honor I never imagined when I started my research. An honor for which I am grateful for.

Getting this second edition released was no small feat. I thought originally I'd have it finished in towards the middle of 2013, but life got in the way. In between the chaotic nature of being self-employed and raising a family, I managed to slowly recheck and verify every fact listed. Unfortunately along the way I managed to find more black serial killers. A few I'd missed in my original search, others surfaced on a monthly basis. So many new black serial killers in fact, I'm sure by the end of this summer there will be at least 8-12 that will surface that will have to wait for the 3rd edition. It's a problem that's not going away, and sadly with the constant race agitating by the media, it has the appearance of picking up speed.

Aside from adding 139 names to this book, I've also made attempts to silence my critics. One such critic, without ever reading my book, dismissed it due to what he called a thin bibliography. As I told him, I could have listed the over 11,000 newspapers and news websites I used, but that would've been a book in itself! Instead I listed a few of my chief news sources, and added additional books I used in researching the subject. I'm quite sure the same guy still won't be satisfied, but I can't win them all. Regardless I'm confident this edition is sound factually, has more references, and has less typographical errors.

My prayer is this book will make it into the hands of every law enforcement officer, judge, criminologist, crime professor, district attorney, psychologist, and news reporter in the land. Not to say, "I told you so!" But instead to be a wealth of information on the subject, in hope it'll prevent further senseless murders. Not only this, but I still have hopes my research will motivate others to pick up on the subject and expand where I've failed, or possibly to write biographies on some of the killers in this book.

Enjoy, and may the memories of the victims of the serial killers in this book never be forgotten. Regardless of who they were, or where they lived, they were someone's child and didn't deserve the cruel deaths they received. May they rest in peace.

Justin Cottrell, June 2015

Chapter 1

The General Perception of Black Serial Killers

Ask the average person about his serial killer knowledge, and almost predictably most will give a similar answer. They will name a few, perhaps as many as ten, but almost exclusively they will recollect only white killers. Amongst the names, you will hear of the monstrous crimes of Jeffrey Dahmer, John Wayne Gacy, Albert Fish, Ted Bundy, Gary Ridgway, to name a few—but nary a black name, save, occasionally, the mention of Wayne Williams or the Beltway Snipers. Comically, some will even name fictional characters like Hannibal Lecter and Buffalo Bill from the hit movie *The Silence of the Lambs* as real serial killers, and draw blanks as to serial killers of any non-white race. Even in cities such as Los Angeles or Detroit, where serial killings are the highest, citizens can rarely name a black serial killer.

Why is this? For decades, Americans have been enthralled by the gory subject of serial killers; as such, they should be able to name a few of the most famous black killers. Yet the problem is not a lack of black serial killers, but instead the ignorance that serial killers can be of another race. Most people assume they must exist but, when pressed, can offer no proof that they do, and thus, in their minds, blacks must be underrepresented in the annals of serial killers in the United States. It is the old adage: what I can't see must not exist.

When I engage people on the subject, they inevitably want to know how many there are, and how bad their crimes were. Before I offer any answers, I usually pose a question first:

GA. DIAG. & CLASS. CTR.
JACKSON, GA

WILLIAMS W JAN 31

How many black serial killers do you think have existed in America, and what do you think their average number of victims was?

After pondering for a moment, most usually posit that perhaps fifteen, and maybe as many as thirty, have ever existed in America, with probably an average kill count of three. Some suggest four would be the absolute ceiling. But when they hear the real statistics, they are always stunned. I get looks of shock, horror, doubt, surprise, and even disgust, with most asking how I can be positive. I go into detail about the data, and give an explanation to why the number is so high. Fortunately, most people walk away satisfied that they have learned a new tidbit of information. On rare occasions, probably less than one percent of the time, ridicule and name calling are dished out, and the facts are discredited as racist. While this is the minority opinion for those with whom I have spoken, it still exists and is surprisingly most often dished out by whites, not blacks. Most blacks with whom I have spoken are not ecstatic to hear what I have to say, but they accept it, because they are already well aware of the high murder rate among blacks in their neighborhoods and communities. Therefore, they are not ordinarily surprised or offended when shown the information. One kind black lady even told me, "I've always been told blacks are too stupid to be serial killers. I guess that theory is wrong." I agreed and told her that most serial killers are of average intelligence and do not stand out in a crowd, regardless of their race. They hide in plain sight; otherwise they would be unsuccessful and caught after their first murder or two.

The truth is that black serial killers do exist, and in much higher numbers than most people would ever imagine. It is not highly speculative to posit this idea, either. The annals of American history have left an ample supply of source material via court records and media reports to validate this proposition, yet, for the most part, these are overlooked, forgotten, ignored, or suppressed to keep this closely-guarded secret hidden.

This perception changed slightly, however, after John Muhammad and Robert Malvo were apprehended in Washington, D.C., for the Beltway Sniper attacks in 2002. After the most intense manhunt in U.S. history, the killers' identities were revealed, and to the embarrassment of the FBI criminal profilers and media outlets, which had everyone on the lookout for a white killer, the killers were black.

Within hours of their discovery, the news media began interviewing black citizens and professionals as to their opinion. Without exception, most of the responses were nearly the same. Blacks were shocked that a serial murderer could be black; they claimed to have never heard of such an atrocity. Here are a few examples of their reactions.

This is not typical conduct for us. I mean black folks do some crazy stuff, but we don't do anonymous violence. That's not in our history. We just don't do that.[1]

White guys have pretty much cornered the market on mass murders and serial killing.[2]

There aren't any black serial killers.[3]

"People were like, aw, he's black," said Christine Kendrick, 49, the black owner of the shop in Camp Springs, Md., a town close to where the arrested man once lived. "It doesn't make sense. It doesn't sound like our M.O."[4]

"When I first heard that they were African-American, I didn't believe it," said Dr. Karen W. Sigel, a white physician in Bethesda. "I felt they must have gotten the wrong guy. I guess we all have our own prejudices."[5]

While some answered with bewilderment, many blacks accepted that the killers were from their race. However, not every black accepted the killers' capture with joy. Some denied the allegations and shook them off as a case of mistaken identity. A black cab driver, who was a recent transplant from Kenya, told a journalist, "This sniper is no black man. The police are looking for a crazy white man. Someone like the Unabomber. Serial killings? Black people don't do that."[6]

The general consensus amongst blacks in the media, however, was acceptance, but at the same time shock that blacks could be responsible for serial murder, which is often thought of as the most heinous of crimes. Donna Britt, with the *Washington Post*, shared her discontent: "As thrilled as I am that suspects have been caught, I'm surprised by their blackness. Ted Kaczynski, John Wayne Gacy, Ted Bundy and others helped me to feel as culturally distanced from those who commit serial murders as I've felt personally outraged by 'brothers' who've shot innocents during drug drive-bys."[7]

Like most blacks, Mrs. Britt had felt that her people were distant from serial killers and that the capture of the Beltway Snipers was an aberration, possibly even a fluke or one-time event. Just as quickly as they had accepted that blacks were capable of serial killings, they dismissed the snipers' actions as the actions of individuals, and not a symptom of a greater problem. Further, in Mrs. Britt's article, she discounts the notion of black serial killers as a human problem: "That it's high time black folks became as adept as white people at accepting that those who look like them do unspeakable things. These individuals' actions don't 'reflect badly' on us as a group. They reflect badly on us all as human beings."[8]

While it is true that the serial killer is a human problem which does not just affect the white race, the failed old canard that the existence of black serial killers is now indicative of a human problem, not

Beltway Snipers

something that should cause concern within the black community, is just an effort to downplay the existence of black serial killers. As Phillip Jenkins wrote, "African-Americans make up a significant number of recorded serial killers, far above what might be expected from public perceptions and recollections."[9] Therefore, it is not at all an assault on the black community to posit this idea, but instead a call for awareness to help shed light on this rising epidemic.

While the capture of the Beltway Snipers stirred a quick fervor of research to find more black serial killers, it died quickly as people shook off this idea as simply a human problem. Now, almost a decade later, most of the general public is back to square one, assuming whites have the market on serial killings, thereby making it a white problem. In fact, there are some people who feel so strongly about this idea that they feel every white in America could possibly be the next big serial killer.

They will pop off with colorful quips like, "Watch out—he might go postal and be the next Bundy." While this is often said in fun, the implications are that whites are the ones who snap and go on for months or even years on serial killing sprees. No one says this about blacks, for fear of the ridicule or arguments which this statement might bring.

Law Enforcement

Those sworn to protect and uphold the law do not fare much better. Even officers who have taken criminology classes and have graduated with a degree typically will name ten to fifteen serial killers, but rarely name one who is black. If they do, it is back to Wayne Williams and the Beltway Snipers, or possibly one who was caught in their local area. None will acknowledge that black serial killers exist in large numbers. But this is not a part of a grand conspiracy: police know that blacks commit violent crime, but they just assume that blacks are responsible for gang-related murders or one-time murder events, not serial murders.

When a serial killer strikes a black neighborhood, oftentimes the police assume the first few victims are a result of gang violence or random crime. Phillip Jenkins documented this phenomenon: "If you have a body that turns up in the street, and it's black, the cops usually say, it's a gang thing and not the victim of a serial killer."[10] Because of this assumption, in many cases additional victims are killed before police realize they are dealing with a serial murderer. There are cases when it takes a dozen or more black victims before police admit they have got a serial killer, whereas if the victims are white, they are prone to suspect a serial killer after just a few bodies turn up. This is not because of racist cops, but instead because they falsely assume both that most serial killers are white and that serial killers always kill within their race. The black community has not failed to notice this problem, either. With almost every capture of a black serial killer, they show their frustration, as this gentleman did when Antwan Pittman was captured: "If it was someone of a different race, things would have been dealt with the first time around; it wouldn't have taken the fifth or sixth person to be murdered. All these women knew each other and lived in the same neighborhood; this is the sign of a potential serial killer. When it didn't get the kind of attention it needed, it made the African-American community frustrated."[11]

Another common assumption by police, especially when a black prostitute goes missing (a common victim of black serial killers), is that the person will return home when she feels like it or when her drug-induced high dissipates. This was clearly illustrated after the discovery of eleven black women's bodies in Anthony Sowell's home in 2009. "They belittled it and made jokes," said Barbara Carmichael about her repeated and failed efforts to file a missing-person report about her daughter Tonia, whose body was the first of the eleven found in Mr. Sowell's house to be identified this week. "They told me to wait a while because she would return once all the drugs were gone."[12]

But even after a black female drug addict or prostitute's body is found, oftentimes police suspect the foul play may be because of a dispute over drugs or sex. Prostitutes are berated by customers who want to beat women, or who pay for sex and then kill the prostitute to get their money back. Some of these men continue this behavior, while for others it is just a one-time event. Aside from this, when a body is found and there is evidence of drugs in its system, unless there are apparent signs of murder, police initially assume it is an overdose. Therefore, it is not until police have numerous examples of unsolved murders, in some cases as many as a dozen or more, that they consider the murders may be as a result of a serial killer. Oftentimes it is after the medical examiner finds the evidence of foul play connecting several deaths.

As a result of these actions, police usually take a bad rap as being racist or uncaring towards the black community. A black police officer who was responsible for helping bring down Eddie Lee Mosley, suspected of killing thirty-three black women in Florida, touched on the subject. He believed that had Mosley killed white ladies, he would have been caught quickly, but since he was raping and murdering blacks, he was ignored. In an interview he said, "Mosley was bigger than Gacy. Bigger than Bundy. But he wasn't doing college girls. And he wasn't hiding the corpses under his house. He was doing it in neighborhoods where nobody cared."[13]

However persuasive his argument might appear, this dilemma has a twofold explanation. First, in certain areas, such as the neighborhoods where Mosley hunted his prey, are often so rife with crime and other murders that police most often are overburdened with a heavy case log. As a result, it is not so much that a murder victim's killer is ignored, but that he is prioritized by the order in which the report is received. Couple this with the renowned tendency of citizens in this type of neighborhood's refusal to talk with police, or even testify against a murderer, and the end result is that police often are left with unsolved murders. In other interviews, this same officer even admitted his department was overloaded with murders that were more easily solved, while Mosley's took a serious commitment of energy and resources the department sometimes did not have. He also mentioned that many of Mosley's victims were found in a severely decayed state; twice just the skulls were found. While he alluded that his department was overloaded with cases during this time, he acknowledged that a freshly killed victim, where police had a better chance of catching the killer with DNA evidence, took precedence over skeletal remains, where the killer's DNA was likely nonexistent.

But an even bigger part of this picture is that police in general have a perception that black serial killers are a rare occurrence; consequently, they do not usually consider them to be an option when investigating their crimes. Combine this with the unwillingness of witnesses to cooperate with police—as the chief witness in Anthony Sowell's case did, when she took thirty-six days after he attempted to rape her, before she went to police—and it becomes clear that the answer is not that police do not care, nor that they are racist, but instead that they are trying to solve

Anthony Sowell

crimes with what information they have available. Coupled with their assumption that a black is more likely to be a spree-killer or mass-murderer than a serial killer, and it is little wonder why police are left scratching their heads when the bodies start turning up in their town, left behind by a black serial killer.

But this all depends upon the municipality involved, and the department's history with dealing with serial killers, too. Police in Detroit or Chicago, who have dealt with their fair share of black serial killers, upon discovering two to three unsolved murders of black victims in close proximity, are more than likely to consider a black serial killer. Contrarily, in a city that has never had a black serial killer, police may not believe they have one until the body count is higher and evidence or eyewitness reports point to the identity of the killer. However, even in cities such as Los Angeles, which have vast experience in this area, if a black serial killer spreads his victims over a large area, it further confuses investigators, making police sometimes slow to accept the possibility of a black serial killer.

There are numerous other factors involved, and I am not trying to make a case that police are inefficient in their work, only that most officers and investigators are used to dealing with black murderers who kill in one event. It is what they have been taught and what the media and Hollywood portray, and until they either learn by experience or research about the reality of black serial killers, they will continue to assume their significance is diminutive.

Now, this problem does not happen just at the bottom level, with patrolling officers and detectives, but is instead an upper-management problem, carried from top to bottom in every law enforcement agency in the country. Notwithstanding, the Federal Bureau of Investigation, which has set the standard of what a serial killer is and is not, is most often the source of this belief.

When a municipality realizes they have a serial murderer roaming the streets, the FBI is one of the first calls they make. Their serial murderer division has helped police profile numerous serial killers and keeps the most up-to-date database of serial murderers in the world. However, their serial killer profiling techniques have failed numerous times, because of their assumption that serial murders are restricted to white males, twenty to forty-five years old. Vaughn Orrin Greenwood and Edward Arthur Surratt are leading examples of the numerous cases in which FBI profilers gave a description of a deranged white killer, when in reality the killer was black.

The FBI agent who coined the term "serial killer," Robert Ressler, has shown the bias FBI profilers have with serial killers on numerous occasions. When asked to testify in the case of Henry Louis Wallace, who was black and killed at least ten black women, he had this to say in 1996: "Here, we have a black man killing black victims. There are very few non-white serial killers."[14]

When Los Angeles was faced with trying to sort out the Southside Slayings, which would later prove to be the work of at least five to six black serial killers, Ressler confirmed what he had said three years prior: "There's so few of them. There's almost nothing to study there."[15]

While Agent Ressler did much to help investigators track down white serial killers with his profiling theories, he surely knew better about black serial killers. He had access to the largest database of serial killers in the world, which has among its ranks a few hundred black members. He was still with the FBI when Atlanta police sought help in developing a profile for the Atlanta Child Murders, of which Wayne Williams would later be accused. It was under Ressler's lead that the FBI corrected the Atlanta police and issued a profile describing a black male killer that would later fit Williams perfectly. Why, then, did he not inform the court properly? The only answer that can be surmised is, perhaps, that he was afraid of being labeled a racist or a victimizer of blacks.

However, in the years since Ressler's retirement, the FBI's stance changed after the Beltway Snipers were apprehended. They had made an embarrassment of themselves by profiling the snipers as white, which had hundreds of officers searching for a thirty-five-year old white male in a white minivan. As a result of this public failure, they slowly began revising their approach to profiling killers by not ruling out the possibility that other races were capable of serial murder.

Indicative of their reaction was Robert McCrie, who was chairman of the Department of Law, Police Science, and Criminal Justice Administration at John Jay College in New York City: "We are surprised about his race because the public bought too readily impressions that were offered by some of the profiling pundits. Profiling makes wonderful movie material, but as a way of helping police solve complex crime, the profiling approach doesn't offer much."[16]

Candice Skrapec, an assistant professor of criminology at Fresno State University, agreed: "This reminds us that we cannot put too much stock in a profile because it could send us in the wrong direction." Not only did she say that; she also recognized that she had been wrong. "For the most part, except for race, my profile was very accurate. I, too, was thinking in terms of a white male."[17]

Being the authoritative agency on serial murder, the FBI realized something had to be done. Their theories, which had worked great on profiling infamous white killers like Ted Bundy and John Wayne Gacy, were now suspect to racial bias, which meant people were dying needlessly because of their standard one-size-fits-all serial killer profile. As of 2008, their latest release on serial murders, they added this verbiage at a symposium on serial murder. "Contrary to popular belief, serial killers span all racial groups. There are white, African-American, Hispanic, and Asian serial killers. The racial diversification of serial killers generally mirrors that of the overall U.S. population."[18]

While the latter part of this statement is in error, at least they now publically recognize killers as coming in all colors, sexes, and creeds (covered in Chapter 5). Now the task is for police departments to begin accepting this idea instead of holding on to the tired maxim they were once taught. From what I can tell, some larger cities have already begun taking steps to consider a black suspect just as quickly as a white when serial murder surfaces.

Books about Serial Killers

One would expect that if anyone could accurately track the number of black serial killers, it would be authors who write on the subject. The good news is that Philip Jenkins plowed a portion of this field in 1993, and has since had assistance from other authors, such as Anthony Walsh and Michael Newton, in including information about black serial killers in their books. Despite their valiant efforts, it has taken almost two decades for their work to be accepted, but even now at times it is ignored.

In the late nineties, it was commonplace for authors to disregard black serial killers as an infrequent anomaly. For example: "Serial killings are almost always committed by white males. There are very few blacks involved in this type of murder because class resentment is far more likely to occur to a person with a good education than someone without an appreciation of how society works. It is projected that as the education level of blacks improve there will be more black serial killers."[19] While the author did recognize how blacks would eventually commit serial murders, by the time his book was published in 1999, there were already hundreds of blacks who had been convicted of serial murder.

As of 2002, this problem was not any better, as many books on the subject either neglected to mention black serial killers or dismissed them as irregularities. A case in point can be found in a book that does mention Jake Bird, who was black, and one of the most prolific killers in America. "Jake Bird was an anomaly: he was an African-American serial killer. FBI profilers have determined that an overwhelming 85 percent of all serial killers are white males. Female and black serial killers are a rarity."[20] How the author can claim that 15% of serial killings are due to black and female killers, but then claim that black serial killers are rare, is disingenuous but all too common in books on serial murder.

Just as with the FBI, after the Beltway Snipers, authors writing on the subject began listening to Jenkins, Walsh, and Newton. Soon, others began to include their findings in their books. Now it is difficult to find a well-researched book on the subject of serial killers which does not mention their work. While this is great, the only problem is that they simply regurgitate what these men wrote almost two decades ago, without joining in the work and helping cultivate other parts of the field.

However, even as recently as 2011, even though these findings are now almost universally accepted, sometimes their research is dismissed on grounds that black killers are victimized because of race, instead of actually being guilty, as the following quote illustrates:

Walsh argued that despite the common criminological and public per-
ception of most serial killers being white, itself developed largely from
biased media portrayals and news reporting, there is actually an over-
representation of African American serial killers, and as such this must
be reported on truthfully. **However, we argue that black-on-black**
crime does not occur in such huge numbers as some would have you
believe, and in claiming that it actually is a common occurrence actu-
ally serves to mask black and minority ethnic victimization at the
hands of white offenders. *It does this via attention diversion strategies,*
as well as failing to raise questions about the criminal justice system
who not only fail to respond to the needs of black and minority ethnic
victims, but who also serve black and minority ethnic victims an ad-
ditional portion of oppression and victimization.[21] *[Emphasis mine]*

This ploy is not a new one, and it will be discussed in detail in chapter three. But even as late as 2011, Wayne Williams, a black man who was convicted of two murders (but is implicated in killing up to twenty-nine), is still considered a casualty of victimization and racism by some. He is not alone, though: similar cries have been made for Mark Goudeau, Harrison Graham, Vincent Darrell Groves, and numerous other black men who have been found guilty of serial killings. However, in each of these cases, and in numerous others where victimization or racism has been touted, DNA evidence, eyewitness accounts, physical evidence, and even confessions stand this canard on its sour head.

Despite occasional pleas of victimization and racism, for the most part, current authors are doing an excellent job by including information about black serial killers in their books. However, despite their valiant effort, the public perception is impacted to a greater extent by what Hollywood and the mainstream news media produce. This will be covered in the next chapter in detail, but it is another sad period in the annals of history that entertainers and biased reporters sway public attention more than facts and true stories. Therefore, the general public's perception on this issue is unlikely to change until what they view on television changes.

ENDNOTES

[1] White, T.,Willis, L.,& Smith, L., *African Americans grapple with race of sniper suspects: Relief at capture, worry about repercussions*, Baltimore Sun. October 25, 2002. Retrieved from http://articles.baltimoresun.com/2002-10-25/news/0210250165_1_serial-sniper-serial-killers-black.

[2] Charles, N., *Black serial killers: A rare breed*. Harlem Times, p. 1. November 2, 2002.

[3] Kimberley,M., *John Ashcroft and the bloodthirsty actions of a bible quoting prosecutor*. Black Commentator. November 20, 2003. www.blackcommentator.com/65/65_fr_justice.html.

[4] Holmes, Steven A., *The Hunt for a Sniper: An Assumption Undone; Many Voice Surprise Arrested Men Are Black*, New York Times, October 25, 2002.

[5] Ibid Holmes.

[6] Britt, Donna, *Racial Naiveté Emerges Amid Attacks*, The Spokesman Review, October, 25, 2002.

[7] Ibid Britt.

[8] Ibid Britt.

[9] Jenkins, P. *African Americans and serial homicide*. In R. Holmes & S. Holmes (Eds.),*Contemporary perspectives on serial murder*, p. 20, 1998.

[10] Ibid Holmes.

[11] Kotz, Pete, *Why the Media Loves Missing White Women (Hint It's Not Just Due to Race)*, True Crime Report, October 25, 2009, retrieved 1/6/2012: http://www.truecrimereport.com/2009/10/why_the_media_loves_missing_wh.p hp

[12] Urbina, Ian and Maag, Christopher, *After Gruesome Find, Anger at Cleveland Police*, New York Times, November 5, 2009.

[13] King, Jonathan, *Remembering the Dead; Obsessed with Justice*, Broward Bulldog, November 20, 2009.

[14] Associated Press, *Witness: Suspect Doesn't Fit Profile*, Morning Star, December 14, 1996. p. 8b.

[15] Lighty, Todd and Kiernan, Louis, *South Side Slayings Defy Myths About Serial Killers*, Chicago Tribune, August 10, 1999.

[16] Ibid Holmes.

[17] Ibid Holmes.

[18] *Serial Murder: Multi-Disciplinary Perspectives for Investigators*- Produced by the FBI in July 2008. http://www.fbi.gov/stats-services/publications/serial-murder.

[19] Falk, Gerhard, Murder, *An Analysis of It's Forms, Conditions, and Causes*, 1990, page 85.

[20] Wolcott, *Martin Gilman, The Evil 100*, 2002, page.129.

[21] Patel, Tina, *Tyrer David, Race, Crime and Resistance*, 2011, page. 135.

Chapter 2

Bias Against Reporting Black Serial Killers

Americans are impacted by what the mainstream media reports and what Hollywood produces, even if it is a pale comparison to what really takes place in the world. In the minds of millions, they have no need to doubt these experts, who entertain them with vivid stories and detailed special effects, but should simply sit back and enjoy the show. As a result, the public assumes these outlets are staffed by specialists who hold advanced degrees in reporting and story-telling; therefore they *must* tell the truth, especially when it concerns crime. The truth is that, regardless of the facts, there are some stories the media and entertainment industries choose to willingly ignore. They are considered "too hot to touch," and subsequently avoided or downplayed.

The Media

In this age of political correctness, the mainstream media is king in keeping their bias from ever stepping where they will be deemed racist or bigoted. While they claim their reporting is truthful and fair on all matters, the reality is that this is often not the case, especially when it comes to black crime. To most casual observers, most news broadcasts and newspapers are bare on the subject, which leaves the appearance that black violent crimes are an infrequent occurrence.

When thinking about this subject, I am reminded of a job I had years ago that required considerable travel. Having grown up in a law enforcement family, I was accustomed to hearing stories about black crime that often did not make the cut for the nightly news. When I would travel to cities that had a much higher black population than my hometown, I was amazed that the nightly news left viewers with the idea that their town did not have much crime. However, when I turned to the middle part of the paper—where the boring stories are put—it would be a different story: there would be stories about murders that did not pass muster to make the nightly news. However, more newsworthy crime stories, committed by white criminals, were front-page news, and always were placed at the front of the broadcast, unless the black criminal was abused in some manner or police brutality was suspected.

Consider the reporting surrounding the Rodney King debacle. Almost everyone in America and the civilized world knows the name of Rodney King, because of the media's pulling of the public's heart strings by over-reporting that he was a target of racism, police brutality, and victimization. While they cleverly refrained from discussing his criminal history, or the fact that he was threatening officers, they focused instead on how he was a victim of the white man's oppression and had been nearly beaten to death by four white cops. Nowhere did a major media outlet tell the public that Rodney was a major catalyst in provoking the police with his behavior and attitude, acting in such a threatening and combative manner that officers thought he was strung out on PCP.

In subsequent years, despite winning a 3.8-million-dollar lawsuit, when Rodney was arrested time and time again, and if the media actually chose to report, they downplayed the arrests and blamed each new event on the trauma he had received because of the white officers who had beat him in 1992. Everything surrounding Rodney was the white man's fault, even the environment in which he was raised, and even the terrible choices that he had made as an adult. Nowhere did the mainstream media suggest that Rodney was responsible for his behavior and should be required to answer for his missteps. Instead, in the next breath, they would let the world know the four white cops were responsible for their behavior and should be reminded continually of it.

Pit Rodney's story against Reginald Denny. Rodney's story sparked the infamous 1992 LA riots, which caused over one billion dollars in damages and cost at least fifty-three lives. In the midst of the chaos, a media helicopter captured the beating of Reginald, a white truck driver, as he was dragged out of his truck by black men. As the cameras rolled on live television, millions of viewers were horrified as they watched his head being beaten with a fire extinguisher as others kicked him repeatedly. Despite suffering permanent physical damage and being left for dead by the men, he did nothing to provoke the attack on him or his semi-truck.

Whilst the media trumpeted the race card for Rodney, when it came to Reginald, they ignored him in general and chose to use the same race card for his attackers. They were victims of the white man's tyranny, and were acting out their rage toward seeing Rodney's beating by white cops. The same tactic was used in explaining the actions of thousands of rioting blacks and Hispanics. Through the PC lens of the media, it appeared that in every action surrounding the LA riots, blacks were victims and not responsible for their actions, whereas all whites were guilty by association, simply because Rodney's attackers had been white.

In an even more telling twist in his story, in 1993, while still being pretty banged up, Reginald appeared on the Phil Donahue show with one of his attackers. It was expected of him to forgive and forget what had happened to him, and to show no malice towards his attackers. Contrast this with Rodney King, who, even today, when interviewed is allowed to say how disappointed he is with the LAPD, and is often asked leading questions to show how upset and unforgiving he is towards his assailants. So on the one hand, Reginald must be the better man and show humility and forgive his attackers publically, but on the other hand, Rodney is encouraged to hold a grudge against his attackers and be the poster child for white police brutality. Their tale is hardly a fair and balanced story: Rodney King the criminal is an unsung hero for taking a beating, while the innocent Reginald Denny is ignored and forgotten for taking an even worse beating.

The reader may wonder how this story ties in with black serial killers. The key is the media bias. The media uses the same tactics when reporting black serial killers, by downplaying the events and circumstances surrounding the killings. When reporting on a black serial killer, most often a tidbit will be added to the story describing how black sociopaths are rare, or that they do not fit the *modus operandi* for serial killers. It is usually as an aside or minor comment. A typical response might be "His type is rare," or "He doesn't fit the model of a serial killer." In saying this, the media leads the viewer to believe that the killer is in a rare, elite class not often frequented by blacks—that he must be an anomaly.

When news broke of the apprehension of George Waterfield Russell, Jr., in 1990, papers in the Northwest spun webs of this type of misinformation. Most fell back on the same tale: that he was an extraordinarily rare example of a serial killer. Even as late as 2003, this rumor was still being displayed in the Seattle Times: "Russell is an African American, unusual in the world of serial killers."[1]

Another example was seen when the *New York Times* broke the story of the capture of the Beltway Snipers. "Should police charge Mr. Muhammad and his young companion, this would be one of the few times a black person has been accused in the serial killings of whites. In this case, a number of blacks were killed as well."[2] The *Times* has one of the largest and easiest-to-use newspaper databases in the world. The reporter could have just done a simple search of their database, and it would have yielded numerous examples of black serial killers. Instead, the public was left with the impression that they hardly exist, because a seasoned reporter said so.

Misinformation is not the only tactic the media uses in their un-derreporting of this topic. An all-too-common but increasingly common practice is to not quote crime statistics whenever they pertain to blacks as the perpetrators. Fearing public attacks by black groups such as the NAACP,[3] they commonly refuse to release statistics that may portray blacks in a negative light. Instead, the viewer is left with the impression that the black mug shots they see on the nightly news are not symptomatic of a larger problem. In the rare event the media does tread into unwholesome waters and report on statistics, they are usually wise to use a black reporter and play the victim's card, or else risk severe public fallout.

But often, even without reporting statistics, the media fails to adequately detail the crimes committed when a black perpetrator is involved. Up until the mid-seventies, it was

Lonnie David Franklin

common practice for media outlets to list the race of suspected criminals, but with the exception of whites, that practice has fallen into the chasm of being racist. For instance, when white serial killers are apprehended, their picture flashes on every media screen in the country, but that is not the norm with blacks. While there are some instances when a black serial killer's identity will be shown in the national media outlet, as Lonnie David Franklin, his story is not the norm. Oftentimes the killer's picture is shown locally, but if the Associated Press picks up the story, it becomes back-page news with no photo or racial description.

When the story of Vincent Darrell Groves broke, few people outside the Denver area knew of his race or what he looked like. It was second-page news at best, and did not even warrant more than 250 words in most instances for Colorado papers. And with a name that would just as easily fit a white man, most people falsely assumed he was just another depraved white killer. However, if a white man had committed between fourteen and eighteen murders in brutal fashion as Groves did, his face would be as easily recognizable as Jeffrey Dahmer's or Ted Bundy's to the average American.

But this problem is applicable to a killer not only after he is apprehended, but also prior to his arrest. Take, for instance, the case of the Four Acres Homes Killer who plagued the Houston, TX, neighborhood and took the lives of up to ten black women. Despite being an almost entirely black neighborhood, and despite police telling the public that they were looking for a black male and even providing a physical description, the media in Houston oftentimes failed to give a description of the suspect. Instead, many of their reports told the concerned citizens that a serial killer was suspected, but they went no further. Rarely was race mentioned or the police sketch of the possible suspect given. This failure to give an accurate description made the general public go into default mode, looking for the blonde-headed, blue-eyed status quo.

This problem was documented by Dr. Schlesinger, who has been studying black serial killers since the mid-seventies: "That is a total, total myth that there are no black serial killers. There have been black serial killers for many, many years, but they haven't been publicized. The media simply chooses not to focus on them."[4]

Comparisons between coverage for dozens upon dozens of black serial killers who committed crimes similar to their white counterparts could be made. But for the sake of time, only a few will be considered.

Most every American is familiar with the story of Jeffrey Dahmer, the serial killer who raped and murdered seventeen men and boys in Wisconsin, famous also for cannibalism. Within days of his capture, every media outlet in the country was displaying his picture, and within months his story was featured on primetime news documentaries. As a result, dozens of books have been written about him, and at least three full-length movies about him have been made. He is unmistakably one of the most well-known serial killers of all time, because he dabbled with cannibalism. However, in the eyes of the media, he fit the stereotypical description of the degenerate white sociopath.

Roughly one decade after Dahmer, two black serial killers were caught who had crimes that either approached the ferocity of Dahmer's or met his taste for human flesh. Yet, despite the monstrosity of their crimes, few people outside their immediate area heard much about them.

The first was Marc Sappington, also known as the Kansas City Vampire. He had been inspired by Dahmer's crimes, and over a three-week period killed four of his acquaintances. He earned his nickname for eating the leg of one of his victims and for drinking the blood of others. Yet, despite the common vein of cannibalism, outside Kansas City his story did not see the light of day and never made the national news.

Just a few years later, the story of Maury Troy Travis broke in St. Louis, MO. He bragged about killing seventeen prostitutes in his basement torture room, where he videotaped himself raping, torturing, and killing his victims. Police now suspect him in up to twenty-two murders and reported that his torture chamber was like something from a horror movie. Yet, aside from his being the first serial killer caught as a result of internet tracking, his story received little coverage outside the St. Louis

Marc Sappington

area. When his story was picked up, as it was in the *New York Times*, instead of focusing on his crimes, they focused on how nifty technology was that an IP address could be used to track down a killer. In fact, his story has received so little media attention that the identities of four of his victims have never been publically revealed. As with Sappington, his story was second-page news at best, and generally ranked towards the bottom of newsworthy articles.

Another good illustration is between Ted Bundy and Carl Eugene Watts. Both killed primarily attractive white women in numerous states, and both had sensational stories surrounding their trials. However, while the charismatic Bundy was white and charmed his 30-35 victims, Watts snatched his 44-100 victims without saying a word to many of them. While they both killed in brutal fashion and showed no compassion for their victims, Bundy is known worldwide, while Watts is generally known only to people interested in serial killers. However, despite the similarity of their cases, one was suppressed by the news media, whilst the other is a celebrity.

The contrast between John Wayne Gacy and Eddie Lee Mosley is another great evaluation that illustrates the lack of equal reporting by the news media. Both are suspected of killing the same number of victims, thirty-three, over an extended period of time. The major difference is that Gacy was white, and his story has made him one of the most well-known killers in history. His story has spawned over a dozen books, inspired numerous fictional characters, and has even been the basis for four fictional movie killers. However, Mosley's story did not even get reported on a national level, aside from the fact that DNA testing freed two innocent men who had been convicted of eight murders he committed. In fact, Mosley's story was so taboo to the media that even in his hometown of Ft. Lauderdale, FL, where most of the murders happened, he did not make the front page. Their reasoning: they did not want to highlight another black man doing bad things. Because of their action, the AP did not pick up on the story, and despite his being suspected in raping over 300 women, his tale has faded into obscurity.

When comparing the white and black serial killers, a connection between early serial killers needs to be made as well. Ed Gein and Jake Bird are good enough candidates who represent opposite ends of the media spectrum. Gein was caught in 1957, convicted of killing two people. But he is more famously known as a body snatcher, stealing body parts to create trophies and fashioning their skin into keepsakes. His story would also be inspiration for Buffalo Bill of *The Silence of the Lambs*, Norman Bates of *Psycho*, and Leatherface of *The Texas Chainsaw Massacre*. Despite having only killed two people, his story fills countless books, and his picture is one many Americans recognize as that of a sick man.

Pitted against Gein, Jake Bird is in an entirely different league. He killed or participated in the murders of forty-four people in numerous states, using knives, pistols, and (his favorite) the axe to kill his victims. Up until the capture of Carl Watts, he was the most prolific serial killer in American history. Yet, aside from the courtroom drama surrounding his case in the late 1940s, hardly anyone knows of him. Usually the only remembrance is that his crimes helped perpetuate the axe-murderer campfire tales of old. Despite mutilating and dismembering people with axes, and having killed forty-two more people than Gein, it is the white serial killer that is remembered and the black that has almost vanished.

Finally, consider the stories of Gary Heidnik and Harrison Graham. Both serial killers were caught in 1987 in Philadelphia, prowled the same neighborhood, and lived roughly three miles apart. Heidnik's story would be told nationwide, and would later be another inspiration for the character of Buffalo Bill. His crime was killing two black women and keeping four more as prisoner in his basement. By comparison,

Heidnik & Graham

Graham, who was black, killed at least eight women, stored their bodies in his apartment for months, and even had sex with their corpses. However, despite that Graham by far committed the worse of the two crimes, it was Heidnik's mug on news channels for months, not Graham's.

In comparing stories such as these, it raises serious questions about the media's motivation for highlighting white serial killers and ignoring black serial killers. While the answer is multi-faceted, Jenkins does offer three possible explanations, while Walsh adds one in addition.

Jenkins documents possible motivation due to the fear of public backlash if the media were to refer to the black serial killer with a negative name, such as "monster" or "animal."[5] Walsh comments that this might be plausible, but he feels the media can quote another person using a negative title, putting the liability on the other party and eliminating negative reaction to the news media.[6] While Walsh's explanation does hold water, the news media is still hesitant to quote other people assigning negative titles to blacks, for any reason to avoid having their phones and e-mail accounts flooded with complaints.

The second explanation Jenkins gives is that police agencies do not take serial killing crimes as seriously if the victims are not white. He lists Jarvis Catoe, a black killer, and Albert Fish, a white killer, as examples. In both examples, the killers did not get caught until they switched from killing black victims to white victims. While these two cases may seem to illustrate his point, it plays into the hands of the black agitators of the world. Walsh disagrees (as do I) with this point, as both cases are rare examples. There are numerous black serial killers who killed white victims that did not raise any more police suspicion when they killed whites than when they killed blacks. The complete list is in chapter five, but includes the following: Jake Bird, Carl Eugene Watts, Vincent Darrell Groves, Kendall Francois, Donald Eugene Borders, Lamar Baskin Jr., Nathaniel White, David L. Washington, Timothy Wilson Spencer, and many more examples.

Jenkins's last reason is that the majority of the country is white and they make up the largest demographic of media viewers. As a result, he posits that they are interested in seeing white people killing white people and are not concerned with what happens in black culture. But again, this plays into the hands of the agitators by allowing them to play the victim card and to label the media and audience as racist. A good argument to dispel his idea is that even in predominantly black cities, where a news staff is predominantly black, the trend to report white serial killers still prevails. Even worse, black newspapers, such as the *Afro-American*, which supposedly cater to the news blacks want and need to here, still fail to highlight black serial killers. In the few instances in which they mention a black serial killer, their motivation is to show bias or racism against the black community.

Anthony Walsh takes notice of Jenkins's reasons, but he thinks a different explanation is more likely: "Although all of Jenkins's reasons must play at least a part, we believe that the primary reason for the lack of coverage of African American serial killers, like the lack of coverage of African Americans in other sensitive areas, such as organized crime and hate crime, is that the print and electronic news media...largely ignore them. The media have tended to avoid more than minimal coverage of heinous crimes committed by African Americans at the same time as they extensively publicize the same kinds of crimes committed by Whites."[7]

To substantiate his point, he makes a comparison of the trial of the four officers who beat Rodney King against the Yahweh ben Yahweh Cult. The latter was a cult led by an enigmatic guy with a messiah complex; they executed four of their own and at least twenty-three whites that they labeled as "white devils." The contrast is that Rodney King's trial sparked the aforementioned riot in LA, as well as smaller ones in Seattle and Atlanta, and is permanently etched in the minds of Americans because of its constant media attention. By contrast, when the Yahweh cult trial was taking place at the same time, even television channels in Miami—where the trial was held—chose to broadcast the King-beating trial. No riots broke out, and outside the realm of people re-searching cults or serial killers, the group's name is unknown.

Walsh goes on to make an excellent point. "Few doubt that the media response would have been quite different if a group of Whites had been on trial for hunting down and killing 'Black devils.'"[8] He further substantiates this point by quoting a black columnist Armstrong Williams. He was commenting on the lack of attention for the case of the Carr brothers, who were black and killed five whites in heinous acts: "...largely because the victims were White, which meant no Jesse Jackson screaming into his megaphone."[9]

The point is well taken, but it is not just restricted to the media. Gary LaFree documented this problem in the academic world of criminology as well. "Despite the centrality of race issues to criminology research and policy for the past three decades, most criminologists have ignored race in explanations of crime. There are some compelling reasons for this. Wilson claims that many researchers have avoided race-related research on crime because of the earlier sharp criticisms aimed at scholars, who directly confronted these issues."[10]

The significance of this is that the mainstream media often takes its cues from academia. If it is acceptable discussion amongst the experts, then it is deemed newsworthy. However, if such news is shunned, the media will look the other way and refocus their attention on less sensitive stories.

In one of the most unpublicized examples of black-on-white crime of the new century, five blacks were found guilty of raping, torturing, and murdering Christopher Newsom and his girlfriend Channon Christian in Knoxville, TN, in 2007.[11] They had been carjacked; but instead of simply stealing their car and letting them go, the thugs took them back to a small house. Thinking they were going to be harassed for more money, the whites offered what they had to be let loose from their captors. However, it was not about money any longer: the thugs wanted to act out their violent tendencies. They started with Christopher while his girlfriend was locked in a bathroom. He was sodomized with a large object, possibly a chair leg, which severely damaged his anus cavity. After this, he was blindfolded, bound, and gagged, and then shot in his head, his back, and his neck multiple times. Not satisfied that he was dead, the blacks set his body on fire in a train yard near the house.

As bad as that may seem, his girlfriend received far worse treatment. She was held hostage for the better part of a day, being repeatedly gang raped by the four men and sexually tortured by the one woman. The latter torture was savage and committed with a large broken chair leg. Her mouth, vagina, and anus sustained horrific injuries that would have required extensive surgery had she lived. After beating her over the head with the chair leg, a cleaning solution containing a large amount of bleach was poured down her throat, over her wounds, and in her vagina. Finally, a plastic bag was placed over her head, her hands and feet were tied, and she was placed in a trash dumpster, where she slowly suffocated to death over several agonizing hours.

Despite this horrific story, outside of Knoxville, little to no media attention was garnered. In fact, were it not for the internet, the crime would not have ever been known outside these states. Country singer Charlie Daniels would speak out: "There are probably not five stories in the country that could possibly be more important than that one during the time it was going on. It is totally, completely unfair to the memory of these young people not to inform people about what happened to them."[12]

Compare this crime to the crime that rocked the nation in 1999. In Jasper, TX, three white men were found guilty of dragging James Byrd to death over a three-mile stretch of dusty road, which decapitated the man and severed one of his arms.[13] Every media channel was quick to pull the race card, claiming it was a blatant hate crime perpetrated by white supremacists. After the crime, Jesse Jackson spent a few days consoling the family, and offered this at Byrd's funeral: "Brother Byrd's innocent blood alone could very well be the blood that changes the course of our country, because no one has captured the nation's attention like this tragedy."[14]

Soon after, Jackson called on the town to erect a statue of Byrd to help eliminate hate. His funeral drew in the heads of the NAACP from every direction: state senators, Senator Maxine Waters, a member of President Clinton's cabinet, Jesse Jackson, Al Sharpton, militant black Muslims, the New Black Panthers, and others. Moreover, the funeral procession even received air time on national news.[15] The New Black Panthers succeeded in rallying a small band of fifteen or so local blacks to march around town with rifles and shotguns to guard against a white supremacist uprising. Yet, no one outside their family and friends showed up to Christopher's and Channon's funerals, and there was no suggestion of a statue, no call to arms by white citizens, and no media coverage of their funerals. Their memory was forgotten, as if they never existed in the eyes of the media, as if their attackers were run-of-the-mill criminals.

While Byrd's death was tragic and senseless, by comparison, his torture did not last nearly as long as Channon's. But, as the media does, Byrd's case was sensationalized, which led to hate-crime legislation that would later include his name. Yet, this hate legislation did nothing for the murderers of Christopher and Channon. In fact, the police were quick to tell the local media that it was not a hate crime, just a bad situation. Soon after, the defense attorneys worried that someone might hold a rally at the courthouse, speaking out against black-on-white crime, which would necessitate moving the trial to another part of the state.[16] Yet if the roles had been reversed, protestors would have been welcomed and given media airtime to voice their opposition.

So the murders of Newsom and Christian were downplayed as a group of blacks who made a bad choice, which drew no national media attention and no support to prosecute them as perpetrators of a hate crime. Had the races been reversed, however, everyone knows what the outcome of the media coverage and hate crime prosecution would have been. Yet, the NAACP, which was so quick to attend the funeral of Byrd, rally marches for his cause, and demand justice for his attackers, rode the PC ticket on these murders. "Whether it is black, white, or Hispanic, there is no way in the world you cannot view what has taken place and not feel remorse for the families. At the same time, you cannot cast judgment as to who did it or who did not do it. That is not our place."[17] But before Byrd's trial, they revealed that they do cast a stone of judgment when the roles are reversed: "These cowards should never walk the street again as free men."[18]

Furthermore, the parents of the blacks were not expected to write a letter of remorse or condemnation for their actions. But in Byrd's case, the ringleader's father did write such a letter and released it publically, because, had he not, he would have been condemned in the media for raising a racist. Every white supremacy group within 100 miles of Jasper was questioned by the media and officials to see if there was a connection, or if they had helped to instigate the crime. In contrast, no black supremacy group, such as the members of the Black Panthers in Memphis or Knoxville, were questioned or harassed by the media after the deaths of Christopher and Channon.

The whole world knows about the town of Jasper and the sad tale of Byrd, but the world has passed by the Knoxville tragedy. There was no call from President Bush to their families, as Byrd's family got a call from President Clinton. Instead, there was silence, and then a quick movement to less controversial subjects. As black author Walter E. Williams said:

> *What can we say about people who exhibit moral indignation at a racist white attack but remain silent when there is a racist black attack?*
>
> *There is only one answer: hypocrisy and moral bankruptcy.*
>
> *What can we say about news people who go to great lengths to publicize white-on-black murders, but remain silent about black-on-white crime? Again, nothing less than dishonesty and deception.*[19]

Because of the wide array of stories like this, Walsh is definitely on to something, but I think it is far bigger than he surmises. By all appearances, there appears to be a well-orchestrated effort by the mainstream media to tarnish the image of the white male, while at the same time improving the image of the black male. It is nothing new, but is the fruit of the Civil Rights Movement, practiced to show the black's struggle to compete with the whites and to be accepted and viewed as his equal. This double standard helps to elevate the black man to the pinnacle of society, but cuts white man at the knees; it is a painful double standard that is a form of anti-white racism.

To do this, it is a classic case of bait-and-switch. If a black man is found guilty of a violent crime against a white, lawyers beg the court to lessen his sentence because he is a product of the white man's blatant racism and oppression. They argue that if blacks would not have been subjugated by whites, then they would commit less crime, even arguing at times that they suffer from an unproven condition called "Post Traumatic Slave Syndrome."[20] Along these lines, some black commentators have suggested that when a black man kills, it is a suppressed and vestigial part of his memory from his ancestors' enslavement, and that the blame clearly lies not in him for his crime, but with his ancestors' wicked slave masters. Not to be outdone, some people have even argued that black criminals would not be criminals if they had been afforded the same opportunities in life that whites have. Inexplicably, even when a black man admits that he had race-based intentions in killing a white, he is entirely ignored, and the media pundits claim he was confused and did not really mean what he said.

Now, pit this against the case of a white male who kills a black, even if it is in self-defense. When it hits the news media, even if there is not an inkling of racial hatred in the white man's heart, there is usually a line said that police are investigating to see if it is a possible hate crime. No one calls this practice into question. It is as if white suspects must pass a race litmus test but not blacks, because the general perception is that blacks are not capable of racial hate crimes. This is clearly illustrated in a recent opinion piece in the *Chicago Tribune*, in which one of the papers editors let it be known: "There are good reasons not to identify the attackers by race. It's the newspaper's sound general policy not to mention race in a story, whether about crime or anything else, unless it has some clear relevance to the topic....Why do you care so much about the attackers' race? If you fear or dislike blacks, I suppose it would confirm your prejudice. But otherwise, it tells you nothing useful."[21] In this rare admission by a media outlet, he essentially says that race is not important when reporting black crime. However, if a white serial killer surfaces and has black victims, the media does not hesitate posting a picture on their front page to inform the world of his whiteness, just as they did with Gary Heidnik: "three of the six women were prostitutes, one was retarded, and one was illiterate. All of the victims were black. Heidnik was white."[22]

Even Jesse Jackson, one of the media's go-to guys for hate crimes and black rights, recognizes this. He has always been quick to tell the world of the oppression of the black people, while being careful to skate the PC line by not pointing out the obvious pattern of black crime in America. Nevertheless, he has been able to say things like this: "We must face the number one critical issue of our day. It is youth crime in general and black-on-black crime in particular. There is nothing more painful to me at this stage in my life than to walk down the street and hear footsteps and start thinking about robbery. Then look around and see somebody white and feel relieved....After all we have been through, just to think we can't walk down our own streets, how humiliating."[23]

While this sort of admission by Jackson is rare, at least he ac-knowledges the role of identifying race and its connection to crime trends. He does not do this to demonize blacks, or with racist intentions, as the *Chicago Tribune* suggested, but to help his people at identifying and solving the problem. Jackson is allowed to say this and is even commended for it, receiving awards and honors for his work. However, if the media were to take the same stride, they would be labeled as racist, and there would be a call to fire the reporters involved in putting the story together.

This problem is not a new one, though, but over a century old: the idea that race is a social construct, lacking any biological existence. However, while the media wants us to think this is the case, especially when reporting on black-on-white crime or black serial killers, where they claim the race of the perpetrator is not important, they nonetheless insist that race is important if the roles are reversed. The race of Byrd's murderers was important, because it made for a good story and helped the government to crack down on militias and pro-white groups, even while claiming that MLK's dream had not been accomplished yet. In Heidnik's case, race was important because it took the focus off the constant stream of murders committed in the black neighborhoods near his home that earned Philadelphia the ominous moniker Killadelphia. Instead, the message was clear: race was important because a deranged *white* serial killer was stalking innocent blacks and keeping them as sexual slaves in his basement.

While this problem could be discussed in far greater detail, the point is that when it comes to black serial killers, the oft-used ploy is that race is not a concern. However, if the serial killer turns out to be white, then race is important. The very best time to use the race card is when the serial killer is white and the victims are non-white, as in the case of Dahmer and Heidnik.

With a generation of media that claims to preach egalitarian principles for mankind, this makes my head spin. They claim race does not exist, but they find it useful to pull the race card to make a point at the expense of whites. I have to remind myself that in our current society, there seems to be a strange combination of George Orwell's *1984*, where books are destroyed for being politically incorrect, and Aldous Huxley's *Brave New World*, where society no longer has a need for books: people take what the media says in regard to serial killers as the final word. Because of this, most people do not stop for a moment to think that blacks might be capable of dreaming up new, dastardly killing methods. And if they do, they have been so thoroughly stricken with the venomous bite of political correctness from these media outlets that they only dare whisper it within the comfort of their home and with the shades drawn.

The Entertainment Industry

Like the news media, the entertainment industries have a severe case of amnesia with the history of serial killers, to an even worse degree than media outlets. It is not from a lack of interest in serial killers as the bad guy in books or movies, either. On the contrary, serial killers as the arch-villains are one of the most common horror and thriller themes on the market. This notwithstanding, true crime stories detailing the crimes of serial killers are in the highest demand ever in history.

Before dissecting the bias against reporting black serial killers in these industries, let us refer to Jenkins's third point again. He stated that the white majority of America wants to be entertained by stories about whites killing whites, and have no interest in stories portraying blacks as serial killers. From a simplistic point of view, on paper it does make sense that racial groups have a tribalist mentality and generally favor their own. That may have been the case prior to the Civil Rights Movement, but, since 1965, white America has been given a cultural enrichment program of unprecedented proportions. To conquer what leftists called "racism," they argued that whites must experience diversity firsthand and embrace the multicultural society of the future. As a result, almost half a century later, most white Americans have bought into the idea that race no longer exists, or that it is an invalid category. Mixed-race relationships and marriages among whites are one of the greatest proofs of this frame of mind. Therefore, Jenkins's point falls short again, because the majority of white America bought into the belief that race is insignificant, and therefore do not care what race of killer they see in a movie or read in a book.

The entertainment industry's chief goal is to make money. If it can sell, they will produce it, regardless of how taboo or unwholesome it may be to the public. However, serial killers are not a subject on which producers and authors feel they cannot make money; they can and have done so, when they choose to produce works on black serial killers. Therefore, it is not that their product does not sell, but simply that they have bought into the same politically correct lies as the mainstream media. In an effort to go along with what is popular and considered non-offensive, they focus their attention on white serial killers, because, when it comes to them, there is never a chance of offending anyone.

But for those who think the proof is in the pudding, look no further than shows that portray violent crime. One that does a fairly decent job in portraying crime from a variety of races is the History Channel's hit show *Gangland*. They portray primarily Latino and black gangs, but on occasion they have an Asian or white gang detailed. In each gang covered, they detail their narcotics trade, murders committed, and numerous other crimes. Despite portraying the minorities in a way from which self-appointed politically correct experts would detract, the public watches the show and gives it high marks for accurately documenting the growing gang problem.

There are other documentaries that have detailed crime by minorities with much success as well, but, for some reason, Hollywood refuses to touch the black serial killer issue. Even documentaries on serial killers stay with the party line by focusing on whites. Another hit documentary show, *Wicked Attractions* (on the Discovery Channel), details serial-killing duos who murdered their victims together. Yet, despite having forty-two episodes, only one black couple was aired, Alton Coleman and Debra Brown. And remarkably, they were not even called serial killers, but instead spree-killers, despite their having killed eight people across numerous states over several months. In any case, the point is that their crimes were explained in great detail on the show, and that

Alton Coleman and Debra Brown

episode received positive reviews equal to their portrayals of white serial-killing duos.

But, despite receiving positive reviews, and despite the ability to sell programs to the general audience, Hollywood as a rule avoids casting serial killers as black. As for full-length films made in America, there has been an almost countless array portraying a serial killer as the bad guy. The best list I have found claims that there are over 450 movies on the subject. But even that number might be low, as there were three I found missing from the list: not because of some conspiracy, but because there are so many that it is tough to keep track. But if the number is rounded to 450 movies for simplicity's sake, only five from that list starred a black serial killer. Two were films detailing the D.C. Sniper; two were horror movies with a demon-like black killer in the Candyman series; and the last was *Switchback*, starring Danny Glover as a fictional killer. This equates to just over one percent of all serial-killer movies portraying a black one. As will be discussed in the next chapter, this figure is not even close to representative of what is actually observed in America. A more accurate number would be around 225 films of 450, to be proportionate with the true percentage of black serial killers.

An example of this bias was seen in the 2008 release of the B movie called *The Baseline Killer*. It was based on the nine murders Mark Goudeau committed from 2005 to 2006 using a pistol. The film was supposed to tell the story behind the crimes, with a little bit of artistic license. However, instead of portraying the killer as black, he was portrayed as a demented white guy in tactical gear who hunted his victims with a high-capacity assault rifle. While the movie received little attention and was seen mostly online, it is clear that they changed the killer's race to fit the stereotypical movie serial killer. Had they done the same with a white serial killer, the public would have been outraged, and lawsuits would have likely been filed against the movie producers.

Not only is the role of black serial killers almost nonexistent, but these same movies portray blacks as the lead detectives or FBI profilers who hunt down white serial killers. While there are several examples, Denzel Washington in *Fallen* and Morgan Freeman in *Seven* are two of the better known films. Now, I am not trying to deny that blacks fill these roles in real life, but instead I want to point out how disingenuous it is to portray blacks often in the positive roles but hardly ever in the negative. Why is it acceptable to portray a black as the lead investigator, but not as the serial killer? Both roles are filled by blacks in real life to some extent, but it is clearly unacceptable to say that we can cast blacks as a positive role model but not as the villain.

As for television shows, whether it is *CSI, Dexter, NYPD Blue, Hillstreet Blues*, or any other modern drama, the serial killers are almost exclusively cast as white, and the blacks in the show fill the positive place of investigators or profilers. The best example of a show that tracks serial killers is the hit show *Dexter*. It is a show about a white serial killer who by day is employed as a blood splatter technician and by night leads a double life as a killer, eliminating other serial killers and murderers who have evaded justice. While numerous fictitious serial killers are portrayed over the six seasons, in each case, the killer is always the white, middle to upper class, average-looking, suburban, neighborly type. And even further, to walk the politically correct line, the producers make sure that even the ordinary murderers whom Dexter dispatches are either white or (on one rare occasion) Hispanic. The one episode in which Dexter has a black voodoo high priest (Jimmy Sensio) on his killing table, he lets him go, because he does not have the heart to kill a man committed to his religious system. This theme is seen again in the sixth season, where Dexter has his sights set on killing a black guy who had admitted to killing years before. But after befriending the man, seeing him rehabilitated and living the life of a street preacher, Dexter has a change of heart. Contrast this with the oodles of white people whom Dexter eliminates: even when they have left their dark past behind and are no longer killing, they are guilty and deserve only death, no matter how they plead.

As underhanded as that may seem, the show's directors do not hold back for their best trick of all. In the one instance in which police think they have finally got a black serial killer, the viewer learns that it is a sham. The alleged killer turns out to be a black cop, Sergeant Doakes, who had proof that Dexter Morgan was a serial killer called the Bay Harbor Butcher. Yet, to escape justice, Dexter frames Doakes and makes it appear he is the Butcher by planting his fingerprints on the murder weapons. Soon afterward, Doakes dies in an explosion in a Florida swamp, but when investigators arrive, one makes the remark of how rare black serial killers are in the real world. Dexter remarks under his breath, "Obviously not as rare as we're told."[24] At the end of the show, a scene of Doakes's funeral is shown, where only a few family members and two friends are in attendance. As this is the only funeral for a serial killer they portray on the show, there are no parades, grieving friends, or a show of the police force; that is all absent because he was viewed as a serial killer in the eyes of police.

The producers of Dexter knew what they were doing in touching sensitive issues. In the tale of Sergeant Doakes, they substantiated the common notion that black serial killers do not exist. But even further, they taught that if one is caught, it is highly likely that evidence has been tampered with and that he has been framed by either police or a white killer. Moreover, as the two other black killers whom Dexter let go suggests, black men are able to change and thus are not to be held accountable for their crimes. There is never a mention of white killers changing; even in the instances in which they had proven to Dexter that they lived a kill-free life, far from their murderous past, they were still killed without question. In the minds of Dexter's producers, blacks are either framed for murder or need a second chance, while white killers are always guilty and need eliminated from society.

This message is clear and has been received by viewers who have given the issue of death penalty and amnesty a better look. As a result, viewers with whom I have spoken are quick to condemn white killers in real life to a speedy death, but suggest that blacks need a second chance and that the evidence had better be double-checked. Like the producer's double standard, viewers take the show's message and embrace its implications as if it is the standard for serial murderers.

This just proves what most people already know about the film industry. Hollywood is concerned neither with little details called facts nor with getting history straight; they are there to make money whilst shaping the public's opinion. Relying on their fallback, they claim they are presenting a historical adaptation, or a fictional tale, embellished to enhance the movie-going experience. But when they ignore this topic, it should be understood that the same people who want you to believe that light-saber technology is scientifically valid in the not-so-distant future are storytellers who warp reality to make an easy sale with moving scenes and computer-generated graphics.

As the public forks over their hard-earned cash to Hollywood to view garbage that bears no resemblance to reality, they show how they are perfectly happy being entertained to death, regardless of how factual the story is. As Neil Postman, the author of *Amusing Ourselves to Death*, often said: "We are the best entertained, least informed society in the world." If Mr. Postman were still alive, he would see that the problem has not gotten better, but is far worse than when he coined that phrase.

The inspiration for Hollywood movies can be found in the thousands of fictional books produced each year. On the subject of serial killers, countless stories have been published, sometimes drawing their characters from real-life stories. But as with Hollywood, the novel based off the story of a black serial killer is a rare occurrence. When an author does choose to use a black villain, he often has a difficult time publishing his story, not because of his writing abilities, but because publishing companies consider this a forbidden subject. Authors who wish to proceed with such a story oftentimes publish with a smaller company which does not have a large market share, or they choose to self-publish, narrowing their potential readership down even further. As a result, the book sells a fraction of what it would if they had chosen to portray a white serial killer.

This is a bit problematic, because well-known publishers have no problem publishing books that defame whites or destroy traditional European values. For instance, it is considered kosher if a lead character is a white serial killer and does things that Christians would find offensive and blasphemous. Yet, this same publisher would most likely turn his nose up to the story of a black serial killer, even if there is not one offensive idea found in the book. Therefore, authors are between a rock and a hard place in the world of fiction writing. Do they try to publish the story they have spent time developing into a fine-shaped masterpiece, but are told cannot be published? Or do they change the race of the killer to white, gain acceptance by a national publisher, and land a possible hit seller? Most often the choice is to continue the status quo, make the serial killer white, entertain the masses, and reap the dividends.

The world of nonfiction books is almost as biased, making it difficult to get a book published about a black serial killer. Take Dahmer[25], for example: a search turns up twenty-eight books written about his crimes, as well as three comic books—not to mention his inclusion into every book on the subject of serial killers written in the last two decades. Yet, a search for books on Carl Eugene Watts provides a

Carl Eugene Watts

whopping one book (one which I highly recommend).[26] In fact, a search of all black serial killers combined produces only twelve nonfictional books detailing their crimes, while a usual search for whites produces hundreds. This problem is also seen in books that portray several serial killers. The heavyweights in the white serial killer world are always there, along with the minor whites who killed two to five victims, but the blacks are either conspicuously excluded or have an extremely meager showing. A book written in 2007 on my shelf details fifty of the more famous killers in the U.S. and Europe, but only two are black (Wayne Williams and the Beltway Snipers), with the typical exaggeration that black serial killers are almost nonexistent.

The one difference the nonfiction world does offer is that some of the books detailing black serial killers have been published by major publishers. Consequently, the exclusion of books on the subject is not quite the same as in the fiction world, which is probably as a result of the general acceptance on the part of criminology authors that serial killers can be black. Thankfully, the few books detailing the crimes of the black serial killers are of excellent quality, providing detail to the crimes while being respectful to give the victims' stories.

Conclusion

To sum up the bias against reporting black serial killers, it is my firm conviction that there is a purposeful and well-constructed effort in the media, reinforced by Hollywood, not to let the public know that black serial killers are among us. While this effort is a multi-faceted gem, the primary thrust is to demonize whites and at the same time exonerate black criminals by appealing to victimization or racism, all in an attempt to help blacks obtain equality. Hand in hand with the black equality movement, media outlets are always fearful to portray blacks in a negative light, and rarely does the AP carry news of black serial killers, because it conflicts with the prevailing view that all serial killers are white.

As a result of this underhanded technique, the people responsible should be exposed by the families of the victims for failing to bring honor to their lost ones' memory. Yet, because the media fails in this regard, more helpless victims are unnecessarily lost because police and citizens are focused on finding white serial killers. Which is more important, a public outcry against the media, or the loss of someone's loved one? The answer is painfully obvious.

ENDNOTES

[1] Ho, Vanessa, *Northwest No Breeding Ground for Serial Killers, Writer Says,* Seattle-Post, November 6, 2003.
[2] Holmes, Steven A., *The Hunt for a Sniper: An Assumption Undone; Many Voice Surprise Arrested Men Are Black,* New York Times, October 25, 2002.
[3] Oftentimes the NAACP is one of the first to get publically frustrated when bodies of blacks start turning up, and police refuse to publically announce a serial killer might be responsible. However, most of the time, they are quick to make a fuss that it's likely a white killer hunting blacks.
[4] Holloway, *Lynette, Of Course There Are Black Serial Killers, The Root,* July 16, 2010, http://www.theroot.com/views/course-there-are-black-serial-killers.
[5] Jenkins, P. (1998). *African Americans and serial homicide.* In R. Holmes & S. Holmes (Eds.), *Contemporary perspectives on serial murder* (pp. 17-32).
[6] Walsh, Anthony (2005). *African Americans and serial killing in the media: The myth and the reality.* Homicide Studies 9:282.
[7] Ibid Walsh, p. 283.

[8] Ibid Walsh, p. 283.

[9] Williams, A. (2002, October 23). *Hate crime reversed.* www.TownHall.com

[10] LaFree, Gary, Race and Crime trends in the United States 1946-1990, in *Ethnicity, Race, and Crime* edited by Darnell F. Hawkins.1995, p. 170.

[11] Mansfield, Duncan, *Critics Say Media Ignoring Slaying of Knoxville Couple, The Tuscaloosa News*, May 20, 2007.

[12] Ibid., Mansfield.

[13] Cropper, Carol Marie, Town *Expresses Sadness and Horror Over Slaying,* New York Times, June 11, 1998.

[14] Firestone, David, *Speakers Stress Healing at Service for Dragging Victim,* New York Times, June 14, 1998.

[15] Associated Press, Town *Questions Celebrities' Interest in Dragging Death,* Victoria Advocate, June 21, 1998.

[16] Ibid., Mansfield.

[17] Ibid., Mansfield

[18] Siemaszko, Corky, *Death for Drag Suspects? Texas Cops Mull Deal in Probe of Horror Slaying*, New York Daily News, June 11, 1998.

[19] Williams, Walter E., *Double Standards Fomented by Hypocrisy*, Reading Eagle, January 7, 1990.

[20] Associated Press, *Lawyer Uses Slave Syndrome Defense*, Moscow-Pullman Daily News, May 31, 2004. [Thankfully this defense was rejected by the judge, on grounds it was unscientifically proven.]

[21] Chapman, Steve, *Race and the 'Flash Mob' Attacks*, Chicago Tribune, June 8, 2011.

[22] Associated Press, *Ridge Signs Death Warrant*, Pittsburgh Post-Gazette, March 21, 1997.

[23] Johnson, Mary A., *Crime: New Frontier - Jesse Jackson Calls It Top Civil-Rights Issue*, Chicago Sun-Times November 29, 1993.

[24] Season 2 episode 12.

[25] Tithecott, R. *Of men and monsters: Jeffrey Dahmer and the construction of the serial killer.*, The University of Wisconsin Press, 1997.

[26] Mitchell, Corey, *Evil Eyes, The Most Insatiable Serial Killer Ever*, 2006.

Chapter 3

Proof That Black Serial Killers Exist

The evidence that black serial killers exist in great numbers, despite what we have been told, is available at the click of a mouse. But, unlike researching white serial killers, it is often very difficult, chiefly due to the lack of articles reporting their crimes. Another problem is that there are no less than sixty on my list who each killed five or more people but were not even listed as serial killers. Instead, they were listed as mass-murderers or spree-killers, even if their crimes spanned a decade. Couple this with the lack of racial identifiers in the media outlets, and it does make the task daunting. However, the information is there, and while I feel I have found the biggest part of it, I am sure I have not uncovered it all.

Because of the lack of information, most people assume that white serial killers comprise the vast majority and probably number in the thousands in America. In the research I have slowly accumulated, I have found just over 855 white serial killers from 1860 to the present. Of this number, it is unclear how many are of Hispanic, Asian, or American Indian origin but mistakenly listed as white, because (surprisingly enough) in the eyes of most criminologists, serial killers are either white or black. For the sake of erring on the conservative side, I have chosen to assume they are all of European extraction and stick with the number 855. I was able to find some non-white killers who were not black, and in an attempt to get the full picture, I should note that I found seventy-seven Hispanic serial killers and eleven Asian killers.

The reader has probably been itching to know how many black serial killers there are, and for good reason. In my database, I have been able to confirm 982 killers who fit the description of a serial killer. This number is shocking to people hearing it for the first time, especially since this number slightly exceeds the number of white serial killers. Thus, before analyzing the data, let me explain my criteria for what constitutes a serial killer.

The old FBI standard for serial killers involved any murderer who kills for lust, pleasure, or money on three or more occasions, over a one-month span, in three or more locations, with a cool-down period between at least two of the killings. When I began my research, these were the criteria to which I adhered. But, after noticing that I was counting only those murderers with three or more kills, whereas the data I had been given on white serial killers followed the new FBI standard, I changed to keep things fair. The new standard is just like the old, with the exception that instead of three kills, serial killers are those who commit only two murders, with a significant cool-down period between kills; more importantly, serial killers can commit their murders in one location, which makes the old standard problematic in many serial killing cases (Gein, Dahmer, Heidnik, Gacy, and others).

It must clearly be stated that, according to this profile, a serial killer is not the same as a mass-murderer. A mass-murderer is someone who murders on one occasion, such as the killer in the Virginia Tech Massacre, Seung-Hui Cho, who killed thirty-two people and wounded twenty-five others.[1] His attack was horrible, but it was a one-time affair. Therefore, for the purpose of my research, I carefully weeded out any black mass-murderers that often plague internet serial killer databases.

I have been careful not to include people who killed in self-defense; as well, I have not included people who killed while following orders in the military. For instance, Edward Arthur Surratt is in the database for killing nineteen people across numerous states.[2] In addition, he was a decorated Vietnam vet who claimed to have killed Vietcong while stationed in Vietnam. Yet, whatever number he killed while in Vietnam is irrelevant to this research, and was not included in his overall total, because it falls under the category of following military orders.

What is included in my database are black men and women who killed on two or more occasions, whether the motivation was greed, lust, pleasure, revenge, or money. This would include gang members such as

Stanley 'Tookie' Williams, who killed at least four people in robberies when he was a Crips gang member.[3] This description would also include hit-men such as the infamous Best Friends Gang of Detroit, who claim to have assassinated over 100 people in the eighties and early nineties for profit. Some may think that this is a liberal inclusion, but they must understand that Bonnie and Clyde, the infamous gangsters who killed and robbed their way across the country, are considered to be an example of a serial killing duo. If their addition to white serial killing databases is accepted, then, to be fair, black robbers and gangsters must be included as well. Likewise, researchers of white serial killers include famous mafia hit men, such as Richard "The Iceman" Kuklinski, who claimed to have killed over 250 men for profit.[4] Therefore, the inclusion of black hit men should not be seen as a problem.

Tookie

One group I have allowed to stay is what I call "modified spree-killers." Usually, a spree-killer is someone who kills numerous people in different attacks, in a short time span, with no cool-down between the crimes. (An example would be a guy who kills a person and then drives to another part of town to kill more people.) What I call a modified spree-killer/serial killer is a man who kills numerous people on different occasions, but all within one month. There are actually very few of these in my database, probably less than ten. In all of them, the reason they are typically profiled as serial killers, besides the fact that the murders do not appear random, is due to a cool-down period between their murders, when they preplanned how they would commit their later crimes. There are over thirty other black spree killers of whom I am aware, but they did not pass this criterion. However, the brunt of my research still stands if this small group is removed, and my initial reason for including them was based on the precedent set by other authors who have included them within their research on serial killers.

The last thing critics may attack is my choice to include killers who have killed only two victims. While this may seem gratuitous on my account, I am simply following the path made by researchers of white serial killers. One of the poster boys for degenerate serial killers is Ed Gein, who has been the inspiration for books and movie characters.

Despite the ferocity of his crimes, no more than two murders have ever been attributed to him. Likewise, Paula Sims was a white woman who killed her two infant daughters, three years apart; and she has become a poster child for murderous parents. If Gein and Sims have been deemed worthy to be included in the annals of serial killing history, then blacks meeting the same minimum requirement should be included as well. It is hard not to consider a two-victim black murderer like Connie J. Williams as a serial killer, after he kept his first victim under his bed and methodically sawed his second into pieces. Likewise, it is difficult not to consider a two-time murderer like William Gerald Mitchell as a serial killer. He attempted to kill three women, and was successful on his fourth. Not satisfied that she was dead, he cut her body into pieces. In his second murder, he raped, beat, and then strangled his victim. Wanting her to suffer, he let her hang onto life only to run over her three times with his car. She was close to death, so he decided to finish the task by carving up her body, making her unrecognizable.

But, if critics insist that this database must be built entirely of killers with two victims, as if I have artificially increased its numbers, then they are wrong. In my database, there are 242 killers who killed on two known occasions. Of that list, twenty-three attempted to kill other people, while more than a dozen are suspected of additional murders. But even if we exclude them from the database, 740 others fit the three-or-more-kill criteria. Moreover, if this same principle is applied to white serial killers, their number is reduced by a similar factor.

However, in an effort to squelch any additional dissenters who would accuse me of loading my database with gang killers and hit men, I offer the following. Both categories make up a minority in the database, with ten known black hit men and sixty-three known gang-related serial killers. Even if I remove those from the diminished list of 740 serial killers, there remain 667 confirmed killers who killed three or more people and were not connected to a gang or acting as professional hit men.

But even after going to these great extents, I am sure that there are people who will still try to discredit my research on technicalities. While I fully admit I am very capable of making mistakes, I have given extreme care not to list anyone falsely. Therefore, I researched court records, sought confessions, and read eye-witness accounts before adding a name into the database. The task at times was excruciating, but such efforts must be done to insure no one is falsely accused.

Another mention is noteworthy. There are books still in print, as well as internet sites, which detail some black serial killers but still include men who have been exonerated of their crimes by DNA or a lack of evidence. Jerry Frank Townsend[5] and Frank Lee Smith[6] are examples of men commonly listed on sites and in books who have been cleared by DNA. While the books written prior to their release are understandable, in some of the recent republications of these books these men are still listed. Another person I have removed from my list is Loving Mitchell, noted as having killed over thirty people with an axe across the Midwest in the early part of the 1900s. I removed him because he was never tried for the crimes, but was later released before he died of old age in East St. Louis.[7] Therefore, I encourage other authors to exclude these men from their books and make mention to readers that these men are innocent of the crimes they were convicted of committing.

Lastly, before examining the evidence, I wish to answer one more objection. Some critics may use the cases of the aforementioned exonerated men as proof that my database has flaws. But I am not the judge, jury, or investigator to determine if a killer is guilty. Fortunately, too, with the steady stream of advances in DNA technology, as well as increased awareness of falsely imprisoned men, it is getting harder for an innocent man to pass through the system. In fairness, if any person in the database is at some time found innocent and exonerated of their crimes, he will be removed from the list. But as it stands, everyone on the list has been scrutinized to remove any doubt about their inclusion.

The Database

For the purpose of keeping things simple, I will use the full data-base number of 942 killers. If the reader chooses to eliminate the two-only killers, gang killers, or hit men, that is his choice. But even with those eliminated, the realization that black serial killers make up a significant part of American serial killers cannot be dismissed, nor can the fact that in every decade since the 1960s their numbers have increased.

Before diving into the research, it should be noted that there has been no proof for Hispanic or Asian serial killers prior to 1940. While there were possibly a few Hispanic hit-men creeping around in the late 1800s, no proof thus far has been found. Similarly, the information on white serial killers provided to me included only those killers from 1930 to 2010. Killers since 2010 have been easy to determine, and when one pops up he is immediately added. Prior to 1930, searching has been a bit problematic. I have made searches in books and old newspaper articles in an effort to get a firm grip on the true number of white serial killers. While my numbers prior to 1930 may be in slight error for white serial killers, the numbers are not going to substantially skew the data.

The following table has the starting decade for serial killers, which indicates the decade in which the killers marked their first kills. But this number can be deceptive: consider the case of Lester Harrison, who marked his first kill in prison in the 1950s but did not commit his additional six murders until the 1970s.[8] Nonetheless, Harrison's case is an exception, not the rule. Most serial killers killed within only one decade, while others began killing towards the latter years of one decade and were apprehended early in the next decade. There are some examples of killers, such as Jake Bird or Lonnie Franklin, who have killings that spanned multiple decades, but again they are the exception.

Some may wonder why we should worry about the start era. The purpose is to track trends in the rise or decline of their ranks, so that criminologists can attempt to determine what causes contributed to these trends. Another advantage is that it allows researchers to compare racial groups side-by-side in a given decade, to see if all races followed the same trends.

On the left-hand column is the start decade for the killer. To the right of this column, each of the four major racial groups is listed, with the corresponding number of killers beginning in a given decade. To the right of the races is the "TOTAL" column, totaling the number of serial killers from a given decade. The last column is one of the most important to understand black serial killers. "% BSK" is an abbreviation I use to notate the percentage of black serial killers in a given decade. For instance, in 1870, there were ten serial killers who began their crimes: six white and four black; therefore, the percentage of black serial killers who began in 1870 is 40% of all serial killers.

TABLE 3.1- Serial Killers By Race						
DECADE	**White**	**Black**	**Hispanic**	**Asian**	**TOTAL**	**% BSK**
1860	1	1	0	0	2	50.00%
1870	6	4	0	0	10	40.00%
1880	5	4	0	0	9	44.44%
1890	9	9	0	0	18	50.00%
1900	7	14	0	0	21	66.67%
1910	7	18	0	0	25	72.00%
1920	6	10	0	0	16	62.50%
1930	20	12	0	0	32	37.50%
1940	18	13	1	0	32	40.63%
1950	30	13	0	0	43	30.23%
1960	76	39	1	0	120	35.83%
1970	218	154	11	2	385	40.00%
1980	245	213	30	3	491	43.38%
1990	158	239	19	4	420	56.90%
2000	40	184	10	2	236	77.97%
2010	9	51	6	0	66	77.27%
TOTALS	**855**	**982**	**78**	**11**	**1926**	**50.99%**

According to Edward Hickey, black serial killers make up 22% of all serial killers,[9] while an early study by Newton found that they made up only 16%.[10] But a look at the column to the right, however, shows that nowhere from 1870 to present have black serial killers dipped below 28.57%. In fact, the average over the 150-year span shows that blacks comprise 50.99% percent of the total and slightly exceed white serial killers by 6.60%. However, this does not mean that their work was inaccurate or that their numbers were flawed, but instead that their research was not as complete. Jenkins noted that the field of studying black serial killers was seriously lacking and consequently that the numbers would rise with further study.[11] I have therefore spent countless hours poring over old records to derive these numbers. This task was further complicated by the rather recent invention of the word "serial killer" in the 1970s.[12] Prior, serial killers were identified as "slayers," "multiple-killers," "mass-murderers," or simply "murderers." Thus, instead of an assault on their labor, my updated percentages should be viewed as a continuation of their fantastic work.

Now, when considering just the decades of 1930-2000, the most accurate recent university study prior to mine was conducted by Radford University in 2010. Their research listed 317 black serial killers in those decades, making up a total of 27.1% of the total number of killers from these decades.[13] I do not intend to take away from their superb research, but after investigating their database, I found a few minor flaws, in addition to the fact that they had missed many killers in their research. (Their numbers did include the two-kill-only serial killers, however.) Covering the same time period, my database has 836 killers, amounting to 48.55% of all serial killers during that time. Again, they did fine work; but it took me almost two years before I discovered the search variables needed to find many of these killers in the news media.

Now, even if my numbers are rejected, the truth remains that blacks are overrepresented as serial killers demographically, even with the lower numbers as proven by previous authors. In the chart below are the demographics of the United States population from 1860 to present. Note, the category of other is significantly underrepresented, because in early census forms, Asians, Hispanics and American Indians were most commonly listed as whites. Even today, the white population percentage (72.4%) is in error, because numerous Hispanics with a small portion of white ancestry have been listed as white. Regardless of this formality, it does not affect the black population, which has remained fairly constant in the last 150 years and stands at 11.49% of the national total over time.

TABLE 3.2- U.S. Population 1860-2010			
DECADE	White	Black	Other
1860	85.60%	14.10%	0.30%
1870	87.10%	12.70%	0.20%
1880	86.50%	13.10%	0.40%
1890	87.50%	11.90%	0.60%
1900	87.90%	11.60%	0.50%
1910	88.90%	10.70%	0.40%
1920	89.70%	9.90%	0.40%
1930	89.80%	9.70%	0.50%
1940	89.80%	9.80%	0.40%
1950	89.50%	10.00%	0.50%
1960	88.60%	10.50%	0.90%
1970	87.50%	11.10%	1.40%
1980	83.10%	11.70%	5.20%
1990	80.30%	12.10%	7.60%
2000	75.10%	12.30%	12.60%
2010	72.40%	12.60%	15.00%
AVERAGE	85.58%	11.49%	2.93%

If Newton's number of 16% is used, this number is still over-representative of the historic percentage of black population by a factor of 1.39 (16% of serial killers divided by 11.49% of the population). However, if my number of 50.99% is used, it illustrates that blacks are represented 4.44 times their average percentage (11.49%) of the population in this time frame! To make the number starker: this means that blacks are overrepresented 444% when it comes to serial killers—that blacks are more likely to be serial killers than any other race.

Detractors may quibble that representative statistics do not matter in the real world, but I would argue that they clearly do. If whites historically were overrepresented fourfold in any crime, that figure would be used to stereotype whites as potential candidates for that crime. Committees would form, politicians would swear to fix the problem, and plenty of intellectuals would write studies in an effort to curb the trend. However, with this subject, none of that has been done. Of course, I am not suggesting blacks should be disenfranchised by claiming that they are all potential serial killers. Instead I am more interested in proving that whites do not have the market on serial killings, but are in fact underrepresented. This stands in direct opposition to the common perception of serial killers today.

To illustrate this disparity, consider the following chart illustrating the percentages of serial killers by decade by race. Due to the relatively small number of Asian and Hispanic serial killers, their numbers have been combined. Also, if each of the three racial bars for any given decade is added together, they total 100%.

Chart 3.1-Percentage of Serial Killers By Decade

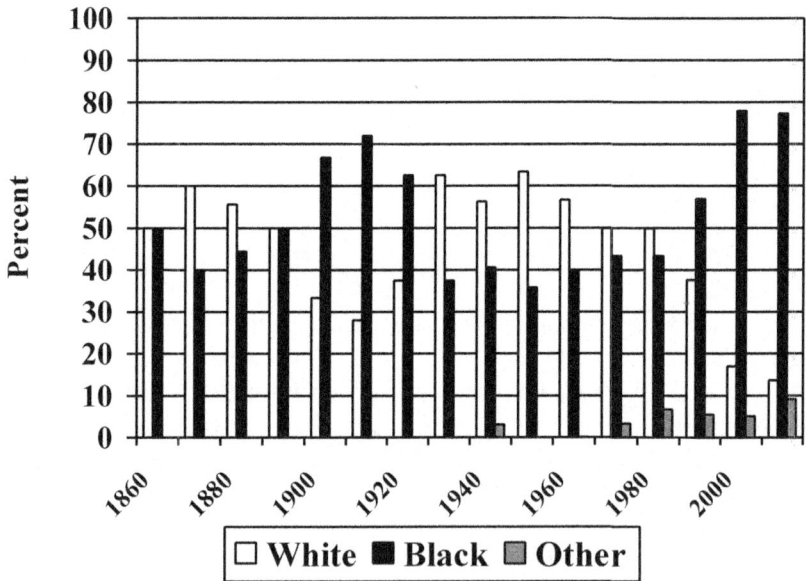

Some will question these statistics with the argument that whites still make up roughly half of serial killers in the U.S. My answer is: rightfully so! White Americans do make up the majority the U.S. population, and therefore it is logical to assert that they should make up half or more of serial killings—and they do. However, even though they make up the majority of serial killings, they are still underrepresented. Referring back to Table 3.2, the historic white population over the past

150 years is 85.28% of the total population. Now, according to Table 3.1, whites were accountable for 854 of the serial killers from a total of 1,869 killers in this time period. This means that whites account for only 44.39% of all U.S. serial killers, or, better stated, that they are underrepresented by a factor of 1.87. When compared with blacks, who are overrepresented by 444% in comparison to their population, white serial killers are under-represented at only 44.39% of their population's total.

Crime statistics like these cannot merely be dismissed as meaningless or inconsequential; these measures are an important means of analyzing trends and drawing conclusions. They are helpful in determining what groups are more likely to commit a given crime, that law enforcement may better counter crimes before they begin. Similarly, state and federal programs designed to help restrain criminal behavior through education draw on stats like these as well.

I am not arguing for investigators and criminologists to forget about white serial killers, for they still kill every year and will continue to kill. Instead, I am making a case that blacks must be considered as possible suspects when bodies start turning up. No longer can blacks be eliminated as suspects simply because they do not fit the outdated and irrelevant serial killer profile of yesterday. In fact, when analyzing the data further, it becomes evident that the number of black serial killers is steadily on the rise.

Below is another chart that pulls the aforementioned numbers on black serial killers together, with a few new columns. On the far right of the chart is the overrepresentation factor column ("OverRep Factor"). This column is the factor by which black serial killers are overrepresented in a given decade in comparison to their percentage of the population, which is represented in the column to its left marked "Historic Black Population." This number, as before, is derived by dividing the percentage of black serial killers in a given decade by the corresponding percentage of the population for the same decade. The overrepresentation factor could also be illustrated by dropping the decimal and adding a percent sign: e.g., 4.44 is the same as 432% overrepresented.

	Black Serial Killers	TOTAL Serial Killers	% BSK	Historic Black US Population	OverRep Factor
TABLE 3.3- Black Serial Killers by Decade					
DECADE					
1860	1	2	50.00%	14.10%	3.55
1870	4	10	40.00%	12.70%	3.15
1880	4	9	44.44%	13.10%	3.39
1890	9	18	50.00%	11.90%	4.20
1900	14	21	66.67%	11.60%	5.75
1910	18	25	69.57%	10.70%	6.73
1920	10	16	62.50%	9.90%	6.31
1930	12	32	35.48%	9.70%	3.87
1940	13	32	40.63%	9.80%	4.15
1950	13	43	28.57%	10.00%	3.02
1960	43	120	33.62%	10.50%	3.41
1970	154	385	39.84%	11.10%	3.60
1980	213	491	42.68%	11.70%	3.71
1990	239	420	55.64%	12.10%	4.70
2000	184	236	77.68%	12.30%	6.34
2010	51	66	70.21%	12.60%	6.13
TOTAL	**992**	**1926**	**50.99%**	**11.49%**	**4.44**

When analyzing this data, we can make some interesting observations. Most evident: in the past 150 years in America, blacks have never been underrepresented according to their population, but in each decade are overrepresented by at least a factor of 3.02 (in 1950), and at most a factor of 6.73 (in 1910). If the common ploy was correct in asserting that blacks are not good serial killers, then they would be underrepresented in this chart in at least one decade—but instead the opposite is true.

To understand this better, consider the following tables. Chart 2 illustrates the historic black population when compared to the percentage of serial killers for each decade. Note in the chart that the historic percentage of the black population has remained consistent for the past 150 years, while the percentage of black serial killers has fluctuated greatly, but is still far greater in every decade than their general population.

Chart 3.2- Black Serial Killers
Compared to Black Population

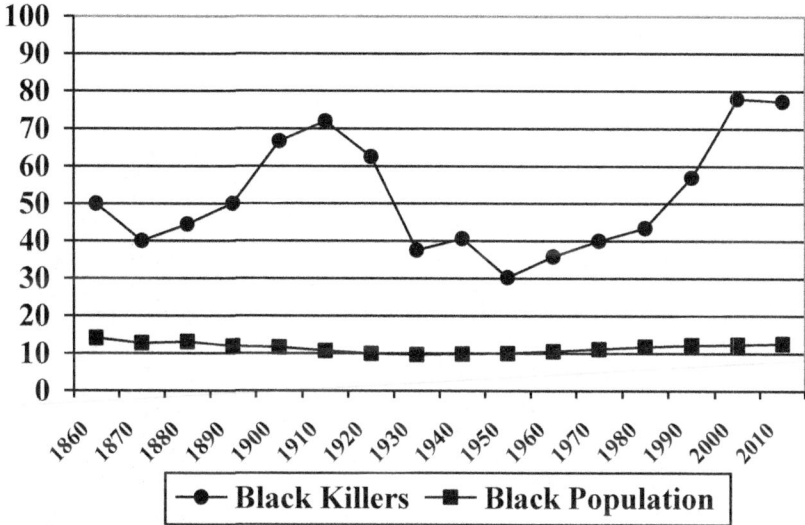

Chart 3.3 includes the same information and format as chart 3.2 but documents white serial killers and the white population. Just as before, the line with squares illustrates the historic population, while the more erratic line with dots is the percentage of killers for each decade. Just as with the black population, the white population has remained fairly consistent, but has seen a decline over the last four decades. However, the conclusions of this chart are the opposite of the previous chart, because whites are always underrepresented in comparison to their population.

Chart 3.3- White Serial Killers
Compared to White Population

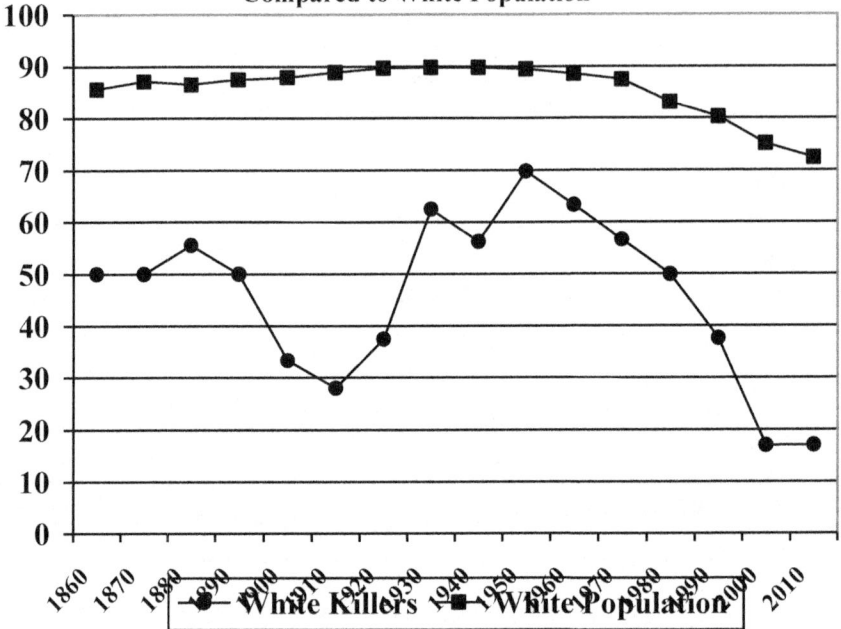

Serial Killer Rates

When I first began studying serial killers, I was interested in knowing the rate of serial killers in relation to the overall US population. To my surprise, I have yet to see anyone give this a serious attempt, and have seen numbers as high as $1/1,000^{th}$ of one percent to as low as $1/1,000,000^{th}$ of one percent. I put a pencil to my figures and have discerned that from 1860-2000, 0.000093% of the US population have been serial killers. This is much lower than I expected, equivalent to approximately 1 in 1,076,732 people. This is in line with the FBI's estimate that, at any given time, there are fifty or so serial killers roaming America, or about 250 to 300 per decade. To keep from detracting from the theme of this chapter, the chart with my findings for the US population can be found in Appendix I.

When I was doing the math to determine the serial killing rate, I was curious to know what the rates for blacks were in comparison to white serial killers. To begin, as previously mentioned, serial killers are a very rare occurrence in the US, less than a one-in-a-million chance overall. However, as Table 3.4 on the nest page illustrates, when the rate is broken down into two groups, the rate increases for blacks while decreasing for whites. The lower the number is in each column, the higher the rate is in relation to each group's population. I derived these numbers by dividing each group's population in a given decade by the number of serial killers their group had in the same decade. For instance, in 1970 the black population was 22.6 million, whereas there were 154 serial killers in that decade, yielding a rate of 1 in 146,753. (Note that I dropped the decade of 2010-2020, since it has not been completed: its small tally seriously skews the data and gives errant numbers.)

As can be seen, in 1980, both whites and blacks reached their highest rate, with blacks having 1 in 124,413 and whites having 1 in 768,864. This means that whites in 1980 were just under one-and-a-half times the 140-year average (1.40 times), but blacks were still 6.17 times the rate of whites during the same span and 8.65 times higher than the average. When the bottom row is considered (the average over the 140-year span), whites are at 1 in 2,064,297, which is 1.87 times less than the average historical serial killer rate. Blacks for the same 140 year span however, are at a rate of 1 in 239,477, or 4.50 times higher than average, or 450% higher. (This number is slightly higher than the 431% previously listed, because the decade of 2010 was dropped for this figure.)

TABLE 3.4 SERIAL KILLER RATES
(Note rates below are one person per number listed)

DECADE	BLACKS	WHITES
1860	4,441,830	26,922,537
1870	1,220,002	5,598,230
1880	1,645,198	8,680,594
1890	832,088	6,122,362
1900	631,000	11,675,994
1910	434,876	13,545,845
1920	1,050,000	18,380,623
1930	991,667	5,564,337
1940	992,308	6,567,493
1950	1,153,846	4,498,068
1960	439,535	2,089,891
1970	146,753	815,362
1980	146,753	768,864
1990	125,523	1,263,836
2000	188,043	5,286,516
AVERAGE	**239,477**	**2,064,297**

While there is a rising trend of serial killers for all races from 1930 to 1980, there is a more drastic curtailing of this trend in 1990 among white serial killers. In whites, due to the drastic drop in serial killers each decade, 1990 saw the rate almost cut in half, while 2000 was cut almost four and a half times what it had been in 1990. In 2000, white serial killers were at a rate 4.90 times lower than the 140-year average. Blacks had a descending trend in their ranks from 1990-2000 as well, but did not see near the drastic drops whites did during the same span, and in 2000, blacks were still 5.72 times the average rate.

Overall in the 140-year span, blacks only saw four decades (1860, 1870, 1880, and 1950) when their rate was lower than the national average (1 in 1,099,188 people). Whites were above the average in all decades except 1970 and 1980, during which their ranks swelled to their highest numbers. This trend, contrary to the general perception of serial killers, shows that blacks represent a ratio higher than whites in every decade. To better understand this, Table 3.5 below compares the rates of both groups in relation to one another. Since, in every decade, the rate was lower for whites, the table lists the factor by which blacks were higher in each decade. Since blacks were higher in each decade, the ratio was easy to obtain. I obtained the factor by dividing the white rate for each decade by the black rate. For instance, in 1980, the 1-in-768,864 rate of white killers was divided by the 1-in-124,413 rate of blacks, yielding that the black rate was 6.23 times higher than the white rate. Again, I dropped the data for 2010, as the decade is not yet complete.

TABLE 3.5 DIFFERENCE IN RATES	
DECADE	**Factor by Which Blacks Were Higher**
1860	6.06
1870	4.59
1880	5.28
1890	7.36
1900	18.50
1910	31.15
1920	17.51
1930	5.61
1940	6.62
1950	3.90
1960	4.75
1970	5.56
1980	6.18
1990	10.07
2000	28.11
AVERAGE	**8.62**

It is important to remember that these are not ratios comparing white serial killers to black ones. Instead, this is merely a comparison of the rates between the two groups. If both groups were in accord with their population in each decade, the numbers would be one in each decade, for a 1:1 serial killer ratio.

The Early Trends

1865 marked the first example of a serial killer in my database. From 1865-67, a young black man known only by his last name of Fitzgerald admitted to killing five men in Tennessee and Mississippi. His victims were three white farmers and two free black men. After killing his final victim on April 12, 1867, a lynch mob comprised of both blacks and whites apprehended him after a long chase on the 18th.[14] What happened next has not been preserved in records, but it is suggested that the lynch mob disappeared with him in the night.

There is some evidence of possibly two earlier black serial killers prior to 1865, but I have not found sufficient data to confirm they were found guilty of their crimes. Therefore, Fitzgerald is the earliest official in my record, which brings up an interesting subject. Why did black serial killers surface after the end of the War Between the States?

Early social commentators from both the left and the right agree that black crime took a serious rise during Reconstruction, starting in 1865. On one side were authors such as Charles Otken, who held that this rise in crime could be attributed to blacks thumbing their nose at the Anglo-Saxon laws and people.[15] On the other were guys like W.E.B. Du Bois, who felt that blacks were trying to find their place in their fight for equality. Despite their difference of opinion on solutions, Du Bois admitted that, prior to emancipation, crime among blacks was far less; he believed the more recent crime was a problem to be solved by better education, which would elevate blacks to an equal social status.[16] While authors like Otken spoke highly of education, Otken also recommended Christian teaching, saying that blacks needed to be happy earning wages as laborers on plantations and not concerned about equal social status. It is apparent that the two sides were opposed, but they both agreed that black crime rose sharply in 1865, almost overnight, and steadily continued to climb into the 1900s. Frederick Hoffman's assessment of this rise is salient: "During slavery the Negro committed fewer crimes than the white man, and only on rare occasions was he guilty of the more atrocious crimes, such as rape and murder of white females."[17]

Just three years later, Du Bois gave a fairly detailed analysis of this rise as well. "A study of statistics seems to show that the crime and pauperism of the Negroes exceeds that of the whites; that in the main, nevertheless, it follows in its rise and fall the fluctuations shown in the records of the whites, *i.e.*, if crime increases among the whites it increases among Negroes, and *vice versa*, with this peculiarity, that among the Negroes the change is always exaggerated—the increase greater, the decrease more marked in nearly all cases."[18]

Du Bois goes on to lament that his people, while representing less than one eighth of the population in 1890, committed more than one fifth of the violent crime.[19] The pattern he documents, and which others like Otken detail in depth, corresponded with the rise of black serial killers after the war. In 1870, the number had risen from the lone serial killer in 1860, to four blacks who began their hunt for victims. Every decade afterward would see a maintaining or steady rise in their ranks.

Du Bois was not the only black man who noted this problem. Booker T. Washington also hung his head low when addressing how his people had embraced criminal behavior. "The increase in the amount of Negro crime in the United States during the period of 1870 to 1890 was so rapid and so marked that it made a great impression on the public, North and South."[20]

Through the eyes of these men, it is easily seen that black crime, especially murder and rape, rose dramatically from 1865 to 1900. Along with this trend, some blacks took to serial killing. Some, such as Sam Grant, were hit men roaming the Wild West and getting paid to headhunt. Others, such as Sam Steenburg and Antonio Richards, were classic sociopaths, each killing at least eleven people and admitting that they craved killing. The correlation is that black serial killers arose in conjunction with the violent crimes.

As to the reason why blacks began serial killing, some suggested that discharged black soldiers, who were disgruntled for a variety of reasons, became the worst criminals and most depraved murderers.[21] Some argued that blacks addicted to liquor were more disposed to criminal behavior.[22] While both of these ideas may have played some small part, both could be used to justify white criminal behavior as well, which did not see near the spike black crime did during this time. Social scientists began looking for the root of the problem and came up with a twofold interconnected explanation to pinpoint the problem.

The first thing they noticed was the disdain some blacks had for laws, which they felt were an extension of slavery by whites.[23] Even blacks such as Du Bois and Washington felt that blacks were more inclined to forsake the entirety of the law because of the minority of laws with which they disagreed. Their solution was for blacks to obey the laws and to petition lawmakers to change any laws that put blacks at a disadvantage. But connected with this lawlessness was a noticeable pattern of broken homes, which most agreed were a result of black men who forsook their duty to be industrious after slavery ended. Therefore, most commentators agreed that some if not all criminal behavior in blacks was born in fatherless homes, where children were not taught respect for laws or how to properly make a living.[24,25,26] This problem was widespread throughout the country and was not an indictment against all blacks, but instead was an admonishment for irresponsible black men to stop their criminal behavior, to have pride in holding a job, and to care for their family with love. In one of Booker T. Washington's more popular and moving speeches, he touched on this subject and gave a practical solution.

> On the Negro's part we have a duty. Our leaders should see to it that the criminal Negro is gotten rid of whenever possible....I have no hesitation in saying that one of the elements in our present situation that gives me most concern is the large number of crimes that are being committed by members of our race. The Negro is committing too much crime North and South. We should see to it, as far as our influence extends, that crimes are fewer in number; otherwise the race will permanently suffer...In this connection let us consider the classes of Negroes that do not commit crime and are seldom charged with crime. They are those who own homes, who are tax-payers, who have a trade or other regular occupation; they are those who are in professional service; those who have received education and such business men and women as those who compose this organization....I have named the classes that do not commit crime. Which is the class that is guilty, as a rule, of criminal action? They are the loafers, the drunkards and gamblers, men for the main part without permanent employment, who own no homes, who have no bank account, who glide from one community to another without interest in any one spot. One of the practical courses that men such as those who compose this business league, our

leaders in the pulpit and every sphere of life, should pursue is to try to get hold of the floating class of our people and see to it that their lives are so changed as to make them cease to disgrace our race and disturb our civilization. We cannot be too frank or too strong in discussing the harm that the committing of crime is doing to our race. Let us stand up straight and speak out and act in no uncertain terms in this direction.[27]

This criminal class of which Washington spoke is the very class that birthed black serial killers. In almost every instance prior to 1900, black serial killers were not tied down to one location, but instead were always fleeing from their crimes. Some killed in one or two states, while others, such as Frank Johnson and John Clark, killed in at least five states. After 1900, the problem still persisted but was not as widespread, yet was seen in Jake Bird's story of killing 44 people in at least 11 states over a twenty-year span. This trend did slow down after 1900 as more black men strived to adhere to what Washington and other black activists said. However, the problem still surfaces in our modern age in small part, as new killers surface every decade who drift from one kill to the next.

Trends from 1900 to 1960

From 1900 to 1949, black serial killers made up the majority of serial killers in the US. Of the 125 known serial killers, 67 were black, which was 53.60% of the total. They outnumbered white serial killers 1.15 to 1. But as their numbers had steadily risen from 1860 to 1900, from 1900 to 1950 their ranks hit a plateau that produced between eleven and fifteen new killers every decade. This pattern held steady until 1960, when their numbers took a drastic increase.

From 1930 to 1950, the number of black killers in each decade was between 12 and 13, yet in each decade their overrepresentation dropped from 3.878 in 1930 to 3.02 in 1950. While the number of black serial killers did not change significantly, that of whites did. In this same time span, white serial killers jumped from 20 in 1930 to 30 in 1950 (see Table 3.1). In addition to this, the overall black population grew from its all-time low of 9.7% in 1930 to 10% in 1950. Thus the drop in overrepresentation factor was not due to a decline in black serial killers in this time period, but instead due primarily to a rise in white serial killers, in combination with the rise in the total black population.

Perhaps the most useful tool when trying to find a trend in serial killers is the percentage of serial killers a given race represents in a given decade. In Table 3.1 earlier in the chapter, the abbreviation *%BSK* is used to mark this column. Prior to 1930, blacks made up the overwhelming majority of serial killers, but from 1920 to 1930 their percentile took a dive from 62.5% to 35.48%, even though their number increased by two in the same span. During this same period, white serial killers increased by a factor of 3.33, from 6 in 1930 to 20 in 1940. Numerous reasons for this explosion in white serial killers have been posited, but most likely their numbers rose as a result of the stress of the Great Depression, in combination with a drastic decline in large cities of traditional European family values. The black population, while affected to some degree by the Great Depression, was accustomed to living in poor conditions, and they had never taken as a whole to European values, which is why their population remained fairly steady during this same period. Whites in large cities, on the other hand, were bankrupted financially overnight, causing many to forsake their values and turn to criminal endeavors to survive. As property crimes rose, so did violent crimes, with some even turning to serial murder. In addition to this, the effect of WWI has to be a minor contributing factor. As young fathers went into battle only to return in a coffin, a portion of the population was raised by single mothers. As noted by Booker T. Washington, when a father is not around to instruct his children, the children stand a greater chance of turning to lawless criminal activity as adults.

The Trend Skyrockets

For both white and black serial killers, their numbers both increased over twofold in 1960 from the previous decade. When seeing a severe spike like this, people want to know the causation behind the jump. There were possibly several factors at play, some which blacks and whites shared and others which catered to one group or the other. The hard fact is that, in the 100 years prior to 1960, there were only 208 known serial murderers, yet from 1960 to present, there have been 1,718.

1960 marked the release of Alfred Hitchcock's *Psycho*, a controversial film which would shape all movies in the serial-killer genre that followed. At the time of its release, the Motion Picture Production Code, known also as the Hayes Code, set moral censorship guidelines for the motion picture industry. These guidelines had restricted anything morally unacceptable, such as nudity, sexual scenes, extreme violence, murder techniques, and other questionable or taboo topics. Stephen Prince gave a good description of what the code did with the subject of violence: "The section of Principles and Plot makes reference to 'murder,' 'cruelty,' 'brutality,' and 'repellent crimes' and cautions filmmakers not to give these such attention as to make viewers 'accustomed' to them. The subsection on Plot Material refers to 'brutal killings', which are not to be shown as justified; 'criminals,' who should not be heroized; and 'methods of committing crime,' which should not be dwelt upon lest some viewers learn techniques of law-breaking."[28]

By the time *Psycho* was released, the Hayes Code was crumbling fast, with filmmakers pushing harder to stretch their interpretation of the code with what they called "artistic license." When Hitchcock's film was sent for approval, he wrestled with the Code board over numerous things, but gave little concession to their demands. After getting approval by minimally cutting what was required, his film set the new standard for violence. While the film is quite tame compared to modern standards, the images of Norman Bates killing his victims brutally, in conjunction with the sexual innuendos, was something that had never been shown before. French film critic Serge Kaganski described how the film was received by the public: "The shower scene is both feared and desired. Hitchcock may be scaring his female viewers out of their wits, but he is turning his male viewers into potential rapists, since Janet Leigh has been turning men on ever since she appeared in her brassiere in the first scene."[29] I would argue not only that it inspired men to rape, but also that it gave them imagery for how a serial killer pulls off a crime and disposes of a body.

Soon afterward, other filmmakers followed suit, bringing new films that portrayed violence each year, showing different murder techniques and themes which filmmakers claimed were intended to shock viewers. While viewers were riveted, a new phenomenon took place. In horror films prior to 1960, viewers left the theater often with thoughts of how they would get out of a situation if they were the victim. However, with the onset of more violence and the presentation of the methods used by killers, people began thinking of how they would improve on the killer's tactics and avoid being caught. This was not particularly new, and it should not be construed as sociopathic behavior, only as reflecting people's innate curiosity to place themselves in a variety of roles, including the killer's. But Hollywood helped fuel this idea, providing visual imagery to stir the mind and leaving a portion of the audience wondering how the crime could be perfected. In generations later, as with the hit show *Dexter*, viewers would even find themselves sympathizing with the killer, rooting for him as he avoids capture.

Hollywood has argued for years that their films do not encourage violence, but instead portray it as an artistic means of entertainment. However, the truth is that in every decade since the 1960s, there have been copycat crimes in which the criminal tells the court that his inspiration was a motion picture or television show. Take, for instance, Nathaniel White, a black serial killer of six: "The first girl I killed was from a 'Robocop' movie... I seen him cut somebody's throat then take the knife and slit down the chest to the stomach and left the body in a certain position. With the first person I killed I did exactly what I saw in the movie."[30] But aside from stories like this, generations of children and young adults have taken to acting out their favorite films for fun, even making their own mini-movies, as was the craze during the days of the 8 mm film festivals. While most of these films and acting sessions were innocent, there were some that portrayed the serial killers from films such as *Psycho* or *Dirty Harry*. Therefore, it is a reasonable argument to assert that the spike in serial killings for both blacks and whites was in some portion influenced by the increase in violence in films in the 1960s.

Hollywood was not the only influence on this spike, however; there were other factors that have to be considered. For both white and black serial killers, the influence of the sexual revolution must not be underestimated. Sigmund Freund, in what he deemed his Hannibal-esque struggle to overcome the traditional views of Europe,[31] taught that people needed to embrace sexual taboos. Later, this idea would be picked up by Alfred Kinsey, and then by Margaret Mead, who encouraged the age-old sexual taboo practices which had been frowned upon by the Occidental people, asserting that they needed to be seen as enriching and fulfilling.

Slowly, as a result of all their work, other authors began to write on the subject; and soon, the traditional sexual values of old—that a man and his wife were to be united in monogamous heterosexual union—were slowly eroded. This revolution gained lots of momentum through the forties and fifties, eventually coming to full speed during the sixties. Young people everywhere were breaking sexual prohibitions, thereby marking it as the Decade of Love—not because of real love for one another, but because they chose to venture into ideas once unmentionable.

Along with this sexual revolution, other more sinister taboos were explored, such as rape. Once considered the evilest of things that could befall a woman, some women took to fantasizing about being the victims of rape, while others staged their sexual encounters to mimic mock rapes. By the 1980s, pornographers had picked up on the topic and began making films portraying women getting raped, oftentimes violently. Sometimes, along with rape, another forbidden idea began to be explored: autoerotic asphyxiation. This revolting and dangerous practice involves oxygen being deprived from the brain during sex for an increased stimulus, whether via suffocation, strangulation, or even hanging. As expected, people died occasionally from this practice, sometimes by accident but other times as a means of suicide. Both of these taboos would in later years spawn the genre of pornographic snuff films, staged films in which one or both of these practices would be used to mock-kill a person. While this genre of film is a minority in the porn industry, it still has a somewhat large following. One black serial killer, Maury Troy Travis, made his own snuff films in which the women really died.

During the 1960s, the pornographic industry, which had been a closet industry reserved for red-light districts and dark alleyways, began to become more widely known. This morally depraved industry claimed to be for entertainment purposes, but as they explored each dark idea, more and more people began experimenting on their own to see if it felt as good as portrayed. One of the more popular of the dark taboos was torture, which had once been reserved only for swanky brothels, full of ladies clad in leather with whips in hand. But as the production of torture films rose, so did the number of serial killers encouraged by them. Lester

Harrison, a black serial killer from Chicago, would watch a torture porn flick before the murder and rape of each of the six women he attacked.

Even without pornography, the sexual revolution taught a generation of Americans that it was acceptable to thumb their nose at forbidden things. The revolutionaries told people that they were not beholden to a set of moral confines; they were accountable to themselves and to no one else—especially not to an outside force like God. In their minds, the recipients of the sexual revolution made their own destiny, which meant that they made their own policies about what was right or wrong. Therefore, not only did the heirs of this revolution question sexual practices, but they began to question other off-limits subjects like suicide and murder. As people tested the fences, many began to reason that if they made the rules, then it was acceptable to murder, regardless of what a governing body and its stuffy old laws said.

Hollywood did not help this problem either, but instead helped fuel it, by portraying humans as disposable blobs of matter. With this sort of encouragement, serial killers were made, not simply because they were born with some chemical imbalance, but because they were taught that some human life was meaningless and that they should take a nihilistic approach to laws. It is safe to say that serial killers of every stripe, to some degree, are a product of the society that made them.

Also in the 1960s was another revolution, one which had gained momentum in prior decades, was encouraged by the success of the sex revolution, and came to fruition in 1964. The Civil Rights Movement was supposed to be a peaceful movement which protested for the rights of blacks as they sought equality in a white society. But while its leaders may have peacefully demonstrated, oftentimes the recipients of their message did not; they heard the words and acted in an effort to throw off what they felt were their white oppressors. It therefore bears mentioning that black serial killers took their first serious rise in the same decade as this movement, more than tripling in number from 12 in the 1950s to 39 that started in the 1960s. But when looking at the startup years for each, the tale is even more telling. From 1960 to the end of 1963, there had been seven blacks who began serial murdering, a number that would have been on track with the prior decade. 1964 was the year their numbers spiked, with 36 killers beginning their crimes from 1964-1969.

One can't rule out the impact the Civil Rights Movement had as a major contributing factor as to this increase.

When looking at other violent crimes, the trend is the same. While blacks did commit crime prior to the 1960s, there was a sharp increase in their overall numbers in the years leading up to the Civil Rights Movement. And while these numbers did plateau in the 1960s, the important point is that they were sustained, not seeing any drop until the mid- to late 70s.[32] It is safe to assume that there is some correlation between the Civil Rights Movement and black serial killers. While this may have primarily been within militant Black Muslim groups, these groups nevertheless were fueled by this movement before spinning off in their own direction.

The last significant contributing factor to consider is one which most of the younger generation take for granted: the interstate highway system. While some may assume it has been around as long as the automobile, the truth is that it is a relatively new system. Before the passing of the Federal Aid Highway Act of 1956, there were paved roads in existence, such as the famous Route 66. However, the interstate system made intra-state and cross-country travel faster by eliminating stops, allowing a relatively continuous speed when traveling from point A to point B. In conjunction with automobiles' being made more comfortable for longer trips, this allowed serial killers to travel farther and wider in their search for quarry. Along with the building of interstates came the shift from rail transportation of goods to trucking companies; this influenced some truckers to become serial killers, able to murder in states far from their home without fear of their crimes being tracked. While vastly improved roads played into serial killers' hands, it was not until the 1980s when most states finally completed their roads. However, the start was in the early 1960s, which, along with the previous causes, provided a clear avenue for killers to travel unheeded from one kill to another.

When trying to assess what caused the 1960s spike in serial killers, these factors must be considered a part of the equation for both black and white killers. However, there is another additional minor factor that has been suggested. Most killers who began in the 60s were young men, born prior to or during WWII. It is possible that the death stories the servicemen brought home from both WWII and the Korean War may have calloused some killers towards human death, making them more susceptible to become killers. While this may have factored into some serial killers' psyches, there was no notable spike after WWI or after the War Between the States.

While the 1960s saw a spike in serial killers, the 1970s experienced an explosion. In the 1960s, white serial killers grew by 250% from the previous decade, while the black ranks grew by 331%. In the 70s, the numbers were even bigger, with white killers growing from 76 to 218 for a 286% increase. Blacks saw unprecedented growth too, jumping from 43 killers to 154 for a 358% increase. Neither of these figures was even close to being representative of the increase in overall US population, which was only 13.3% for this time period. The only indicators of this increase were those factors that arose in the 1960s, but in the 1970s they became larger and more widespread. For instance, pornography increased more than tenfold in sales, whereas, with the demise of the Motion Picture Code, Hollywood saw a dramatic increase in the number of slasher-styled serial killer films.

Corresponding with this, police-themed television shows, which in earlier years had a whimsical touch and portrayed little investigative work, became more serious in the 1970s, oftentimes involving what actual police fieldwork was like. While the media's depiction of the investigation usually paled in comparison to actual police work, there is a possibility that serial killers picked up bits of information from this genre of show and tried to use it in an effort to evade police. It was during the 1970s that these dramas first began to mirror the real police work, and it was through these shows (and movies like them) that people learned the value a well-placed fingerprint is to detectives. However, as with the other factors this cannot be singled out as the primary cause, but only as a piece of the puzzle that helped influence this massive increase in serial killers.

Another factor to consider in this leap, at least in black serial killers, is the rise of the black gangs. Many of the famous black gangs, like the Crips, Folk Nation, and the Black P. Stones, started off in the decades prior to the Civil Rights Movement as non-violent groups. However, after 1964, some of these groups began to dabble in the sale of illegal drugs and went to murderous means to protect their turf and to show their dominance. Along with this, some older Civil Rights groups did not take the drug route, but instead became belligerent black militias. Some of these groups, like the Black Mafia, focused their aggression on other blacks, while others, like the Angel of Death cult (Zebra Killers), began hunting whites. Both the drug-pushing gangs and the militant groups would spawn countless gangs over the next four decades.

But critics may balk and point out that those 218 white serial killers comprise a much greater number than the 154 black serial killers from the 1970s. This is true, but while the 1960s saw black serial killers account for 35.83% of all serial killers, the 1970s saw that number rise to 40.00%. This means that blacks were overrepresented by a factor of 3.60 in comparison to their population, while whites were still underrepresented by a factor of 1.55 in relation to their population. While critics will always be quick to point out that white serial killers have outnumbered blacks from 1930 to 1980, they fail to notice that in the history of white serial killers, whites have never killed in proportion to what their population represents. The closest they came to that was in the 1950s, where they were still underrepresented by a factor of 1.28. By comparison, however, remember that blacks have always been overrepresented by a factor of at least 3.02.

In the 1990s was the first significant downturn in white serial killers. In just a matter of a decade, their numbers decreased by 23.34%. Some will claim the reason is that many have not been caught, which is possibly true. However, even if every unsolved serial killer case from the 90s brought only white killers to justice, the number would not rise much above the current figure. With the advent of DNA analysis and the continual rise in technology surrounding it, the number of unsolved murders decreased dramatically in the 90s. Also, every unsolved murder is not a result of a serial killer; many are committed by one-time offenders. However, even if the number were to rise, it would be only slightly, which would not be significant for the purpose of comparison.

During the 1990s, while white serial killers decreased, blacks rose by 13.52%. Along with this increase, the percentage of serial killers who were black rose as well. Whereas the 1980s saw blacks represent

43.38% of all serial killers for that decade, the 1990s saw the number increase to 56.90%.

Some have been curious as to what caused the decrease in white serial killers in the 1990s. Again, there is no definitive answer, but there are contributing factors. As mentioned earlier, the 1990s brought about the reliability of forensics DNA evidence in court, in addition to improved methods of gathering and preserving physical evidence. Along with this, as a result of the higher number of murders in the 1980s, the 1990s saw an increase in police-force size around the nation. As a result, it is reasonable to assert that white serial killers became scared that they would be caught.

Awareness about sociopathic behavior became more readily known as well. People began to learn what the warning signs were, in addition to possible factors that contributed to making someone a serial killer. Documentaries and books on the subject told millions about this phenomenon and documented the punishment of serial killers. As stated earlier, most of these resources focused almost exclusively on white killers, who for the most part earned a death sentence for their crimes.

These aspects probably helped curb many potential white serial killers, but blacks' numbers did not drop much. In the late 80s and early 90s a new music genre, gangster rap, hit young blacks and did much to shape their mind about the world around them. While there were a few early examples from the mid-80s, the first big song to hit the scene was "Straight Outta Compton" by N.W.A. in 1988. Other acts soon followed, with Snoop Dogg hitting the scene in 1993 and taking the genre to an entirely new level of violent lyrics and ideas.

Many of these rappers had grown up in a violent inner-city environment, where many had connections with gangs and some were gang members themselves. Their music glorified killing as a way of life, being an easy means to eliminate people with whom they disagreed or had a bad business deal. From the beginning, this genre had a heavy insistence that the police represented "whitey," whose sole purpose was to "get a brother down" and

Sir Mario Owens

to further oppress blacks in their struggle for equality. As a result, some songs encouraged killing police, raping white women, and even killing whites at random, all in an effort to show their authority and assert that they would not be beaten down.

Sometimes these themes even carried over to the album covers, as with Ice T's 1993 release of *Home Invasion*. On the cover is a horrifying scene taking place inside an underground storage bunker, in which we're left to surmise a race war is underway on the outside. Inside the bunker a white teenager is seen dressed in African garb while listening to rap music on his earphones, with drug paraphernalia nearby. In the background, his dad lies dead with the butt of a rifle against his head in the hands of a black intruder. Just behind him and to the right is his mother, in her undergarments and with her breasts exposed as she is being raped by another black intruder; and another is guarding the door. This sort of imagery had a powerful effect on young black men, especially those who grew up fatherless and looked to whatever role model was the hippest and most daring.

Police across the county have noted the tendency of black criminals to mirror the behavior depicted by gangster rappers. In Colorado Springs, police noticed the connection of violence to gangster rap,[33] while in Houston, TX, in 1993, a black teenager, inspired by a song by Tupac Shakur, shot a police officer in his car.[34] There are dozens of additional examples, but rap artists deny that their music promotes violence, all despite the constant stream of young criminals claiming gangster rap as their inspiration.

While it is difficult to track how many serial killers were influenced by gangster rap, there is an indication that at least two were influenced. Ralph McLean killed two law enforcement officers in separate events, and severely wounded another. After a shootout with police in which he was killed, a search of his apartment yielded his adoration for gangster rap, including his own lyrics boasting of his gratification when killing white cops. Sir Mario Owens, guilty of killing three people, was the first serial killer to get a MySpace page in prison, and he made national news because of it. A look at his musical interests on the page shows solely gangster rap, with most of the artists inclined towards violence against whites or police. However, whether gangster rap was a major contributing source fueling black serial killers in the 1990's or not, it cannot be ruled out as insignificant. It is hard to argue against this, because many rappers have paid tribute to convicted murderers in their songs, with at least one serial killer, Pistol Pete Rollack, memorialized for the eight murders he committed. Sadly, though, the music industry and artists do not dispute that this genre glorifies murder, but simply insist that it has a benign effect on the listener.

The last two decades' stories are still being written, as there will be occasional news of a serial killer apprehended who began in the new millennium. However, there are still sufficient numbers to enable us to accurately track trends. Significantly, we can note that a serious rise in violent gangs occurred in the late 1990s, one which shows no signs of slowing. Therefore there are numerous gang members who have not been apprehended, or have only been charged with one murder, despite having committed several, and with the constant onslaught of gang members turning up in the news on a daily basis, it is difficult to keep up with each one fitting the description of a serial murderer. For instance, there are eight Hispanic serial murderer between 2000 and 2010, whereas there are probably dozens of Latino gang members in and out of prison who easily qualify for inclusion into the list. In years to come, as further information comes to light about them, they will be added to the list for future publications. But even without them, there is already a notable trend established even with the expected future inclusion of additional serial killers of any race.

For the decade of 2000-2010, white serial killers decreased by 53.89% and were underrepresented by a factor of 4.21 times less than their population. During the same time, blacks had an increase of 21.07%, but there were still 4.60 times more black serial killers than whites: overall, blacks accounted for 77.97% of all serial killers from 2000-2010! Despite this fact, it was in this decade that the race of the Beltway Snipers was revealed to the public, and the general perception by both authorities and the public was that black serial killers did not exist or were at least severely underrepresented. On the contrary, in that decade blacks killed by a factor of 6.34 times their population, when compared to the 12.3% of the population they comprised. In no way can this be construed as "underrepresented." Remember as well that whites were underrepresented by a factor of 4.21, which means that they ranked at a rate that is only 17.86% in comparison to their population. 100% would indicate that they were perfectly represented, yet they were closer to one fifth of that figure.

Another factor to consider, which will be covered in the next chapter, is murderers who kill again after they are released from prison. The decade of 1990-2000 saw a serious rise due to repeat offenders. In conjunction with that, there are numerous black serial killers who were only recently convicted, due to a resolution of an unsolved murder via DNA. Consequently, it is reasonable to assume that the number of 184 known black serial killers for the decade of 2000-2010 will rise as murderers are paroled and as more cold cases are solved. For instance, just in the few years between the release of the 1st and 2nd edition of this book there have been 137 black serial killers that have surfaced! Some started their crimes as early as the 1980's and were recent parolees, but there was a sizable portion that were new killers.

Our current decade is proving to be no different: barely halfway thru as of this second edition, already there have been 66 serial killers that have surfaced in this decade thus far. Of these, nine are white, fifty-one are black[35], and six are Hispanic, which means (obviously) that black serial killers outnumber whites by a ratio of almost four-to-one. If this dangerous trend continues, it's not unreasonable to expect the decade of 2010-2020 to produce 200 plus black serial killers. Compare this to the falling number of white killers, which by all estimates will likely be closer to 45. The percentage of black serial killers (77.27%) shows no signs of deviating this decade.

Based off the current available information for this decade, blacks are overrepresented by a factor of 6.13 when compared to their population, which currently sits at 12.6% of the total population. By comparison, white serial killers are underrepresented by a factor of 5.31. If these stats are depicted graphically, with 0 representing 100% of representation (e.g. if 12.6% of serial killers were black), the results are startling: blacks would be located at positive 6.13 while whites would be below negative 5.31. These opposite ends of the spectrum are not anomalous, but indicate a trend showing white serial killers falling in number, while blacks are maintaining or gaining in their numbers. The following table illustrates this trend. For the sake of clarity, zero represents perfect representation with the population, a one-to-one ratio. A factor above zero is the amount overrepresented, while a negative factor indicates the amount underrepresented. Notice that as one group gets farther from the norm, the other goes in the opposite direction, while as one gets closer, the other gets closer as well. Also note that at no point in the last 150 years are black serial killers underrepresented or white killers overrepresented. They consistently stand at opposite ends of the field.

**Chart 3.4- Comparing Black Serial Killer
Overrepresentation with
White Serial Killer Underrepresentation**

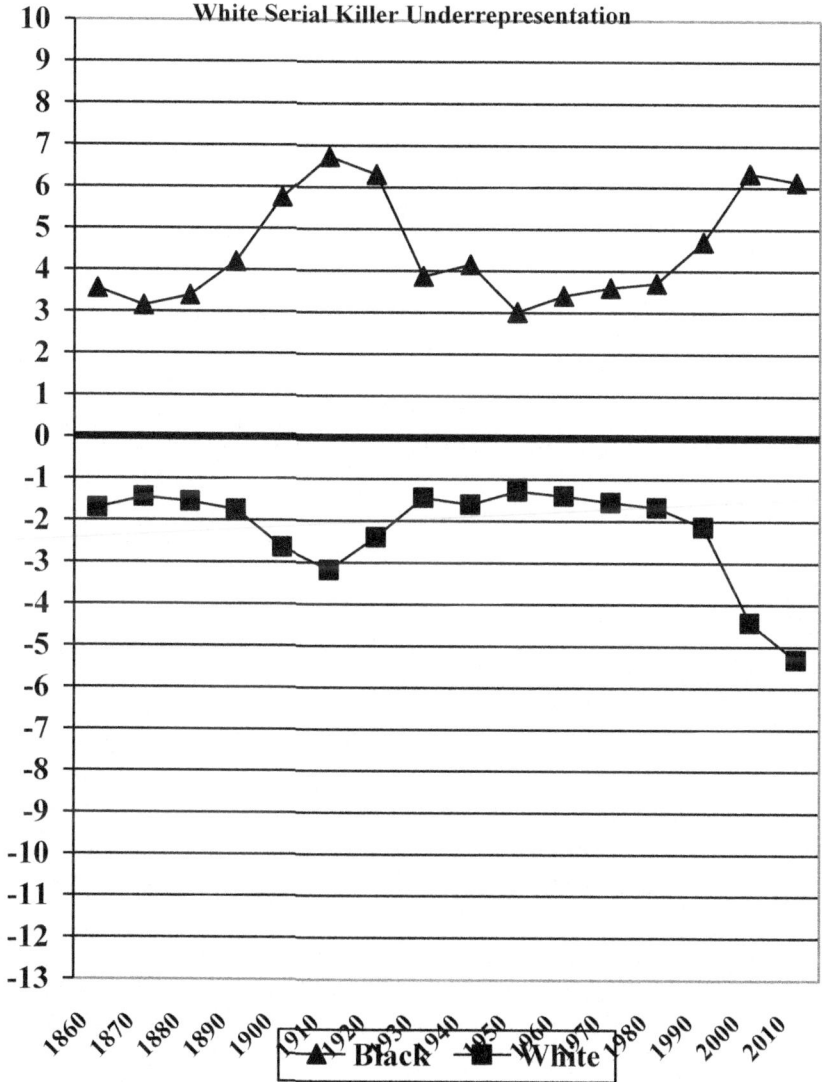

Accepting the Facts

With black serial killers now constituting the majority of killers since 1990, it raises the question: when will we see truth and fair reporting by the mainstream media on this subject? When will movies start portraying knife-wielding serial killers who are black? The answer does not look good; as mentioned in the previous chapter, there is an outright war against the white male in America. If he does not recognize blacks for their grand achievements, he is damned, and if he points out any negative achievement, as contained in these figures, he is even more damned. It is the classic "damned if I do, damned if I don't" paradox.

I have been called racist, bigot, liar, hateful, inbred, redneck, undereducated, stupid, and a host of other derogatory names for just pointing out these obvious facts. This has led me to conclude that some people view facts as racist if they portray blacks in a negative light, but enriching, meaningful data if they demonize whites. Proof of this can be seen in the recent MLK Parade Bomber debacle from Spokane, WA. Kevin Harpham was convicted to thirty-two years in prison for supposedly planting a pipe bomb on the parade route for an MLK day parade in January 2011.[36] It is unknown and highly speculative if the device would have done much damage, or if the device would have even been capable of detonation. Yet, his face was pasted on every new channel in the land for eleven months, from the discovery of the backpack that held the bomb to his conviction. His face has become the new face of hate, and Jesse Jackson proclaimed his normal rhetoric when asked about the impact of the MLK Parade Bomber: "Today we have achieved freedom in America, now we need to achieve equality."[37] Soon after Harpham's arrest, the NAACP arrived with much pomp and fanfare in Spokane to march against hate, despite the fact that not a soul was injured.[38]

Yet, where were Jesse Jackson, Al Sharpton, and the other black activists proclaiming that Joshua Julius Anderson was the new face of horrible serial killers when he was caught in 2007?[39] Where was Joshua's face on national news when it was discovered that he had raped a sixty-nine-year-old woman of his race and then forced her fifty-one-year-old son at gunpoint to have sex with her? Why did his story not make news for weeks during his trial when it became known that, after killing this woman, he ate part of her brains and then burned the two bodies beyond recognition? Why did his story make barely a ripple outside Oklahoma, despite his having killed five to seven people from 2006 to 2007? The answer to each question is clearly because he is black; his story would be construed as strumming up support for a harmful stereotype towards all blacks. Yet, had Anderson been white and committed the same crimes on white people, he would have been the next Jeffrey Dahmer, and Hollywood producers and authors would have stood in line to be the first to tell his story. But this man is unheard of. While the citizens of Spokane are bound to hear about Kevin Harpham every MLK Day for years to come, Joshua Anderson is already forgotten by many in Tulsa.

Black detractors will argue that the reason for this inequality is because Anderson's victims were black; had they been white, we would all know his name. While this answer is intuitively appealing to some, it is baseless and easily proven wrong, for there are dozens of mostly-unknown black serial killers who killed only white victims. For instance, in 2005, Gary Sinegal raped and killed five elderly white women in the vicinity of Port Arthur, TX.[40] Yet aside from a few initial snippets on national television towards the middle of the broadcasts (where non-important news is inserted), he is unheard of. Outside of the Houston area, news of his trial was never mentioned in the national news media. Even in local channels, it was not front-page news, whereas during Kevin Harper's trial in Spokane, every channel in Spokane and Seattle markets aired him as a top story. This is not fair and balanced reporting, but an example of the prejudice against white criminals and the media that has been scared to portray black criminals accurately. The double standard exists, and it has no future signs of cracking.

My hope is that the subject of black serial killers will not be a taboo subject. It should be that both blacks and whites can look at the data, agree that the crimes are horrible, and then work together in an attempt to slow the rising trend. Instead, whites are accused of racism and lambasted if they mention black serial killers, even as the media suppresses a serial killer such as Sinegal or Anderson.

ENDNOTE

[1] Veale, Jennifer, *A Family's Shame in Korea*. Time Magazine. April 22, 2007. Retrieved September 16, 2008.

[2] Gemperlein, Joyce, *Surratt Gets 200 Years and Life*, Pittsburgh Post-Gazette, October 28, 1978.

[3] *Stanley Williams Deserves to Die for 1979 Murders*, Bakersfield Californian, December 7, 2005.

[4] Holmes, Ronald & Holmes, Stephen, *Serial Murder, 3rd Edition*, 2009 p. 140

[5] *Townsend Set Free After 22 Years*, The Miami Herald, June 16, 2001.

[6] O'Boye, McMahon, & Friedberg, *Death Row Prisoner Dies; Now, DNA Test Clears Him*, South Florida Sun, December 15, 2000.

[7] An excellent blog detailing the crimes, and fairly substantial proof that Loving Mitchell didn't commit them, can be found at http://gettingtheaxe.blogspot.com/search/label/Lovey%20Mitchell

[8] Associated Press, *Seattle Woman is Stabbed*, Lewiston Evening Journal, August 14, 1973.

[9] Hickey, Edward, *Serial Killers and Their Victims*, 1997, p. 136

[10] Newton, Michael, *Serial Slaughter: What's Behind America's Murder Epidemic?* 1992, p. 49.

[11] Jenkins, P. (1998). *African Americans and serial homicide*. In R. Holmes & S. Holmes (Eds.), *Contemporary perspectives on serial murder* (pp. 17-32).

[12] Ressler, Robert K.; Thomas Schachtman. *Whoever Fights Monsters: My Twenty Years Tracking Serial Killers for the FBI*. 1993, p. 29.

[13] Class notes for Psychology 405 taught by Michael Aamodt at Radford University. Downloaded 1/6/2012: http://maamodt.asp.radford.edu/Psyc%20405/Student%20Notes%20-%20Serial%20Killers.pdf

[14] *Arrest of Boy Accused of Five Murders*, New York Times, May 4, 1867.

[15] Otken, Charles, *Ills of the South*, 1894.

[16] DuBois, W.E.B. & Eaton, Isabel, *The Philadelphia Negro: A Social Study*, 1899.

[17] Hoffman, Frederick, *Race Traits and Tendencies of the American Negro*, 1896. p 217.

[18] Ibid, Du Bois, p. 20.

[19] Ibid., Du Bois. p. 14.

[20] Washington, Booker T., *The Story of the Negro: the Rise of the Race From Slavery, Volume 2*, 1909. p. 88.

[21] Fleming, Walter Lynwood, *Civil War and Reconstruction in Alabama*, 1905. p. 762.

[22] *The Negro's Progress in Fifty Years*, American Academy of Political and Social Science Vol. XLIX, Editor Emory R. Johnson, 1913.

[23] Ibid Otken, p. 222.

[24] Ibid., Otken.

[25] Ibid., Du Bois.

[26] Stone, Alfred Holt, *Studies in the American Race Problem*, 1908.

[27] Washington, Booker T., in a speech before the National Negro Business League entitled, *Law-Breaking Negroes Worst Menace to Race*. August 1906, reported in the Atlanta Constitution Paper, August 29, 1906.

[28] Prince, Stephen, *Classical Film Violence: Designing and Regulating Brutality in Hollywood*, 2003, pgs 30-31.

[29] Kaganski, Serge, *Alfred Hitchcock*. Paris: Hazan. 1997.

[30] Karen Freifeld, *Tale of Death Suspect says 'Robocop' sparked spree*, Newsday, August 6, 1992.

[31] Armstrong, S, *Freud's Hannibal: New Light on Freud's Moses*. ,Psychoanalytic Review, 2008, 95:231-257.

[32] LaFree, Gary, Race and Crime trends in the United States 1946-1990, in *Ethnicity, Race, and Crime* edited by Darnell F. Hawkins.1995, pp 181-182.

[33] Frosch, Dan, *Colorado Police Link Rise in Violence to Music*, New York Times, September 3, 2007.

[34] Moreno, Sylvia, *Stakes High in Murder by Rap Fan*, Dallas Morning News, June 21, 1993.

[3535] As of June 2015, there are an additional five serial killers where eye witnesses list the suspect as black. In addition to this, there are another 15 or so serial killers leaving a string of bodies in cities like Detroit, Atlanta, New York City, and Gary, IN. Police suspect the killers are black, but until their apprehension it's still speculative.

[36] Clouse, Thomas and Cuniff, Meghann, *White Supremacist Arrested in MLK Bomb Plot*, Spokesman-Review, March 10, 2011.

[37] Graman, Kevin, Jesse Jackson: *MLK Bomb Planter 'More Sick than Mean'*, Spokesman Review, February 7, 2011.

[38] Graman, Kevin, *NAACP Leader Coming to Spokane*, Spokesman Review, March 28, 2011.

[39] Braun, Bill, *Jury Hears of Suspect's Confession*, Tulsa World, October 23, 2008.

[40] *Sinegal Sentenced to Life in Prison*, Port Arthur News, April 9, 2007.

Chapter 4

Breaking Down the Black Serial Killer

Just as their white counterparts, black serial killers are hiding in plain sight. Whenever they are caught, their neighbors are surprised and often shocked that the person they knew, even chatted with on occasion, had a dark secret. Also, as their white counterparts, black serial killers come from a wide array of socioeconomic backgrounds, from dirt poor to residents of upscale neighborhoods. Some were loved as a child; others were abused. Some have below average intelligence; others are above average. The common theme is that they are sick monsters who enjoy killing others and who do not care whether their victims suffer or die quickly.

Despite evidence that serial killers come in all shapes and sizes, having representatives from all races, the assumption is that most are white. The classic description of a serial killer, the drawing board used by criminal profilers until the last decade, generally looked like this. :

- White, middle-class male, average build, in his mid-30s
- Intelligence: average to above average intelligence
- Childhood: abused to some degree, possible bed-wetter, enjoyed torturing animals
- Trigger Event: Some traumatic, life-changing event set him off
- Killed each time in a different location

This system was problematic, however, as it effectively indicted a large portion of Americans as prime serial killing suspects. It proved to be a failure from the start as each category was systematically disproven, time and time again, as the stereotypical mold was shown to be faulty. Not only did serial killers of other races surface, but serial killers older and younger than the norm were prevalent. Soon, authorities became aware of female killers, killers who were mildly retarded, and killers who killed their victims in one location. Some were the products of loving homes; others grew up in dysfunctional homes. The profile needed to be discarded.

Yet, instead of abandoning the failed profile, the FBI and most police agencies kept plowing forward, claiming that anyone who fell outside the narrow scope of this profile was an anomaly. This was the case for Derrick Todd Lee. Police in Baton Rouge were originally looking for a white serial killer, despite the fact that the victims were white: "Derrick Lee's ethnicity may have helped him escape capture for a while. The task force looking for a suspected serial killer initially released a composite photo of a white man. Two days after authorities said the killer may not be white, Lee was arrested."[1]

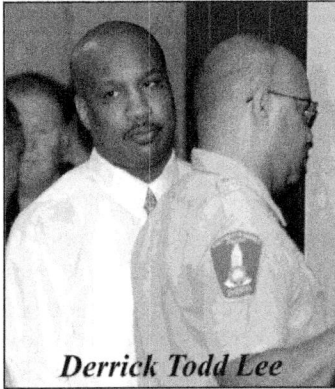

Derrick Todd Lee

As more anomalies like Lee surfaced, the FBI finally conceded. They adopted a new, more general policy which allowed police the flexibility to entertain the possibility of serial killers from a variety of walks of life, from any of the races. Essentially anyone who has a pulse and is able to commit murder fits the new profile, which, despite its generality, is a major improvement over the old biased version. "Contrary to popular belief, serial killers span all racial groups. There are white, African-American, Hispanic, and Asian serial killers....All serial murders are not sexually-based. There are other motivations for serial murder including anger, thrill, financial gain, and attention seeking."[2]

Just as with the old serial killer profile, there is no fool-proof mold that fits all black serial killers. However, certain generalizations can be made when comparing them to their white counterparts. But even with those, there are numerous examples that fall outside of the norm on one or all generalizations. The truth is simply that there is no one size that fits all black serial killers.

Intelligence

The first question when people ask about any serial killer is: What is his intelligence? The answer is that both black and white killers fall within the norm of their respective race's average intelligence. There certainly are killers who fall outside this range within both races, but it is often falsely assumed that serial killers are all of super intelligence. Classic examples are Ted Bundy and Gary Heidnik, who had IQs of 136 and 130, respectively; but these are both exceptions and not the norm. In fact, a study of known serial killer IQ tests by Radford University has found only twenty-one serial killers with IQs higher than 127, and another study indicated that many killers fell below 100.[3]

An example of the far spread can be seen in looking at the lowest and highest IQs for serial killers in each race. (It should be noted that 70 is considered the breaking line for mild mental retardation.) For the blacks, the lowest intelligence found in this database goes to Eddie Lee Mosley, who tested between 44 and 63, with most agreeing he was closer to 51[4]. For the whites, the lowest of which I am aware is Simon Pirela, with a score of 57[5]. Both of these are well into the range of mild retardation, which, lawyers argue, proves that they cannot differentiate between right and wrong; yet it should be noted that they both knew how to murder, how to rape, and the difference between life and death.

On the high side for whites, Ted Kaczynski had an IQ between 155 and 165, which is considered genius level. For blacks, George Waterfield Russell, Jr., and Cleophus Prince appear to have been two of the smartest in my database, yet their respective IQs are unknown but reported to be higher than average. However, both Russell and Prince, despite their higher-than-average intelligence, used strangulation as their kill method, which was once considered a trait of lower-intelligence killers. This is proof that even intelligent killers use disorganized killing methods, meaning that there is no necessary or prescriptive mold that corresponds a killer's intelligence to his kill method.

When comparing the intelligence of white serial killers to blacks, however, there is a difference, but it follows the standard norm for each race's intelligence. *The Bell Curve*, which is the preeminent source for racial intelligence and its relationship to different aspects of life, lists blacks' average IQ as 85 and whites' as 100.[6] Contrary to what some internet sites claim, black serial killers most always fall into the average for their race's respective normal IQ, not below. In an effort to show that there are no black serial killers, some internet sites suggest this, but in doing so, they greatly demoralize blacks in the process. Blacks are smart enough to be serial killers; the notion that they are not needs to be dropped.

This is important, because to mention blacks and serial killers in the same breath is oftentimes a double-edged sword. On the one hand, blacks do not like the idea of their people being serial killers, but on the other, they are insulted if they think it means that blacks are not smart enough to fill the role. No race wants serial killers amongst their ranks; it is akin to having the proverbial crazy psychotic uncle in the family. But blacks must accept that their race has produced its fair share of serial killers, each sufficiently intelligent to end the life of many people.

Trigger Events

Psychologists spend a large part of their time interviewing serial killers trying to identify a trigger event. Quite simply, this is an event or series of events that had a negative and possibly traumatic effect on a person, making him snap and become a serial killer. Examples could be the death of a loved one, the loss of a job, being molested as a child, being rejected as a child, dropping out of school, or any other major, life-changing event. While a trigger event makes for great stories and movies, in reality it is often tough to assess the legitimacy of any one event triggering a person to kill. In some cases, it is found; in others, it is not as readily noticeable, but is perhaps a combination of several things.

With black serial killers, there are documented trigger events in a few cases, but for the most part, they appear as a whole to have fewer major trigger events than white killers. They do appear to exist, though, as in the case of Vincent Johnson. He was abandoned by his birth parents and raised by a foster mother, who then abandoned him in his formative teen years[7]. For Kendall Francois, it was possibly the constant teasing he received for being overweight as a child[8]. For Lemuel Smith, it could have been the five serious head injuries he sustained as a child[9]. Edward Arthur Surratt lists his trigger event as having to kill in Vietnam, but he may have suffered from PTSD as well[10]. Yet with each of these cases, it could have been other factors as well: it is difficult to know for sure.

Now, these are each textbook examples of trigger events, but one more, not always associated with serial killers, must not be ignored: drug abuse. The violent behavior that is associated with drugs such as heroin or cocaine is amplified when a user has come down from his high and is looking for the next fix. Lester Harrison, Benjamin Atkins[11], Cory Morris[12], Vincent Darrell Groves[13], and Shelly Andre Brooks[14] are each examples of drug abusers who made their first kill while either high or in search of the next high. After their first kill, they had crossed a bridge, and

Cory Morris

killing to get the drug they desired was no longer an obstacle. While some may argue that drug abuse does not qualify as a good trigger event, it is hard to argue that drugs do not impair judgment and create a false reality, even when a user is between highs. This softened state of critical thinking and impaired decision making has started many a drug user down the path of serial killing. Therefore, the power of mind-altering drugs cannot be underestimated in their effect to help create serial killers.

There are examples of white serial killers who suffered a drug-induced trigger event, but in comparison to black killers, they are fairly well outnumbered. For instance, for each of the gang-related serial killers and hit men in the black database, most of their kills were drug-related in some capacity. Even the killers who were drug-dealers were still addicts themselves, willing to kill those who owed debts, or to eliminate a rival. Aside from this, those who killed prostitutes lured their victims with drugs, and were often users themselves. Currently, a study of the killers in my database is being conducted to see how many drug abusers there are. It is a long, tedious adventure, but from the findings so far, it appears that at least half, and possibly as many as two thirds or more, were habitual users.

Motivation

Sometimes the edges of a trigger event are so blurred that it is hard to distinguish between a trigger and the killer's motivation. Drug abuse is an example that could fall into both categories. However, aside from this, there are definitive motivators that drive each serial killer to commit their crimes. Sexual lust, financial gain, revenge, hate, thrill, and pleasure are all motivators, and will be explored in detail. Some killers, however, are driven by a combination of several of these factors.

Amongst the black serial killers, rape is a common motivator, as it is seen in 342 of the 982 killers on the list, or 34.82%. Occasionally, rape appears to be the only motivation for some serial killers. Other times, robbery is the first motivation, but while robbing a female, the perpetrator decides to rape before he kills. However, not every serial killer who rapes also kills on every occasion. Eddie Lee Mosley is the poster child for this: by police estimates, he raped around 300 women, but he only killed at maximum thirty-three, or about ten percent of those he raped.[15] Maury Troy Travis is another example of a killer who did not kill all whom he raped. The drive for serial killers to murder some of their rape victims while letting others go will probably never be solved, but it could be because a murder victim reminds them of their first kill or of someone they hate. However, opposite of this problem was Carl Eugene Watts. He killed as many as 120 victims yet only raped a small number of them, perhaps as few as five[16]. Carl is an exception from the norm for most rapist-serial killers; in all other cases, if a killer rapes one victim, he rapes the majority of them.

Probably a close tie with rape for motivation is money, as it is present in over half the killers on the list. This subject, however, can be difficult to grasp fully. There are hit men who torture and kill their victims for profit on one end of the spectrum, but on the other side is the home invasion robber who rapes and kills his victims. Both are driven by a lust and greed for monetary gain to kill their prey. But, oddly, not every serial killer who robbed did so with each of his victims. Edward Arthur Surratt, for instance, robbed on a few occasions, and even raped a few victims, but in other circumstances, he only killed before leaving the scene. Like rape, it is not entirely known why a serial killer sometimes robs some whom he kills, then other times does not. Perhaps in some of these instances, robbery is a secondary motivation, with the thirst for blood being the primary motivator; and after killing the victim, the killer sees something of value and decides to steal it.

The primary motivator in all serial killers, regardless of their race, is a hunger for death. Sometimes this thirst is due to hate towards a group of people and the drive to eliminate them, as with the Zebra Killers, De Mau Mau, and the Yahweh ben Yahweh cult's hatred for whites. But this hatred is not present only in cults. Carl Eugene Watts killed relentlessly because he thought his victims had "evil eyes," even going to the means of burning their belongings to release their evil spirits. Like Carl, Shelly Brooks and Maury Troy Travis felt the urge to eliminate crackhead prostitutes, despite both men being crackheads who enjoyed the company of prostitutes.

This thirst for blood is not just restricted to hate; other times, black killers do it for a thrill or a high. Inspired by Jeffrey Dahmer, Marc Sappington killed and ate parts of his victims to duplicate the Milwaukee Cannibal's crimes, in an effort to see if there was a euphoric high in killing. Like Sappington, Quincy Jovan Allen, who called himself "Weird Man," was inspired by the stories of white serial killers and drawn to kill for nothing more than a cheap thrill. While both of these are also examples of copycat criminals, even professional killers often became hit men simply by the idea of a thrill. Wayne "Silk" Perry, a notorious black hit man who made between 30 and 120 hits (some place the number as high as 300), told officers he enjoyed nothing more than killing. But in every serial killer, even if their motivation is at first financial gain, they enjoy killing and the feeling of power and authority it gives them, or they would not kill at all.

Victim Selection

The old, tired adage investigators have used for serial killers is that they are male, tend to kill within their race, and choose female victims whom they can easily overpower. While this description does seem logical, and while it is for the most part descriptive of white serial killers, it is problematic for blacks. A detailed look at the racial selection of victims by black serial killers will be examined in the next chapter, so this section will offer only a minor treatment.

Most investigators assume that black serial killers murder within their race with little deviation. The truth is that their victims are represented fairly equally from both black and white races, and individual killers usually favor either one race or another. Rarely is there a black serial killer who has victims that are an even mixture of both white and black; it is usually one or the other. The ramifications of this are huge: if police properly understood this, it might prevent the wanton waste of human life, when white victims started appearing in their jurisdiction, to consider a black criminal profile alongside a white suspect.

Just as in racial selection, the sex of the victim is not uniform; it is not always males choosing delicate females who are easily overpowered. Only about five eighths of all victims were female. While there are examples of large black men overpowering small women, there are also examples of small black men who had a passion to kill equal or larger black males. Therefore, no normative or decisive judgment should be rendered that makes all black serial killers fit into a preconceived mold. At best they are eclectic, choosing whatever victim gets in their way first, whether it be a random victim or someone pre-planned. For instance, Lonnie David Franklin, while having possibly as many as sixty-nine female victims, only had one male victim of whom police are aware.[17]

Unusual Behavior

When people read about serial killers, they usually want to know how bad it was, to know what sort of gross, unusual behavior the killer exhibited. Common amongst these are posing bodies, overkill, storing bodies, torture, mutilation, cannibalism, and necrophilia. Each of these items offers a look into the depravity of the killer, but the latter three are amongst the most unthinkable items in most cultures. We will take a brief look at each of these items, with a few examples of each from the database.

Posing bodies is something found in numerous white serial killers and occasionally in blacks as well. It can be as simple as making the victims appear to be sleeping, or setting them in a chair to appear alive. But it can also take a sinister path that can include morbid sexual practices or posing the victim in a grotesque manner. In most cases, the interpretation is known only to the killer, appearing strange to the rest of the world. Vaughn Orrin Greenwood is an example of this. He posed each of his eleven victims by putting some of their blood in cups, sprinkling salt around their heads, writing cryptic signs on their faces, and placing their shoes next to their bodies.[18] George Waterfield Russell had a flare to pose his victims in unimaginable, grotesque ways (though he also would place them in normal positions)[19]. With his first victim, he placed her nude body in the classic sleeping pose used to place people in caskets, lying on her back, with a plastic top over one eye and a pinecone under her crossed hands. His second victim was the most disturbing. The victim was nude and her head was wrapped in plastic, covered by a pillow. Her legs were spread towards the door, and a 12 gauge shotgun was inserted deeply into her vaginal cavity. With his third victim, he posed her sitting in bed nude and appearing to read the book, *The Joy of Sex*, with a sexual toy shoved down her throat. While Russell's examples are amongst the worst known in any serial killer, there are numerous other examples where black serial killers posed their victims taking baths, sitting in chairs, or sleeping in bed. Anthony Jackson even went to the extent of nailing one of his victims up in a closet after he had stabbed and strangled her to death, to make her appear alive.

Overkill is a behavior in which the killer keeps stabbing, shooting, or beating his victim, even well after death has occurred. There are abundant examples of this amongst black serial killers, but with so little data on many of them, it is hard to determine an exact percentage of those who practiced this behavior. Nonetheless, there are still times when the media reports this behavior or when it is detailed in a court document. Craig Price is an example. In his first murder, he strangled a thirty-nine-year old woman to death and then stabbed her fifty-seven times with steak knives, often breaking them off in her body and then getting another to start again. After he was finished, he moved to her terrified daughters and stabbed each of the young girls up to thirty times, even crushing the younger girl's skull almost flat with his foot. Two years later, he repeated such wicked behavior by stabbing another woman sixty times after he had strangled her to death.[20] Derrick Todd Lee stomped some victims after their death, and in another case, after stabbing a woman eighty times, he beat her dead body with a clothes iron and almost decapitated her with a butcher knife.[21] William Gerald Mitchell had already cut a woman into pieces in 1974, but for his next victim in 1995, he beat her to near death, strangled her until she was unconscious, ran her over with a car three times, and then mutilated her body beyond recognition with a large knife. There are other examples, such as Donald Kline stabbing his victim forty-one times, or Dawud Majid Mu'Min stabbing one victim in the neck fifteen times with a large metal spike he had made.[22] But the media is often hesitant to release this information, fearing that it might induce panic or gross out the viewers.

Along with overkill, torture is usually present, but it likewise is often not reported in the media, and can generally be found only in detailed court records. There are over 100 cases in my database where torture to some degree has been rendered, but for the remaining killers it can be difficult to determine whether victims were tortured. It could be argued that rape is a form of torture—rightfully so—which would mean that over half of the list participated in torture. However, even if rape were excluded, there are still examples of these serial killers tormenting their victims. A classic example is Maury Troy Travis, who held his victims captive in his basement and chained to a post. He would videotape himself beating, stomping, slicing, and raping his victims, having them submit to him as their master. He repeated this between seventeen and twenty-two times, and while he is one of the most extreme examples for a serial killer of any race, there are other lesser examples in my list. Morris Mason nailed the feet of his victims to the floor while he robbed them, after which he set them on fire. Ahmond Dunnigan's last victim was tortured over a three-day period, where she was set on fire, shocked with jumper cables, forced to drink bleach, sexually assaulted, and drowned in a cooler full of water.[23] Of the other killers, over 200 beat their victims before killing them. Matthew Macon, Elroy Chester, Gregory Davis, and Jeffery Lee Guillory are but a few examples.

Made popular by movies and books is the practice of killers storing the bodies of their

Michael Anthony

victims. Cory Morris kept the bodies of some of his victims in his RV, while Renee Bowman stored the bodies of her two daughters, whom she had killed a year apart, in a freezer. Michael Anthony kept one body under a pile of clothes and another in a freezer in his basement apartment, where drug addicts would come to party and hang out. Kendall Francois methodically bathed and prepared the bodies of his victims before storing them in the attic or crawlspace. Both Harrison Graham and Anthony Sowell stored the bodies of their victims throughout their homes, with little regard for the stench about which neighbors had complained. Connie J. Williams killed his landlord and then kept the body under the bed in which he slept for a month, before police discovered it after odor complaints from neighbors. These are the known examples, but generally speaking, most black serial killers dispose of their victims quickly, to lessen the chance that they could be caught.

Also made popular by slasher films and by shows like *Dexter* is the serial killer's mutilation of a body. While most killers simply kill their victims and flee, there are examples of blacks who spend the time to cut up their victims. Robert Alston decapitated one of his victims after her death, and in another instance left the victim's head and arm near a conspicuous bush to be found. Samuel Ivory and Alonzo Robinson are two other killers who enjoyed decapitating some of their victims. As for cutting their victims, Ben Mathis carved his victims beyond recognition with a butcher's knife, while axe murderers like Jake Bird would often hack off his victims' limbs. Connie J. Williams cut the head and limbs from his wife's body and then buried them in separate places far from his home. As far as I can tell, this phenomenon was most widely seen in the earlier examples of black serial killers, amongst those who used an axe or hatchet. Not satisfied merely that their victims were dead, they would dismember and disfigure the bodies so badly that some were never identified.

When Jeffrey Dahmer was caught and he admitted to eating a bicep from one of his victims, people were shocked that a serial killer could eat part of his victim. It was this almost unmentionable practice that propelled Dahmer to be one of the most revolting serial killers of all time. But what most people do not know is that there are examples of cannibalism amongst black serial killers as well. Almost two decades prior to Dahmer's capture, Lester Harrison killed and ate part of his victim in a Chicago park. And after Dahmer's crime, both Marc Sappington and Joshua Julius Anderson ate part of their victims, with Sappington even drinking the blood of three of them. Yet, because of the media bias against reporting black serial killers, everyone is left thinking that Dahmer is the only example. While there are other white examples, from what the data shows, their numbers are about equal in America.

The last unusual practice to consider is necrophilia, or sex with a corpse. This unthinkable crime is rarely seen in serial killers of any race, but it does happen. According to the figures I have, there are six known examples of white serial killers who participated, which equates to 0.7% of their ranks. By comparison, there are fourteen confirmed examples in black serial killers, with almost as many suspected of it. This would equate to 1.5% of all black serial killers who did necrophilia to at least one of their victims. The list of those known to participate is the following: Cory Morris, Winston Mosley, Sonny Pierce, Harrison Graham, Norman Roye, George Russell, Carl Watts, Theodis Hill, Anthony Sowell, Vincent Johnson, Benjamin Atkins, Johnny Ray Johnson, Sidney Brinkley, and Andre Crawford. The worst of these was Andre Crawford, who performed this sick ritual with each of his eleven victims, sometimes returning to a body repeatedly over a period of several days.

While each of the above practices after death is unique and sickening in its own way, the general consensus is that blacks are not capable of such unspeakable atrocities. Instead, we are told that this revolting behavior is committed by guys like Dahmer or Gein, which idea is reinforced by movies like *Silence of the Lambs*, making people think that only white killers are capable of such ghastly acts. Extreme examples of degenerate behavior are not limited to whites, but have been perpetrated by serial killers of every race.

Methods of Killing

When serial killers are discussed, people inevitably want to know what method of killing they used. Was it a knife, a gun, a rope, their bare hands? The answer is all the above (and much more) when discussing black serial killers. However, it is difficult to make a definitive number of how many killers used which means. I have been able to accurately detail what methods each killer used, but more than half on the list employed multiple methods for their victims. Sometimes a different method was used on different victims, and sometimes, a killer might have used several tactics on each victim.

But if the most popular methods are discussed, shooting is number one, while strangulation and stabbing follow closely behind. Other killing methods, in order from greatest frequency to least, are as follows: beating, killing by axe, suffocation, killing by hammer, bludgeoning, killing by machete, burning, drowning, hanging, running over by automobile, killing by hacksaw, and killing by pliers (oddly enough). Some stabbed with screwdrivers, others strangled with bras or cords, some bludgeoned with bricks, one beat a woman to death with a toaster, another with a toilet seat, and one even sliced a throat with a broken bottle. Essentially, they used whatever means necessary to kill their victim, no matter how crude they would seem.

This brings up an interesting discussion about the difference between organized and disorganized killers. Disorganized killers are usually characterized by spur-of-the-moment decisions, grabbing whatever weapon they find to make their kill, often having to use their bare hands. They also care little for hiding the body, and in most cases simply flee. By contrast, organized killers usually plan out their killings and have a deep concern about leaving evidence behind, making an effort to clean the scene and dispose of the body. But while this may seem clear-cut, the truth is that an organized killer sometimes digresses to disorganized killing or shows disorganized traits. They may spend days conceiving of their crime, analyzing every detail, and then show little regard for physical or DNA evidence left behind.

For the most part, most of the black serial killers would fit into the disorganized category, with some deviating to have organized traits. A typical story is Anthony Baalam's: his victims were prostitutes, and after sex, he strangled them to get his money back. Others, like Carl Watts, would drive the streets, looking for the right girl. When he found her, he would attack her with whatever he had—a knife, a screwdriver, his hands, her shirt, or anything else, even if it required drowning her. He would then leave the area with no concern for cleaning up the crime scene. His behavior is typical of the list, and represents over three quarters of the total.

Almost the entire remainder of the list is comprised of mixed killers who displayed both traits. Sometimes they displayed differing traits on the same kill; other times, they would be more organized in one kill and fly-by-night in the next. Most of the hit men on the list could be considered mixed, as they took time to plan out their kills and shot most of their victims, but rarely did they take the time to dispose of the body. In other cases, a killer would strangle or bludgeon the victim with a rock, but then take meticulous care to hide the body away from the murder site. Some, as with Edward Surratt, showed concern at times for cleaning the crime scenes, but at other times would blast away and leave evidence everywhere. Others, like Shelly Brooks, became angered when giving prostitutes money and felt cheated. After killing his victim by blunt trauma or strangulation, with most, Brooks took the time to dispose of their bodies in a vacant building.

Anthony Balaam

For truly organized killers, there are few examples on the list. Maury Travis would be a good fit, as he lured his victims, disposed of their bodies from his home, and cleaned the crime scene, even going as far as repainting the walls. Aside from him, however, it is a tough call as to which killers would fit, because even the most organized killers seemed to always show some degree of disorganization. But even with white serial killers, the organized killer is the minority on their list as well.

Victim Count

Everyone wants to know how many victims the black serial killers have taken. Unfortunately, there is not a definitive number, but the answer can be provided as a range. For instance, Maury Travis admitted that he killed seventeen women, but police suspect the number could be as high as twenty-two. Therefore, the low for him is listed in my database as seventeen victims, while the high is twenty-two, with a mean average of 19.5 victims. His story is not isolated to black killers, either, but is prevalent among the white serial murderers as well. Gary Ridgway admitted to killing forty-eight women, but police suspect him of killing as many as seventy-one, while some criminologists think it could be as high as ninety. Thus, before discussing averages, it must first be understood that the average is simply these lows and highs put together and divided by two, just as you learned in grade school.

For the black serial killers, on the low side, there are a total of 4,199 victims. That is the absolute lowest this number could get, based on the evidence. If that number is divided by 982 killers, that gives us an average of 4.276 victims per killer. On the opposite side of the equation, the high side has 5,922 possible victims, with some possibility that the number could increase in a few instances. This would mean that, on the high side, there is an average of 6.0305 victims per killer. In total, the average number of victims per killer would be 5.15.

Some reading this number might dismiss it, thinking that the number is lower than that of their white counterparts. But the truth is that it is almost the same, if not slightly higher by a few hundredths of a percent. Most people have the misconception that white serial killers all have thirty, forty, or even 100 victims, when in reality most have fewer than five kills. Sure, there are whites who have those inflated numbers, but so have black killers.

To help understand the numbers better, it helps to take a look at the twenty most prolific serial killers from both whites and blacks, comparing them side by side. Since I have spent most of my time researching black killers, getting their numbers was just a few simple clicks of the mouse to sort the information. The whites were a bit more difficult, because different experts disagree on their kill numbers, so I came up with a list which I think best represents their ranks. For both, the method and criteria were simple: I found the most prolific killers on the high side of the numbers and listed them in descending order from one to twenty. It should be noted that three of the serial killers in the black table are groups of people who killed together, while the white table is solely of white individuals. Had there been a group of whites who killed in numbers high enough to grant access into their top twenty, they would have been added. Moreover, for clarity's sake, if a killer has confessed in full of his crimes, and if he is not suspected of having more victims, this number is listed as both high and low. Also, in fairness, hit men for either group are not included, as both lists would be comprised of most professional assassins.

Table 4.1 Top White Serial Killers

	First	Middle	Last	Victim Low	Victim High
1	Gary		Ridgway	48	71
2	Randy	Steven	Kraft	16	65
3	Michael		Swango	4	60
4	Donald		Harvey	37	57
5	Amy		Archer-Gilligan	5	48
6	Ted		Bundy	36	44
7	Thomas	Eugene	Creech	9	42
8	Billy		Gohl	2	40
9	Belle		Gunness	5	40
10	William		Bonin	21	36
11	Paul	John	Knowles	18	35
12	Gerard		Shaefer	2	34
13	John	Wayne	Gacy	33	33
14	Bruce	A	Davis	8	32
15	Jane		Toppan	11	31
16	Dean		Corll	27	29
17	Charles		Cullen	18	29
18	Patrick		Kearney	21	28
19	Herman		Mudgett	11	27
20	Earle		Nelson	22	25
			AVERAGES	**17.7**	**40.3**

Table 4.2 Top Black Serial Killers

	First	Middle	Last	Victim Low	Victim High
1	The Human Five Cult, Church of the Sacrifice			49	300
2	Zebra Killings (Death Angel Cult)			23	270
3	Carl	Eugene	Watts	44	120
4	Kenneth		Williams	35	75
5	Lonnie	David	Franklin	19	68
6	Jake		Bird	44	44
7	Michael		Hughes	12	44
8	Savage Drug Ring			12	43
9	Lexington Terrace Boys			9	40
10	John	Floyd	Thomas	30	39
11	Alabama Axe Murders			36	36
12	Brandon		Tholmer	12	34
13	Eddie	Lee	Mosley	25	33
14	David	Lance	Bruce	6	32
15	Wayne	Bertram	Williams	25	31
16	Nate		Craft	30	30
17	Cleamon		Johnson	13	30
18	Chester	Dewayne	Turner	17	24
19	Maury	Troy	Travis	17	22
20	Grady		Brooks	19	20
			AVERAGES	**23.85**	**61.75**

Notice that the murders for the top twenty killers of each race do not differ a great deal. For each race, the twentieth slot is held by guys who each killed far above the minimal number to be declared a prolific serial killer (8-10 kills is considered prolific). Additionally, if the Zebra murders are dropped, the black serial killer list still has three men whose kill totals either surpassed or are almost equal to the number one slot on the white list. The point is, of course, that blacks have a great deal of prolific serial killers amongst their race; it is not just restricted to whites. Further, both the average low and average high of each race's most prolific killers place black killers in a higher position than whites. If an average were to be taken from each list, the top twenty whites would have an average kill count of twenty-nine, while blacks would have an average of 44.8. This shows that blacks can be just as prolific killers as whites, and in just this comparison, they have an average kill number which is 35.26% higher, just from the data on this list.

Some might say that this proves nothing and is not important, because statistics and data can be skewed. I will agree that data can be manipulated to reflect a variety of conclusions, but my approach is simple: let the data speak for itself. The numbers represented in each category are those established by police and criminologists, not by me. But more importantly, even if the experts erred in their numbers for either race, the thing to remember is that black serial killers are just as able to take life in high quantities as whites are. Trying to argue otherwise is actually a slight towards blacks and, in an underhanded way, an attack on them, inadvertently telling them that they are not crafty or wise enough to become a prolific serial killer like Ridgway or Bundy.

I discussed in chapter two the disparity in the media between reporting black serial killers and white ones; and it is further manifested by this data. The *New York Times* is a good gauge of a story's popularity in the Associated Press. It is the widest circulated newspaper in America, reporting on all news topics. If a story has made the *New York Times*, it is a safe bet that it has made it into almost every newspaper in syndication in the U.S. at the time.

A search of the *New York Times* database[24] of every issue since 1851 pulls up some interesting figures. Of the top twenty white killers, all but two received an extensive write-up in their paper, and some received write-ups from the time of their capture to their execution. And of the two not worthy enough to get the NYT's attention, one did get mention in reference to other murderers. A search of the top black serial killers should pull some similar numbers, but it does not. There are only five of the twenty who were sufficiently newsworthy to receive mention, but only two of those had extensive coverage. One was Lonnie David Franklin, because of the need to identify photos of possible victims; and the other was Wayne Williams, because of the allegations that he was framed by racists. Had Franklin and Williams not had those unique attributes about their cases, it is likely that their stories would not have passed muster to be national news.

Fair and balanced reporting, then, covers 90% of the top white serial killers, but only covers 25% of the top black ones. And even worse, the number of articles for many of the white killers was greater than the total number of all the articles for the five black killers represented. And this is called equality? Why did Bundy deserve more articles in the *Times* than the entire list of blacks put together? Surely Carl Watts, who killed an estimated total that doubled Bundy's, should merit at least one article. But the press is silent on a killer who is easily one of the most prolific killers in US history. If Watts had taken the life of one of my loved ones, I would be utterly outraged at this disproportionate coverage.

A search of the *LA Times*, the second biggest American newspaper, pulls in similar numbers. All of the white killers were listed, and some black killers were dropped while others were added. This cannot be interpreted as reporting the truth to the public, no matter what excuses are given. It is yet another clue into the media's bias to veil the reality that black serial killers exist.

Female Black Serial Killers

When most people think of serial killers, they assume the suspect is male. This is because most serial killers are in fact male, and because the males tend to be the more aggressive of the sexes. This assumption is true most of the time, but with every rule about serial killers, there is always an exception.[25]

When I began compiling data on this subject, the one void I noticed was the lack of females in my database. For quite some time, the only ones I had were Debra Brown, the accomplice of Alton Coleman, and Pearl Jackson, who had participated in the Alabama Axe Murders. It was some time before I found an individual serial killer who was a woman, but once I found my first, others soon followed. Currently there are twenty-eight women on the list, about 2.9% of the total number. Interestingly, one third of them killed either their children or their husbands. This figure is much higher than in male killers; out of the 954 males, only a small handful killed their family. Below is the list, with a brief description of their crimes. (Some of this information is duplicated in the next section on killing family members, but I have decided to retain it in both places.)

-   **Wanda Jean Allen** beat and shot her roommate in 1981 in Oklahoma City. After serving a four-year sentence, she was freed, and she murdered again in 1988. She became the first black woman executed after the US Supreme Court lifted the ban on executions.
-   **Marie Arrington** committed her first murder by slaying her husband in 1964. The second was a woman she shot and crushed with her car.
-   **Clementine Barnabet** carried out some of the most obscure yet prolific murders of the early 1900s. As the high priestess of a voodoo cult, she admitted to authorities in 1912 of personally murdering 19-22 people with an axe and of participating in another twenty-one murders with her handful of followers. Authorities verified her story, and she served for life in a Louisiana prison. At least one member of her cult murdered two more families after her arrest. The court determined based on her testimony the group was responsible for at least 49 murders, but perhaps as many as 300.
-   **Mitchelle Blair** Both victims were her children, killed 9 months apart. The first was her 9 year old son, who she severely tortured for 2 weeks prior to his death. The second was her 14 year old daughter, who complained about her mom killing her brother. Both victims were found in deep freezers.
-   **Renee Bowman** had two adopted daughters whom she killed in 2007 and 2008. She kept their bodies in the freezer.
-   **Debra Brown** was the accomplice of Alton Coleman in their cross-state murdering spree that left eight dead in 1984.
-   **Celeste Carrington** murdered two people and attempted a third while committing robberies in the San Carlos, CA, area in 1992.
-   **Shavonda Charleston** did the unthinkable in 2000. Over a five-month period, she murdered her four young daughters, aged between a few days old and five years.
-   **Latine Marie Davidson** killed her two children: the first by strangulation in 1983, and the second by drowning in 1985.
-   **Josephine Gray** was a "black widow" killer who killed her husbands to collect on insurance policies. Her first victim was her first husband in 1974, her next was in 1990, and her last was in 1996. While she was suspected in the first two murders, it was not until the third that the police found evidence that indicted her. She was tried for all three, but due to her age, she was only slapped with an insurance fraud conviction, which puts her parole around the age of ninety.

- **Donetta Hill** was a crack-addict prostitute who in 1990 murdered two customers in separate events. She used a claw hammer in their homes in order to steal for her addiction.
- **Marie Eileen Huber** joined her boyfriend and another man to commit murder, all in order to fix the social injustice against them. In total, she killed at least five people.
- **Pearl Jackson** was a part of the murderous band of Alabama Axe murderers from the early 1900s. Together, they hacked at least thirty-six to death, and they left many more maimed for life.
- **Banita Jacks** stabbed her oldest daughter to death in late May or early June 2007. Over the next ten to thirty days, she killed her remaining three daughters by beating them and then strangling them. She then lived with their decomposing bodies until January 2008, when officials came to evict her from her house.
- **Patricia Ann Jackson** killed a woman in 1966, then another in 1981. Both women were stabbed to death.
- **Carolyn Ann King** in the only instance of a black and white serial killing duo. King enlisted her white boyfriend to help her brutally kill at least two people, and possibly a third, in two different states.
- **Robbin Monique Machuca** participated in the above murders with Marie Huber.
- **Kimberly Lagayle McCarthy** was an in-home health care provider who beat and stabbed two patients to death in 1988 and a third in 1997 in Dallas, TX.
- **Lethisa Morgan** Shot her first victim in early 2010 in Texas. She then fled to South Dakota where just six months later she killed her second victim, stabbing him 37 times.
- **Caroline Peoples**, along with Angel Wright-Ford, posed as Chicago prostitutes in 2004 and murdered four prospective customers.
- **Mary Perkins** poisoned her husband, her best friend, and her friend's baby from 1955-1956 for insurance money. She was suspected in seven other deaths, but it is inconclusive if she was the killer.
- **Debra Sue Tuggle** suffocated four of her children from 1974 to 1982 and killed two additional people.
- **Annette Washington** murdered two of the women for whom she provided in-home health care in 1985 and 1986. She had plans to murder others, but she was caught after stabbing her last victim over ninety times with a butcher knife.
- **Linda Ann Weston** murdered at least three victims. Each was kept imprisoned in a closet and was beaten severely. They eventually starved to death. One victim was beaten with a hammer and bled to death slowly.

- **Carol Wilkins** shot her Kenyan boyfriend point blank in the face in 1992. After serving a sentence for his murder, she sliced the throat of a man in 2008 in Nebraska.
- **Dorothy Williams** killed three elderly people, one woman and two men, from 1987-1989 in Chicago.
- **Blanche Wright** was the accomplice of Robert Young. Together, they killed six people for money in the Bronx from 1974 to 1980.
- **Angel Wright-Ford**, along with Caroline Peoples, posed as Chicago prostitutes in 2004 and murdered four prospective customers.

Killing Friends and Family

It is rare when any serial killer chooses to murder a close friend or a member of his own family, but it does happen. Blacks are not excluded from this either, but are equally represented when compared to white serial killers. Most killers make at least some attempt to remove their crimes from their home turf, often venturing far away from home to commit their

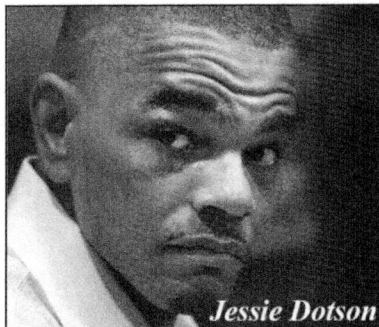
Jessie Dotson

crimes. But this unique group, which never ventures to kill outside their close circle of influence, is among the most unforgiving of killers, hurting the ones who love and care for them, killing them without remorse.

Some of the most tragic stories involve a serial killer who killed their own children. It tears at my heart to imagine people so sick as to eliminate their own flesh and blood and dash their progeny's chance to continue their family line into the future. Sad as that may be, it has happened with black serial killers on more than one occasion. Below is a list of the killers on my list who have killed friends or family members. There are others who killed their next-door neighbors, but it is not known how close their relationship was with the victims.

- **Marie Arrington** committed her first murder by killing her husband in 1964.
- **Renee Bowman** killed her two adopted daughters in 2007 and 2008. She kept their bodies in the freezer.

- **Shavonda Charleston** did the unthinkable in 2000. Over a five-month period, she murdered her four young daughters, aged between a few days old and five years.
- **Davon Crawfod** brutally murdered his wife and two children in 2009. He had a prior murder in 1995.
- Dewitt Crawley was a paroled murderer when he raped his sixteen- and eighteen-year-old nieces, killing one by hanging her and the other by stabbing and drowning her. When their father arrived home to find their bodies, Crawley stabbed him over sixty times with a pair of scissors and an ice pick.
- **Darin Davis** killed his infant daughter in 1994. After serving fifteen years, he was released, only to kill another infant daughter.
- **Von Clark Davis** stabbed his wife to death in 1970. After his release, he shot his girlfriend to death in 1983.
- **Latine Marie Davidson** killed her two children, the first by strangulation in 1983 and the second by drowning in 1985.
- **Jessie Dotson** was paroled for a 1994 murder. A few months later, he killed six friends and family members. He shot his brother and three friends, and he stabbed to death his young nephews.
- **Robert Ford**, a.k.a. Noah Arnold, slew his best friend during an argument. He went on to kill four other people.
- **Josephine Gray** was a "black widow" killer who killed her husbands to collect on insurance policies. Her first victim was her first husband in 1974, her next was in 1990, and her last was in 1996. While she was suspected in the first two murders, it was not until the third that the police found evidence that indicted her. She was tried for all three, but due to her age, she was only slapped with an insurance fraud conviction, which puts her parole around the age of ninety.
- **Paul Harrington** murdered his wife and two children in 1975, but was found innocent by reason of insanity. In 1999, he murdered his new wife and three-year-old son. He told police, "They should have put me away then," when asked about the previous murders.
- **Thomas Hawkins** had already murdered twice when he raped and murdered his fourteen-year-old niece
- **John Ruthell Henry** murdered his first wife in 1975. He was released in 1983 and remarried. In 1985, he murdered this wife and her five-year-old son.
- **Banita Jacks** stabbed her oldest daughter to death in late May or early June 2007. Over the next ten to thirty days, she killed her remaining three daughters by beating them and strangling them. She then lived with their decomposing bodies until January 2008, when officials came to evict her from her house.
- **Andrew Jett** murdered two girlfriends twenty years apart.

- **James Donald King** murdered his first wife in 1967. After release, he married again and killed his second wife in 1988.
- **Mary Perkins** poisoned her husband, her best friend, and her friend's baby from 1955-1956 for insurance money. She was suspected in other deaths in her family, but it is inconclusive if she was the killer.
- .**James Pugh** shot his best friend in an argument, and went on to kill eleven in a mass murder years later.
- **Theodore Rodgers** shot his girlfriend in 1978, and served five years. In 2001, he killed his wife in a daycare.
- **Arthur Lee Sanford** murdered two of his girlfriends, one in 1983 the other in 2003.
- **Debra Sue Tuggle** suffocated four of her children from 1974 to 1982.
- **Henry Louis Wallace** murdered ten women he counted as friends, including one who he said was like his little sister.
- **Connie J. Williams** had already served time for another murder when he stabbed his wife in 1999 in Philadelphia. Angered at her, he cut her body to pieces with a hacksaw and buried the parts in two separate locations.

There may be more of whom I am unaware, but these are the killers I have noted to break the vow of family and friend with murder. While these murderers are in the minority, the only purposes in listing them are to bring recognition to the crimes for the families that suffered and to make people aware that white serial killers are not the only ones to kill their own friends and family.

Killing in the Home

Americans were shocked when Dahmer's story broke, mostly because of the gruesome nature of the crimes. But one reason that many people were shocked was because he killed the men and boys in his own home. His neighbors did not suspect what he was doing up late making strange noises, or what the unpleasant odors wafting out of his apartment were. They were horrified when their worst nightmare came true, and they realized that the smells and commotion had been from his dark side. However creepy this was, serial killers who keep their work at home are rare. Most choose to keep their dirty business far from their place of serenity.

The following is a list of killers who killed, and in some instances stored, their victims in their homes. Each of the killers from the previous list has been omitted to avoid duplication, but they should all be added (with the exception of Henry Louis Wallace, who killed his victims in their homes).

- **Michael Lee Anthony** stored the bodies of two women he had killed in his basement apartment.
- **Kendall Francois** murdered and then stored the bodies of eight to ten women in his home.
- **Lester Harrison** kept the remains of seven women he had murdered in his home, and an eighth he hid next door.
- **Cory Morris** stored the bodies of seven women he had killed in the RV in which he lived.
- **Anthony Sowell** killed and stored the bodies of eleven black women in his Cleveland home.
- **Maury Troy Travis** lured between seventeen and twenty-two women into his basement torture chamber to be killed.
- **Wayne Williams** killed at least some of his twenty-nine victims in his parents' home.

Murdering as a Group

Serial killers are usually portrayed as reclusive loners who keep to themselves, shunning friendships and even family. There are instances, though, when a serial killer teams up with another individual who shares similar beliefs, and the two act as one killing machine. Most commonly, one will be more dominant and recruit the other by appealing to his devotion or love, bringing him into the killer's sick world. Some may think that these killer pairs are sole products of the white serial killer realm, perhaps pointing to the killer teams of Henry Lee Lucas and Otis Toole, or of Dean Corll and his two young lover-accomplices. But the truth is that black serial killers are equally represented in this area as well. Blacks usually are thought to have only the Beltway Snipers, and Alton Coleman with Debra Brown. Yet here are all the serial killer duos from the list with a brief description of their crimes.

- **The Baltimore Duo** was led by Jerry "Black Jerry" Williams. As a team, he and Anthony Ayeni Jones murdered between twelve and fifteen people in Baltimore from 1994-1997. Police speculate the number could be higher.

- **The Beltway Snipers**, John Allen Muhammad and Lee Malvo killed twelve people in a three-week crime spree in Washington, D.C., and are implicated in at least four additional murders.
- **The Bronx Assassins** were a duo led by Blanche Wright in which she and her sidekick Robert Young killed at least six people from 1974-1980 for money.
- **The Brooklyn Murders** were the work of the duo of Cory Gist and Lamont Fleming. As part of a drug organization in Brooklyn, NY, they killed four to five people together.
- **Brown/Coleman** was the team of Debra Brown and Alton Coleman. In a four-state area, the pair murdered eight people in 1984. They also raped, robbed, and beat other people, in addition to stealing cars.
- **The Buffalo Killers** were the team of Milton Jones and Theodore Simmons. Their crimes involved killing two priests in separate attacks, both of them execution-style, in 1987.
- **The Cook Brothers** were the brutal duo of two brothers, Anthony and Nathaniel Cook. From 1973-1981, they killed between nine and ten white people in Toledo, OH.
- **The Crack Dealers** is a generic name for a duo of crack dealers who grouped up to eliminate any competition. From 1990-1992, the pair of Arleigh Carrington and Tony Chatfield murdered at least two, and probably five or more, competitors.
- **The Drug Murders** were committed by the twin brother team of Shaheem and Raheem Johnson. They killed at least five people in Virginia, Pennsylvania, Maryland, and New York from 1995-1997. These are the known murders; the number could be higher.
- **The Ford/Donnelly Team** consisted of Robert Ford and Mike Donnelly. They had met in prison in WA, where Donnelly was serving time for two murders while Ford was serving time for one. After parole in 1923, they headed to Idaho where they killed a man together in the village of Hope. Ford would later be hanged for the crime, while Donnelly got another life sentence. Before his death, Ford admitted to killing five people in his life, and he gave a detailed account of each murder.
- **The Grave Murderers** were two of the earlier examples in the database. In 1946, Robert Bradley and William Lisenby lured three black men on separate occasions, promising them sex with a white woman. Forcing the men to dig their own grave, they beat them with a shovel and then disfigured their bodies with an axe before burying them.
- **The Haley Brothers** was one of the more brutal duos. Reginald and Kevin Haley beat, tortured, and killed at least eight white people in California from 1979 to 1984.
- **The Hooker Murderers** are in a unique category, one of the few serial killing duos comprised of only women. In 2004, Caroline Peoples and Angel

Wright-Ford posed as prostitutes to lure victims to rob and kill. By the end they had killed four black men.

- **The Indy Drug Killings** were committed by a duo in Indianapolis in 2005. Jarvis Brown and Gabriel Jordan killed at least four people together.
- **The Jennings/Johnson Team** had already murdered separately, and both are individual black serial killers in their own regard. Police still do not know how Wilber Jennings and Alvin Johnson knew each other, but they teamed up to rape and murder an elderly white woman in Fresno, CA, in 1983.
- **Jones & Reardon** earn the prestige of being the earliest duo in the database. From 1870 to 1879, they committed between five and seven murders across Tennessee. Caught in 1879 trying to sell the cufflinks of one of their victims, they both confessed to other murders together. After confessing their crimes in full, a lynch mob stormed the jail and hanged them from a railroad bridge.
- **The Louisville Dou** of Jerald Garrett and Billy Richardson committed their murders over a three month span, and killed at least three. Police suspect them in additional murders.
- **The Nashville Murders** were committed by Gdongalay Berry and Christopher Davis. Together they killed three people between 1995 and 1996.
- **The New Haven Murders** were done by the brutal duo of Robert Bradley and William Lisenby, who in 1946 killed at least three and possibly more people.
- **The New Orleans Drug Murders** were committed by the team of Terrance Benjamin and Winston Gilmore, in which they killed three to four people.
- **The Palmetto Murders** was a series of robberies committed by Earnest Houston and Charles Edward Shoates in 1970. In their wake, they left four white people dead.
- **The Penn Brothers** were the duo of William and his younger brother Thomas, who killed six white people in Richmond, VA, in 1966.
- **The Revenge Murders** were committed by Sir Mario Owens and Robert K. Ray in 2002. Angered over a girl, the two killed three people in two separate incidents in Colorado.
- **The Richmond Killing Spree** was a vicious seven-day killing spree in 2006, in which Ray Joseph Dandridge and Ricky Jovan Gray terrorized both black and white families. They tortured and beat the families, raped the women, and killed nine people in all.
- **The St. Aubin Street Massacres** occurred on St. Aubin Street in Detroit. From 1988-1990, the street was rocked by two separate massacres. In the first in 1988, Mark Lamont Bell and Jamal Latiff Biggs executed two people. In 1990 they struck again, killing six people in one bloody massacre. Police believe that each committed more murders, but so far no witnesses have come forward.

- **The Virginia Killers** were the team of Joshua Andrews and Jamel Crawford, and they killed three people from 2000 to 2001.
- **The Wichita Massacre** involved the Carr brothers, Reginald and Jonathan, as they led one of the most brutal examples of black-on-white crime. In December 2000, they murdered five people. One was left for dead, three women were raped, one man was beaten, all were robbed, and a group of five friends were forced to participate in an orgy at gunpoint.

Serial killer duos are rare, and teams of three killers are only documented in one or two instances with white serial killers. However, black serial killers have not failed in this category, as there are seventeen different groups which had three or more members killing together. Some of these groups had as many as a dozen members working in unison for a common goal. If a white serial killing group of a dozen members existed, the National Guard would be called and the FBI would be involved in bringing this group to swift justice—especially if they were killing blacks. Not so when the races are reversed. In any case, here is the list with a brief biography for each.

- **The Alabama Axe Murders** helped give rise to the campfire horror stories of axe-wielding madmen. From 1919 to 1923, central Alabama was ravaged by a team of axe murderers who maimed dozens and left thirty-six people dead. Eleven people are thought to have been a part of the gang that killed both whites and blacks, but only five were ever charged for the crimes. After apprehension, Frank Glover, O'Delle Jackson, Pearl Jackson, Peyton Johnson, and John Reed were charged with the murders, but their leader, an unknown black man, was never caught.
- **An Armed Truck Robbery** happened in 1996 in Los Angeles, CA, where three friends, who each already had other murders on their record, joined to kill the driver and guard of an armored truck, stealing its contents. Roshone Colston, Kendrick Loot, and Bruce Millsap were arrested soon after.
- **The Best Friends Gang of Detroit** was probably the most prolific black killing group in US history, with police estimates of over 100 murders in the Detroit area. They provided muscle for the drug kingpins and started a drug war when they tried to move in on the drug business themselves. Over twenty-three men were charged with a variety of charges, including mass-murder, but only a few were convicted of murder. Most of the killers either ended up dead themselves or were sentenced on lesser charges. Police have been able to determine, based off the surviving members' testimonies, which men of the group were the most notorious. The Brown brothers Ezra, Terrance, Gregory, and Reginald, as well as Nate Craft, Darryl Hardy, Michael Williams, Patrick Jackson, Lonnie O'Bryant, Charles Wilkes, and Sta-

cey Culbert, are the names most commonly given. Each killed at least three times, and some, like Craft, claimed to have killed thirty. The remaining members are either out of prison or will be released in the near future.

- **The Black Mafia** was a band of Muslim extremists operating out of Philadelphia. Police are unsure of the exact number of murders this group committed, but it is thought to have been over forty, committed from 1971 to 1986. Most heinous was their execution of five children and two adults in 1973 in what is known as the Hanafi Murders. Among the group, these men stand out as serial murderers: Ronald Harvey killed between nine and twelve people, Samuel Christian between three and six, Russell Barnes between three and six, and Joseph "JoJo" Rhone between two and three.
- **The Briley Gang** was comprised of three brothers: James, Anthony, and Linwood. In 1979, they terrorized the streets of Richmond, VA, and killed a total of twelve white people.
- **The Bronx Killings** happened in 1980 by a trio of disgruntled young men seeking to get to the top, robbing and killing their way to success. After killing eleven people, Thomas Aikens, William Jackson, and Michael McFarlane were apprehended.
- **The Clifford Jones Drug Organization** was one of the most lucrative and deadly groups to hit Detroit. Police confirm that at least six and possibly as many as fifteen enforcers killed fifty to sixty people from 1983-1992. This number is the conservative figure; some experts theorize that the number is actually closer to 130.
- **The DC Hitmen** were a professional group of assassins led by Wayne "Silk" Perry. Along with his two accomplices, Tyrone LaSalle Price and Michael Antony Jackson, they killed between 30 and 120 people from 1984 to 1993 in Washington, D.C. Police have tied at least thirty murders to them, but have tried them only on nine. The evidence, however, points to the larger figure as more accurate, but some speculate that the number could approach 300.
- **The De Mau Mau Gang was** a militant group of black Muslims who felt that they needed to kill whites to avenge the problems of their people. Over the course of 1978, the eight members of their gang assassinated at least twelve or more people in Chicago, IL, and Nebraska.
- **El Rukn** was one of the most notorious groups of in the history of Chicago. Originally founded by Jeff Fort as the Black P. Stones, the group as a whole committed between 65 and 180 murders from 1974 to the late 1980s. It is unknown how many participated in the killings, but three have been pinpointed as serial killers. Earl Hawkins committed between ten and fifteen of the murders, and Derrick Kees clocked between five and ten, while Charles Edward Bey is estimated to have committed four to eleven. To Bey's credit, he is the only one of the primary killers who left his past behind and tried to lead a productive life far from drugs and violence.

- **The Human Five Cult**, also known as the Hand of Death Cult, was a cult that operated along the Southern Pacific Railroad that ran between Lafayette, LA and San Antonio, TX from 1911 to 1912. They brutally murdering black families as they slept with an axe or hatchet, only on Sunday nights. After the massacre the killer would put a bloody handprint on the victim along with a Bible verse. They believed that the only way to free people to go to heaven was through voodoo enchantments combined with killing them. Clementine Barnabet was the only one caught, but she said that there were four others involved. After being arrested, there were three more families that died by the cult, which was thought to be run by her brother. She admitted to killing seventeen with an axe, but claimed to have participated in forty murders. Another possible suspect was the leader of the cult, King Harris, who gave orders to kill on the nights people were murdered. The total for the group, who called themselves The Sacrifice Church was at least forty-nine, but authorities think it may have approached 300.
- **The Mall Murders** were committed by a group of misfits who felt that society owed them for the misfortunes they had suffered in life. In 1991, Vincent Hubbard, Marie Huber, Robin Machuca, and John Lewis took to the streets of Los Angeles to get their revenge by robbing and killing whoever they felt owed them. In the end, they killed five people.
- **Murder, Inc.**, named after the infamous mobsters of the thirties and forties, was a group that racked up numbers of which their namesake would have been proud. From 1990 to 1999, the group as a whole racked up between forty and sixty-five murders in the Washington, D.C., area. The leader, Kevin Gray, pulled the trigger on nineteen to twenty-two of these, while his chief sidekick, Rodney Moore, accounted for ten to twelve kills.
- **The Preacher Crew** was murderous group of extortionists in New York City. Operating from the early eighties to the late nineties, the group murdered as many as fifty people. The group was led by Clarence "The Black Hand of Death" Heatley, and the lead killer was a police officer named John Cuff. Heatley admitted to killing three to six victims, but he is suspected in many more., and Cuff confessed to ten murders. Their standard MO was to torture the victim and then shoot him; afterwards, they would pour acid over the body to hide any distinguishing marks.
- **Racist Killings** were committed in 1970 by a trio of young black men who headed south with revenge on their minds. They were led by Ben Chaney, whose brother was killed by the KKK. He and Martin Rutrell killed between four and five random white people in a two-month span. The driver of the car, L.L Thompson, never pulled a trigger but died in a police shootout.

- **Shakedown Entertainment** was the rap and hip-hop music business of Willie Edward Mitchell. In 2002, he led Shawn Earl Gardner, Shelton Lee Harris, and Shelly Martin to help him kill five people.
- **The Yahweh Cult** was active in Miami, FL, from the mid-seventies to the late nineties. In 1980, they killed one of their defectors, which was soon followed by the deaths of three more. It eventually got to the point that every member of the cult (eighty at the time) had to kick or hit before he was ritualistically killed. Soon after, their leader Yahweh ben Yahweh (Hulon Mitchell, Jr.) ordered his enforcers to kill the "white devils," who he taught were a curse from God to hurt blacks. Except for Robert Rozier, the names of his enforcers have never been made public, because the murder charges against the cult were dropped. Police attribute the deaths of four of their members, and at least twenty-three whites, to these enforcers.
- **The Zebra Killers,** a.k.a. the Death Angels, were the most prolific group of serial killers in American history. Their numbers were unparalleled by any other group. It is known that, from 1973 to 1974, the group killed at least twenty-three white people, whom they called blue-eyed devils. Police suspect them in at least seventy-eight murders in the San Francisco area, but the group claimed to have killed more. Based on the testimony of one of the members and independent research, many experts believe that they could be responsible for 270 or more murders across several states. The dilemma with this group is that only five men were brought to justice, despite that their group was much larger and that there is proof of many more people's involvement in the murders. Many feel that the five men were scapegoats and that the twenty-three murders for which they were convicted do not represent the true size of their criminal enterprise.[26]

The last two groups and the De Mau Mau Gang each had the same agenda and similar beliefs. They believed that a vast white conspiracy was in place to eliminate the black race, the true children of God, from the planet. Below is a sample of a speech given to the Zebra Murderers, as documented by one of the leading researchers on this cult before they started their rampage:

"A thousand years ago, near the holy city of Mecca, there lived an evil black leader named Yakub. He desired to create a race of weak people that he and his ancestors could rule forever. To do this, he began to study the black race. He learned that in every black man there exists two germs: a black germ and a brown germ. He found a way to separate the brown germs from the black germs, and he put the brown germs into all the healthy, strong girls among his followers who were at least sixteen years of age. As they produced babies, he had the black ones separated and fed to

wild beasts, but he had the brown ones carefully nursed and raised to adults. Then he passed a law that blacks who were alike could not marry; only those who were unlike could marry. Black had to marry brown. Dark had to marry light, and light had to marry lighter.

"Yakub was pleased because he saw his people becoming weaker and weaker, while he and those who ruled with him remained black and strong. For six hundred years there continued this process of grafting brown from black, and lighter brown from darker brown, until finally the original black blood had thinned so much and become so weak that the germ it carried lost all its color and became white. Weak, wicked white."

From the audience came several low grunts of disapproval. The speaker nodded agreement with them.

"By the time the descendants of Yakub realized what had been done, it was too late. The grafted white devils had spread over the earth and were teaching lessons about a new, mysterious god that no one could see until after death. Soon eighty-five percent of the people on earth were being taught about this mystery god. They were being taught by ten percent who were clever and crafty and desired to lead them. Only a scant five percent of the earth's population remained righteously believing in the true god, Allah."

The speaker raised his forefinger like a vengeful sword. "For four hundred years these white infidels have spread their false religion over the land like a great dirty plague, trying to put out the light of Allah. Christians and Jews alike are guilty of setting up rivals to Allah. Both are black-slave-making religions dedicated to the mental destruction of the black man. They are the enemies of Allah and they are the sole people responsible for leading astray nine-tenths of the world's black population!"

"Evil!" one of the men in the audience said loudly.

The speaker's eyes widened even more. His voice grew raspy, hissing. "For four hundred years this grafted white devil has controlled the earth and manipulated the black man. For four hundred years he has castrated black men, raped black women, and stomped the heads of little black babies!"

"Devils!" said a voice in the audience.[27]

Some will dismiss this as the ramblings of a lunatic who has not an inkling of research or history to back his wild claims. However, despite his ridiculous claims, this speech and subsequent ones were the motivation for young, misguided black men to lash out and kill the "blue-eyed devils." Instead of being the peace-loving egalitarians which the whites of San Francisco thought all blacks in the city were, this group was fueled by inaccurate hate speeches given by men wishing to start an insurrection.

Gang Murder

Some of the most difficult serial killers to track are those functioning in gangs across the nation. True gang numbers are difficult to pin down, because oftentimes the fine line between a die-hard gang member and a gang affiliate is blurred. It can thus be hard to track down which gang members did the killings and which ones acted alone in independent murders. Therefore, when it comes to serial killers within the gang underworld, I have always treaded lightly, and for some time I would not even include them in my list. If we could accurately know which gang member pulled the trigger in every event, then everyone in America would be surprised, even law enforcement officials. I am quite sure that there would be a list of black gang members stretching to the hills, as the old-timers would say, who would qualify as serial killers. However, in lieu of such a list, I have done my best with the available resources to provide the most accurate information I can on this obscure group of killers.

Benson Cadet
Terrorist Boyz

One of the problems presented is trying to determine when a gang member is a serial killer. Oftentimes, one will blast a gang rival and get caught, but it is difficult to prove whether that was his first kill or the last in a long line of murders. Occasionally there will be a blip evidencing that the killer is implicated in other murders, but as most often is the case, no follow-up report will ever be issued on the killer; and sometimes, police can never pin the crime on the killer, because no witnesses will come forward to testify. On other occasions, the initial report will claim that there are other murders which the police attribute to the killer, but because the killer received an adequate prison sentence, he is never brought up on the other charges. All in all, it is a frustrating avenue to travel, but the task does uncover numerous interesting stories.

Another difficult thing to ascertain is how many of the black serial killers were gang members. The truth will probably never be known, because while some in my database claim to be gang members, most committed their murders independently of any gang function. In some of the few cases I have found, these serial killers were members of gangs that had not killed, and their fellow gang members shied away from the killer or sometimes even testified against him in court. It would be like a white member of social club committing serial murder: his acts would not be representative of the social club but the man's own. Therefore, it is important to recognize that serial killers belonging to gangs did not necessarily kill as a part of their gang.

An example of this would be Stanley "Tookie" Williams, who killed at least four people in robberies which his Crips gang committed. Fellow gang members told him not to pull the trigger, but since he was the shot-caller for the gang they did not question him. Tookie's case shows something else too. His gang had killed a few rival gang members before, but at this time, the Crips gang was still in its infancy. Tookie's murders of non-gang members brought things to a new level for LA gangs. While his original set at the time disapproved, it did not take long before other gangs in LA began killing during the course of robberies. Even his original set had a change of heart, and some of them went on to murder non-gang members themselves.

Some black gangs who killed numerous people for profit, for territory, or out of cold blood have been brought to justice. While their numbers only represent a fraction of the gangs in America who kill on a regular basis, this list is my attempt to try to bring awareness to this rapidly increasing phenomenon. The following list is not a list of individual gang members who acted on their own, but instead of gangs who acted together as a whole. Sometimes they might send one to commit a murder, and other times the entire set, so the number of murders for each person differs based on his varied involvement.

- **The Boyle Street Boys** were a small gang in Chester, PA. From 2000 to 2001, the trigger men, Andre Cooper and Vincent Williams, killed between three and four people.
- **The Cash Money Brothers** were a small gang set in Brooklyn, NY, that had a reputation for violence. Connected to more than a dozen murders, Damion Hardy, Dwayne Meyers, Eric Moore, and Abubakr Raheem committed four to five together.
- **The Chapel Hill Hoovers** were responsible for at least three to four murders at the hands of Cornet Pokey Meekins and Jamarcus D. Warren. There were other gang members and more murders, but these two are responsible as a team for most of the murders.
- **The Crip Set**, a small set of Crips from Louisiana, rolled through Texas in 1998, and in a one-month span killed three white people. There were three members present, but Damon Smith and Kenneth Tatum did the killing.
- **The Down Below Gang** was a black gang from San Francisco. From 2004 to 2005, the five main members committed at least nine murders and possibly more. Robert Calloway, Edgar Diaz, Emile Fort, Don Johnson, and Ricky Rollins acted as a team in these murders.
- **The International Robbing Crew** was a brutal gang from Atlanta that terrorized the streets from 2005 to 2008. Charged with nine murders, the total number is thought to be thirty. The four main killers worked as a team and consisted of Carlos Drennon, Maurice Hargrove, Edward Morris, and DaQuan Stevens.
- **The John Doe Gang** was a group of approximately one dozen members who committed fifteen to twenty-two murders in Miami, FL, from 1995 to 1998. The leader, Corey Smith, is responsible for six of these murders, while Julius Stevens committed either two or three.
- **The LA Boys** were a group of Los Angeles gangsters transplanted to Buffalo, NY. From 2003, they left a path of over fifteen dead on the streets, and possibly more. Daryl Reese Johnson led the charge with seven or eight murders to his credit, while Donald Sly Green had two or three.
- **The Lexington Terrace Boys** were a notorious gang from Baltimore, MD, led by Keon Moses and his go-to guy, Michael Lafayette Taylor. They killed between nine and forty people from 1998 to 2002. There were others involved in some of the murders, but these two stood out as the lead killers for the gang.
- **The M Street Crew** ravaged the streets of Washington, D.C., from 1998 to 2004. Larry Gooch was the leader, and he killed either five or

six people. Tommie Dorsey and Jonte Robinson each had two to three murders to their credit.

- **The Newton Street Gang** was shooting up the streets of Washington, D.C., from 1988 to 1990. In that timespan, the gang killed more than a dozen people, but the four main enforcers killed eight to ten. Anthony Goldston, Mario Harris, Mark Hoyle, and John McCollough acted as a deadly team.

- **The New Towne Gang** was a criminal street gang comprised of Cory Johnson, James Roane, and Richard Tipton. In a three-month span in 1992 in Richmond, CA, they assassinated eleven people who were rival drug dealers or who owed them money.

- **The Poison Clan** was a twenty-three-member gang based in Richmond, VA. From 1988 to 1994, a group of five killers among the gang killed between eight and ten people. Led by Devon Dale Beckford, his brother Dean Anthony Beckford and members Leonel Romeo Cazaco, Claude Gerald Dennis, and Richard A. Thomas worked as a cohesive killing team. The gang is thought to be connected to other murders.

- **The Rolling 90s** was an LA gang that moved drugs into Oklahoma and Tennessee. Only two members were convicted of serial murder: Eben Payne with eight murders and Jamal Shakir with nine. There were others implicated in other murders, but they were never tried.

- **The Savage Drug Ring** was one of the most vicious gangs in Philadelphia history. With ties to over forty murders, the core group of killers was tried on twelve of them. Kaboni Savage was the leader, and his accomplices were Lamont Lewis, Robert Merrit, and Steven Northington.

- **The Terrorist Boyz** were a gang that kept the Miami police on their toes from 2000 to 2003. With ties to possibly as many as twenty murders, police are positive that the primary group killed between twelve and fifteen victims. Johnny Charles led the charge, along with Benson Cadet, Max Daniel, Walkens Flowers, and Frantzy Jean-Marie.

- **Young Boys, Inc.** was one of the notorious Detroit gangs that left a path of devastation. In the eighties, they were responsible for between sixty-eight and eighty-five murders as a group. They were led by Milton David Jones, who later wrote a book about his experience. He was a charismatic leader who contract-killed for drug dealers by hiring black teenagers to do his dirty work. The theory was that the kids could not be prosecuted because of their minor status. In the end, at least nine were charged with many of the murders, and most are still behind bars. Milton Jones had six to ten murders to his credit, while Eugene Mitchell led the pack with five to twelve murders. James Earl Butler had three to five, Charles Victor Obey had two to six, George Young had three to five, Curtis Napier had three to six, Spencer Tracy Holloway had two to four, Farod Mallory had three to four, and Raymond Canty had three to six.

- **89 Family Bloods** was another ruthless LA gang that thrived on violence in the eighties and nineties. The shot caller was Cleamon Johnson, a.k.a. Big Evil, and in his time he killed between thirteen and thirty gang rivals. His group became one of the most feared in LA, and his brother Timothy would later become the shot-caller after Big Evil was arrested. Timothy soon earned the reputation his older brother had for blood, earning the name "Sinister." Police have confirmed that he killed four people before he was murdered by a rival gang, but now they suspect that the number could be closer to twenty. Before Big Evil left the gang, he recruited a young neighbor, Michael "Fat Rat" Allen, who would kill for the gang as well. Before his capture by police, Fat Rat had killed at least three people, but he has indicated that the number might surpass twenty.

There are other examples of gang members who killed for their gang, like Kody "Monster" Scott, who killed twelve people, and Pete "Pistol Pete" Rollack, who killed eight. Yet they are not listed, because while they did ride for the brand, they were alone in carrying out the murders and are thereby listed as individuals. In closing, there are rumors of many other black gangs across the US that have killed numerous people, but are still on the streets. If they are ever brought to justice and their crimes revealed, any that qualify will be added to the database.

Pistol Pete Rollack

ENDNOTES

[1] Peabody, Zanto, *Stories Emerge on Suspect in LA. Serial Killings*, Record-Journal, June 1, 2003

[2] Serial Murder: Multi-Disciplinary Perspectives for Investigators- Produced by the FBI in July 2008. http://www.fbi.gov/stats-services/publications/serial-murder

[3] Aamodt, Mike, *Serial Killer IQ*, Radford University. Downloaded 2/2012: http://maamodt.asp.radford.edu/Serial%20Killer%20Information%20Center/Serial%20Killer%20IQ.htm.

[4] Friedberg, Ardy and McMahon Paula, *Murder Suspect Unfit for Trial Psychologist Says*, Sun Sentinel, November 17, 2001

[5] Ibid reference 3.

[6] Herrnstein, Richard J., and Murray, Charles, *The Bell Curve*, 1994, page 276

[7] Celona, Larry, *Brooklyn Strangler Admits Killing 5*, New York Post, August 6, 2000.

[8] Gado, Mark, *Nightcrawler,* Rosetta Books, 2011, Chapter Four.

[9] Foley Davis, *Lemuel Smith and the Compulsion to Kill: The Forensic Story of a Multiple Personality Serial Killer*, New Leitrim House Publishing, 2003.

[10] DeLauter, Lori, A KILLER CONFESSES: Edward Surratt Admits Quilt in Six Area Slayings, Beaver County Times, February 24, 2007.

[11] Bradley, Alan, *The Benjamin Atkins Story: America's Most Prolific Serial Killer*, Kindle Edition, 2013, 27 pages.

[12] Wagner, Dennis, *Man Who Confessed to Phoenix Killings Suspect in Oklahoma*, Tucson Citizen, April 15, 2003.

[13] Court of Appeals of Colorado, *People of the State of Colorado vs. Vincent Darrell Groves,* October 8, 1992, No. 90CA109, page 1312.

[14] State of Michigan Court of Appeals, *People of the State of Michigan vs. Shelly Andre Brooks*, June 28, 3008, No. 277652, Wayne Circuit Court.

[15] King, Jonathon, *The 15-Year Hunt for a Serial Killer*, South Florida Sun, October 30, 1988.

[16] Mitchell, Corey, *Evil Eyes: The Most Insatiable Serial Killer Ever,* Kensington Publishing Corp, 2006.

[17] Mather, Kate and Blankstein, Andrew, *LAPD to Post 'Grim Sleeper' suspect's photos on Facebook and Twitter*, Los Angeles Times, October 18, 2012.

[18] Isaad, Virginia, *It Happened this Week in L.A. History: The Skid Row Slasher Strikes*, LA Magazine, November 30, 2012.

[19] Olsen, Jack, *Charmer: The True Story of a Ladies' Man and His Victims*, Avon Books, 1995.

[20] Lang, Denise, *A Call to Justice: A New England Town's Fight to Keep a Stone Cold Killer in Jail*, Avon Publishers, 2000.

[21] Musta Susan D. and Clayton, Tony, I've Been Watching You: The South Louisiana Serial Killer, AuthorHouse, 2006.

[22] Smith, Leef, *Man Executed by Virginia for 1988 Dale City Slaying*, Washington Post, November 14, 1997.

[23] Vogell, Heather and Rankin, Bill, *A Death Case Derailed, Atlanta Journal-Constitution*, September 25, 2007.

[24] To perform the search yourself, go to www.nytimes.com, and type the name into search. You'll have to adjust the settings to search all papers since 1851,

and it's helpful to put the name in quotation marks, to help narrow down the search.

[25] For more information on the subject in general, I highly recommend Murder Most Rare: The Female Serial Killer by Michael Kelleher.

[26] Howard, Clark, *Zebra- The True Account of the 179 Days of Terror in San Francisco,* 1979

[27] Ibid., Howard, pp. 20-21

Chapter 5

Comparing Black and White Serial Killers

A general assumption is that serial killers always murder intra-racially, or within their race. Experts and the media offer this without any quantifying statistics to back their claim. As a result, those who are less informed generally accept this without question. The media will say things like, "Most serial killers, black and white, kill within their race....Cleophus Prince Jr. was unusual in that he murdered six white women in San Diego in the 1990's."[1] Even experts offer statements like the following: "White serial killers tend to prey on white victims; blacks on black."[2] As a result, when a rash of homicides pop up in a town, all connected to the same killer, police assume that white victims point to a white killer and black victims to a black one. The truth, however, is that this assumption is only half-true.

For whites, the FBI's mantra about serial killers murdering in-traracially is generally true. Of the 855 known white killers, there are nineteen examples of their killing interracially and preying solely on non-white victims. This equates to only 2.22% of white serial killers who choose victims outside their race. In addition, only thirty-one white killers who killed an even mixture of black and white victims can be found, only 3.62% of the total. If the two groups are tallied, we can see that whites either kill outside their race or have no racial preference for their victims only 5.84% of the time. This leaves 805 killers who murdered almost exclusively within their race, or 94.15% of all white serial killers. Thus, whites do fit the FBI's assumption of intraracial murder.

But when compared to black serial killers, an obvious disparity arises. Of the 982 killers, only 396 were black-on-black murders (40.32%), which is a considerable drop compared to the rate of white in-traracial murders. Contrary to white killers, there were 316 black killers who chose to strictly kill whites, which is 32.17% of those on the list, a rate 14.5 times higher than white interracial killers. Of the remaining 270 black killers, 248 (25.25%) killed an equal share of whites and blacks. The remaining twenty-two killers (2.24%) slew victims whose identities are unknown at this time. This means that 57.42% of black serial killers have chosen to kill outside their race, compared to 5.84% of the white killers.

To illustrate this, consider the following graph, which demonstrates the disproportion between the victim selection of white and black serial killers. The numbers to the left of the graph represent the percentage of killers, while the boxes under the graph represent the different racial categories. These categories are self-explanatory, with the exception of "Varied," which refers to a fairly equal mixture of both races. Notice that white serial killers almost always kill within their race, whereas blacks kill outside their race at a much higher rate.

Note also that there are times in which one of the killers killed over a dozen victims of one race, and then for some unknown reason chose a victim of another race. Both Chester Turner and Maury Travis are listed as having killed only black victims, yet both men murdered at least one white victim. Likewise, Carl Eugene Watts and Derrick Todd Lee killed exclusively white victims, except in one instance each when they killed a black female. To solve this dilemma, the victim's race assigned to each killer reflects the majority killed. If a killer had a fairly equal race selection, he was considered to fall into the "varied" category.

Chart 5.1 Serial Killer Victim Race Selection

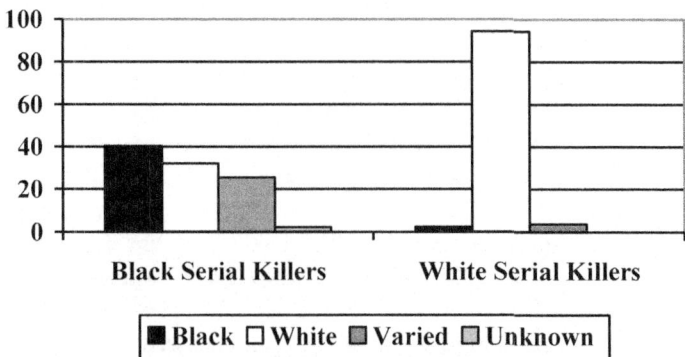

If the FBI would distribute these sorts of statistics instead of relying on their fallback rhetoric about victim selection, the subject of black serial killers would be more frequently discussed, and, more importantly, there might be a drop in their numbers. However, the FBI is not interested in public perception or how a void of information may affect the public; they live to follow their agenda with no regard of its implications. Hoover set this precedent when he took the reins of the FBI, and even years after his death, they show no deviation from this protocol.

The Racist Serial Killer Conundrum

As a result, not only do people assume that serial killers stay within their race for victim selection, but serious ramifications transpire whenever a white serial killer deviates from this norm. When Jeffrey Dahmer was caught, it was quickly publicized that a majority of his victims were black (ten of seventeen), and the media spun off reports that he had been a racist killer despite his having also killed young men who were white, Latino, and Asian. "Jeff Dahmer was a racist, and we know that there are policemen who dislike blacks," said Rev. Michael Champion, a black non-denominational minister in Milwaukee.[3] Numerous quotes from black citizens and family members were printed: "Many of us in Milwaukee are beginning to ask ourselves if this is a blatant case of racism and insensitivity."[4] This blitz of media quotes had a dramatic effect in making blacks nationwide feel that Dahmer was a racist white killer who hated blacks. There were numerous articles and headlines that appeared nationwide over the months following his arrest:

-   *Murder Spree Called 'Racist'*[5]

-   *Dahmer Victim's Family Sues City, Citing Racism*[6]

-   *2 Black Officials Call Dahmer Killings Racist*[7]

-   *Dahmer Case Raises Racism Complaints*[8]

Within a matter of days, black activists in Milwaukee were jumping on their soap boxes, screaming that something had to be done.

The head of the Black Panther Militia in Milwaukee was certainly vocal: "A blind man can see this is a race crime. The majority of his victims were black. He hates black people, period."[9] Moreover, later in the article, he threatened violence against whites and possible riots if racial conditions in Milwaukee did not improve by 1995. Soon afterward, black elected officials formed a coalition and called for a federal investigation of Dahmer's case, the Milwaukee police department, and the Wisconsin court system, on allegations that the system was full of racism from the top down. They alleged: "The mayor, the Police Department, the attorney general and other public officials have allowed institutional classism, racism and homophobia that exists in our government offices and other city and state departments to continue, and they must be held accountable."[10]

Lawsuits were soon filed against the police officers who had let one of Dahmer's victims, Konerak Sinthasomphone, return back to his apartment. But instead of filing on grounds of negligence, the lawsuits were on the grounds of racism, because the boy was Laotian. The department did eventually dismiss the officers on grounds of negligence, not racism, but that did not stop citizens and black officers for the next decade from charging the department with racism. Some even said that the problem arose because there were not enough black cops.[11] They would even go so far as to suggest that Dahmer would have killed less if police would have cared more about black victims of homicide.[12]

The court system was also attacked by the media, black activists, and the victims' families. They wanted special rights and privileges apportioned to the families affected, privileges not normally afforded to any families regardless of their race. Some complained that they wanted free parking close to the court building, despite Milwaukee County not offering that service in other court cases.[13] Additionally, they wanted court passes given to black activists who had helped fuel the charge of racism, on the grounds that they were counselors. Since it was a closed court session, they were denied the passes, just as any nonfamily member, witness, or other part of the court system would have been in other trials.[14]

But the biggest racism charge was because only one of the fourteen jurors was black, which the media fueled by churning out the complaints of families and black activists. Jeanette Robinson, who was a black counselor for some of the families, said: "One black juror! The law says you should be tried by a jury of your peers. A jury of your peers! Who did this man go to bed with and eat up?…There should be at least half blacks and gays on that jury."[15] County Supervisor Elizabeth Coggs-Jones, along with her aid Michael R. McGee, told the district attorney to "start dealing with the issue of racism,"[16] due to the lack of blacks on the jury panel. But to the chagrin of these protestors, civil rights lawyer Arthur Heitzer told the press that the reason there was only one black juror was because blacks are less likely to be registered voters and because they change their address too frequently, not because the court system was racist.[17]

During the trial, the confession of Jeffrey Dahmer was given and later printed in newspapers far and wide. Many papers reported that his victim selection was not racial: "In his confession, he said he selected victims not because of race but because he wanted a certain type of body."[18] But this still did not stop the racial momentum in the eyes of the black community in 1992, which was already a turbulent time with the LA riots and smaller race riots in Seattle and Atlanta. However, in the eyes of most whites, Dahmer was nothing more than a sick monster that had a taste for flesh and for killing young men; to them, his crime was not racial but repulsive.

By 1994, Dahmer's story was still being told in biopics on every major media channel, and books which gave the gritty, nasty details of his crime were hot sellers. On November 28, Dahmer and Jesse Anderson, who was made famous for killing his wife and blaming two black men, were beaten to death by Christopher Scarver. Despite Scarver's being black and having previously said that the justice system favored white and victimized blacks, officials were quick to rule out any racial motivation for the murders. However, after further investigation, they concluded that racial motivation could not be ruled out. Soon, it was reported: "Milwaukee County jail officials were particularly concerned about the attitude of black prisoners who considered Dahmer 'a racist killer' because most of his victims were young, gay black men."[19] Ultimately the charge of racial motivation was dropped altogether against Scarver after officials became convinced that other black prisoners had paid him to carry out the murders. However, blacks within the prison system and outside the prison walls all held their head a little higher, knowing that Dahmer had been killed by a black man—poetic justice in their eyes.

What the Dahmer case illustrates is that blacks are passionate when members of their race are victims of a white serial killer. However, even after it had been proven that his crimes were not hate crimes, Dahmer still bore the mark of a racist within the black community. As a result, everything revolving around the case, even small details which everyone normally accepts as the beliefs of a depraved sociopath, were considered racist.

Pit Dahmer's case against the Yahweh ben Yahweh cult trial in Miami, which happened during the same time. Through the extensive testimony of over 160 witnesses, many of whom were defectors from the cult, it was learned that the black cult leader ordered his followers to kill "white devils."[20] Yet, despite the blatant racial motivation behind the crimes, there was no public outcry from the families of the estimated twenty-three white victims. They did not accuse police, prosecutors, judges, or other officials of legitimizing racism. Instead, they gladly paid for their parking, sat in the courtroom without their grief counselor by their side, and waited for the verdict to be issued. But while there was never a charge of racism directed at the cult, this did not stop blacks from wondering if the cult had been racially profiled and framed by white cops. In an effort to keep the PC detractors happy, the FBI issued a statement that they had not harassed blacks or committed any form of racism in having white agents arrest black suspects.[21]

When the verdict came back from a very diverse jury that all murder charges were dismissed and that Hulon Mitchell (Yahweh ben Yahweh) and a few other members would serve small sentences on lesser charges; the families were upset, but they did not accuse any of racism. When Mitchell was released just a scant decade later, there was disappointment, but there was no outcry by the families, white activists, or the media that this racist was out on the street and might order the killings of more whites. There were no protest marches, calls on Congress, or human-rights groups yelling through mega-phones. It was business as usual in the media—stories about Hollywood starlets, the stock market, the habits of the president's dog, and other standard media fluff.

Some might argue that the reason the Yahweh cult did not garner as much attention or attract the charges of racism is because it was a group activity committed by several members. However, one person killing due to racial hatred is not as severe compared to a group working together as an organic unit. And Dahmer admitted from the beginning until his death that he was not a racist, but was rather attracted to black men. Hulon Mitchell, on the other hand, ordered his enforcers to bring back the ear, nose, or finger of the white devil to earn a blessing from him and to help elevate their status in the Book of Life (which ironically was a three-ring binder).[22] Even in his personal files, and in his three-ring binder "Book of Life," investigators found hate-laced documents against the "white devils" whom Hulon loathed.

This dichotomy is not just limited to Dahmer's case, but also has been seen in every white serial killer who has killed black victims in the past two decades. With the apprehension of each, the same rhetoric of racism fills the media, with blacks accusing police of not properly doing their jobs because the victims were black. When white serial killer Larry Bright was convicted of killing eight black women from 2001 to 2003 in Peoria, IL, blacks were appalled and blamed the police. This quote, from an article detailing his conviction, was typical: "Black leaders alleged then that authorities were slow to launch an investigation into the deaths and disappearances because of the victims' race and lifestyles. Many blacks also felt victimized because Bright is white."[23] Bright's case did not garner as much attention as Dahmer's, but the overtones of racial hatred did slowly melt away when it was discovered that he had a passion for black women. But the point is that these accusations were still present from the onset by default, simply because he was white and the victims were black.

Another example was seen in 2010 in Flint, MI. Black citizens were on high alert for a racist serial killer who was targeting blacks. The news media far and wide carried a composite sketch in August of the serial killer's possible identity, which featured a large white male in a baseball cap with a well-kept goatee and a menacing stare. Based on eyewitness accounts, police warned for residents to be on the lookout for a stocky white male in a green blazer with a cream-colored stripe. The media suggested, because the suspected killer was white, that the "attacks may be racially motivated."[24]

Within days of releasing the sketch, police had Elias Abuelazam in custody on August 11, where he was charged with killing five people in eighteen attacks. Citizens were outraged because the five dead were all black, and of the eighteen stabbed, only two had not been black. Black leaders began crying foul and charging Elias with racism, with many calling for a crackdown on white racists. Much to their embarrassment, Abuelazam turned out to be a citizen of Israel, working here on a green card—not the typical American redneck as the original profile had suggested.

Despite this, the media still carried headlines like this: "Israeli Eliasa Abuelazam Appears in US Court Accused of Racist Murders."[25] To observant eyes, it was obvious that he was not a white American accused of the crime, but to most, they saw the buzzword "racist" and assumed that he must be another backwoods white supremacist. Riding on this wave of momentum, the Michigan branch of the NAACP hosted a public forum where the police were questioned as to why they had not released more information prior to the release of the sketch.[26] But because the police chief was black, they were hesitant to throw accusations of racism against the department, instead focusing on their not properly informing the citizens of Flint. The chief did remind citizens that stabbings are a regular occurrence in Flint, which has a crime index just over three times the national average, so it took police time to connect the crimes. However, this did not stop citizens in the taped question-and-answer period to accuse the department of racism, particularly by not properly protecting black citizens from white racists.

The dilemma is not that Abuelazam killed blacks, but instead that, from the beginning, it was pegged as a racially motivated crime, possibly even a hate crime. However, as stated previously, there are 299 black serial killers who killed mostly whites, yet there has never been the charge of hate or racism thrown out in any of their cases. It is as if any white killer who ventures outside his race is automatically a racist, but it is accepted as normal behavior for blacks to kill whites. This double standard is both appalling and unfair to the general public—they deserve better; they deserve the truth.

Pit this against the story of Roy L. Williams. On January 27, 1988, he told friends of his hatred for white people and that he was going to kill the first white man he saw. Within days he had gunned down a white man he had never met, James McDonnell, on the streets of Philadelphia. He then ran to Massachusetts, where, a few months later, he killed at least one other white man before he was apprehended. Despite the local press coverage on his case, some of which did mention his motivation, no one dared call him a racist. He was charged with murder but was not even considered a suspect for a possible hate crime. Even the Pennsylvania Supreme Court, when reviewing his case during the appeals process, acknowledged his motivation, but they refused to acknowledge that it was a hate crime. Instead, Williams was analyzed by psychiatrists to see if there was something else motivating him besides hate.[27]

Consider the story of Mark James Robert Essex, the disgruntled sniper who killed nine and wounded ten more. After leaving the Navy, he openly voiced his hatred for white people and began hanging around the black militant group, the Black Panthers. On New Year's Eve in 1972, he snapped after telling friends he was going to kill honkeys, and he went to snipe police officers as they were leaving the station. After killing one officer, who (ironically) was black, he wounded two others and fled. One of those officers would later die from his injuries.

Mark Essex

Police were baffled at who the attacker was and were looking for clues. On January 7, Essex returned and was involved in a firefight with police for over eleven hours as he holed up on the roof of a hotel. As the battle drew to a close, he stepped out and received a volley of bullets into his small body. As he knelt down, he arched his back, looked to the sky, and said, "Power to the people. Power to the people. I'm gonna get me three more white honky."[28] Upon saying that, he expired.

When recovering Essex's body, police learned his identity and went to his apartment. Upon entering his small domicile, they encountered racist graffiti covering much of the walls. Single words like "Africa," "hate," "blood," and "Congo" were spread across the walls in a disorganized fashion. More ominous were phrases like "Shoot to Kill," "Justice is Black Justice," and "Hate White People Beast of the Earth."[29] Elsewhere in the room, they found Black Panther literature and notes he had scribbled about his hatred for white people, including his plan to kill dozens more white victims, starting with the police. In their minds, it was an extreme case of racial hatred that had fueled his desire to kill.

The news media was reluctant to carry a story about a racist black man killing whites, so the emphasis on his motivation was toned down, and it shifted to the source of his frustration. Instead of thousands of articles and hours of newsreel showing dismay for Essex's racist actions, they focused on how good a boy he had been, the church in which he grew up, and the fact he had grew up in a mostly white town in Kansas. Friends from his childhood, his minister, and his family were interviewed, and each showed contempt at the idea that he was a racist. Instead, all voiced that Essex was a nice but confused young man. None of his new friends, the black militant type, were interviewed. The media was afraid of what their testimony might do to tarnish the image of Essex they had constructed as an all-American guy who made a bad choice.

Within days of his death, the media began focusing on what triggered Essex. From the testimony of his family and childhood minister, they began to paint a vivid tale of racist subtleties directed at him for growing up in an all-white town, but they focused most of their attention on racial abuse at the hands of a few whites with whom he served in the Navy. They told of the inequality he faced, which frustrated this young lad to begin hating the white race as a whole due to the actions of a few. His mother was given adequate press time, and she would say incendiary things: "A clear signal for White America to get off the seat of its pants and do something. If this terrible thing will awaken White America to the injustices that blacks suffer, then some good will come of it."[30]

No one in the media was willing to pin Mark's racist problems on him; instead they each shifted the focus onto white sailors. But despite their continuous blame game, no adequate proof was found to substantiate their story. They just kept strumming the victim card every time his name was mentioned for the next two decades. Only one newspaper that I can find had the guts to lay the blame solely on him. From a small paper in Washington, PA, they lambasted the mainstream media for their tactics: "To insist that society is to blame for his death is captious reasoning. No way will I buy that. The guilt lies within the bullet-shattered body of the young black from Kansas."[31]

Imagine that this tale had been reversed, with Essex belonging to a white supremacist organization, hating blacks by hunting them and painting racist graffiti over his walls. If that were the case, everyone knows what the outcome would have been. They surely would have interviewed his family and childhood friends—but not to see how good a boy he had been, just to see if they were the source of his racist sentiments. No blame would have been placed on his military record; instead, they would have searched to see if he had any connection to the South, if he was the descendent of a Confederate soldier, or if his ancestors had owned slaves. The media would have made every effort to prove that his racism was ingrained in him from birth and not a reaction to the actions of others. Even worse, there is a high likelihood lawsuits would have been filed against his family and friends.

Modern-Day Lynching

This problem is not merely restricted to these cases; it has manifested itself in almost all of the black serial killers with white victims: there is a total media blackout. In most of the cases, it requires extensive digging to reveal the identity of the victims before the story can even be properly understood. Sometimes it is much more than a black who killed whites; there is often a deeper, hidden meaning that only rises after further investigation.

Such is the case of Javier Victorianne, a name most of the country holds as insignificant, a name that does not raise any red flags. Javier was a large black man; he was 6'4" and over 240 pounds of lean muscle. He easily intimidated people with his size, but he won them over with his charm. On July 29, 1999, he took a white female, Maria "Lisa" Boyd, to his hotel room to chat. After she refused his offer to have sex with him, he became angry with her and hit her over the head with a lamp. While she was dazed, he tied three different ligatures around her hands and raped her, despite her pleas. Once finished, instead of letting her go, he fashioned a necktie into a makeshift noose and hanged her to death in the closet. Her body was found the next day, but Javier was nowhere to be found.

Almost a year later to the day, he met sixteen-year-old Amanda Hoffman at a party, where he was handing out business cards advertising himself as a talent scout. The young white girl decided to follow him to a nearby park to learn more about a potential job. Once at the park, he overpowered her and raped her in the moonlit hours. She pled for her life, but Javier took her overalls, fashioned them into a noose, and hanged her from a tree, where her body was found seven days later.

He was caught not long after when he tried his trick on another helpless white woman. She was able to escape and alert authorities after kicking him in the face and stomach numerous times. After comparing his DNA with the database of unsolved rapes and murders, he was a positive match for the two murders. He patiently awaited his trial for over seven years in the county jail before it went to trial. After a three-month trial, he was sentenced to two death sentences and implicated in the murder of a mildly retarded white woman in 2000.

Outside the town of Riverside, CA, this story was not big news. It made no newspapers outside the Los Angeles area, and if it were not for his story being posted in pro-death penalty internet forums, I would not have found it. Every local news agency that had carried it has deleted their original stories, but thankfully they are preserved on numerous sites in full, describing his atrocious crimes.[32]

Compare this to an early case, almost two decades prior to Javier's. In 1981, the nation heard of the brutal attack and hanging of a young black man by a small group of Ku Klux Klan members in Mobile, AL. The leader of the local Klan chapter had been outraged that a black man, Josephus Anderson, who had shot a white policeman, had his case declared a mistrial. Upset, he told his fellow Klansmen that if a black could kill and get away with it in Mobile, then surely a white man could too.

Encouraged by their leader's speech, Henry Hays and James "Tiger" Knowles took to the streets, driving around in search of a victim. They spotted Michael Donald, figured he was a likely target, and kidnapped him. After driving to the woods near Hays's home, they beat him with a branch and then put a noose around his neck. They slit his throat before hanging him and left his body to be found the next day.

Initially, police thought that it was a drug-related crime, due to an ongoing drug war in the area. Unsatisfied with police answers, his mother called Jesse Jackson to lead a protest march in the streets to get the black community involved. Threatened by the negative media attention, police quickly contacted the FBI, who eventually located the killers two and a half years later.

More protest marches followed prior to the killers' capture, and Jesse Jackson told a crowd of marchers at a Selma-to-Montgomery reenactment of MLK's famous march: "If they lynch any more black boys in Mobile, it's fighting time. When they kill 24 black babies in Atlanta it's fighting time."[33] The crowd reacted in overwhelming support, applauding Jackson in the midst of his bid for the presidency. The latter part of his quote would later prove false, as it was in reference to the belief that black children in Atlanta had been killed by the KKK. Those murders would later be proven to have been committed by black serial killer Wayne Williams.

After the conviction, Michael Donald's mother still was not that satisfied that only her son's killer had gotten a death sentence, while his two accomplices received a life sentence with no chance for parole. She contacted Morris Dees at the Southern Poverty Law Center in Montgomery, AL, about a possible lawsuit. In 1987, the SPLC won that suit with a seven-million-dollar award against the United Klans of America, the organization to which the killers had pledged allegiance. This bankrupted the organization, despite evidence that they did not have prior knowledge of the crime. In later years, Donald's story would be told in books and TV biopics, detailing the hate his killers had for him. In 2006, the street on which he was kidnapped was renamed in his honor.

Contrast Donald's story with the aforementioned lynchings of the two white women. In both instances, the killers picked a victim outside their race, and the victims were each beaten and then hanged to death. The difference lies in the fact that Donald died at the hands of KKK members in the deep South when blacks were heavily campaigning for equality and the elimination of any white nationalist group. In Donald's case, the NAACP, Jesse Jackson, the SPLC, and the mainstream media were quick to rally and throw in their support. But with Javier, there were no lawsuits against his family, no public marches of whites in the streets of Riverside protesting black-on-white violence, and no national reports that a hate crime had been committed. Instead, the story was known only to the friends and families of the victims and to authorities handling the case.

These are not the fair scales of justice that black egalitarians have demanded for the last 100 years. Instead, whites who commit vile crimes are painted as racist, and their families and associates stand to lose big after their conviction. Blacks, however, can commit a similar crime or worse and be forgotten, and in some twisted perversion of justice, they can be occasionally portrayed as victims themselves.

Another example is the story of the Carr brothers. After the trial of the two, in what was one of the vilest crimes in recent history, Michelle Malkin noted that the trial of Hollywood actress Winona Ryder attracted more news articles and television airtime than did this horrific tragedy.[34] David Horowitz said, "The fact is that the Wichita horror is but one of many spectacular lynchings of white people by black racists, which the nation's moral watchdogs choose to ignore."[35]

Most will ask who the Carr brothers were and what crimes they committed.

In December 2000, the city of Wichita was rocked by what would later be called the Wichita Massacre. Two black brothers, Reginald and Jonathan Carr, had recently moved to the town, and instead of getting jobs, they decided to try to make a

Johnathan Carr

career of robbery, rape, and murder. On December 11, after already having robbed and beaten a well-known white high school baseball coach, they robbed, raped, and shot a white woman named Ann Walenta. Satisfied with their take, they took a few days off to celebrate and prepare for their next heist.

On the snowy, blustery evening of the 14th, at a home shared by three young men, the Carr brothers decided to enter. They had chosen the home mostly at random; based on the number of cars in the driveway, they assumed it would be a good haul. After bursting through the front door, they demanded the five white people, three men and two women, to stand still or get shot. The victims complied with the men's orders and put their hands in the air.

At this point in most situations, people assume that the robbers ask for money, the victims hand it over, and the story ends. But that is not what the Carrs had in mind. Instead, they had the victims strip naked and then forced the victims to perform various sex acts with each other over a period of three hours, all while the Carrs laughed and drank the booze from the home.

Finally satisfied with the show, the Carr brothers took turns raping the two women and beating the men. The victims offered to empty their savings accounts to pay the robbers to leave, at which point the Carrs agreed to receive their money.

Reginald Carr

One by one, the victims were forced in the nude or little clothing to drive through the icy roads, with a gun to their heads, to the nearest ATM. Once this task was complete, they set to raiding the home for other valuables. It did not take long for them to find an engagement ring, which one of the men was going to give to his girlfriend that very night. It was still in its box, hidden in a jar of coins, and he begged for them at least to leave that one item, so he could still give it to her. The Carrs mocked him and threatened to beat them all again, and said that his girl would have to get another ring.

Despite having told the victims that they were not going to die, the Carrs forced the three nude men into the frigid trunk of a car and put the nude women in the back seat. After driving for a while, they arrived at a remote soccer field on the edge of town, covered in wind-blown snow drifts. The victims were forced out of the car and were marched onto the field, where they were lined up and told to get on their knees in the snow. Under the light of headlights dimmed by blowing snow, each person was shot execution-style in the back of the head. Not satisfied that they were dead, the Carrs drove over the bodies several times. With their wicked deed complete, the Carrs fled the scene, satisfied with their haul.

This story may have gone unsolved, or more victims may have fallen, had it not been for one of the victims. She was a courageous woman, and by fate the bullet had ricocheted off her hairclip. She did, however, take the full weight of the truck, which caused serious injuries, but she remained calm and played dead when the Carrs kicked the bodies before leaving to see if they were dead.

Certain that the Carrs were gone, she ran towards Christmas lights she saw in the distance. Occasionally, she had to hide in a roadside ditch as cars approached, fearful that it was one of the murderers driving by. After running the grueling distance in near-zero conditions in the middle of the night, with snow pelting her face, she made it to the house. The occupants were shocked to see a naked young woman shivering and bleeding on the front porch, so they let her in and covered her in blankets as they called 911. Despite all that she had been through, she remained calmer than the couple and was able to guide police via the phone to the scene and to describe what the killers looked like.

When this happened, I was living a little over three hours south in Oklahoma City. The initial reports were on the three major networks in our area, but after that it did not make news again. When the trial took place, it did not even make our local news, but instead we heard repeatedly about a handbag that Winona Ryder had stolen.

Compare this to the news of the BTK killer, Dennis Rader, who was caught in Wichita in 2005. Our local news carried the story from the time of his capture to his trial, always updating us with every new detail. The fundamental difference between Rader and the Carrs is that the latter were black and killed white victims, which is politically incorrect to discuss or broadcast as legitimate news. BTK was a white serial killer, and his victims were either white or Hispanic, which makes for prime news. Had the Carr brothers been white and their victims black, every news channel in the country would have carried their story, and the streets would have been congested with satellite news trucks. But as it was, the story did not even rank enough to be carried in the major newspapers or magazines, and it has yet to be made into a movie or TV documentary.

Looking for a White Suspect

The media is not the only guilty party when a black serial killer begins his killing spree. Oftentimes the police are responsible for releasing the initial story, telling people to be on the lookout for a white killer when in reality the killer is black. Sometimes this is just a simple case of ignorance on the part of police, while other times it is because of an errant description given by a witness. For instance, the original order given by police for the killings committed by Derrick Todd Lee was to be on the lookout for a white thirty-five-year old male in the area.[36] Media outlets carried a composite sketch of what they thought he looked like, but when he was caught and his identity was revealed to be black, he seemingly vanished from the national media attention.

When police were researching the murders committed by Edward Arthur Surratt, they had compelling evidence that the killer was black due both to hair samples found at the scenes and to eyewitness accounts. However, because of the account of one shaken woman who thought that her husband's killer might have been white, the police ignored their prior conclusions and focused the search on a white male. The woman did tell police that it happened so fast she could not be sure, in addition to the fact that she was awakened from deep sleep by the gunshot that killed her husband. Her story was enough to send police after a white suspect, despite already having Surratt as their chief suspect. This caught the media's attention and helped fuel the search for a white killer. When it later turned out that Surratt was responsible, his name fell into obscurity because he was black, despite his having killed nineteen white people.

Gregory Davis

In 1987, four elderly white women had been brutally raped and murdered outside Jackson, MS. There was one eyewitness account from a woman who survived the attack describing a black male as her attacker. Police quickly discounted this, claiming that she could not have been sure because her glasses were knocked off.[37] This left residents of the area on the lookout for a white serial killer. However, after Gregory Davis was caught and he confessed to the crimes, the media reports conveniently dropped the race of the victims, leaving those not following the case to assume that the killer and victims were of the same race. No mention was made of possible racism, but instead the media focused on how good a student Davis had been, and how pleasant a person he was to be around.[38] Included in these feel-good stories, which portrayed Davis as hardly able to be the monster that mutilated the bodies of his victims, was a picture of him from high school, smiling and jovial, meant to leave the reader feeling sorry for him. Prior to his arrest, this story was the talk of the South along with increased gun and door lock sales, but afterwards, it was displaced by more important things, like the story of Sen. Gary Hart's affair with Jessica Hahn.[39]

The Litmus Test

The story of the Atlanta Child Murders of the late seventies and early eighties also had undertones of being a white racist conspiracy. In 1982, Wayne Williams was convicted in the murders of two black adult males, and because of physical evidence, the unsolved deaths of twenty-seven black children from an inner-city housing project were also cleared by police. The FBI had been called in to assist because children were the victims, and they quickly drew up a profile. Despite the urging of the black mayor and black politicians in Atlanta that the killer had to be a member of the KKK or some other secretive white racist organization, the FBI stated that the pattern of crime seemed to point in the direction of a black suspect.

After his capture, the killings stopped just as quickly as they had happened, despite the pleas from the community that they felt Williams was an innocent man. However, this did not stop a whirlwind of interest in his case in the thirty years that have followed. Many blacks in Atlanta are still convinced that Williams is innocent, that he was somehow framed by the Klan. They say things like: "It must be some white guy in a cop's uniform or some uniform of authority."[40]

Just as the Williams story was fading away from media attention, CBS aired a two-part documentary in 1985 attempting to show that Williams was a scapegoat for white supremacists. The docudrama was highly watched, receiving 28% of the viewing audience, which put it in the top spot for the week according to Nielsen ratings. Critics called the film deplorable, a poor attempt at uncovering the truth: "The script has all the skill of a 3-year-old fingerpainting on the wall. If CBS had been serious about producing a documentary, the network was bound by ethics, to say a little common sense, to increase the scope of the original investigation."[41] But critics alone were not the only ones outraged; the film, in its attempt to make Williams seem innocent, made the Atlanta police and judicial system (which had a high number of blacks at the time) appear to be incompetent. This outraged citizens of Atlanta and members of the force.

After the film, Williams' attorney was encouraged that he would have public sentiment, so he appealed the conviction on grounds that there was a conspiracy to cover the KKK's involvement.[42] He spun stories about documents being destroyed, the Klan drinking beers with the investigators during the trial, and other such tales. His attempt was shot down, but this did not keep him from trying the same tactic over the next few years.

By 2000, the world had almost forgotten about Williams, and his attorney had shifted gears after failing on his prior appeals. The Showtime Network came riding in to save the day with a documentary called "Who Killed Atlanta's Children?", hosted by Gregory Hines and

James Belushi. The film made a mockery of the justice system and again attempted to show Williams as an angelic victim of racial hatred towards blacks. Here is a description of the drama: "The film suggests the Georgia Bureau of Investigation turned up possible Ku Klux Klan links to some of the killings, then covered up or destroyed the evidence. Agents are shown laughing chummily with Klan members during 'interrogations' and throwing boxes of evidence into the furnace....The film also suggests that political pressure led police and prosecutors to cover up the Klan investigation for fear race riots would break out and Atlanta's image would be tarnished."[43]

Just as with the 1985 documentary, the show was watched by a large audience, and just like its predecessor, it failed miserably as well.

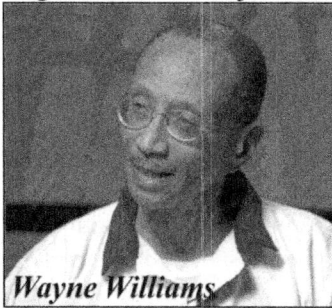

Wayne Williams

Critics complained that it looked like a hack-job version of *The Naked Gun*, while others said that the producers did not answer any of the questions they posed, but only showed their lack of credibility.[44] Even Williams' lawyer, while appreciative of the film, showed his discontent; even he was no longer using the worn-out Klan angle in his appeals.[45]

All these films managed to do was cement in black minds across the nation that Williams was framed. This further fueled the belief that black murderers are frequently framed by racist white cops. To this day, Williams still maintains that he was framed, and most blacks who are aware of his case agree. For instance, moved by the story, the black police chief of DeKalb County reopened the investigation of five of the murdered children in May 2005. The case uncovered nothing new, but instead led investigators back to square one: Wayne Williams. In fact, in 2010, DNA found in one of the children's bodies was proven conclusively to be none other than Williams'.[46]

When considering cases like Williams, sound logic has to be applied. Despite what critics of the case may think, the FBI called it right. They speculated that it would be near impossible for a white man to sneak into an Atlanta ghetto and steal a black child in broad daylight once. But to repeat the action twenty-seven times and cap it off by kidnapping two adult black males, and somehow to plant carpet samples from Williams' home and the trunk of his father's car onto each victim—they correctly reasoned that that was impossible. This has not slowed critics though, who imaginatively contend that anything is possible and that the Klan was behind this.

The irony in Williams' case is that the evidence which detectives used to pin the murders on him was comparable in quantity to the evidence used to convict dozens of white serial killers before his time. Yet, while many of the whites have had documentaries made detailing their crimes, in no instance have the films suggested that the men were framed or otherwise innocent. With the white serial killers, they are portrayed as rabid monsters, unable to control their primal urge to kill, while Williams is portrayed as a gentle, small black man who would not hurt a fly. It is just more of the one-sidedness that the mainstream media and Hollywood portray, by casting the white killer as guilty and the black man as innocent.

Williams' case has become the litmus test for all black serial killers ever since. Even though few have made national news, whenever they are reported in the local media there is always the suspicion that the killer might have been framed. In the case of Mark Goudeau, the Baseline Killer, his supporters have claimed that police planted his DNA on the victims. In other cases, despite overwhelming evidence—comparable to catching a child with his hand in the cookie jar—blacks are quick to scream foul and allege that there had to be some element of police dishonesty at play.

But one area where the Williams litmus test most always rears its ugly head is at the time of execution. Whether it is a serial murderer or (as in the case of Troy Davis) a single-time murderer, the tactics blacks use are always the same. Mysteriously, witnesses recant their testimony years after the fact, jurors spread rumor of jury-fraud, DNA evidence gets questioned, physical evidence is doubted, and confessions are abrogated by the killer. Perhaps worst of all, anything that can be used as a technicality is blown out of proportion by the mainstream media in an attempt to have the sentence commuted or even absolved. While I agree that no one wants the blood of an innocent man on his hands, and that every effort should be made during the trial to validate the evidence and testimony, the time to do this is not as the inmate is marching to the execution chamber. Yet, in this perversion of fairness, it is rare when a white man is sentenced to see a huge public outcry to halt the execution and demand a new trial. But this tactic is used frequently with black killers.

The Victim Card

In some instances, it is not the crime itself that brings the black killer to public attention and fame (or infamy), but the pleas to spare his life on the basis that he is a victim. As with the aforementioned Marx Essex, a common ploy with black serial killers is to look towards external forces instead of inward volition as the motivating factor that drove them to kill. With white serial killers, physiologists do look at outside mitigating forces, but ultimately, in almost every case, they place the blame on the killer. While this does happen in some instances with black serial killers, there is a higher frequency of relying on external stimuli alone, used in an attempt to exempt the killer of his crimes. Family and friends will rally behind the black serial killer and claim that that is not the person they knew, as if it were not possible for him to be the monster he is portrayed to be. But what they do not realize is that they have played into one of the greatest tricks serial killers have: to blend in to such a degree that even their own families do not notice the animals they have become. This does not stop the media from rushing from story to story and portraying black serial killers as victims, even if it is right before their execution. The case of William Henry Hance is an example.

Hance murdered four young black women from 1977-1978. His case started off with public outrage after he had forged a note claiming to be a group of seven racist white men who would keep killing black women until the Stocking Strangler (Carlton Gary) was caught. Blacks outside Fort Benning, GA, were terrified and on vigilant watch for these white racists as black activists spun stories about how this crime was a crime against blacks nationwide. However, when Hance was caught and found to be black, his name slipped into obscurity as if the crime never happened, and the officials reeled in embarrassment for buying his story.[47]

Just before his execution, his name resurfaced—yet not as a serial killer, but instead as a victim. Despite overwhelming evidence and his full confession, his defense claimed that the entire trial should be thrown out because of a rumor. Fifteen years after his trial, one female juror claimed that a male juror said that Hance would be "just one more sorry nigger that no one would miss."[48] In addition, the lone black juror said she was forced to recommend the death penalty in spite of her reservations. The governor of Georgia and the courts did not agree that a rumor, unrevealed until years after the trial, was a valid reason to halt the execution. Hance was executed on March 31, 1994, but this only fanned the flames that he was a victim of a corrupt white man's system. His death was seen as a great racist tragedy: "Our judgmental shortcomings include our colossal inability to crawl out of the muck of racial prejudice."[49]

Alton Coleman committed eight murders, seven rapes, and numerous burglaries across the Midwest in 1984. Once caught, he was the only man at the time to have concurrent death sentences in three states. As his execution drew near in April 2002, his attorneys filed an appeal that he was a victim of blatant racism. They claimed there were not enough black jurors, and that some of the prospective but dismissed juror candidates had been black.[50] Their claim was that since the trial in question concerned a white victim, white jurors would be more apt to issue a death sentence because Coleman was black. Unmoved by this argument, the court system ruled that the execution must take place.

Unsatisfied with this answer, the lawyers tried a different approach. A psychologist issued an opinion to the courts that Coleman should be kept alive to be studied and that he was really the victim. The lawyers "argued that Mr. Coleman should be spared because of his troubled childhood, including organic brain dysfunction caused by his mother's drug use before his birth and growing up with an abusive mother and grandmother."[51] Again, the court was unmoved, and it maintained that Coleman should be held accountable for his crimes, no matter what his upbringing was. He was executed on April 26, 2002.

One serial killer's execution probably received more attention than any other. The infamous Crips leader Stanley "Tookie" Williams was sentenced to death for killing four people in robberies in the late seventies. After getting locked up, he achieved celebrity-like status by writing children's books, and media outlets were lining up to interview him. His story was sensationalized with television biopics, memorialized in rap songs, and told in countless internet blogs; and it even earned him a nomination for the Nobel Peace Prize. The common push in most of the stories was that Tookie was a rehabilitated man who had done enough work to detour kids from entering gangs to atone for his own murderous sins. It was told that he was repentant for his crimes. Yet in reality, they rarely reported that Tookie denied his crimes, even as he lay on the execution table.

As his execution neared, the media and radio hosts in California predicted that riots would break out if Gov. Schwarzenegger did not grant clemency. Many set up websites with petitions to the governor, black rappers and movie stars proclaimed his innocence, Jesse Jackson spoke with Schwarzenegger on behalf of Tookie, and amnesty groups were at a deafening roar to release him. The common theme was that Tookie had been convicted by a majority-white jury, in which case this was an obvious example of racism. The *LA Times* reported that Tookie's case was complete "with its racial overtones and compelling theme."[52] Even Tookie suggested that his trial was a set-up, in realty a conviction of his founding the Crips gang. Unconvinced that Tookie was apologetic for his crimes and noting that he could not be repentant if he never admitted guilt, Schwarzenegger denied the appeal for clemency. After the execution, black commentators and bloggers were calling this the greatest example of legal lynching in history. The family members of Tookie's victims disagreed and unanimously felt that they finally received the closure they deserved.

Not only does the victim card get played before execution, but it also is utilized in many cases from the beginning. One of the most famous examples was Wayne Williams, as was previously discussed. There are many others besides him, but for the sake of space just a few will be considered.

Charles Duffy was found guilty via DNA evidence of having killed four black women, and he was implicated in the deaths of two more. In an interview at a popular website for serial killers, he was asked about his crimes and prison sentence. He responded about avoiding the death penalty by working with the authorities, but as for his sentence, he called the prison system "legalized slavery, legalized murder."[53] Then, when asked what he would do if released tomorrow, his answer was simple: "Find me a pistol."[54] That leaves little doubt as to what his next task would be.

Carlton Gary, the Stocking Strangler and the contemporary serial killer in Georgia with William Henry Hance, is another example. He had raped and murdered nine elderly white women, which provoked fear throughout New York and later Columbus, GA. From the beginning, he accused the legal system of being racist. He continually burst out in court, hurling insults at the judge and prosecutors. During one outburst he shouted, "All that's missing (in the trial) are a tree and some hoods. The only difference I see is that most of you just wear suits and don't wear hoods."[55]

Soon after receiving his death sentences, he was sent to county jail to await delivery to the state penitentiary. While he was there, the sheriff recorded the following behavior in his file: "Gary resisted being shackled, hurled racial slurs at the two white deputies, and threatened to kill them and their mothers, according to the typed reports."[56] This behavior continued into prison for years before he finally settled down.

When the matter of his execution arose, the first roadblock was the accusation of racism during the trial. Everyone involved was interviewed, and all denied that any racism had occurred other than what Gary had exhibited. While the charge of racism against Gary was eventually dropped, it was not before every bit of evidence against him was called into question. His last execution date in 2009 was issued a stay, and he is currently still on death row while the evidence and testimonies from thirty-two years prior is tested for accuracy. So far, this painstaking and expensive process had dragged on slowly, being hampered by new allegations of racism that surface from time to time. But thus far, the evidence still points to Gary as the killer.

Perhaps one of the strongest black serial killers on record, capable of breaking handcuffs, bench-pressing over 500 pounds, he even ripped a cell door off a jail cell once, had a similar story. As an amateur bodybuilder and boxer, Damon Chapple was traveling through Spokane,

WA, when he decided to stay to see what the city offered. After suffocating a white drug dealer by bear-hugging him, and then raping and beating a seventy-eight-year-old white woman to death four months later, he was finally arrested. From the start, he said the system was racist. While in prison, he almost killed a cell mate while raping him, and he had to stand trial. At his trial, he blurted: "Sure be glad when you get this Klu Klux Klan [sic] meeting over with; I'm getting tired."[57] Aside from this, he threatened to kill jurors, the judge, his attorney, and even a journalist for being white.

William Gerald Mitchell was a paroled murderer who had brutally cut a female friend into pieces in 1974 in Mississippi. A few years

William Gerald Mitchell

after parole, he viciously killed a white woman in Biloxi, MS, in one of the worst cases of overkill on record. While this story did not make any headlines, his appeal did stir up a few stories. Mitchell alleged in 2002 that his case should be thrown out because they did not move the trial to a county with a higher black population. He claimed that "it was imperative that he be tried in a county where the racial make-up was more favorable to him."[58] The court denied his appeal, telling him that the jury represented a fair cross section of the county in which the crimes were committed. This has not stopped him from trying a similar tactic in other appeals.

Another noteworthy case to mention is that of Anthony Sowell. Just prior to the jury's sentence recommendation, he was allowed to speak to the court about what made him a serial killer. Throughout the half-hour testimony, he answered a series of questions that his lawyer and he had previously discussed. The judge noted that his testimony was not to be used to sway the jury, but was instead Sowell's time to publicly confess and give his reasons. His attorney hoped it would sway at least one of the jurors to vote against the death sentence. Throughout the questions, Sowell stated how he was a product of a home without love, one where he was severely punished for the smallest infractions. His conclusion was that although he murdered eleven women, ultimately he was not responsible; instead, his mother's lack of love and the evils of white society were to blame. He was a hapless victim in his mind. The jury was unmoved, and they voted collectively for the death penalty.

A potential hiccup happened after his trial in August 2011. Just days after receiving the death sentence, his lawyer requested a new trial based off a juror's comments to the media after the trial. She had told the press that it gave her the creeps when Sowell would occasionally wink at her during the trial. In addition, when asked about having to walk through the home that contained the bodies of eleven black women, "she became overwhelmed with a sense of the horrible events that occurred inside the house and had to take a moment to regain her composure before continuing."[59] In the eyes of the defense attorney, this was grounds for a new trial. Yet, if Sowell had been white with white victims, he would have probably said that the woman needed to suck it up. It may very well be this little hiccup in Sowell's trial that will cause serious problems with his execution in the future. His defense already attempted to establish that he killed only because his mother never loved him and because he was not afforded the same benefits as whites. Hopefully his execution will come and go quickly, but a bumpy ride may be ahead.

The point with each of these cases is not that white serial killers do not claim ludicrous things, for they do too. Instead, it is to show the value that race holds with the black killers. The media fails to report the race of most black serial killers, claiming that race does not matter. However, race becomes very important during and after the conviction as a means to portray the killer as a victim of racism. To my knowledge, no white serial killer (or for that matter, no white murderer) has ever attempted to use racism against him as an appeal. Sure, white killers use other tactics—which blacks use as well—but claiming racism is not one of their tools. Posing as the victim of racism during the investigation or trial is a tactic unique to black killers. It is especially prevalent when a black serial killer had white victims. There is almost an expectation, during either the trial or the appeal process, that racism towards the killer will be mentioned. This same notion is not afforded to white serial killers with black victims, but instead is reversed by painting them as the racist.

Lessened Prison Sentences

When a white killer is brought to trial, it is almost a given that he is facing either the death penalty or a life sentence with no chance of parole. If there is no death penalty in the state where he is tried, he will receive multiple life sentences, sometimes totaling a term hundreds of years long. However, when a black murderer is brought to trial, the sentence is not always a guarantee, even if he is a serial murderer.

According to the FBI Uniform Crime Reports, black males made up 52.5% of all homicides from 1980-2008.[60] (This does not mean that whites make up the other 47.5% of the total, for one should remember that Hispanics, American Indians, and sometimes Asians are counted as white by the UCR.[61]) Compare this to the number of inmates from each race who have been executed during roughly the same time, and the results are vastly different. From 1977-2010, 56.72% of prisoners executed were white, while only 34.35% were black.[62] This means that white death row inmates were executed 1.25 times more than the number of homicides their group committed during the same time period. By contrast, blacks were executed 1.528 times less than the percentage of murders they committed.

Now, granted, not every death row execution was a result of murder, nor did every homicide conviction result in a death row sentence. But these numbers do indicate a trend that whites are executed in greater numbers in proportion to their murder rate than blacks. If the number of death sentences for this same time period is factored in, the trend continues to display the same results. Of the 7,879 death sentences given, 3,816 were given to whites (48.43%), while 3,225 were given to blacks (40.93%).[63] Whites receive a death sentence almost on par with the percentage of murders they committed, only about 1.06 times higher. Yet, blacks were underrepresented by 1.28 times their murder percentage. This may seem trivial, but when charted, the results show the rift between the two camps.

Chart 5.2 Homicides Compared to Death Row
Convictions and Executions
1977-2010

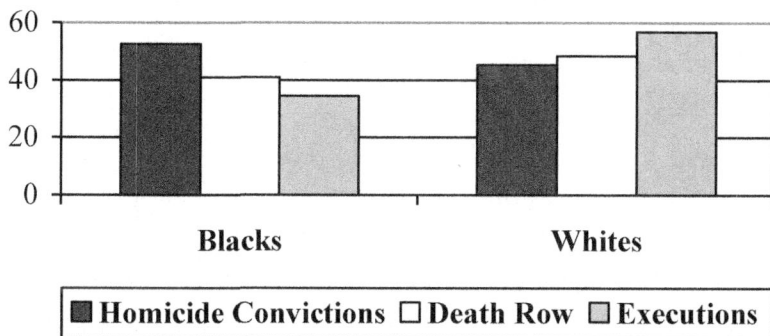

| ■ Homicide Convictions | □ Death Row | ▨ Executions |

While blacks murdered disproportionately high in comparison to their population, they received far fewer death convictions and even fewer executions. On the other hand, whites, who are seriously underrepresented, received death sentences more frequently and were executed most often of all (700 times compared to 424[64]).

I am not trying to suggest all black serial killers avoid the death penalty, because there are plenty who are on death row and some who have been executed. But instead, I am simply making a point about this trend. Further, by comparing the existing data provided by the U.S. Department of Justice to serial killers, we can see that the trend for serial killers is similar. Statistically, white serial killers have a greater chance of making it to death row and of being executed when compared to blacks.

But this was not always so. Prior to 1960, most serial killers received a death sentence and were executed within a short time after their trial. However, in our modern times, when appeals can stretch twenty-five or more years, even white serial killers are often slower to be executed. In the future, I will conduct a study comparing the average time between white and black serial killers on death row. From the preliminary data, there is no question that black serial killers spend more time on death row and exercise more appeals. Additionally, there is a greater chance that blacks' sentences will be commuted to life.

There are numerous instances in which blacks have been convicted of murder but issued a sentence of manslaughter or second-degree murder. With this lessened sentence, most only serve a few years and are released from prison only to murder again. These are the ones I have found thus far[65].

- **Tony A. Ables** was convicted of murder in 1971, and he served until 1983. Five months after his release, he raped and murdered an elderly woman. A few years later, he murdered again, and his last known murder was his girlfriend in 1990. Police believe that he may have committed several more murders.
- **James F. Allen** murdered a Chicago police officer in 1969. Soon after his release he began murdering again, and killed at least two people. Police suspect the number could be as high as four. He's serving life in prison now.
- **Howard Arthur Allen** killed an elderly white woman in 1974, but was paroled in 1985. In 1987, he raped and murdered two more elderly white women.
- **Wanda Jean Allen** beat and shot her roommate in 1981 in Oklahoma City. After serving a four-year sentence, she was freed, and she murdered again in 1988. She became the first black woman executed after the US Supreme Court lifted the ban on executions.
- **Ronald Keith Allridge** served six years for a murder he committed in 1977. In 1985, he killed a white customer in a restaurant in Ft. Worth, TX.
- **Daniel Ray Bennett** beat a man to death in 1988 in Las Vegas. After his release he murdered again, this time for hire. Police now suspect him in a total of four additional murders after his prison term.
- **John Henry Brown** was sentenced for killing a man in 1963. After his parole, he killed again in 1986.
- **Willie A. Brown** murdered a man in 1979 and served until 1994. After his release, while working as a gay prostitute he murdered between two and four men in Michigan. He is now serving a life term.
- **Jerome Butler** killed a black man in 1974 in Houston, and he was released in 1984. In 1986, he got into a cab, at which point the driver recognized him as the killer of his friend. After riding in the cab for a few blocks, Butler wielded a pistol and shot the cabbie in the back of the head.

- **Robert Joe Butler** committed his first murder in 1955 in Texas and served a short prison sentence. After his release, he murdered again in 1971 to garner another short sentence. His final murder was the fatal stabbing of his wife in 1992 in Kansas. He died in prison.
- **Xavier Chase** murdered his girlfriend in 1991 and served seven years. In 2007, he murdered an ex-girlfriend and her new boyfriend.
- **Phillip Delbert Cheatham** served a short sentence for a 1994 murder, with the charges reduced to manslaughter. In 2003 he murdered two women, and is suspected in one additional murder.
- **Davon Crawford** served time for a 1995 murder. After his release he married and had two children. His lust for blood raged again and one night he snapped and murdered his family.
- **Lucious Crawford** had a long history of violence against women, and served time for attempted murder and rape. After his first murder in 1993 he served time again. After his last release he murdered at least additional women.
- **James Crowson** is in a rare category for serving two life sentences. After being paroled for the first sentence, he murdered again.
- **Dewitt Crawley** stabbed a friend to death in 1971. After serving a short term in prison, he was released, and he killed his two nieces and brother-in-law in 1983 in Philadelphia, PA. He raped both nieces, hanged one to death, stabbed and drowned the other in a tub, and stabbed his brother-in-law with scissors and an ice pick over sixty times.
- **James Edward Daniels** served time in New York for a murder he committed in 1964. From 1979 to 1984, he murdered at least two more people, and police estimate that the number was four. His final murder was of a New Jersey state trooper in 1984, and he died in a car crash shortly afterward. Daniels had ties to the New Black Panther Party.
- **Curt Davis** was sentenced to 40 years for a 1989 murder. After serving just 18, he committed a triple murder in 2012.
- **Darren Davis** killed his infant daughter in 1994. After serving fifteen years, he was released. After meeting a new woman, she became pregnant, but after his daughter was born, he killed her as well.
- **Von Clark Davis** stabbed his wife to death in 1970. After his release, he shot his girlfriend to death in 1983.
- **Tyrone Eugene DeCastro** had served eight years for a murder charge when he was released. Soon after release, he killed a married couple.
- **Mike Donnelly** was a convicted two-time murderer who had killed two Justice of the Peace officers in 1911. He met Robert Ford in prison in Tacoma, WA, and when they were paroled together in 1923, he participated in a murder in Hope, ID.

- **Jessie Dotson** was paroled for a 1994 murder. A few months later, he killed six friends and family members. He shot to death his brother and three friends, and he stabbed to death his young nephews.
- **Stanley Faison** beat a man to death in 1965 and threw his body in the Detroit River. After being paroled in 1973, he was in and out of trouble for holding people hostage, assault, robbery, and drug-related charges. In 1987, he stabbed a woman to death and almost killed her boyfriend.
- **Stephen Lamar Fields** was paroled in 1978 after having served a short sentence for bludgeoning his best friend to death with a barbell. Within months he had killed again, murdering one of his sister's friends. He tied her to a bed and raped her, then forced her to write him checks to drain her bank account. Afterwards, he shot her and went on a rampage where he tried to kill two prostitutes.
- **Robert Ford** had etched his first murder in 1915, and he served time in a Washington prison until 1923. He had received a lessened sentence for manslaughter instead of the second-degree murder for which the prosecutor argued. After his release, he killed a man in Hope, ID, for which he was later executed. He claimed a total of five murders in his life.
- **Gregory Gibson** was only thirteen when he bludgeoned a ninety-year-old white widow to death with a hammer. He was sent to a state school, but he was released at age eighteen with no criminal stain on his record. Within months he killed another elderly white woman.
- **Kenneth Griffin** murdered in 1968 and was released on July 9, 1974. On September 11, 1975, he murdered two white people in a robbery. He was sentenced to death, but he later had his sentence commuted to life in prison. He was released in 2008 at the age of sixty-three.
- **Vincent Darrell Groves** is one of the most prolific killers in Colorado history, killing at least fourteen women. After serving merely five years for a murder charge, he was released in 1987. Over the next year, he killed at least six women and possibly more. After his arrest, police tied him to seven more murders prior to his first conviction.
- **Kenneth Hartley** murdered his fifteen-year-old girlfriend in 1987, and he was released in 1991. Three months after release, he shot a friend in the head. He has been made semi-famous for having a younger brother play in the NFL.
- **William Gary Harvard** committed his first murder in 1979, but he was out of prison by 1983. In 1986, he committed another murder by shooting a man. He was released in 2001, but within a few months he was caught selling cocaine and then stealing a car. He died in prison in 2005.
- **Steven Hayward** was sentenced for a murder in 1988. After his parole a few short years later, he committed a double murder.

- **Thomas William Hawkins, Jr.,** served a six-year sentence for raping and murdering a fifteen-year-old black girl. After release, he murdered two more times, even killing his niece.
- **Steve Douglas Hayward** shot a man in 1988 and was paroled six years later. Just four months after his parole, he shot another man, and he is suspected in one additional murder.
- **John Ruthell Henry** murdered his first wife in 1975. He was released in 1983 and he remarried. In 1985, he murdered his next wife along with her five-year-old son.
- **Walter Hill** committed his first murder in 1951 and brutally beat a fellow inmate to death in 1958. After his release, he shot a man and two others after the man refused to let him marry his thirteen-year-old daughter. Hill was forty at the time. He was later executed in 1997.
- **Anthony James Hipps** attempted to murder a man in 1975, but he did not serve any prison time. In 1978, he murdered a man, but he was paroled in 1991. In 1994, he committed his second known murder, and he is still serving time in a North Carolina prison.
- **Richard Hilliard Jackson** murdered his infant stepson in 1972. He received a 10 year sentence, but only served 23 months in a halfway home. In 1977 he beat and strangled an elderly woman to death.
- **Steven Jefferson** murdered a 30 year old woman in 1991 and served 13 years in prison. After release he murdered a 36 year old woman.
- **John Jenkins** was convicted for a 1980 murder in Detroit. After serving a minimal sentence, he was back on the streets as an enforcer for a drug kingpin, where he murdered as many as twelve more people.
- **Andrew Jett** murdered his girlfriend in 1992. Just a few months after his release he murdered his new girlfriend.
- **Alvin Johnson** killed a white man in Oregon in 1973 and served a ten-year sentence. Within days of his release, he killed two white people, one in Utah and one in California.
- **David Lee Johnson** served a six-year sentence for his first murder, and he was released in 1984. He went right back into prison for an assault where he almost killed the victim. After being paroled in June of 1994, he committed another murder in November 1994.
- **Eddie James Johnson** served a meager one-year sentence for murder in Illinois from 1975-76. In 1987, after being fired for poor performance, he kidnapped a coworker and a woman with her young daughter. After driving them to the woods, he bound their hands and executed them.
- **Raymond Eugene Johnson** shot a man in 1996 and was released in 2005. In 2007 he beat a woman and her infant daughter to death and lit their house on fire.

- **Joe Willie Jones** was convicted of murder in 1947 in Louisiana. After his release, he murdered again in 1980, shooting a man four times. He was later paroled again. He almost killed two people in a drunk driving accident in 1996.
- **Arthur James Julius** was convicted of a 1972 murder, and he was suspected in possible other murders. In 1978, for reasons that escape all imagination, he received a one-day pass to visit family. He raped and killed an adult cousin, and he was sentenced to death. He was executed in 1989.
- **Darrell Steven King** murdered in 1998, but he was paroled shortly thereafter. In 2007, he murdered just eight months after parole.
- **James Donald King** murdered his first wife in 1967. After release, he married again and killed his second wife in 1988.
- **Edward Lewis Lagrone** served seven years for murdering in Ft. Worth, TX, and he was released in 1984. In 1991, when he was thirty-six, he impregnated a ten-year-old black girl. Without provocation, he went to her house to kill her two aunts and wound her father.
- **Curtis Martin** committed one of the most brutal murders in Oakland history in 1994. After serving only six years he killed three more victims, two of which were toddlers.
- **Robert Henry McDowell** raped and murdered an elderly woman in 1972. After his release, he murdered a four-year-old girl with a machete and assaulted her fifteen-year-old aunt with nunchucks and the machete, causing her to need over 300 stitches and extensive reconstructive surgery. He received a death sentence, but he later had his sentence commuted to life based on a technicality.
- **Elton Ozell McLaughlin** shot a man in cold blood in 1974, and he received a lessened term of manslaughter. After parole, he murdered a black couple and their five-year-old daughter.
- **Leroy McNeil** killed in 1977 in Raleigh, NC. After serving a short term, he was released to kill again. In 1982, he killed between three and five young women. He later died in prison in 2008.
- **Gregory McKnight** murdered in 1991 and served only six years. After his release he murdered at least two more times.
- **William Gerald Mitchell** murdered and mutilated a woman in 1975, receiving a life sentence. After serving only fourteen years, he was set free. In 1995, he kidnapped a woman, raped her, beat her, strangled her, ran her over three times with a car before she died, and then mutilated her body with a knife. He is currently serving on death row, but he is trying to get his sentence thrown out.
- **James Lewis Morgan** was convicted of beating a person to death in 1976, and he received a life sentence. After his release, he killed a man with a beer bottle and attempted to kill others.

- **John Murray** murdered in 1978 and served time until 2011. He was suspected of a few prison murders, but they were never proven. Three months after his release he murdered again.
- **Michael Wayne Norris** committed murder in 1979 and was released on May 28, 1986. On November 12, 1986, he shot a black woman and her two-year-old son to death.
- **Louis Oliver** killed in 1962 and, soon after his release, murdered again in 1981.
- **Edjuan Payne** served 15 years for a 1987 murder. He murdered again in 2010.
- **Raymond Perry** was convicted of a New Jersey murder in 1989. After his release, he killed another man in 2009.
- **Clifford X. Phillips** murdered in New York in 1972, but the charge was reduced to second-degree manslaughter, leading to his release in 1976. In 1982, he murdered an affluent white woman in Houston, TX, by strangling her with a phone cord. He was later arrested in Los Angeles.
- **Wallace Pless** killed his first man in 1917 and served five years in a Florida prison. In 1956, he killed a young couple for the thrill of killing. His sentence was overturned in court based on the allegation that he did not receive a fair trial, despite his confession and the evidence. In 1964, he murdered his last two known victims and spent the rest of his days in prison.
- **James Pough** killed a friend in an argument and received five years of probation, and he was not even considered a felon afterwards. On June 27, 1990, he was angry that he could not make his car payment, so he stormed into a GMAC finance office and killed eleven people.
- **Reginald Powell** killed a cab driver in 1984 and was sentenced to life in prison. After release in 2008, he murdered a woman in her home in 2011.
- **Dalton Prejean** was just fifteen when he recorded his first murder. Because he was a minor, he was sent to a school for juvenile delinquents. In 1977, he shot a Louisiana state trooper in the head twice.
- **Charles Henry Rector** was still on probation for a 1974 murder and rape charge, and he was awaiting parole when he murdered again. In 1981, he raped a young white woman and then shot her and drowned her to death.
- **Walter Reed** served almost eleven years for a murder committed in 1970. In 1982, just nine months after his parole, he murdered again. He was released from prison in 2011.
- **Eugene Rhoiney** murdered for the first time in 1969. After his release he murdered less than a year later, and is suspected in numerous other deaths.

- **Alexander Robinson** was convicted of a 1974 murder. After being released in 1980, he killed two people just four months later. He was last released from prison in 2007.
- **Steven J. Robbins** was convicted for murder in 1968, but he was paroled just a few years later. In 1975, he murdered again and was sent away for a short prison term. After release, he murdered again in 1982, and he served until his release in 1995. These murders were all committed in Chicago, and after his release he moved to neighboring Gary, IN. In 2001, he committed his fourth murder, and he is now serving a life sentence.
- **Theodore Rodgers** shot his girlfriend in 1978 and served five years. In 2001, he killed his wife in a daycare.
- **Irvin Rogers** punched his wife's seventeen-month-old daughter, who had Down's syndrome, to death in 1987. After serving just two years, he was out of prison. In 1991, he beat his girlfriend's eight-month-old boy to death, breaking his ribs and lacerating his liver in the process.
- **Vernon Lamar Sattiewhite** murdered in 1977 but served only two years. In 1986, he hunted his ex-girlfriend before kidnapping her from work and shooting her in the parking lot.
- **Arthur Lee Sanford** murdered his girlfriend in 1983 and was paroled in 2002. In 2003 he murdered his new girlfriend.
- **Zeno Sims** murdered a man in 1990 and was sentenced to prison. After his release, he murdered a young woman in a fit of road rage.
- **Wilbert James Smith** was convicted for a 2000 murder, but only served seven years. In 2008 he committed a double homicide that was the most gruesome police in Huntsville, AL had ever seen.
- **Tommy Lee Stewart** raped and murdered a woman in 1971, but he was released in the early eighties. In 1986, he raped and murdered an eighteen-year-old woman and her mother in Port Arthur, TX. He did not confess to the latter two murders until 2008, when his DNA was tested as positive in their murders. Police speculate that he might be connected to other murders.
- **Alex D. Thomas** shot a man to death in 1978. While serving time he was convicted of murdering again in 1985 for slicing an inmate's throat. After his release he raped and murdered an 18 year old girl. Her head was bashed almost flat with a crowbar, and she was almost decapitated with a knife. He is suspected in other prison murders.
- **Troy Tyrone Thomas III** murdered a man in 1981. After his release he murdered a popular college professor.
- **Earl A Thompson** committed his first murder in 1979 and was paroled in 1988. In 1992, he killed again but was paroled in 2007.
- **Clarence Victor** strangled a woman in 1964. After serving a short sentence, he was released. Soon afterward, he slashed the throat of another

woman and served another short sentence. After being released for a second time (for good behavior), he beat a woman to death in 1987. At his third trial for murder, he escaped the death penalty because of a low IQ.

-   **Clarence Walker** marked his first murder in 1945 and was in prison until 1962. After release, he began a murder spree from 1963 to 1966 which took the lives of eighteen women and girls. But these murders were not attributed to him until 1970, when he was serving a 320-year sentence for numerous rapes. He served out all his days in prison.

-   **Maurice Walker**, while just sixteen years old, clocked his first murder in 1984. After his release, he murdered again in 1996.

-   **Tony Walker** was released from prison in 1980 after serving five years on a murder charge. In 1992, he showed up at the Dallas home of an elderly black couple with whom he was well acquainted. Trusting him, they allowed him to enter, at which point he raped the woman and then clubbed them both to death.

-   **Tyrone Walker** murdered a woman in Lawrence, KS in 1989. In February 2011 he was released from prison. By June 2011 he had murdered a woman, beating her then strangling her with her shoelaces. He's suspected in additional murders.

-   **Pearison Ware** committed his first murder in 1966 and served four years in a Florida prison. In 1990, he stabbed a man to death in the neck. He later died in prison of old age.

-   **Charles Edward Washington** was convicted in a double homicide in 1977. After an early release in 1981, he murdered again in 1985. Remarkably, he was released again in 1990, but he was sentenced to life in prison for an armed robbery in 1991, and he currently has an assault charge pending.

-   **Dameon Lareese Wesley** murdered his best friend in 1994 and served 19 years in prison. Just months after his release he raped and brutally murdered his girlfriend's 13 year old niece. Police have tied him to one more murder just prior to this.

-   **Darius Wilcox** had already served a sentence for murdering a person for a car in 1992. After release in 2004, he picked his criminal activities up again. On February 3, 2008, he kidnapped four people and executed one of them.

-   **Connie J. Williams** murdered his landlord in 1974 and stored his body under his bed. He served seven years for his crime. He later murdered his wife in 1999 and sawed her body into pieces.

-   **Donald E. Williams** served 15 years for a 1994 murder. One month after his release from a halfway house in 2009, he murdered his girlfriend.

- **Larry Lester Williams** served a seven-year sentence for a 1981 murder. In 2004 he murdered again.
- **Ronnie Keith Williams** was convicted of murder in 1984, and he had a history of raping children. He was released in May of 1992, but he murdered again on January 26, 1993, in Florida.
- **Tom Williams** served nine years for a murder in Georgia, and he was paroled in 1949. In 1954, he was working for the warden of a prison camp where he had served, and he murdered the warden and his wife as well as two other white men in town.
- **Fred Willis** murdered a black prostitute and served ten years. Soon after his release, he repeated the crime again.
- **Carl W. Wilson** murdered in 1975. After serving only part of his life sentence he murdered again in 2004.
- **Jessie Lee Wise** killed a man in 1971 and received life in prison, but he only mustered twelve years before release. Four years later, he bludgeoned a woman to death.

Aside from these, there are at least three instances of killers who were found innocent on reason of insanity or a technicality, only to repeat their murder.

- **Paul Harrington** murdered his wife and two children in 1975, but he was found innocent by reason of insanity. In 1999, he murdered his new wife and three-year-old son. He told police, "They should have put me away then," when asked about the previous murders
- **Joseph Eli Moss** was acquitted on a minor technicality on a 1978 murder. The prosecuting attorney chose not to retry the case. In 2007 he murdered again.
- **Winford Stokes** was found innocent by insanity for killing two women in 1969. In 1978, he killed another woman.

Given the steady churning out of black murderers from the nation's prisons for time served or for good behavior, it is difficult to know how many men walking the streets have murdered again, possibly even multiple times. If the men listed had been properly sentenced in the first place, many lives would have been spared. However, this problem is not just isolated to these killers who killed again after their release. Even

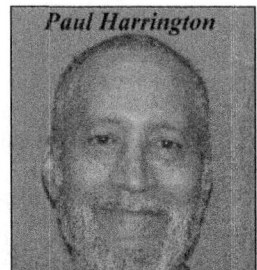

Paul Harrington

black serial killers with just a handful (or dozens) of murders have been given lessened sentences. In some instances, it is because of jurors who do not have the heart to condemn the black killer to death. Other times, it is because of the judge or even the prosecuting attorney.

- **Antwaun Ball** and his partner brutally murdered five people. Despite his confession, and the evidence against him a judge dismissed his murder charges. The reason the judge gave, is because additional charges for drugs would keep him off the street for a few years.
- **John Brooks** gunned down nine people in a five-month murder spree in the mid-eighties. In 1995, his two death penalties were commuted to life in prison, because his defense said that he was not smart enough to understand his crimes.
- **Lorenzo Gilyard** had killed at least thirteen women and girls, but the prosecutor struck a deal that if he agreed to a non-jury trial, they would push only for life in prison and not for the normal death sentence.
- **Freddie Glenn** murdered two white women and one white man in Colorado Springs, CO, in 1975, one of whom was Kelsey Grammer's sister. Despite the brutality of his crimes, his death sentence was commuted to life in prison with chance of parole in 1978. He was up for parole in 2014.
- **James F. Horton II** had a prior murder record in Illinois before he murdered in California in 1984. In 1995, he was spared of death when his sentence was commuted, because his lawyer argued that he had not been properly represented on his first murder charge. Not satisfied with this, his Jewish lawyers fought to have his sentence thrown out on a technicality. In 2010, Horton walked free and admitted to news reporters that he was guilty of both murders, saying he was the luckiest man on earth. The reason for his release, the court ruled, was because he did not have proper representation in his 1974 murder case; thus his confession and the physical evidence in his 1984 case could not be accepted in court. The prosecuting attorney tried to have him brought to trial again, but it was not allowed, because the first prosecutor in his 1984 case was still employed by the district attorney's office.
- **Reginald McFadden** dared the judge to sentence him to 1,000 years in prison for his murders. The judge only sentenced him for twenty-five years to life.
- **Gregory McKnight** committed several murders, and for his last two, the judge ordered that there was not enough money in the county for a death-sentence trial. This marked the first time in history that money had dictated the outcome of a trial publicly.
- **Michael Melvin** was charged with a quadruple murder in 2004 in New Jersey. After he killed both witnesses to the murder in separate incidents, the case fell apart and charges were dismissed. He was prosecut-

ed by the federal court for the last murder of the witness and received a measly sixteen-year-sentence, with an 85% chance of early parole for good behavior. Fortunately, additional witnesses have come forward for the earlier massacre, and the state may press charges, though it has not yet. There is a high chance that he might be free within the next few years if nothing materializes in his case.

- **Winston Moseley** killed three women in the 1960s and was a confessed necrophile. He has been up for parole review fifteen times, but thankfully has been denied each time. Yet, there may come a day when he is paroled automatically.

- **Eddie Lee Mosley** has never been prosecuted for the murders (up to thirty-three) and rapes (over 300) he is thought to have committed, because the judge held that his intelligence was too low to prosecute. Yet, he had been tried and sentenced for rapes and burglary charges prior to being suspected in murders.

- **Christopher Peterson** was convicted of seven murders with no doubt that he committed the crimes. However, the death sentence was commuted to 120 years with chance for parole, because he alleged that the police forced his confession out of him instead of waiting for him to confess.

- **Craig Price** was not yet sixteen when he brutally murdered four whites, two women and two girls, in separate attacks three years apart. He was due to be released by state law at age twenty-one. Thankfully, he opened his big mouth and bragged that he would make history upon his release; and a group petitioned the court to keep him an additional ten to twenty-five years. It is highly likely that he will be paroled while still in his forties or younger, so the odds of him murdering again are very likely.

- **Beoria A. Simmons** kidnapped and raped four young white women from 1981-1983, leaving three of them dead. After years of appeals, the court reduced his sentence to life in prison in 2010. Despite his confession and his apology to the families for his crimes, the court deemed that there was not enough evidence for a death row conviction.

- **Jerry Jerome Spraggins** was sentenced for only one of the three murders for which he was charged. While the jury acknowledged that he was guilty of the other two, he was sentenced only to a term of thirty years to life.

- **Roy Gene Smith** was convicted of killing two victims and sentenced to death. His sentence was later commuted to life, because the state ruled that the jurors had not heard about the poverty-stricken neighborhood in which he grew up.

- **James Edward Swann**, known as the Shotgun Stalker, killed four and wounded five others in a two-month period in 1993 in Washington,

D.C. Eric Holder, then Attorney General of D.C., dropped all charges and had him sent to a mental hospital. Holder said in an interview that Swann understood his actions but was a likely candidate to kill again because he was non-remorseful. He reckoned that Swann should be studied and should receive mental help instead of prison.

- **TwDarrel Toney** was already wanted for gunning down a man in 2003 in New Orleans when he shot two men with an AK-47, one of whom had been his best friend. The jury could not agree on a sentence, and he was charged with manslaughter, receiving a forty-year sentence.
- **Carl Eugene Watts**, the most notorious serial killer in US history, was given a plea bargain that if he told investigators about his murders, he would not be tried for them. Despite confessing dozens, he went to prison on a burglary charge. He was up for parole numerous times, but he was denied. He was facing a mandatory parole in 2006, but, thankfully, another state prosecuted him before the parole.
- **Larry Lamont White** admitted to killing two young women in June 1983, and he gave a vivid description of his crimes and the location of his murder weapon. He was convicted and given a death sentence in Kentucky for his crimes. In 1987, because of a US Supreme Court decision, his sentence was thrown out, for an attorney was not present at his police questioning. The court ruled that he could not be brought to trial for the murders again, but the court did allow him to stay in prison for a burglary charge. In 2008, DNA pointed to him for the murder of a third woman he killed in January 1983. He has admitted to the crime and will spend the rest of his days in prison. Had it not been for this break via DNA, he would be freed before 2016.
- **Carol Wilkins** shot her Kenyan boyfriend point-blank in the face in 1992. After serving a sentence for the murder, she sliced the throat of a man in 2008 in Nebraska. Despite her murderous history, and despite that both murders were proven to be premeditated, she received only a twenty-year sentence on a manslaughter charge for her latest murder.

There are numerous other instances when a death penalty was not issued for a variety of reasons, but instead a life sentence was given. Sometimes this is because the state does not have a death penalty, or in some cases it is because the killer's IQ is low. But there are oodles of black serial killers serving now who will have a chance for parole, including no less than four in this decade alone.

When a black serial killer is brought to justice, whites do not take to the streets and march for justice to be served or rally to get his trial brought to primetime television, regardless of his victim's race.

Instead, for the most part, whites catch the initial TV spot covering the story, and then they forget about it and often miss the trial. They are unaware of the numerous lessened sentenced that have been handed out in the past twenty years. If the same action was done proportionally to white serial killers, black leaders would take to the streets, and all the acronym organizations (ACLU, NAACP, SPLC, ADL, etc.) would petition a higher court to overturn the sentence and issue a much more severe sentence.

If a white serial killer were given a lessened sentence with chance of parole, as Winston Moseley did, the public outrage would be unbearable. Investigative news channels would criticize the officials and demand to have answers for the public, reporters would dig for every gruesome detail of the murders to publicize, black civil rights leaders would form committees to petition the Supreme Court, civil lawsuits would be filed against the killer, and riots would break out in cities across the nation. Yet, because killers like Moseley are black, no one gives the subject a second thought, save the families of the victims and diehard researchers of their crimes. This is why there is such a high repeat rate amongst black serial killers.

It is high time that black serial killers be held just as accountable for their crimes as white serial killers. The world needs to know, and we need not fear the truth. If a black killer had half-a-dozen white victims, we have the right to know; this information should not be suppressed and voided in the mainstream media. To tell such stories is no more an indictment against the black race than white serial killers are to whites. Bad

Walter Ellis

things happen, and serial killers plague every race in every culture in the world. The information about black serial killers in America should not be suppressed by the media.

Black Serial Killers Who Killed Only Whites

Following is the lengthy list of black serial killers who have murdered only white victims. Many of these names are unknown outside the area where their crimes were committed, and even then, some will be surprised that these killers lurked the streets of their town. I am sure that this list will be disputed by critics; I fully expect it. But the reality is that, even if a few of these men's names were removed from the list because of some technicalities, the truth remains that black serial killers murder outside their race far more frequently than whites. Therefore, instead of trying to find a minuscule problem that I overlooked, remember that each of these killers took innocent lives which can never be given back. My point in presenting this list is not to slight black people, but to raise awareness in both the black and white communities about this injustice that is rarely reported. In closing, if this imbalance were reversed, and if white serial killers enjoyed murdering outside their race, as a white man I would welcome and appreciate a black author bringing this subject to my attention. I would do my best to tell other whites in my small attempt to curb such a dangerous trend.

In this list, the tables are fairly self-explanatory, but the last column does need a bit of background. Sometimes it is difficult to track the true number of victims a killer had, and a low and high must be established. This problem exists in serial killers of every race; many times a killer is convicted of a certain number of murders but suspected beyond a reasonable doubt in additional murders, thereby necessitating the need for a low and a high.

Table 5.1 Black Serial Killers Who Killed Whites

First Name	Last Name	Killing Area	Years Active	Victims Low	Victims High
Tony	Ables	St. Petersburg, FL	1970-71	4	4
Keith	Adams	Florida	2001, 2005	3	3
Howard	Allen	Indianapolis, IN	1974, 1987	3	3
James	Allen	Chicago, IL	1969, 1986	3	4
Quincy	Allen	NC, SC, OH	2002	4	4
Ronald	Allridge	Texas	1977, 1984	2	2
Robert	Anderson	Tampa, FL	1912	3	3
Dickie	Anderson	New London, CT	1997-1998	2	2

Emmanuel	Anderson	Chicago, IL	1934-1936	3	3
John	Ausby	Washington, D.C.	1971	3	3
Clinton	Bankston, Jr.	Athens, GA	1987-1988	5	5
Charles	Barr	Memphis, TN	1923-1924	3	6
Jerome	Barrett	Nashville, TN	1975	4	4
Lamar	Baskin, Jr.	Houston, TX	1990, 2002	3	3
Norman	Bernard	Los Angeles, CA	1983	3	4
Brian	Bethell	Florida	2006	3	3
Marko	Bey	New Jersey	1983-1984	2	2
Jake	Bird	16 states	1923-1947	44	44
Rodney	Bixler	Lawrenceburg, KY	2000	3	3
Willie	Bonner	Miami, FL	1992, 1998	2	3
Donald	Borders	North Carolina	2003	3	3
Willie	Bosket	New York	1978	2	2
Charles	Boyd	Dallas, TX	1986-1987	3	3
McArthur	Breedlove	Florida	1974-1978	2	2
James	Brewer	Indianapolis, IN	1977-1977	2	2
Tyrone	Bridges	New Orleans, LA	1987	2	2
Gregory	Bryant-Bey	Toledo, OH	1992	2	2
Leslie	Burchart	Richmond, VA	1990-1996	7	14
Jermaine	Burgess	Philadelphia, PA	2001-2008	4	4
Adrian	Burks	KS, CA	2005-2009	5	6
Pat	Burton	Texas	1897-1899	7	7
Robert	Butler	TX, KS	1955-1992	3	3
Rufus	Cantrell	Indianapolis, IN	1900-1903	6	6
Celeste	Carrington	San Carlos, CA	1992	2	2
Stephen	Carter	OH, HI	1920	2	2
Robert	Carter	Houston, TX	1981	2	2
Damon	Chapple	Spokane, WA	1984, 1988	2	2
Elroy	Chester	Port Arthur, TX	1997-1998	5	5
Sam	Chinn III	NY, TX	1989	3	3
Leonard	Christopher	Philadelphia, PA	1980's	7	8
Tom	Clark	Mississippi	1900-1902	3	3
Willie	Clisby	Birmingham, AL	1978-1979	2	2

Techumseh	Colbert	San Diego, CA	2004	2	2
Jim	Collins	MT, AR	1900-1913	5	7
Fred	Collins	Pennsylvania	1931-1932	2	2
Delmus	Colvin	OH, NY	2000-2005	6	6
Michael	Cook	Cathedral City, CA	1998	2	2
Carl	Cooper	Washington, D.C.	1993-1997	4	4
Herbert	Copeland	D.C., IL, TX, NC	1909-1918	12	12
Keith	Cosby	El Cajon, CA	1985	2	2
Walter	Cotton	Virginia	1900	4	4
Juan	Covington	Philadelphia, PA	1998-2005	3	3
Donald	Craig	Ohio	1995, 1996	2	3
James	Cromwell	KS, Wichita	1987	2	2
James	Crowson	Philadelphia, PA	1957, 1975	3	4
Alva	Curry	Texas	1991	2	2
James	Daniels	NY, NJ	1964-1984	4	7
Earl	Daughtrey	Georgia	1971-1980	3	4
Bernice	Davis	Chicago, IL	1949-1950	3	3
Rader	Davis	Atlanta, GA	1933	2	2
Girvies	Davis	East St. Louis, IL	1978-1980	4	4
Gregory	Davis	MS/GA	1986-1987	4	4
Eugene	DeCastro	North Carolina	1982, 1992	3	3
Leon	Dorsey IV	Texas	1994	3	3
Ernest	Dye	TX, NC	1906, 1911	2	2
Ike	Easley	Joilet, IL	1982, 1989	2	2
Joseph	Ebron	CO, TX	1994-2005	3	3
Walter	Ellis	Milwaukee, WI	1986-2007	9	9
Andrew	Engram	Arkansas	1976, 1997	2	2
Mark	Essex	New Orleans, LA	1972-1973	9	10
Fredrick	Evins	Spartanburg, SC	2002-2003	2	2
John	Ewell	Los Angeles, CA	2005-2010	4	4
John	Ferguson	Florida	1977-1978	8	10
John	Fletcher	Yakima, WA	1987	2	2
Linwood	Forte	North Carolina	1990	3	3
Kendall	Francois	Poughkeepsie, NY	1996-1998	8	10
Quawn	Franklin	Orlando, FL	2001	2	2

Carlton	Gary	Columbus, GA	1977-1978	9	9
Louis	Gaskin	Florida	1986, 1989	8	8
Gregory	Gibson	California	1992, 1997	2	2
Moses	Gibson	LA, AZ, CA	1908-1920	7	7
Freddie	Glenn	Colorado	1975	3	3
John	Gordon	Vicksburg, MS	1895-1897	3	3
Coleman	Gray	Virginia	1984-1985	3	3
Ronald	Gray	North Carolina	1986-1987	4	4
Vaughn	Greenwood	Los Angeles, CA	1964-1975	11	11
Kenneth	Griffin	Gainsville, FL	1968, 1975	3	3
Richard	Grissom, Jr.	KS, MO	1989	4	4
Vincent	Groves	Denver, CO	1978-1988	18	20
Matthew	Guzman	Miami, FL	2010	2	2
Thomas	Hager	D.C., VA	1992-1997	7	12
Kevin	Hampton	Terre Haute, IN	2000	3	3
John	Hardaway	Portland, OR	1996, 2011	2	2
Ralph	Harris	Chicago, IL	1992-1995	6	6
DeWayne	Harris	Seattle, WA	1998	3	3
Lester	Harrison	Grant Park, IL	1951-1973	7	7
William	Harvard	Miami, FL	1978, 1986	2	2
Charles	Hawkins	Ocala, FL	1966	3	3
Steven	Hayward	Florida	1988, 2004	2	3
William	Herring	Raleigh, NC	1994	2	2
Clarence	Hill	New Jersey	1939-1942	6	6
Douglas	Hines	TX, CA	1973-1991	2	2
Ronald	Hinton	Chicago, IL	1996-1999	3	3
Willie	Hodges	FL, AL, OH	2001-2003	3	3
Darryl	Holmes	Greenville, SC	1996	2	2
Leon	Holstem	Florida	1966	3	3
Raymond	Hopewell	Baltimore, MD	2004-2005	5	5
James	Horton II	IL, CA	1973, 1984	2	2
Earl	Jackson	Long Beach, CA	1977	2	3
Anthony	Jackson	Cambridge, MA	1972-1973	8	8
Charles	Jackson	San Francisco, CA	1975-1982	9	9
Leroy	Jackson, Jr.	Chicago, IL	1953-1954	2	2
Eugene	James	MD, D.C.	1948	2	2
Ronnie	Johns	Michigan	1991	4	4

Tivan	Johnson	Florida	1991	3	3
Brandon	Johnson	Little Rock, AR	2008-2009	3	3
Emanuel	Johnson	Florida	1988	2	2
Jay	Johnson	Minneapolis MN	1991	2	2
James	Johnson	Worcester, MA	1992-1993	2	2
Steve	Johnson	St. Petersburg, FL	1963	3	3
Alvin	Johnson	UT, OR, CA	1973, 1983	3	3
Eddie	Johnson	IL, TX	1975, 1987	4	4
Milton	Johnson	Joliet, IL	1983	14	17
Henry	Jones	TN, FL	2002-2003	4	4
Joe	Jones	LA, KS	1947, 1980	2	2
Martin	Jones	Buffalo, NY	1985-1987	2	3
Jesse	Jones	South Carolina	1942	4	4
Jeffery	Jones	California	1985	4	4
Keydrick	Jordan	Florida	1991-1992	2	2
Anthony	Joyner	Philadelphia PA	1983	6	6
Melvin	Keeling	OH, IN	2005	3	3
Horace	Kelly	California	1984	3	3
Edward	Kennedy	Miami, FL	1978-1981	3	3
Carolyn	King	PA, ND, NV	1993	3	3
Thomas	Knight	Florida	1974, 1980	3	3
Keith	Lamar	Ohio	1989, 1993	5	5
Posteal	Laskey, Jr.	Cincinnati, OH	1965-1966	7	7
Derrick	Lee	Lousiana	1992-2003	7	10
Ronald	Lott	OKC, OK	1986	2	2
Laurence	Lovette	North Carolina	2008	2	2
Franklin	Lynch	San Francisco, CA	1981-1987	3	13
Ulysses	Mack	Gary, IN	1929	3	3
Gillis	Mack	Indiana	1929	3	3
Matthew	Macon	Lansing, MI	2004	6	6
Muziwokuthula	Madonda	OH, NM	2009-2011	4	4
Joe	Malone	Texas	1890-1898	5	5
Andy	Mann	Minnesota	1929-1930	3	3
Derrick	Martin	Indianapolis, IN	1992, 2007	2	2

Willie	Martin	Arkansas	1920-1925	7	7
Lamont	Marshall	Grand Rapids, MI	1970-1975	2	7
Morris	Mason	Richmond, VA	1978	2	2
Ynobe	Matthews	Texas	1999-2000	2	2
Kimberly	McCarthy	Dallas, TX	1988, 1997	3	3
Larkin	McCloud	Nebraska	1916-1917	4	4
Jeremiah	McCray	VA, OH, GA, AL	1956-1958	5	5
Robert	McDowell	Smithfield, NC	1972, 1979	2	2
Edward	McGregor	Houston, TX	1990-2005	4	4
Gregory	McKnight	Ohio	1993, 2000	3	3
Ralph	McLean	D.C., MD	1995	2	2
Leroy	McNeil	North Carolina	1977, 1982	4	6
James	Mealey	VA, MD, NC	1900-1903	3	4
Douglas	Meeks	FL, Taylor County	1974	2	2
Antonio	Melton	FL, Pensacola	1990-1991	2	2
Alex	Mengel	New York	1985	2	2
David	Middleton	NV, CO	1994-1995	3	4
John	Mitchell	Florida	1970	2	3
William	Mitchell	Mississippi	1974, 1998	2	2
Tony	Mitchell	Tennessee	2002	2	2
Roy	Mitchell	Waco, TX	1922-1923	6	8
Jessie	Moffett	California	1979-1987	2	2
Kasey	Monroe	Scotland, NC	1995	2	2
Thomas	Moore	Florida	1990-1993	2	2
Arsenio	Morgan	Los Angeles, CA	2007-2009	4	4
Letisha	Morgan	SD, TX	2010	2	2
Winston	Moseley	NYC, NY	1960-1964	3	3
Dawud	Mu'Min	Virginia	1973, 1988	2	2
Huey	Newton	Oakland, CA	1967-1974	2	4
Robert	Nixon	IL, CA	1936-1938	7	7
Dempsey	Nolan, Jr.	IN,CA	1996-1997	5	5
Lyndon	Pace	Atlanta, GA	1988-1991	5	5
Gerald	Parker	Southern CA	1978-1979	6	8
Raymond	Perry	New Jersey	1989, 2009	2	2
George	Perry	Cambridge, MA	1902	2	6

Clifford	Phillips	NY, TX	1972, 1982	2	2
James	Pough	Jacksonville, FL	1971, 1990	12	12
Reginald	Powell	White Plains, NY	1984, 2011	2	2
Marcus	Pressley	Alabama	1996	2	2
Larme	Price	Brooklyn, NY	2003	5	5
Craig	Price	Warwick, RI	1987-1989	4	4
Cleophus	Prince, Jr.	San Diego, CA	1990	6	6
Yusef	Rahman	KS, NY	1987	4	5
Charles	Rector	Austin, TX	1974, 1982	2	2
Willie	Reed	Alabama	1937	2	2
Asbury	Respus	North Carolina	1912-1930	9	9
Antonio	Richards	Louisiana	1884-1898	11	11
Frederick	Richey	Oregon	1984	2	2
Reginald	Riggins	Florida	2009-2011	2	2
David	Roberts	Whiteland, IN	1975, 1977	4	4
Alonzo	Robinson	MS/MI/MA	1926-1934	6	6
Alexander	Robinson	Florida	1974-1981	3	3
Antonio	Rodriguez	Philadelphia, PA	2010	3	3
Robert	Rozier	FL, NY, MD	1985	7	7
Antiono	Ruffin	Augusta, GA	1991-2009	3	3
George	Russell, Jr	Mercer Island, WA	1990	3	3
Charles	Sears	NYC, NY	1981	2	2
Beoria	Simmons	Kentucky	1981-1983	3	3
Gary	Sinegal	Port Arthur, TX	2005	5	6
Warren	Sloan	Fairfield, CA	2012	2	2
Roy	Smith	Houston, TX	1988	2	2
Reginald	Smith	Miami, FL	1994	3	3
Lemuel	Smith	New York	1958-1981	6	6
Clyde	Smith Jr.	Houston, TX	1992	2	2
Timothy	Spencer	Richmond, VA	1984-1987	5	5
Jerry	Spraggins	New Jersey	1981-1983	3	3
Sam	Steenburgh	New York	1870s	11	11
Gary	Sterling	Texas	1988	4	4
Charles	Stevens	Oakland, CA	1989	4	4
Raymond	Stewart	Illinois	1981	6	6
Winford	Stokes	MO, AR	1969, 1978	3	3
James	Stuard	Arizona	1989-1990	3	3

Edward	Surratt	FL, OH, PA, SC	1977-1978	19	19
Alvin	Taylor	Wisconsin	1985-1988	4	4
Norris	Taylor	NC, VA	1979	3	4
Alex	Thomas	California	1978-1997	3	3
Gus	Thomas	Kansas	1909-1910	4	4
Daniel	Thomas	Florida	1976-1977	2	3
John	Thomas, Jr.	Los Angeles, CA	1970-1990	30	39
Anthony	Townser	St. Louis, MO/IL	1993	3	3
Clarence	Trotter	Chicago, IL	1981, 1986	2	2
Michael	Vernon	Bronx, NY	1993-1995	6	7
Clarence	Victor	Nebraska	1964-1987	3	3
Javier	Victorianne	California	1999-2000	3	3
Anthony	Wadsworth	Columbus, OH	2012	2	2
Maurice	Walker	Albany, NY	1984, 1996	2	2
Tyrone	Walker	New York	1993-1996	3	3
David	Washington	Dade County, FL	1976	3	3
Steven	Washington	Tampa, FL	1963	3	5
Johnny	Watkins	Virginia	Nov-83	2	2
Carlton	Watts	TX, MI, Midwest	1972-1982	44	100
Robert	Watts	Indianapolis, IN	1947	5	5
George	Whitmore	NYC, NY	1964	3	3
Darius	Wilcox	Florida	1992, 2008	2	2
Marvin	Williams	Orlando, FL	1994	2	2
Roy	Williams	MA, PA	1988	2	3
Anthony	Williams	FL, NJ	1995, 2000	2	4
Tom	Williams	Georgia	1940, 1954	4	5
Robert	Williams	NE, IA	1977	3	3
Jerry	Williams	Florida	2004-2008	2	3
Kenneth	Willliams	Florida	2000	2	2
Herbert	Wilson	Miami, FL	2000, 2003	2	3
Anthony	Wimberly	California	1984-1985	3	3
Jesse	Wise	Missouri	1971, 1984	2	2
George	Wright	New Jersey	1962	2	2
Moses	York	AR, MS	1890s	2	2
George	Young	Jacksonville, FL	1968	3	3
Herbert	Youngblood	IL, UT	1933-1934	2	2
Unidentified Killer		Bremerton, WA	2011-2012	2	2
Unidentified Killer		MD, D.C..	1991-1998	3	4

The previous list included only 279 of the 316 killers who chose white victims exclusively. The other thirty-seven are groups and gangs who have killed white people; these thirty-seven comprise thirteen different groups in the database. Sometimes it was difficult for investigators to determine exactly who did the killing in each murder, due to conflicting testimonies where each person was trying to pass guilt to others. Other times, it was clear that all in a given group participated equally in each murder. Regardless, here are the groups, along with the pertinent information about the number of victims. Please note that each person in the group may appear to have the same number of kills, which can be confusing. This was for sorting purposes in my database; it does not reflect individual murders, but instead reflects the total for the group. There are two instances, however, as with Linwood Briley and the Armed Truck Robbers, where their numbers differ. Briley has a different number because he committed an additional murder of a neighbor prior to the murders he committed with his brothers. For the latter, each killed a different person in the robbery, and they had additional murders as well. Truthfully, these three could be listed as individual serial killers, but I have listed them as a group.

First Name	Last Name	Gang Name	Known Locations	Years Active	Victims Low	High
Roshone	Colston	Armed Truck	Los Angeles, CA	1995-1996	4	4
Kendrick	Loot	Armed Truck	Los Angeles, CA	1995-1996	3	3
Bruce	Millsap	Armed Truck	Los Angeles, CA	1995-1996	8	8
James	Briley	Briley Gang	Richmond, VA	1979	12	12
Anthony	Briley	Briley Gang	Richmond, VA	1979		
Linwood	Briley	Briley Gang	Richmond, VA	1979		
Milton	Jones	Buffalo Killers	Buffalo, NY	1987	2	2
Theodore	Simmons	Buffalo Killers	Buffalo, NY	1987		
Nathaniel	Cook	Cook Bros.	Toledo, OH	1973-1981	9	10
Anthony	Cook	Cook Bros.	Toledo, OH	1973-1981		
Damon	Smith	Crips Duo	Texas	1998	3	3
Kenneth	Tatum	Crips Duo	Texas	1998		
Nathaniel	Burse	De Mau Mau	Chicago, IL, NE	1978	12	12
Michael	Clark	De Mau Mau	Chicago, IL, NE	1978		
Garland	Jackson	De Mau Mau	Chicago, IL, NE	1978		

Edward	Moran	De Mau Mau	Chicago, IL, NE	1978			
Darrell	Patry	De Mau Mau	Chicago, IL, NE	1978			
Reuben	Taylor	De Mau Mau	Chicago, IL, NE	1978			
Donald	Taylor	De Mau Mau	Chicago, IL, NE	1978			
Robert	Wilson	De Mau Mau	Chicago, IL, NE	1978			
Bill	Reardon	Early Duo	Tennessee	1870-1879	5	7	
Tom	Jones	Early Duo	Tennessee	1870-1879			
Charles	Shoates	Florida Duo	Palmetto, FL	1970	4	4	
Earnest	Houston	Florida Duo	Palmetto, FL	1970			
Reginald	Haley	Haley Bros.	California	1979-1984	8	8	
Kevin	Haley	Haley Bros.	California	1979-1984			
Jerald	Garrett	Louisville Duo	Louisville, KY	2012	2	3	
Billy	Richardson	Louisville Duo	Louisville, KY	2012			
Thomas	Penn	Penn Bros.	Richmond, VA	1966	6	6	
William	Penn	Penn Bros.	Richmond,VA	1966			
Ben	Chaney	Racist Duo	SC, FL	1970	4	5	
Martin	Rutrell	Racist Duo	SC, FL	1970			
Reginald	Carr	Wichita Massacre	Wichita, KS	2000	5	5	
Jonathan	Carr	Wichita Massacre	Wichita, KS	2000			
Yahweh Cult			Miami, FL	1980-1991	23	27	Yahweh Cult
Jesse	Cooks	Zebra Killer	San Francisco, CA	1973-1974	23	270	
Larry	Green	Zebra Killer	San Francisco, CA	1973-1974			
Anthony	Harris	Zebra Killer	San Francisco, CA	1973-1974			
Manuel	Moore	Zebra Killer	San Francisco, CA	1973-1974			
J.C.X.	Simon	Zebra Killer	San Francisco, CA	1973-1974			

ENDNOTES

[1] Kleinfield, N.R., Goode, Erica, *Retracing a Trail: The Sniper Suspects; Serial Killing's Squarest Pegs: Not Solo, White, Psychosexual or Picky*, New York Times, October 28, 2002.

[2] Schechter, Harold, *The Serial Killer Files: The Who, What, Where, How and Why of the World's Most Terrifying Murders*, p. 42.

[3] Associated Press, *Serial Killer's Case Splits Milwaukee*, New Straits Times, August 5, 1991.

[4] Associated Press, *Dahmer Case Raises Racism Complaints*, Times-Union, February 1, 1992.

[5] Associated Press, *Murder Spree Called 'Racist'*, Gadsden Times, July 24, 1991.

[6] Associated Press, *Dahmer Victim's Family Sues City, Citing Racism*, Star News, September 21, 1991.

[7] Romell, Rick, *2 Black Officials Call Dahmer Killings Racist*, Milwaukee Sentinel, February 7, 1992.

[8] Ibid Associated Press, Dahmer.

[9] Ibid Associated Press, Murder Spree.

[10] *Coalition of Black Elected Officials Calls for Federal-Level Investigation*, Milwaukee Journal, July 30, 1991.

[11] Sykes, Leonard, *Black Officers Had Warned of Racial Strife at Academy*, The Milwaukee Journal, August 16, 1991.

[12] Ibid Associated Press, Dahmer.

[13] Ibid, Romell.

[14] Ibid Associated Press, Dahmer.

[15] Ibid Associated Press, Dahmer.

[16] Ibid., Romell.

[17] Ibid Associated Press, Dahmer.

[18] Ibid., Romell.

[19] Walsh, Edward, *Cannibal Killer Beaten in Prison, Ocala Star Banner*, November 29, 1994. First printed in the Washington Post.

[20] Associated Press, *Leader of Black Yahweh Sect Charged in Murder, Extortion, Pittsburgh Post-Gazette*, November 8, 1990.

[21] Ibid., Ref 19.

[22] Associated Press, *Yahweh was Former Cult Leader Linked to 23 Killings*, Milwaukee Journal Sentinel, May 11, 2007, page 4.

[23] Dennis, Jan, *Accused Serial Killer Gets life in Prison*, Associated Press, Mary 30, 2006.

[24] Glod, Maria, Va. *Attacks May be Linked to Serial Killer*, The Washington Post, August 9, 2010.

[25] Mcgreal, Chris, *Israelis Elias Abuelazam Appears in US Court Accused of Racist Murders*, The Guardian, August 13, 2010.

[26] Reported online by various Michigan news channels, retrieved from MINBCNEWS at http://www.minbcnews.com/weather/story.aspx?id=499500#.TxXed_1_mVc

[27] COMMONWEALTH of Pennsylvania, Appellee v. Roy L. WILLIAMS, Appellant, J-141-98, and again in 2004.

[28] Foreman, Laura & Mack, Darrell, *The Private War of Mark Essex: How He Killed 7 in Hate Orgy*, Pittsburgh Press, January 14, 1973.

[29] Associated Press, *Sniper's Room Filled with Anger*, Milwaukee Sentinel, January 13, 1973.

[30] Associated Press, *Mother of Suspect, "Society" Blamed*, Spokane Daily Chronicle, January 11, 1973.

[31] Weirich, Charles, *Society not to Blame for Death of Essex*, Observer-Reporter, January 18, 1973.

[32] Here is a sample site: http://off2dr.com/smf/index.php?topic=2542.0 The victims were identified as white, from a now defunct victim's support page that had shown pictures of the victims, and told in brief their stories.

[33] Associated Press, *Blacks Re-enact Selma-Montgomery Rights March*, Record Journal, April 6, 1981.

[34] Malkin, Michelle, *Winona and the Wichita Massacre*, retrieved from www.TownHall.com.

[35] Horowitz, David, *Black Racism: The Hate Crime That Dare not Speak It's Name*, July 16, 2002, retrieved from www.FrontPageMagazine.com

[36] Full credit must be given to the Zachary, LA, police department. They were the only dissenting vote in the Baton Rouge area to the white profile. From the onset they had Derrick Todd Lee pegged as the killer, but their repeated attempts to prove so were blocked by larger departments and federal officials. In the end, their information and firsthand knowledge of Lee would be what helped convince police of Lee's guilt.

[37] Associated Press, *Residents Arm Themselves as Police Search for Widow Slayer, Kentucky* New Era, April 8, 1987.

[38] Associated Press, *Davis Charged in Spiller's Slaying*, The Albany Herald, May 5, 1987.

[39] A study of every newspaper prior to his capture revealed that it was usually front-page news, even as far away Michigan and Wisconsin. However, after his capture, it did make the front page of his local paper, but in other areas it was placed in the back of the paper, behind Hart's story and the debacle surrounding the Iran-Contra Affair. Even in the Albany Herald, after the initial splash his story faded away, yet the paper kept everyone abreast of every detail surrounding Hart and Hahn's affair.

[40] Rowan, Carl, *Racial Fear Compounds The Horror in Atlanta*, Miami News, March 4, 1981.

[41] Musick, Phil, 'Atlanta *Child Murders' a Frightening Poor Effort*, Pittsburgh press, February 12, 1985.

[42] Associated Press, *Williams Appeal Heard*, The Albany Herald, February 11, 1985.

[43] Woodford, Carol, *Showtime Movie Renews Case of Atlanta Child Murders*, Ocala Star-Banner, July 16, 2000.

[44] Crook, John, *Showtime Bungles Tense Tale of Atlanta Child Murders*, Times-Union, July 15, 2000.

[45] Ibid., Woodford.

[46] *DNA Test Strengthens Atlanta Child Killings Case*, CNN.com, June 9, 2010. Retrieved from http://articles.cnn.com/2010-06-09/justice/williams.dna.test_1_hair-samples-dna-testing-harold-deadman?_s=PM:CRIME

[47] Ressler, Robert, *Whoever Fights Monsters: My Twenty Years Hunting Serial Killers for the FBI,* 1992, pp. 157-181.

[48] Herbert, Bob, In America; Judicial Coin Toss, New York Times, April 3, 1994.

[49] Ibid., Herbert.

[50] *Defense Lawyers Claim Racial Bias*, Toledo Blade, April 17, 2002.

[51] Wilkinson, Howard, *Alton Coleman Finally Faces Justice*, Cincinnati Enquirer. April 24, 2002.

[52] Warren, Jenifer and Dolan, Maura, *Death Watch at San Quentin*, Los Angele Times, December 13, 2005.

[53] Retrieved from Serial Killer's Ink, at http://serialkillersink.net/QANDA/duffy1.php

[54] Ibid., Serial Killer's Ink.

[55] Associated Press, *Stocking Killer Suspect Lashes Out at Judge*, Waycross Journal Herald, July 29, 1986.

[56] Williams, Chuck, *Muscogee County Jail Records Offer Insight into Carlton Gary.* Ledger Enquirer, December 15, 2009.

[57] State of Washington vs. Damon Lopez Chapple No. 23836-5-II, November 9, 2000.

[58] State of Mississippi vs. William Gerald Mitchell, No. 2002-DR-00479-SCT, page 5.

[59] Atassi, Leila, *Serial Killer Anthony Sowell Requests New Trial*, Argues Juror was Biased from the Start, The Plain Dealer, August 15, 2011.

[60] U.S. Department of Justice, *Homicide Trends in the United States, 1980-2008*, page 13. Published November 2011.

[61] Ibid., reference 44.

[62] U.S. Department of Justice, *Capital Punishment, 2010 Statistical Tables, 1977-2010*, page 13. Published December 2011.

[63] Ibid., reference 60, p. 17

[64] Ibid ., reference 60, p. 13.

[65] This data is via available court records. With the sheer number of killers in the database, and the number that murdered in several states, the task of wrangling up the court records for each at this time is a difficult task. However, this subject is proving to be a disappointing subject. While an arduous task to tackle, the more I research, the more names I find that were two, three, and even four time murder repeat offenders.

Chapter 6

Biographies of Thirty-Five Black Serial Killers

Robert Sylvester Alston

On December 15, 1991, police were notified of a body that had been dumped at a cemetery in Greensboro, NC. The body was Louise Elizabeth Williams, a black prostitute who had been raped and strangled to death. Police had no suspects, aside from a witness who described the car Williams got into the night before.

One month later, on the 22nd of January, Alston struck again. This time, the twenty-nine-year-old woman was able to escape her captor, but not until he had raped her. She reported it to authorities, who then quickly arrested Alston.

After his arrest, they found incriminating DNA evidence connecting him to the murder of Williams. He confessed that he had killed her, giving details of where he picked her up and how he murdered her. Police suspected him in other similar murders, but he denied any involvement.

Robert Alston

In April 1994, he was sentenced to forty years for a kidnapping and rape charge and sentenced to life for the murder of Williams. However, police were confident he was responsible for at least a few of the six unsolved prostitute murders they had from 1991-1993. They made pleas with the community for anyone to come forward.

Soon after his conviction, police compared his DNA to that found with the other five unsolved murders. Within a few months, they had a positive connection with the murder of Joanne Robinson, which occurred on April 11, 1991. Her raped and strangled body had been found the next day, but no headway was made until the DNA connection. Alston confessed that he had killed Joanne and received an additional life sentence.

Police still suspected that he played a role in other murders. In 1998, they caught a break when new and better forensic technology matched DNA from two murders to Alston's DNA. These two would prove to be his most violent.

On November 4, 1991, he picked up Sharon Martin, a twenty-six-year-old prostitute. She was never seen again alive. A few days later, her head and right lower arm were found in some brush near a mall and school. The rest of her body has never been recovered.

Five months later, he picked up nineteen-year-old Shameca Warren on April 24, 1992. Her decapitated and severely decomposed body was found in an empty lot on July 23, 1992. Her head was never recovered.

When charged with the new murders, Alston confessed without hesitation. He told of cutting Ms. Martin into pieces, but refused to tell where he had put the rest of her body.

Alston was convicted of the two murders and given two additional life sentences without a chance of parole. At his trial, he smirked and appeared unconcerned with what he had done. The judge in the case said, "You can smirk and grin all you like." Then he asked Alston to help the grieving families present by telling them what he did with the remaining body parts.

Alston refused and said, "I have had time to search my soul. What I did was wrong, and I've made peace with God. Only me and God will have those answers anyone wants to know."[1]

Police do not believe he committed the addition two unsolved murders, but he is still listed as a suspect until proven otherwise.

Robert Sylvester Alston's victims
1. Louise Elizabeth Williams
2. Sharon Martin

3. Joanne Robinson
4. Shameca Warren

Joshua Julius Anderson

On November 5, 2006, the body of Evaristo Tovias was found on a Tulsa, OK, sidewalk. He had a single shotgun wound to the head and had died instantly. Police had no suspects.

Less than a mile away, almost three months later (January 23), the killer struck again. This time the victim was Christopher Moderow. Having been shot multiple times with a .22 pistol, the victim had three dollars stolen from his wallet.

The next day, the killer shot and killed David Gilbert during an argument at a convenience store. The victim was shot in the head with a .22 pistol.

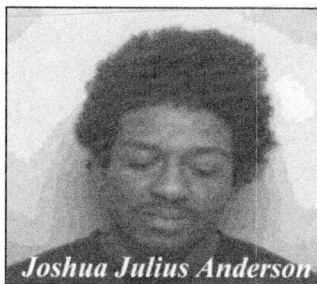

Joshua Julius Anderson

Police knew the three killings had to have been connected, having occurred in a small area in a relatively short time frame. They had put a search warrant out for Anderson, desiring to question him. But he would kill again before they got him.

On February 2, 2007, he committed his worst crime to date, one that is among the most evil and disgusting ever recorded by a serial killer.

He had knocked on the door of an elderly woman's home wearing a bandana over his face. After forcing his way in, he robbed Rose Mary Hobbs of all her valuables. Before he left, he tied her up in the living room. He went and picked up his older brother, wanting him to witness the fun. Later, he would detail that night's event to detectives, not sparing the grotesque details.

He went back to Mrs. Hobbs's home and noticed through a window her son Herbert untying her from her restraints. Infuriated, he burst in the door and demanded they stick their hands up. At gunpoint, he then forced them to strip naked and perform sexual acts with one another.

They begged to be set free, but Anderson and his brother just laughed. Finally growing bored with his sick game, Joshua shot the son in the head, killing him instantly. He then shot the mother numerous times in the chest. As she sat in agonizing pain, he taunted her before putting a bullet in her head. Then, in an effort to impress his brother and to show what he felt was toughness, he ate some of her brains. It is not known how his brother reacted to this, but Joshua later bragged to a friend about eating his victim's brains. Before leaving the scene, Anderson then doused the bodies and home with gasoline and set them on fire.[2]

Despite the horrific nature of this crime, Joshua was spared a death sentence and is currently sitting in McAllister Prison (Big Mac) in Oklahoma, enjoying a life sentence. Police suspect that he may have been involved in two additional murders, but they have no proof yet.

Joshua Julius Anderson's victims
1. Evaristo Tovias
2. Christopher Moderow
3. David Gilbert
4. Rose Mary Hobbs
5. Herbert Hobbs
6. Unidentified
7. Unidentified

Michael Lee Anthony

He should have never been set free, but due to a technicality, Anthony was set free from a fifteen-to-thirty-year rape charge after having served only five years. The state of Michigan does not know how it happened, but someone forgot to record his prison sentence, thereby allowing him early release.

Anthony had a history of violent crimes with a propensity for rape. His neighbors said he was a nice guy, but all knew that he was a serial rapist and stayed clear of him. When it was discovered that he was a killer, they were not surprised.

In 2002, Anthony, who lived in the basement of his eighty-year-old mother's home, had a serious infection in his hand. While being treated in the hospital, police had received an anonymous tip that a possible body was in his quarters. Upon receiving a search warrant for the premises, they soon confirmed their fears.

Next to his bed was a small freezer; inside was the frozen body of Tina Wallace. She had been strangled with a rope that was coiled and placed on her nude, decomposing body.

Michael Anthony

On the floor, under a pile of clothes, lay the body of Toya Lynn Hill. Her decomposing body had been lying there for months, discarded like a piece of dirty laundry.

Perhaps most shocking was that Anthony used his quarters as a hangout for druggies and prostitutes. He was the ring leader they looked up to. They all knew of his wicked secret as well, but they dared not tell for fear of their lives. Instead, they came to get high and ignored the bodies he loved to brag about.

During the trial, Anthony was quite disruptive and unmoved by the families' grief. At one point, he blurted out when photographed by photographers: "You're taking a picture of a black Jesus, your God....I can't stand white folks."[3] At other times he claimed to be a messenger of God.

The court saw through his disregard, though. He was sentenced to two life terms and, to the chagrin of the family, was granted permission to skip the formal sentencing when he would face the families. Outraged at Anthony's missing the trial, the brother of Tina Wallace had this to say: "He may not be able to see my face, but in the years to come, he will see the face of my sister."[4]

Michael Lee Anthony's victims
  1. Tina Wallace
  2. Toya Lynn Hill

Benjamin Tony Atkins (The West Corridor Strangler)

In a nine-month period from 1991-1992, the West Corridor section of Detroit was home to one of the most brutal serial killers the once-great city has ever known.

Born into a life of poverty and crime, Benjamin Atkins grew up without much ambition in life. His mother was a prostitute, often taking her two young sons with her to work, where they would hide in the back seat of her car.

When ten years old, Atkins had his first homosexual experience at the hands of an older man, his caseworker; he violently raped him. This experience set him on a path of homosexual activity, which gradually cultivated a growing disdain for women.

By the time he was twenty-three years old, his disdain had turned into full-festered rage. In October 1991, he sought the services of a prostitute, but his intentions were not merely sexual.

The prostitute realized that he was not a normal customer but a violent man wishing harm upon her. She tried to get away, but he overpowered her and attempted to strangle her while raping her at the same time. The woman, however, proved too much for him and escaped, running naked from the abandoned house where he had her held captive. She would later be the one who turned Atkins in to the authorities.

Benjamin Atkins

As a result of his failed attempt, Atkins changed his plan by targeting small, petite woman who were frail due to being crack addicts. He took to the streets prowling for his next target.

His next victim, Debbie Ann Friday, fit this description and was snuffed out on December 14, 1991. This first murder would set up the pattern he was to follow with ten other women. After strangling the victim unconscious with a cord nearly to death, he would stop to check her pulse. By his own confession, this phase would often last up to ten minutes, as he did not like to rush things. Next, he would strip her and tie her hands behind her back, then latch her legs to two posts. He would then rape her while continuing to strangle her—a process he admitted took quite some time, often over an hour. Occasionally he would stop to check her vitals again, letting his victim regain consciousness, and then he would resume his game until she was dead. He said he would often continue raping for a while after death.

This sadistic killer, who dabbled in necrophilia, haunted the mile-long street where he lived, preying on his victims and always escaping the police. Oftentimes the bodies of his victims were not found for months after death, usually by accident. On one occasion, a demolition crew was removing a dilapidated home when they made their discovery. Other times it was crack addicts or derelicts exploring an abandoned home or motel.

As Atkins grew bolder, the frequency of his attacks increased, and so did the method of choking his victims. He was always trying new techniques he had dreamt up, trying to find a way to make the experience last longer and cause more suffering for the women.

Police were frantically looking for the suspect. They noticed a pattern in each of the eleven murders, and because of their close proximities to one another, they assumed they were all related. However, every tip they received was a dead end. Every suspect they questioned turned up innocent. Finally, they got their big break.

In August 1992, the first woman Atkins had attacked, the one who escaped his clutches, noticed him at a payphone. She notified the police and told them the story that had happened a year before. They were positive that this was their man.

Police then invited the woman to join a police officer on a stakeout near the place she had seen him, waiting for him to return. A few days after they started, Atkins was spotted strolling nonchalantly down the sidewalk. He was arrested without incident and brought in for questioning.

Upon bringing Atkins in, police had little physical evidence to connect him to the crime. They offered him some food and let him start talking. They were surprised at how articulate this street-wise thug could speak, including the depth of his vocabulary as he accurately described each murder down to the smallest minute detail. He described the clothing each victim had worn, the location of the bodies, the method of strangulation, and the pleasure it gave him to kill women.

During the twelve hours it took for Atkins to tell his story, detectives noticed that he acted sexually aroused during much of it. He told them that he would gladly kill again and that he hated women; he wanted to see them suffer as he raped them.

It took two days for the jury to deliberate on the fate of Atkins, with one female holdout who did not want to condemn an innocent man. The other jurors convinced her that Atkins's eighty-seven-page confession, in combination with the physical evidence from the scenes, was a mountain of evidence against him. They finally were in accord: he was guilty with a recommendation to have life without parole. While serving his life parole, Atkins died of AIDS on September 17, 1997, at age twenty-nine.[56]

Benjamin Troy Atkins's victims
1. Debbie Ann Friday
2. Bertha Jean Mason
3. Patricia Cannon George
4. Vickie Truelove
5. Valerie Brown-Chalk
6. Juanita Hardy
7. Unidentified Female
8. Brenda Mitchell
9. Vicki Beasley-Brown
10. JoAnn O'Rourke
11. Ocinena Waymer

Jake Bird (The Tacoma Axe Killer)

Often called an anomaly in the world of serial killers because of the killer's skin color, the story of Jake Bird is one that helped fuel campfire horror stories for generations. However, despite being one of the most prolific killers in U.S. history, after his original story made a blip in the national media, he drifted into oblivion.

In the quiet little port town of Tacoma, WA, on October 30, 1947, Bertha Kludt got the surprise of her life. As she entered her living room in the middle of the day, she was surprised by a fully nude black man wielding an axe on his shoulder. Immediately she screamed in horror, getting the attention of her seventeen-year-old daughter Beverly June and a few of her neighbors.

Neighbors quickly alerted patrolmen near the home. When officers Sabutis and Davies arrived, they were surprised to see a half-naked black man run out the back door of the home and crash through a picket fence. They quickly pursued the man.

The chase led them through numerous backyards and over many fences until they had cornered Bird in an alley. Knowing that he was caught, Bird lunged at the officers with a jackknife, cutting deeply the hand of Davies and stabbing Sabutis in the shoulder. In a reaction to being stabbed, Sabutis, who had been a prize fighter, dropped Bird with one solidly planted left hook to Bird's jaw.

After arresting Bird, the officers and detectives went back to the Kludt residence, where they found the bodies of Mrs. Kludt and her daughter. Police said that it looked like a slaughterhouse, with blood splattered everywhere. They detailed everything they observed in one of the most extensive crime scene reports of its time.

Jake Bird

In trying to piece together the crime from the scene, they arrived at this conclusion. Mrs. Kludt had been surprised by Bird. After telling him to go away, he attacked her and tried to rape her. At this point, they believe her daughter came to her rescue, grabbing

Bird from behind. Bird turned and pushed her into the kitchen, where he bludgeoned her to death with a skillet. He then quickly turned to her screaming mother and chopped her to pieces with an axe he had found in the woodshed earlier.

At first Bird denied any part in the murder, telling officers that an unknown man named Leroy had done it. When they told him that he had left his shoes in the home, he got nervous. When they informed him they had found brain matter and tissue from both victims on his trousers, which he had left at the scene, he finally broke.

His take on the crime was different. He claimed to have taken his shoes off to be quiet in the house, so he could rob the place. After finding a purse and stealing $1.50, he said he was caught by Mrs. Kludt. A fierce struggle between him and the women ensued, in which he said he was forced to kill the women in self-defense. He left out the axe and the bludgeoning and tried to play the part of the victim. Rather comically, he claimed to have assaulted the officers because he felt they would shoot a black man in a mostly white town.

Things proceeded at a normal pace after his confession to the murders. Aside from his defense attorney's wishing to step out at Bird's request, the trial was fairly speedy. Bird had a propensity for courtroom drama and was disappointed that the trial went so fast, hoping that his case would stall and that he would be released.

The prosecutors presented the evidence of Bird's bloody fin-gerprints on the axe and in the kitchen. They then presented his trousers and shoes which were found at the scene. The nail in the coffin was the signed confession presented to the court. The jury took only thirty-five minutes to deliberate and returned with a verdict of murder in the first degree, with a death sentence as the punishment.

On December 6, 1947, Bird was sentenced to be hanged at the Washington State Penitentiary on January 6, 1948. But the day after sentencing, Bird started talking. While en route to the prison to await his death, Bird confessed to twelve additional murders over a twenty-year span. The guard informed the warden, who in turn informed the governor.

A stay of execution was issued on January 6 after the prosecutor in Bird's case heard the confessions from Bird. The stay was to last only sixty days, which they hoped would be enough time to investigate the new confessions by Bird.

Officials took comprehensive notes of Bird's confession, which lasted several days. In the end, the confession was 174 pages of crimes stemming from 1922 to 1947. He admitted to have committed or participated in forty-four murders in Illinois, Kentucky, Nebraska, Oklahoma, Kansas, South Dakota, Ohio, Florida, Wisconsin, Michigan, Utah, New Jersey, New York, California, Iowa, and Washington. He went on to explain that they were committed in a variety of ways: stabbing, axe killings, shooting, strangulation, suffocation, and beating.[7]

Law enforcement officials from those states poured in to interview Bird. Many left satisfied with the details he gave them of unsolved crimes in their states. In a few cases, he even admitted to a crime in which other men had been found guilty. It later came out that one of the men was his accomplice in a robbery, and that Bird had done the killing.

Remarkably, police would learn that Bird had been suspected of axe murders in Omaha, NE, in 1928. After a failed attempt at killing an elderly couple, police suspected him of three additional axe murders from the same week. Despite their efforts, they could never find conclusive proof that he was the murderer. As a result, he went to prison for assault with a deadly weapon and was back out a few years later. During his confessions later in Tacoma, he admitted to the three Omaha murders.

As the sixty days drew to a close, Bird, who had started representing himself alongside his attorney, submitted an appeal to his sentence. He would end up submitting more appeals, which went on for another year and a half.

During this time, he tried numerous attempts to place blame for some of the murders on other convicts that he knew. Authorities would allow him to have supervised phone calls to other prisons to question the accused. His calls sometimes lasting up to an hour and half, he would ask leading questions in a calm voice and try to pin murders on guys who were in prison at the time the murders took place.

Before his death, he also took to studying occult literature. He claimed to have put hexes on numerous people involved in his trial. In the years subsequent to his death, five men involved with the trial had passed away. Some of the media tried to strum support that Bird's hexes had worked, yet most acknowledged that the deaths had no connection to a voodoo hex, but were due to preexisting medical conditions and old age.

In January 1949, the U.S. Court of Appeals denied Bird's final appeal, allowing the judge to issue the sentence. Up until the sentencing, Bird and his attorney had petitioned the U.S. Supreme Court four times, reviewing and denying his last attempt the day before his sentence was carried out.

On July 15, 1949, in front of 125 witnesses, Bird was hanged, dropping five feet from the gallows. His final words were that he wished to seek forgiveness from the victims' families, but, more importantly to him, he said that he "forgave" the world for killing him.

After his execution, his original attorney offered this: "I feel whenever any man 45-years-old gets an idea that no lives are safe to anyone, except his own, that man is a detriment to society and should be obliterated."[8]

Jake Bird's victims
1. Unknown grocer in Los Angeles during a holdup in 1923
2. Harvey Boyd in Council Bluffs, IA, in June 1928
3. J.W. Blackman in Omaha, NE, on November 18, 1928
4. Mrs. Resso in Omaha, NE, on November 19, 1928
5. Greta Brown in Omaha, NE, on November 19, 1928
6. Alta Fulkerson in Highland Park, IL, on June 24, 1942
7. John _____ in South Bend, IN, on September 23, 1942
8. John's wife in South Bend, IN, on September 23, 1942
9. John's son in South Bend, IN, on September 23, 1942
10. Lillian Galvin in Evanston, IN, on October 22, 1942
11. Edna Sibliski in Evanston, IN, on October 22, 1942

12. Marie Manners in Pueblo, CO, on October 1, 1947
13. Unknown man in Ogden, UT, on October 6, 1947
14. Bertha Kludt in Tacoma, WA, on October 29, 1947
15. Beverly Kludt in Tacoma, WA, on October 29, 1947

Eugene Victor Britt

Police in Gary, IN, were baffled by a series of unsolved murders in 1995. They were used to dealing with murders in this high-crime area, but they were usually able to solve them quickly. That year, they had twenty-four dead females, with only a few solved. Little did they know that some of the murders were committed by a serial killer.

Eugene Victor Britt had a violent criminal background. In 1978, he raped a seventeen-year-old girl and served a fifteen-year sentence for his crime. He was released in 1993, and officials were hopeful that he was rehabilitated.

After his release, he found work at a fast-food restaurant a little over ten miles from where he lived. Instead of trying to impress his employer by being a hard diligent worker, he was often late or caught messing around instead of working.

In the spring of 1995, Britt was back to his old habits. At first he began raping teenagers and women, but then he turned to more sinister crimes. Oftentimes a serial rapist will cross over to becoming a serial killer. On rare occasions the first kill is accidental; other times it is an effort to quiet the victim; and most commonly it is an effort to gain full control over the victim. Whatever the reason, once serial rapists make their first kill, they feel a sense of power which drives their appetite to rape and murder again.

Britt had perhaps learned in prison from fellow inmates that it is best to eliminate his rape victims. He did just that in the early spring of 1995. On May 16, Sarah Harrington's nude body was found in a wooded area close to Lake Michigan. She had been strangled to death.

Over the next six months, the bodies of nine more victims turned up, either near his home in Gary or along his route to his job in Portage.

In all cases, the females had been raped and then strangled, their bodies left in the woods or in vacant lots. At least one of his victims was male, a man who is still unidentified to this day.

On September 14, Britt attempted to commit suicide by stepping in front of a train. This was two days after his last murder, and he later said it was because he felt remorse for his crimes. The accident left him with an injured leg, unable to work. He was taken in by a homeless shelter run by a church. It was during his stay here that police suspected his possible role in one of the murders.

On August 22, Brit had murdered his youngest victim. After being sent home early from work for misconduct, he saw eight-year-old Sarah Lynn Paulson playing in a church parking lot across from her home. He lured her near a patch of trees, savagely raped her, and strangled her to death.

During the months after her death, investigators learned from a witness that they had seen a man fitting the description of Britt riding his bike in front of the girl's home. Police began looking for the suspect. On November 3, police found Britt at the shelter and asked him to come in for questioning. When Britt requested his minister to be present, police did not suspect the crimes to which he was going to confess.

After eight hours of confession, Britt had given investigators the gruesome details of ten different murders he committed that year. His confession also led them to locate three bodies of women who had been reported missing. He also willingly let the investigators compare his work uniform with clothing fibers found under the fingernails of his youngest victim. They had a positive match.

Prosecutors felt they had an open-and-shut case. The defendant admitted guilt, provided physical evidence, and wished to plead guilty to his crimes. However, the defense attorneys wanted to prove that Britt was mentally retarded. This made the case drag on for eleven years before a sentence was issued. Prosecutors accurately argued that Britt was fully aware of his actions, since he attempted suicide due to guilt he carried for his crimes. They also argued that his full cooperation with police was corroborating evidence that he knew right from wrong. They pursued the death penalty from the beginning, but in the end, the judge was unmoved and found Britt mentally incompetent.

On November 3, 2006, eleven years to the day after his arrest, Britt was sentenced to a minimum of 245 years in prison with no chance of parole. Upon hearing his sentence, Britt wept to the judge: "I'm truly sorry for my sins and I take full responsibility for my actions, ain't nobody but myself. God knows I'm guilty, God knows I'm guilty."[9]

Eugene Victor Britt's victims
1. Sarah Harrington, age 34
2. Nakita Moore, age 14
3. Deborah McHenry, age 41
4. Michelle Burns, age 27
5. Sarah Lynn Paulsen, age 8
6. Betty Askew, age 50
7. Cleaster "Precious" McNeil, age 29
8. Unidentified male
9. Tonya Dunlap, age 24
10. Maxine Walker, age 41

Shelly Andre Brooks

Shelly was known as a gentle giant in the poor Detroit neighborhood where he grew up. Standing at 6'4" and weighing in close to 275 pounds, he was a monster of a man. People who knew him said he was soft-spoken and polite, but they were unaware of his dark side. He had been homeless for almost a decade and drifted about his old neighborhood, living in vacant buildings or abandoned cars. He collected bottles and cans to earn money, occasionally working odd jobs when they could be found. His biggest expense was paying for prostitutes, whom he often paid with drugs. By his own estimation, he was well-acquainted with over sixty prostitutes in the decade when he was homeless.

In the early summer of 2001, he

solicited Sandra Davis, a fifty-three-year-old black prostitute, for sex. He took her to an abandoned apartment building. After finishing, he demanded his money back, but she refused, which only made him angrier. When she tried to leave the building, he stuck her with a brick in the head repeatedly until she was dead. He then hid her body in a closet and left. The decomposed remains were found on August 31, 2001.

On January 22, 2002, a man removing asbestos from the same building found the remains of Pamela Greer. She too had been bludgeoned with a brick, after which she was wrapped in carpet. Only her legs, whose flesh had been stripped by dogs, were sticking out. Not far from the apartment building, the body of Marion Woods-Daniels was found in an alley on April 14, 2002. Her head had been smashed in with a brick as well, because she dared not to give Brooks his money back. Just eight days later, on April 22, the body of Rhonda Myles was found in another abandoned, dilapidated building. She had been beaten to death with a wooden chair-leg; her body was almost unrecognizable. The killer, however, made a mistake in leaving ample amounts of his DNA on the chair-leg. On November 5, 2002, someone found the body of Thelma Johnson in a vacant lot. She was a known prostitute and had the same pattern of being beaten to death, this time with a large rock or piece of concrete.

By early 2003 the police had a break. They confirmed that there was matching DNA in each of these five unsolved murders. They did not have a suspect yet, but they did have something of substance to start testing possible suspects. But after this, the killings stopped; for nearly three years there was silence. Police were left with five unsolved murders and no serious leads. Brooks would later tell officials that it was because he got a full-time job and moved in with a new girlfriend during this period, so he was not compelled to kill.

On October 18, 2005, the body of Melissa Toston, a thirty-eight-year-old prostitute, was found in a vacant garage. She had been bludgeoned with a concrete block, and then her purse had been stolen. Upon scouring the scene for clues, investigators noticed blood on the block that did not match the victim. But after running it through their system, it was a positive match for the DNA from the other unsolved murders. Police began a frantic search of the area, interviewing everyone who they believed might know something.

On June 5, the last known victim of Brooks was found in a vacant lot less than 1000 feet from the house in which he had been raised. The decomposed body of the woman was never identified. A few days later, he lured another prostitute into an abandoned house. After raping her, he beat her in the head and left. He had assumed she was dead, but in his haste he had not noticed that she was still very much alive but feigning death. After recovering, she went to the police and gave an accurate physical description, telling them that she had always known him as "E."

The description was helpful to police, who caught up to Brooks in July of 2006 as he was prowling about an old abandoned building. After rounds of questioning, Brooks gave a full confession, detailing each of the seven kills. Police then had him take a DNA test. It came back as a positive match on the first six suspects.

Police commented during the trial that Brooks never displayed remorse for his actions. He just stated how he had killed his victims without a hint of sorrow. His lack of compassion led them to suspect him in other murders. At first they thought he might be connected to fourteen additional murders, but they have since cleared seven of them. They have no conclusive evidence yet, but he is the lead suspect in seven additional murders from 1999-2001.[10] When asked if he was involved, he just denied knowing the victims, but he did not deny killing them.

At his trial, Brooks was a different person. After being coached by his lawyers, he concocted a story, alleging that the police beat the confession out of him and that he was innocent. Surveillance recordings of the confession thwarted this effort as they showed him calmly telling every detail of his crimes while the police listened.

Brooks was found guilty of seven murders and implicated in seven more, despite his plea of non-guilty. For his crimes he was sentenced to life in prison without parole.

Shelly Andre Brooks's victims
1. Sandra Davis
2. Pamela Greer

3. Marion Woods-Daniels
4. Rhonda Myles
5. Thelma Johnson
6. Melissa Toston
7. Unidentified woman
8. Seven additional victims whose names were never released

Curtis Don Brown

On the night of May 28, 1986, a Ft. Worth nurse, Jewel Woods, opened a window in her apartment to enjoy the nice evening air. She was described as a pleasant woman who had raised two children and was working on her master's degree. Outside, Curtis Don Brown waited for her to get settled into her routine. As she was drawing a bath, he removed a window screen and reached in to unlock the door. As she came into the kitchen, she was surprised by Brown, high on cocaine, crouching in the corner and waiting to attack.

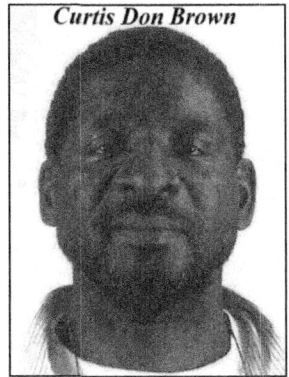

Curtis Don Brown

After chasing her throughout the house, he caught her in her bedroom. He ripped her pants off, raped her, and carried her off. In a patch of tall grass near her apartment, he bashed her head in with a rock and then left her half-nude body to be found the next day. Brown then proceeded back to the apartment to ransack the place, looking for items of value. Finding two purses, he vacated the premises.

At midnight, Brown was hurriedly walking down a private road when officers observed him acting suspiciously. They stopped him for questioning and noticed that he was hiding something in a towel. Brown revealed that he had two purses, one of which had Mrs. Woods's identification. Brown was arrested for purse theft, but he was later charged with murder. He admitted his guilt and was sentenced to life in prison. Police were happy to get another criminal off the streets but did not know he had other dark secrets.

While he was in prison, his DNA was submitted into a database that compared it to cold murder cases in Texas. Police were surprised when they had two positive hits from murders in Ft. Worth. The first was Terece Gregory, a twenty-nine-year-old woman who had been raped and shot in the face on May 29, 1985; she was found in the Trinity River by a fisherman. The other was Sharyn Kills Back, an eighteen-year-old who had been raped and strangled with a rope, found in a storm drain months later.

Police investigated Brown more, and they soon began to suspect him in the deaths of twelve additional women in the Ft. Worth area from 1984-1986, all of which were in close proximity to these murders.[11] Unfortunately, there was no DNA taken from these murders, so they could not prove a connection scientifically. They did note that the manner of death, the similarities in the victims' physical features, and the close proximity pointed towards Brown. However, he never confessed to the murders, as is common with serial killers. Oftentimes killers only confess to the murders in which evidence is strongly against them and deny the other murders. Police hope that, in time, a break in the cases will come through, and either he will confess to these crimes or additional evidence will be found to indict or dismiss him as the leading suspect.

In what was disheartening to the victims' families of the three women known to have been killed by Brown, he was given two additional life sentences to be tacked onto the one he is currently serving. The brother of Ms. Gregory said it best: "The scum is already serving a life sentence for the murder of Jewel Woods. Another life sentence is the equivalent of his receiving no punishment for this crime. It is disgusting, and, as far as I'm concerned, a crime in itself."

Curtis Don Brown's victims
1. Jewel Woods
2. Terece Gregory
3. Sharyn Kills Back
4. Twelve other possible victims

Jarvis Theodore Roosevelt Catoe

On April 12, 1935, a sixty-five-year-old black widow, Florence V. Dancy, was brutally raped and strangled in her home in Washington, D.C. A devoted mother and friend, she was described as one of the kindest souls anyone could meet. Friends also would later say that she was the most beautiful black woman to come out of Pittsburgh.

Initially, another man was convicted of killing Mrs. Dancy, based solely on circumstantial evidence. He would later be released after Catoe's confession and his knowledge of facts which only the killer would have known.

He would wait four-and-a-half years before killing again, which would start a cycle that would last for two years. His next three victims were all mature, older black ladies. The ploy with them was always the same, as he had done in the death of Mrs. Dancy. After ringing their doorbell, he would inquire to see if they still had an apartment to rent based on signage they had placed in their window. With his charm and well-spoken manners, he would be allowed in, no questions asked. Then he would overpower the women with his large, strong hands and violently rape them. After beating them, he killed them, usually by bare-handed strangulation.

In 1941, he changed his tactics and began posing as a taxi driver to prey on younger women. His first victim was a young black woman, Ada Gladys Puller. Police would later find her mutilated body in her home, barely recognizable.

Jarvis Catoe

Two months after the brutal murder of Ms. Puller, Catoe began seeking out young, attractive white women. He struck in March of 1941 and then later in June in the capital city. His last victim, Jesse Elizabeth Strieff, a secretary in the War Department, was found nude in a garbage bin in an alley. She had been raped and then strangled after having mistaken Catoe for a taxi driver.

After the murder of Ms. Strieff, the FBI got involved in searching for the killer in conjunction with a congressional investigation. Feeling heat from the investigation, Catoe fled to New York.

On August 4, 1941, Catoe struck in New York City, killing twenty-six-year-old Evelyn D. Anderson. She had left for work at 6 A.M., but she never made it. Her lifeless body was found, having been strangled by an assailant with large hands. Deep fingernail prints were embedded in and around her throat. Oddly, though, she was his only victim not sexually assaulted.

Within days a valuable watch Ms. Anderson had been wearing appeared in a pawn shop. The man who pawned it swore that he received the watch as a gift from a girlfriend. After tracing how the woman got the watch, the trail ultimately ended at Catoe, a Washington, D.C., resident with large hands.

Since he had already made it back to D.C., police apprehended him on August 29. During questioning, Catoe confessed to murdering a total of eight women he could remember and raping at least six more. When asked how many, he held up his hands, with his large fingers extended, and said, "At least this many or more." With each case, Catoe gave detailed information only the killer would have known. In some instances it was the place the body was found or the manner of death, but he always remembered the clothing color of each of his victims.

When asked, "What makes you do these things?", he was quoted as replying: "I feel like that after reading detective stories about rape cases and looking at pictures of nude women. I did wrong and I'm glad to get it off my mind. I did it and I'm sorry."[12]

Obviously feeling bad for his crimes, he tried on two occasions to end his life, the first by trying to drown himself in his sink and the second time by hanging himself with a belt. During this time he would tell his friends and relatives: "Don't waste money getting a lawyer for me just pray. I have done wrong and am ready to answer for my crime only God can help me now."

Despite his vivid recollection of each murder, Catoe would later recant his testimony. He claimed that the police forced it out of him after severely beating and threatening him while he was sick and weak. When asked to provide proof of said injuries, he could not. The judge and jury did not buy his story.

After a short deliberation of only eighteen minutes, the verdict came back as guilty with a recommendation for the death penalty. The judge agreed and sentenced him to death. On January 15, 1943, Catoe died in the electric chair.

Officials from other municipalities had questioned Catoe about other unsolved murders in their jurisdictions, but to no avail. According to his count, there were more victims. After his death, police believe attributed five more deaths to him.

Jarvis Catoe's victims
1. Florence Dancy
2. Josephine Robinson
3. Lucy Kidwell.
4. Mattie Steward
5. Ada Gladys Puller
6. Rose Simons Abramovitz
7. Jesse Elizabeth Strieff
8. Evelyn D. Anderson
9. Five more unidentified deaths

Nathaniel Robert Code, Jr.

In the mid-1980s, one of the most horrific serial killers in the last century stalked the streets of Shreveport, LA. The gruesome murders he

Nathaniel Code

committed haunted residents and brought sorrow for the families of the unfortunate victims.

At the age of twenty years old, Nathaniel Code had violently raped a young woman. He was quickly apprehended and sentenced to fifteen years in prison. After serving only eight years, he was released for good behavior.

Just seven months after his release, he turned his lust into a far more hideous passion. On August 31, 1984, he snuck into the home of Deborah Ann Ford, a twenty-five-year-old mother of two. After raping her, he stabbed her in the chest nine times, killing her within minutes. The killer was not finished, though; he then sliced her throat in a sawing motion six times, nearly decapitating her. When finished, he placed the body face down in the pool of blood. This last act was seen in each of his crimes and signified ultimate control in his mind.[13]

On June 24, 1985, the body of Wes Burks was discovered in the kitchen of Code's home. Lying in a pool of blood face down, he had been stabbed numerous times in the chest. Code was a leading suspect, but he was never charged.

Less than a month later, the body of Monica Renae Barnum was discovered in her apartment by her mother. She had been bound and then raped by her killer. After finishing, he strangled her to death with a wire hanger. Not satisfied that she was dead, the killer then stabbed her in the chest multiple times before laying her face down into her own blood. Code was named as a person of interest, but he was never charged in the crime.

His next known murder occurred almost a year later and is almost unimaginable. In September of 1985, Code staked out the home of Vivian Chaney for days, learning the household's patterns and be-haviors. He learned that everyone in the house was either blind or mentally retarded. Believing that they were easy targets, he struck on the 19th.

With the air conditioner making noise, he snuck into the home without notice. He first shot Billy Joe Harris, Vivian's boyfriend, in the head in his bedroom. Quickly moving to the other male in the home, he killed Vivian's brother, Jerry Culbert, by shooting him in the chest twice before slicing his throat.

After having taken out what he saw as the biggest threats, he moved on to the females. After capturing both Vivian and her teenage daughter, he bound their hands with electrical cords and covered their mouths with duct tape. It is not known for certain if he raped either victim, but it is assumed that he did.

Carlitha Culbert, the fifteen-year-old daughter, was first to be killed. In front of her mother, he sawed her throat with a large knife, almost decapitating her. Blood spurted onto her mother's dress and the ceiling. He then took Vivian to the bathroom and smothered her to death, then draped her body over the edge of the tub. Remarkably, Vivian's two younger daughters (ages seven and ten) escaped death by hiding from Code. Had he known they were there, they would probably have been killed as well.

In 1986, two additional murders happened in the area near Code's home. He was suspected in both but was never charged. Both bore a striking resemblance to his known murders and to the two previous killings of which he had been suspected. On February 21, the decomposing body of fifty-four-year-old Johnny B. Jenkins was discovered in his trailer. He had been stabbed multiple times in the chest. Towards the end of the year, on December 12, the body of Jake Mills was found on his living room floor. He too had been stabbed in the chest numerous times. Both men were placed face down in their blood.

On August 5, 1987, Code committed his last murder and crossed a line not many serial killers ever dare to go. While his seventy-three-year-old grandfather, William Code, was watching television with two of Code's young nephews, he snuck through a window. Quickly overpowering them with his large body, he bound each with appliance cords or telephone cables. After duct-taping each of their mouths, he killed his family. His grandfather was stabbed five times in the chest, then rolled over and stabbed three times in the back. Both nephews, Joe Robinson (age twelve) and Eric Williams (age eight), were strangled to death with a telephone cord.

The next day, Code was charged with murder in the deaths of his family. A neighbor who knew that Code had been banished from his grandfather's home saw him sneak out just prior to another family member's discovery of the bodies. Code denied any wrongdoing, but he was arrested.

Police would later pin the murders of Deborah Ann Ford and Vivian Chaney on Code, despite his denial. The connection was his fingerprints found at all three crime scenes. The police suspected he was involved in the other unsolved murders, but they were never able to find incriminating evidence aside from the similar kill patterns.

Another behavior of Code, sometimes seen in serial killers, was his following many of his murders. He was at the scene when they hauled the bodies out of Vivian Chaney's home. Likewise, he was on scene as his family's bodies were removed from his grandfather's home. He even sought police and gave a statement, claiming that he did not see anything happen.

On December 28, 1990, Code was sentenced to death for the murders of Vivian Chaney's family. He was not tried on the murders of his own family or the other murders police believe he committed.[14]

A lengthy legal battle has taken place since his death sentence. His death warrant has been issued three times, and he has appealed it numerous times. Currently, Code's attorneys are appealing the court because of the state's lethal injection policy. The families affected all wish to have closure.

Nathaniel Code's victims
1. Deborah Ann Ford
2. Wes Burks
3. Monica Renae Barnum
4. Billy Joe Harris
5. Jerry Culbert
6. Carlitha Culbert
7. Vivian Chaney
8. Johnny B. Jenkins
9. Jake Mills
10. William T. Code (grandfather)
11. Joe Robinson (nephew)
12. Eric Williams (nephew)

Andre Crawford

From 1993 to 1999, the infamous 9th Police District of Chicago recorded 291 murders, an average of almost fifty per year. It was during this murder-filled time that no less than three black serial killers prowled the streets, eliminating black prostitutes without raising much police suspicion. This was due in part to the high number of murders in combination with the large number of black prostitutes who died during this period.

One of these serial killers was Andre Crawford. A known cocaine addict, he lived as a transient in the high-crime town of Englewood, located in the notorious Southside of Chicago. People knew him as "Dre" and regularly solicited for him to perform small jobs, such as shoveling their snow, cleaning their yard, or other small odd jobs. They described him as quiet and considerate, yet they never suspected him as being one of the most prolific serial killers in the area.

In September 1993, Crawford killed his first victim, Patricia Dunn. They had been familiar with each other, having been druggies in the same neighborhood and having hung around the same crowd. Both were accustomed to getting high with friends and then having sexual intercourse. Therefore, Dunn did not think it odd when he offered to pay her for sex with cocaine.

After talking for some time, they strolled to an abandoned warehouse, known as one of the local haunts for junkies and transients. After arriving, Dunn requested that they first get high before having sex. Crawford furiously disagreed, and he beat her to death with a pair of pliers he had in his pocket. When she fell from the beating, he continued striking her until she was near death. He then began to rape the dying woman, but stopped when he noticed the large puddle of blood that began to surround her. He dragged her body to a dry area, later saying, "I didn't feel comfortable continuing to rape her there by the puddle of blood."

Years later during his confession, and again during the trial, he further elaborated on his actions. Feeling nervous, he smoked his cocaine and took a walk to cool off. After feeling better about what he had done, he returned and had sex with Dunn's corpse. This gruesome event was repeated at least one additional time the next day, when he returned yet again to Dunn's body.

This pattern of enticing drug addicts or prostitutes with cocaine continued for six more years and would take the lives of ten more innocent women. In each case, he beat, strangled, stabbed or bludgeoned his victims to death in abandoned buildings or vacant lots. He also admitted to having postmortem sex with the body of each victim while high on cocaine. He visited some of the victims for a few days after their murder for his sick sexual euphoria.

In 1999, investigators got a break in seven of their cases when DNA evidence linking the bodies to the same killer returned positive. They then knew that another serial killer was on the loose. It was also during this same year that Crawford attempted to kill his twelfth victim. She, however, was cleverer than he expected. After being beaten in the head, which would later require fifty-two stitches, he stabbed her in the back a few times with a knife. During the process he also broke her leg, which would later require a surgical rod. However, instead of fighting him, she played dead. Lying in her blood on the ground in a lifeless pose, she played the part well. Crawford, thinking she was dead, performed his appalling ritual and left the scene, hoping to return the next day. After he left, the victim was able to pull herself together and flee the scene, where she sought the help of friends to take her to the hospital.

After hearing this woman's story, investigators intensified their search for the killer. They built a profile of what they thought the killer would be like: a black male aged thirty to forty who used cocaine on a regular basis and was familiar with the neighborhood. They further thought that he knew many of the victims prior to killing them and that he had sex and used drugs with some of them. They also speculated that he frequented the same soup kitchen and possibly homeless shelter as his victims did.

This profile was compared to males in the Englewood area, with a total of 305 that fit this description. After whittling this list down via DNA tests, they had an "A" list of suspects that included Crawford.

Police continued eliminating suspects and were able to get a DNA sample of Crawford from his mother in late 1999. They had a positive match, leading to his arrest on January 30, 2000.

At the station, police began to question Crawford about the seven deaths and one attempted murder. He willingly told his story over the next three days, providing details of each death and how he knew the victim. During his confessions, he also admitted to killing three additional women from whom the police were unable to recover DNA due to their severely decomposed state.

At one point in the confession, Crawford admitted that he had attended a few community CAPS meetings held by police in an effort to solicit any information that might lead to the killer's arrest. He also congratulated the police for a job well done in catching him, but then gloated of being one step ahead of them: "You have to admit, I was pretty good, too. I killed for eight years."[15] This cat-and-mouse game is one in which some killers take great pride; they stay close to the investigation to feel a sense of accomplishment.

Another thing that came out during the gruesome confession was that Crawford took a totem from his victims. In his case, it was their shoes. Unlike most serial killers who take things from their victims, he sold the shoes on the street corner, fetching as much as twenty dollars for each pair.

Initially, Crawford was charged with ten murders and eleven rapes. Investigators would later link to Crawford the murder of Rhonda King, which had been pegged on another black serial killer, Hubert Geralds, Jr. When presented with the evidence, Crawford admitted to the crime and gave information that only the killer would know. It is suspected that he might have committed other murders, but he has never admitted to any additional ones.

The case dragged on in courts for almost a decade, in large part due to Crawford's defense attorneys. Despite his lengthy and detailed video confession and intimate knowledge of the crime scenes, they managed to stall the case by insisting that the confession was forced. They also claimed that the DNA from the victims was a mixture of numerous men, which meant that their client could not be the only suspect. The DNA was tested again and came back conclusively to incriminate Crawford.

When the case finally came to trial in 2009, Crawford had been the longest serving inmate in county history. He entered a plea of not-guilty at the advice of his attorneys. The evidence piled against him was outstanding and more than enough to convince the jury that he was guilty. However, the jury split against the death penalty. One female claimed that religious conviction forbade her from condemning him to death. Another male juror felt that Crawford's rough childhood in a poor environment contributed to his killings, which in his mind made Crawford not liable.

The ten jurors in favor of a death sentence were visibly upset, and after the trial, some openly said that Crawford should die for his crimes. The victims' families were upset as well. The one survivor from this monster said to reporters after the trial in tears: "The courts let him live, and he killed 11 women. I thought he had killed me. How could you let someone like that live?"

Despite the ferociousness of his crimes and the number of victims, this case was unheard of outside of the three-square-mile area he called home. Media outlets that initially released the report of his arrest shied away from the case as it dragged on in court for near a decade. Today, most people in Englewood can name many white serial killers, but the name of Andre Crawford has fallen into obscurity.

Andre Crawford's victims
1. Patricia Dunn
2. Rhonda King
3. Angela Shatten
4. Shaguanta "Pumpkin" Langley
5. Tommie Dennis
6. Sheryl Johnson

7. Constance Bailey
8. Sonji Brandon
9. Nicole Townsend
10. Evander Harris
11. Cheryl Cotton-Cross

Paul Durousseau (The Jacksonville Serial Killer, The Killer Cabbie)

Having grown up in a decent home in the Los Angeles area, Durousseau had no known criminal activity prior to the age of twenty-one. His first offense was for carrying a concealed weapon, for which he received three months' probation. After receiving a subsequent charge just a month later, he enlisted in the U.S. Army, partially to avoid having to marry a woman he had impregnated.

After serving his career in Germany, Durousseau reenlisted in 1996. It was just months after this that Paul's known violent criminal behavior began. On January 6, 1997, he kidnapped and raped a woman in Columbus, GA. Yet, after being arrested in March of that year, he was later acquitted of all charges, freed due to a technicality. He continued serving in the military.

One month after being acquitted, Durousseau kidnapped, raped, and then murdered Tracy Habersham in Fort Benning, GA. Her body was found two days later, bound and naked in a ditch. Just eight days after the body was found, Durousseau's wife gave birth to his second child. However, charges would not be filed until 2003, after DNA evidence connected him with the crime.

On the home front at this time, Durousseau's wife moved to Jacksonville, FL, to escape his violent behavior. She reported him for beating and threatening her, feeling that he might seriously harm her or their two young daughters.

In January of 1999, Durousseau was dishonorably discharged from the army for buying stolen military computer equipment. Soon afterward, he made his way to Jacksonville, hoping he could reconcile himself with his family. However, within three months of his arrival, his criminal behavior started again. His first crime was molesting a fifteen-year-old girl in a city park. Charges, however, were never filed by the victim or her parents, so he was free again.

Paul Durousseau

Feeling as if he was free to commit crimes unimpeded, he murdered Tyresa Mack on July 26, 1999. Like every murder he committed, he gained the woman's trust by seducing her with his charm. After being invited to her apartment, he bound and raped her before strangling her to death with a small cord. Police did not connect him with this crime until 2003, when forensics confirmed that his DNA matched what was found on the victim's body.

Almost two years went by before Durousseau committed another known violent crime. This time, he violently raped a woman in her home on June 24, 2001. He was arrested soon afterward, and he spent only thirty days in jail. He accepted a deal with the district attorney for two years' probation in exchange for keeping his DNA out of the police database. Had his DNA been submitted, he would have been found guilty of two murders, and five innocent women's lives would have been spared.

In August of 2001, Durousseau found work as a school bus driver, despite his conviction for rape just two months prior. This job only lasted a month, though it is not known if he quit voluntarily or was fired. During this same time period, his wife filed a protection order against him and even had him arrested for domestic abuse.

After being acquitted for a burglary charge in October 2002, Durousseau's most fierce rampage began. Within a month-and-a-half span, he raped and killed five young black women, two of whom were pregnant. In each case the victims (all between eighteen and twenty years old) were bound, raped, and then strangled with a cord. Each victim's body was then either disposed in a ditch or buried near the scene of the crime.

Currently, Paul is sitting in a Florida state penitentiary awaiting his execution for his second murder. No execution date has been set as of this time; it may take years for justice to be served. Officials in Germany are currently investigating Durousseau's possible role in murders committed in a similar fashion from the time he was stationed there with the military.[16]

Paul Durousseau's victims
1. Tracy Habersham
2. Tyresa Mack
3. Nicole Williams
4. Nikia Kilpatrick
5. Shawanda McCalister
6. Jovanna Jefferson
7. Surita Cohen
8. Unborn child of victim
9. Unborn child of victim

Kendall Francois (Stinky)

When the story broke on Kendall Francois, psychologists were shocked that a black man was a serial killer. What puzzled them the most was that (yet again) a black man had become a serial killer without a significant trigger event in his life. According to their theories, based around the model of white serial killers, all serial killers needed a traumatic event in their life to provide the catalyst to spark their deadly rampage.

Without a criminal past, Francois assumed the life of a janitor in the Arlington School District of Poughkeepsie, NY, after his release from the army. Having accepted the life of a loner, he quietly worked while still living in the comforts of his parents' home.

On October 24, 1996, something snapped. After having sex with a prostitute, he felt he had been cheated, and in his anger he choked Wendy Meyers to death. His next steps became his haunted ritual for each of his kills: he bathed the body, carefully placed it in a garbage bag, and then stored it in the attic of his parents' home.

A month later, he repeated his ritual from the original kill twice within a two-day span. This time, Gina Barone and Catharine Marsh were added to his gruesome collection.

Francois resumed his predation in January of 1997, his first victim of the year being Kathleen Hurly. Just a month later, police met with Francois to question him as a possible suspect. Police released him, thinking he could not be the killer. But within an hour after his release, he was placing the body of his fifth victim, Mary Healey Giaccone, in his attic. She would not be reported as missing until November 13, 1997.

News of a potential serial killer broke on December 12, 1997. The victims' names were released, and a description of the possible assailant was given. Police were desperate to find their man before he killed again.

Undeterred by the attention his murders were receiving, he tried to kill again on January 23, 1998. This was just five days after police re-questioned him about his possible involvement and asked him to take a lie detector test. He passed the lie detector test but failed to kill his victim. A month later, she filed assault charges against Francois.

In May of 1998, Francois pled guilty to assault charges and was sentenced to serve a small jail term. After serving only seven days of his sentence, he was freed to terrorize the town yet again. Just over two weeks after his release, he was successful in adding the body of Sandra Jean French to his attic storehouse. The next day, he moved the body to his crawlspace.

Kendall Francois

His last murders were committed in August 1998. In the methodic manner in which he killed and stored his prior victims, he placed the bodies of Audrey Pugliese and Catina Newmaster in the crawlspace of his home.

On September 2, 1998, Francois finally broke down and admitted to his crimes. He had attempted to kill another prostitute. After she successfully fought him off, he dropped her off at a gas station where she then told the attendant to call the police. Police brought Francois in for his third questioning about the murders. He admitted to killing many of the ladies.

When police searched his home, they found the decayed and decaying bodies (whose stench was overwhelming) of eight of the ten missing women from the area for whom they were searching. Francois admitted to killing the eight they had found, but he denied involvement in any other murders. Police suspect him in at least two additional murders, each victim having been killed in the same manner, and both being prostitutes whom Francois had frequented. He may be tied to additional missing prostitutes in the area, but no additional bodies have been found to date.[17]

Kendall Francois's victims
1. Wendy Meyers
2. Gina Barone
3. Catherine Marsh
4. Kathleen Hurly
5. Mary Healey Giaccone
6. Audrey Pugliese
7. Sandra Jean French
8. Catina Newmaster

Lonnie David Franklin (The Grim Sleeper)

Since the 1970s, the suburbs of Los Angeles have been plagued with at least thirty-four black serial killers: some were gang members; others solo killers. Many had their crimes solved quickly, with a few taking years to solve, but few took as long as Lonnie David Franklin's. Pegged as possibly the most prolific serial killer in the city's history, his tale has gradually unfolded since his discovery in 2010. Facts and details are still being uncovered, so the story is far from complete, and it will have more information added after he has gone to trial and police have investigated every lead.

He earned the name "Grim Sleeper" after a reporter used the term to describe his crimes, since at one time police believe he had taken an almost decade-long hiatus from killing. It is now known that he did kill a few victims during this time, and police now believe he never stopped killing since his first known murder in 1982. It was in that year that he killed Cathern Davis, but now investigators believe that he most likely started circa 1978 and was a seasoned killer by the murder of Ms. Davis. After this, we know that he chalked up at least seventeen murders by 2006, but that is just the beginning of the story.

In 2010, police were still stumped by dozens of unsolved murders dating from the late seventies to the present. Most of the victims were black women, many of whom were prostitutes. The list had once numbered well over 100, but it was slowly whittled down to a more manageable number. Despite this, they were not closer to solving the remaining homicides. They did notice that eleven of them were connected to one killer via DNA and ballistics, but they had no suspects until they got a big break.

In 2009, police were frantic to find the killer of the ten women and one man, all killed within a short proximity of one another over a twenty-year-span. The LAPD did what is known as a familial DNA analysis, which is a test that looks for paternal DNA markers which are a partial match to the DNA found on the victims. They ran over one million samples before they had a positive hit—Franklin's son in prison showed up as a partial match. Police set up an interview, and he pointed to his father as the suspect, claiming that he had odd habits and was a good fit for the crimes.

In 2010, police began tailing Franklin, learning his moves and habits. They wanted to obtain his DNA secretly without a court warrant in the event that he was not the suspect. After scoping him out, they watched him leave a table at a pizza shop where he had left his crust on a table. A detective swooped in and gathered the discarded crust as evidence. Within days, they had a positive match—he was the killer with less than a one-trillionth chance of error.

After arresting him, police interviewed him in hopes that he would crack, but he instead denied the crimes, saying that he was innocent. His wife, daughter, and neighbors told investigators that he was the nicest man they knew, and that he was not capable of such heinous crimes; they said the police were mistaken. Even when presented the

DNA evidence, which proved without question that his DNA was found in and on some of the victims, they still denied that he was guilty.

Police next moved to investigate his home, but they found little in the house that indicted him. Yet when they went to the garage, which also doubled as an auto mechanic's business, they found further proof that he was guilty. In an old refrigerator, they found a box of Polaroid photographs, most depicting women who were passed out in the seat of a car or naked. As they dug through the photographs, they found pictures of the ten murdered women in the clothes they had been wearing at the time of their deaths. Now the police had physical evidence tying him to the crimes. But this discovery opened the investigation up to further-reaching implications.

Amongst the photographs were 180 (mostly black) women who had no names or dates on the photo, leaving police to wonder if possibly they were homicide victims as well. They posted the unidentified pictures on the internet and hosted a public viewing, asking for help in identifying the women. Slowly the list was reduced to forty-two unidentified, as it presently is at the time of this writing. In addition to the forty-two unknowns, police have identified eight women who were previously unsolved homicide cases. (One still remains a Jane Doe, but police are positive that Franklin was the killer.) Police have attributed their deaths to Franklin.

In addition to this, police were contacted by authorities in Belize, where Franklin's wife was from. It is known that they spent a few years there on at least two different occasions. During the times he was there, seven young girls in the same city where he lived were raped and murdered in a similar fashion to his known murders. As of yet, there has been only a circumstantial connection, but they are working hard to see if any of the DNA from the killer was preserved to compare with Franklin's.

Thus far, this makes for nineteen known murders combined with the seven possible from Belize and the forty-two unidentified photos from his home; and there is the possibility that his murder count might surpass sixty-eight. Only time will tell: hopefully he will confess his crimes in full to give the families closure.

Lonnie David Franklin

As for the identity of the victims, some of the women he killed were prostitutes, but not all. Some were women he had picked up, as was the case of a woman who survived his attack in 1988. The one man, Thomas Steele, was a well-known pimp with whom Franklin was acquainted. It is unknown if he knew Franklin was the murderer or if he had been in an argument with him prior to being shot. So far, police have linked him to the other murders based off the ballistics tying the bullet to the other murders.

What also is known is that, despite his recent capture, he was within the grasp of police on at least two occasions of which they are aware. The first was after the murder of Barbara Ware in 1987. On January 10, they received an unusual call from a black man who remained unusually calm for someone reporting a murder. He told the dispatcher that he had watched a black man put the body of a woman in a church van and leave the feet hanging out. He went on to describe how the body was placed, what was covering the body, and what the contents of the van were. With this intimate knowledge, police felt that the killer was the one who placed the call. But when they arrived, the killer was gone, and they found the body exactly how it had been described. He had come close to being caught but had slipped right through their fingers.

The next close call was almost two years later, in November 1988. A young black woman was walking home from an evening party when a man in a highly detailed orange Pinto hatchback with white racing stripes had stopped to offer her a ride. After playful banter, the woman consented to letting the well-dressed, courteous older man give her a ride. She remembered how nice the interior of the car was, meticulously maintained without even a hint of dust. He told her that he had to stop by his uncle's home around the corner, and then they would be on their way.

After leaving the home, he came back a different man. Instead of the nice, well-spoken gentleman she had met, he had a scowl and spoke in a rude, demeaning tone. He kept calling her by another name, one she recognized as that of a well-known prostitute from the neighborhood to whom she bore resemblance. The woman told him he had the two women confused and he was not the first to make the mistake. But he kept telling her, "You dogged me!" Soon thereafter, he pulled a gun and shot her in the side. Next, she remembered a camera flash and him raping her as she lay bleeding slowly to death, writhing in pain. But somehow she escaped and made it back to her friend's home, waiting for them to get home and take her to the hospital.

Police investigated the extracted bullet from her abdomen and noticed that it was a dead ringer match for the same gun used in a series of unsolved murders known as the Strawberry Murders. Police asked the witness if she could identify her killer, but after flipping through a mug-shot portfolio, she found forty-two men who resembled him but none who were a positive match. But she did remember the car, and positive she had seen it before. After leading police to his home, they interviewed Franklin and searched the premises but found no proof that he was the attacker. For some reason, the police did not bring him in for a line-up to see if she could pick him out as the killer. She eventually let it go, fearful that he might hunt her down and kill her. She would later resurface after he was captured and identify him as her attacker.

But perhaps most shockingly, Franklin was under the nose of the police on more than one occasion. He had been arrested several times for receiving stolen property and assault, but in each case he was let go a short time after incarceration. In one instance, he was released after serving just four months, due to jail overcrowding. And while most prisoners had to give a DNA sample to have on record, for some reason he had been able to skate around the system and walk without giving a sample. In addition to this, he had been a police mechanic for years and worked at the garage closest to where many of the murders took place.

Police are currently trying to identify the unknown women from the photos. Additionally, they are investigating 260 unsolved murders from areas where Franklin has been to see if any have a tie to him. Currently he is not talking, which does nothing to help the case. His trial is set to start in April 2012, but it could be delayed by unforeseen hitches. Any new information will be updated in subsequent editions.

Lonnie David Franklin's victims
1. Cathern Davis, age 32, June 9, 1982
2. Debra Jackson, age 29, August 10, 1985
3. Henrietta Wright, age 34, August 12, 1986
4. Thomas Steele, age 36, August 14, 1986
5. Barbara Ware, age 23, January 10, 1987
6. Bernita Sparks, age 26, April 15, 1987
7. Mary Lowe, age 26, November 1, 1987
8. Lachrica Jefferson, age 22, January 30, 1988
9. Unidentified woman, known from the photos and found dead in 1988. Police have her listed as Jane Doe but are hopeful that someone will come forward with her identity.
10. Inez Warren, age 28, August 15, 1988
11. Alicia Monique Alexander, age 18, September 11, 1988
12. Rosalind Giles, age 26, January 10, 1991
13. Lisa Renee Knox, age 18, May 11, 1993
14. Anita Yolanda Parker, age 27, November 17, 1998
15. Princess Berthomieux, age 14, December 21, 2001
16. Valeria McCorvey, age 35, July 11, 2003
17. Ayellah GBO Dza Ta Marshall, age 17, February 1, 2005
18. Rolenia Morris, age 31, September 10, 2005
19. Janecia Peters, age 25, December 31, 2006

Lonnie David Franklin's possible victims from Belize
1. Sherilee Nicholas, age 13, October 1988, stabbed
2. Jay Blades, age 9, October 1988
3. Samantha Gordon
4. Jackie Malic, age 12, March 22, 1999, stabbed
5. Becky Gilharry
6. Erica Wills
7. Karen Cruz

Alfred J. Gaynor (Big Al)

From 1995 to 1997, the town of Springfield, MA, was riveted and shocked by a series of murders and deaths of young women ruled as overdoses. Over the next fifteen years, one man would eventually admit to killing nine of these women and letting a child die of dehydration.

Alfred Gaynor, known as "Big Al" by his friends and family, was an intimidating, large man known to have a peaceful demeanor. Most knew that he struggled with a crack cocaine addiction; what they did not know was how violent his addiction had made him.

It took Gaynor just over fifteen years after the murder of Vera E. Hallums, to finally admit guilt. On April 25, 1995, he had knocked on the door to her home and asked to sleep on her floor. Having been acquainted with him, she did not mind. But as she slept, the monster in him awoke. He took a pot from the kitchen and beat her unconscious, so severely that it fractured her skull in numerous places. She was not dead, though, and he wanted to rape her before he killed her. He tied a telephone cord around her neck and behind her back onto her hands, so that if her hands moved it would only apply further pressure. As she started to become conscious, before he had the chance to rape, she was strangled as she tried to free her hands. Upon her death, he gave up his pursuit for sex and stole a ring before fleeing.

His next murder was over a year later and has resulted in much speculation and debate since his admission of guilt in 2008. Sometime in early July 1995, he went to the apartment of Amy Smith, who was the girlfriend of his nephew Paul Fickling. Fickling admits to having had a tiff of some sort between himself and his girlfriend upon Gaynor's arrival. He also admits to having left the house or room while Gaynor raped and strangled his girlfriend. It would later come out in trial that Gaynor had intimidated Fickling since his youth and that Fickling was scared that

Alfred Gaynor

Gaynor would kill him, which was the reason why he did nothing to stop Gaynor.

On July 11, 1996, Smith's nude body was found stuffed in a closet. She had been strangled with large bare hands, and a sock was stuffed in her mouth. On a mattress on the floor lay her twenty-two-month-old daughter, dead from dehydration and starvation, having been left unattended. Both Gaynor and Fickling knew the girl was there; they assumed she was Fickling's biological daughter. It would later come out during trial, after a paternal test was ordered, that Fickling was not the girl's father.

Fickling was eventually convicted of second-degree murder in both deaths on November 17, 1998. After Gaynor's 2008 confession, Fickling was granted a new trial and was resentenced on the lesser charge of manslaughter.

It would take Gaynor almost a year before he killed again. In late May 1997, Gaynor was walking home from work one night when a pickup with a man and woman in it stopped and asked if he had any crack. Gaynor said that he had none but knew where to get some. The young woman, Jill Ann Ermellini, left the truck and joined Gaynor as he took her on the search for crack. After stopping by a convenience store, Gaynor picked up two small white rocks on the pavement which resembled crack. He convinced Ermellini that he had found some crack in his pocket, and he offered to share it with her.

After finding an abandoned vehicle in an alley, they climbed in to smoke their drug. Quickly, however, she found out Gaynor's trick and demanded to be let out of the old truck. Gaynor used his large body to overpower the young woman, and he choked her until she passed out. He then stripped her clothes and raped her in the truck. After finishing, he strangled her to death and left her body. When her body was discovered on June 16, 1997, it had decomposed severely. The coroner found traces of cocaine in her system and ruled the death an accidental overdose. The family doubted the official story and was relieved when Gaynor confessed to the crime years later.

Picking up steam, Gaynor murdered again in October of 1997. His victim, Robin M. Arkins, was found on the 25th, the story much like the others. Gaynor had lured her into an alley, promising her crack cocaine. Once his cover was blown, he overpowered her, bound her hands with her shoelaces, and gagged her mouth with a sock. After he raped her, he strangled her barehanded. Her half-nude body was found in an alley and had the presence of cocaine in it. She had abrasions on her face and legs; in her throat was a wad of paper he had forced in.

Just days later on November 1, the body of JoAnn Thomas was found in her home. She too had been raped and strangled. As in all of his murders, Gaynor stole a few valuables to feed his rabid appetite for crack.

Within two weeks, he had murdered again. This time, his target was a friend whom he had known for years. On the morning of November 15, 1997, the eleven-year-old son of Yvette Torres found his mother's lifeless body on the bathroom floor. Aside from a bruise on her chin and on her lip, the death did not look suspicious. The medical examiner found a lethal amount of cocaine in her system and ruled the death undetermined. Gaynor would later admit to raping her and strangling her in the bathroom of her home. After leaving her body, he stole her son's video games, which he would later pawn for more drugs.

Gaynor took a slight cooling-off period from his frenzy of 1997, not resuming until February. In this final month of his murders, he would snuff out the lives of three women and attempt to kill another. The body of Loretta Daniels was found on February 2, 1998, in an alley. On the 11th, Rosemary A. Downs was found in her home dead. His last victim, Joyce L. Dickerson-Peay, was found dead outside a restaurant on February 19. All women were treated the same. They were bound, gagged, and then raped. After he finished, he strangled them to death.

Police had assembled a task force to identify potential suspects and got a big break the day after the death of Dickerson. Gaynor had been identified as the last person seen with Dickerson; police then began tracking his movements. Soon afterward, police questioned him and requested a DNA sample, which later conclusively proved that he was the killer of Daniels, Dickerson, Downs, and Thomas. But he staunchly denied any wrongdoing in any of their deaths, even after his first conviction.

Gaynor was sentenced to four life sentences with no chance of parole. After his sentence was read, he told the court that he was innocent and that he had been framed.

His name would not pop up again until 2005 when he was trying to sell pictures he had drawn for profit. The public was outraged, but he was allowed to move forward in selling his art. He currently has a small website where he sells his art, in addition to autographed pictures of himself in plain clothes, taken in the medium-security prison where he appears to be enjoying life.

In 2008, he dropped a bombshell on the Commonwealth of Massachusetts. After doing some soul-searching, he decided to come clean and tell the world that he was a monster who had killed nine women and let one child starve to death. His reasoning was that he did not want his mother to know the depth of his depravity, so he waited for her death in 2006.

At his new trial, he said, "I know it's hard to understand but I truly am a good person." This statement caused much grief to the families of the victims he killed, but the positive is that this idea pushed him to make a full confession.

During the sentencing in 2010 for these newly confessed murders, the families affected were greatly displeased with the sentence. "This changes nothing," was the common plea, as the judge tacked additional life sentences to those he already had.[18]

Alfred Gaynor's victims
  1. Vera E. Hallums
  2. Amy Smith
  3. Destiny Smith (by neglect)
  4. Jill Ann Ermellini
  5. Robin M. Arkins
  6. JoAnn Thomas
  7. Yvette Torres
  8. Loretta Daniels
  9. Rosemary A. Downs
  10. Joyce L. Dickerson-Peay

Lorenzo Jerome Gilyard

With the advent of DNA analysis in 1984, a new era in solving cold cases emerged. Since that time, the science has improved greatly, increasing the speed at which samples can be studied. The depth of the study has vastly improved as well: what was yesterday's deteriorated sample, too far gone for testing, is today's gold mine. Even samples once deemed too small for analysis are clearing cases in record numbers.

Lorenzo Gilyard

In 2004, the Kansas City, MO, police got just such a break. Amongst their library of hundreds of cold cases were dozens of unsolved homicides whose remaining evidence they had diligently preserved for future analysis. Having initially lacked the funding, they received a federal grant which allowed them to put a serious dent in their cases. In six of the unsolved homicides, they found DNA from the same killer. They were equally surprised when they also had that killer's DNA already on file.

Lorenzo Gilyard was a man with whom they had been well acquainted. From 1969 to 1993, he had been arrested numerous times for assaulting and raping women and girls in the city. Most of the charges had not stuck, and he was free to continue harming innocent women. He was convicted on two of the nine sexual assault charges. He served nine months in 1975 for raping a friend's thirteen-year-old daughter. In 1982 he was sentenced for raping a woman; he served just less than four years. Because of his history, in combination with his known habits of visiting prostitutes, they obtained a DNA sample from him in 1987 to place in their database.

After the police arrested Gilyard, who was working as a manager at a trash collection company, he denied the charges. Police showed him the DNA results, demonstrating that his semen was found in six dead women and his hair on another. But he still steadfastly denied any wrongdoing.

Police began to look into other possible murders he might have committed. They found three prior to his four-year stint in prison, all matching his MO. They soon found three more from after his prison stint.

The pattern was all the same; only the ages and race differed. The victims consisted of eight white and four black prostitutes, ages fifteen to thirty-six, in addition to one thirty-six-year-old homeless white woman. All were found strangled and nude, usually with a sock or piece of paper in their mouth, and with evidence that they had been raped. Some were strangled bare-handed; others with their shoe laces or socks. All had scratches and bruises indicating a struggle to ward off their attacker.

When the case was getting close to trial, the prosecutor struck a deal with the defender. If they would forgo a trial by jury, the death penalty would not be sought. Realizing that the chips were stacked against Gilyard, the defense agreed.

At the trial, Gilyard's defense tried to deny the DNA evidence. When faced with concrete evidence that it was legitimate, they then argued that it was possible for him to have been shadowed by a serial killer who killed after he had had sex. The judge dismissed this as an improbable conspiracy based on a near-impossible hypothetical situation. The prosecutor agreed in his closing argument: "The odds of some unknown person shadowing the defendant and killing those women immediately after he had sex with them defies logic."[19]

The judge eventually threw out the evidence on seven of the cases, saying that it was not incriminating enough to convict but did point to Gilyard as the killer. He did, however, keep the DNA from the original six charges. For those crimes, he sentenced Gilyard to six consecutive life terms without parole. When asked if he had anything to say, Gilyard said, "No matter what I say, it doesn't matter." He was then sent to prison.

It is believed that Gilyard might have quit killing after his last victim in 1993. However, police are not certain that there are not more victims from his extended cool-down periods waiting to be discovered. If there are, Gilyard is not saying so, as he still professes his innocence to this day.

Lorenzo Jerome Gilyard's victims

1. Stacie L. Swofford (white), age 17, on April 17, 1977
2. Gwendolyn Kizine (black), age 15, in January 1980.
3. Margaret J. Miller (black), age 17, in May 1982
4. Catherine M. Barry (white), age 34 (non-prostitute), on March 14, 1986
5. Naomi Kelly (black), age 23, on August 16, 1986
6. Debbie Blevins (black), age 32, on November 27, 1986
7. Ann Barnes (white), age 36, on January 17, 1987
8. Kellie A. Ford (white), age 20, on June 9, 1987
9. Angela Mayhew (white), age 19, on September 12, 1987
10. Sheila Ingold (white), age 36, on November 3, 1987
11. Carmeline Hibbs (white), age 30, on December 19, 1987
12. Helga Kruger (white), age 26, on February 12, 1989 (Austrian National)
13. Connie Luther (white), age 29, in January 1993

Mark Goudeau (The Baseline Killer)

The city of Phoenix, AZ, was on edge from 2005 to 2006 as police were trying to solve fifteen murders which they believed were the result of a serial killer. It did not take police long before they realized that they were dealing with two separate killers, based on the manner of the kills and different gun calibers used by each killer.

One of these killers earned the name "Baseline Killer," because his first killings started along Baseline Road. Of the two serial killers, he had the higher victim count, slaying nine. It would take almost a year before police caught him, but when the dust settled, Mark Goudeau was arrested for being the most prolific serial killer in Arizona history.

Mark Goudeau

His crimes began with raping two teenage girls behind a church on August 6, 2005. Just over a week later, he struck again on the 14th, raping and then robbing a young woman not far from his last rapes. After this he took a brief break from his crimes to avoid raising suspicion.

Perhaps wanting to take his crimes to a new level, he committed his first kill was on September 8, 2005. After following Georgia Thompson to her apartment, police think he propositioned her for sex, based off his behavior with other victims. As with the other victims, she denied him, which set him off. Angered, he shot her in the back of the head with a pistol.

It would not be until December 12 when he murdered again. This did not stop him from at least four rapes and numerous robberies, though. In the evening hours on the 12th, Tina Washing-ton was on her way home when she crossed paths with Goudeau. After refusing his sexual advances, he shot her point-blank in the back of the head and ran.

He struck again on February 20, 2006, this time committing his first double homicide. Inside a snack truck near a large construction site, he attacked Romelia Vargas and Mirna Palma-Roman. But unlike the other murders, there was no sign of robbery, and police doubted there were sexual advances. By all appearances, the crime was just for the thirst of blood.

Taking an almost one-month break, he killed again on March 15, 2006. He kidnapped Liliana Sanchez-Cabrera and co-worker Chao Chou from a restaurant parking lot as they were getting off work. He started with Chou first and left his body on the side of the road. Driving with Cabrera a bit further, he raped her, killed her, and left her body about a mile away.

Two weeks later he struck again, slaying twenty-six-year-old Kristina Nicole Gibbons. After raping her and killing her, he dragged her body to some scrap plywood besides a building. The owner of the business noticed blood on the sidewalk and drag marks in the gravel. Police investigated but found nothing, concluding that it was nothing of significance. A week later, the owner's dog found the decomposed body stuffed between plywood and the building.

Police were frantically looking for clues from the crimes and had begun to connect a few together. They realized a serial murderer was in the area, but few details were released to the public.

On April 10, Goudeau visited a woman with whom he was friends. He had been hitting on her for some time, but she refused his advances, knowing he was married. Paying her a visit, he raped her, leaving his saliva on her breasts, and then shot her. She was found by her eight-year-old son, who had been forced to walk home when she did not arrive to pick him up.

On May 5, police released information that a serial killer was in the area. They said he was responsible for at least five to six murders and possibly more, as well as at least eleven rapes in a small area just a few square miles in size. A $100,000 reward was offered, and a police sketch showed a black man with long hair wearing a bucket hat (a Gilligan-styled hat). Residents were on edge as people were warned not to travel alone and to be on the lookout for anyone suspicious.

On June 29, he struck for the last time. Carmen Miranda was vacuuming her car at a small car wash and talking on her cell phone. Goudeau snuck up behind her, forcing her to an alley 100 yards away. After raping her, he shot her and left her body, but little did he know that the crime was caught on a closed circuit television.

On September 4, Goudeau was arrested for raping two sisters at gunpoint the year before. He was sentenced to 438 years for this crime. About three months after his arrest, police began putting the pieces together and noticed that his DNA was found in a few of the murders and rapes attributed to the Baseline Killer. They compared his photo to the eyewitness sketch and to the video surveillance tape and noted the similarities. They questioned him about the murders, but he denied any connection to the crimes.

After gathering more information and interviewing witnesses, Goudeau was charged as the Baseline Killer. This would set off a whirlwind of controversy as he claimed racism and as his wife claimed that the DNA was planted on the victims by racist cops. But police did not back down: he was their man. He was eventually found guilty of all crimes attributed to him, and was given nine death sentences as well as numerous life sentences, totaling over 1,500 years in duration.[20]

To this day, Goudeau denies any involvement in the murders or rapes, despite his previous record of violence. His wife has set up a website claiming that the police tampered with the evidence and that he just happened to fit their profile. However, no one denies that, after his arrest, the rapes and murders in the area ceased.

Mark Goudeau's victims
1. Georgia Thompson, age 19, on September 8, 2005
2. Tina Washington, age 39, on December 12, 2005
3. Romelia Vargas, age 38, on February 20, 2006
4. Mirna Palma-Roman, age 34, on February 20, 2006
5. Liliana Sanchez-Cabrera, age 20, on March 15, 2006
6. Chao 'George' Chou, age 23, on March 15, 2006
7. Kristin Nichole Gibbons, found on March 29, 2006
8. Sophia Nunez, age 37, on April 10, 2006.
9. Carmen Miranda, age 37, on June 29, 2006

Harrison Frank "Marty" Graham (The Corpse Collector)

The City of Brotherly Love was haunted by three separate serial killers in the 1980s. Among these, Gary Heidnik is the most well-known (and oftentimes the only one known) despite his having killed the least amount of victims. His wicked story would eventually spawn the character of the malevolent Buffalo Bill from the popular movie *The Silence of the Lambs*. Heidnik was white, but the other two men, both black, each killed four times as many victims as Heidnik during the same time frame and in the same general area.[21] Yet the names of the black killers, Harrison Graham and Leonard Christopher, are almost unheard of.

The most gruesome of the three stories belongs to Harrison Graham, known to his friends as "Marty." He roamed the streets of the Philadelphia projects, working odd jobs as a handyman and selling drugs. Often seen shooting hoops with children, he was well known in the area for entertaining everyone with his impression of Grover from the children's television show *Sesame Street*. Getting drunk and dancing in the street just to show off was also a ploy he used to entertain people.

Most never suspected what he was hiding; they simply wrote him off as a zany, happy-natured guy.

On a blistering August day in 1987, he was evicted from the run-down apartment he rented for $90 per month. The apartment building was in a severe state of disrepair, but his landlord could not take the dead, rotting smell that emanated from his cave any longer. He had to go.

Before leaving his apartment, Graham nailed the door to one of the rooms shut and informed his landlord that he would be back to clear out the room in a few days. He warned him not to let anyone in the room, fearing that people could not handle what they saw.

Curious as to what Graham could be hiding behind the door that had "Marty" scratched in ominous letters, he peered through the keyhole. What he saw shocked him, and he notified the police.

On August 9, a police officer was sent to Graham's apartment to investigate. Upon entering the building, he recognized the smell of death. Thinking he would find the victim of a drug overdose, he proceeded to investigate Graham's apartment, which had once been a crackhouse run by Graham.

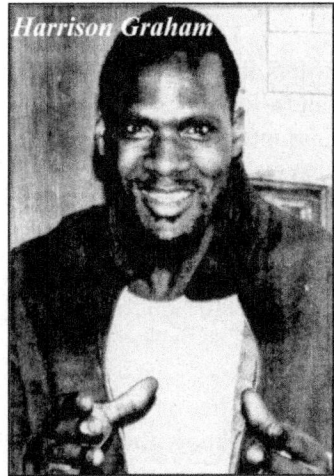
Harrison Graham

Upon entering the apartment, he was confident that he had found the source of the pungent odor, yet he only saw trash in the main part. After searching the poorly lit rooms, he was left with one more, the door marked "Marty." He looked through the keyhole and noticed a woman's body on a mattress. After knocking and getting no response from the room, he called for the medical examiner. When the ME arrived, they pried open the door only to be overpowered by the strong odor that consumed the room. They had to wear masks before they entered.

In the room, which resembled a miniature landfill, they found the nude, bloated body of a black female on a pile of old, worn-out mattresses. Next to the mattress was another bloated corpse. Assuming that both bodies could be possible drug overdoses, they roped off the apartment as a potential crime scene and called for backup to help sift through trash and debris.

Over the next two days, investigators would find the remains of seven unidentified women in the small 10' x 12' homemade mausoleum that Graham used as his bedroom. Some were nothing more than skeleton remains with dried-up bits of flesh on them, while others looked as if they were mummified. One set of remains shocked investigators the most: found between the mattresses on which Graham had slept were the skeletal remains of one of his earliest victims. A few weeks later, police located an eighth victim who had been bound and gagged on a pile of ashes in the basement of a neighboring building. The remains were de-composed so severely that police did not know if it was a man or woman.

Police put out an APB for Graham, looking for him in the places his friends said he hung out. Over the next eight days, they had several sightings of him but always got there too late to make an arrest. Graham's picture was printed in the local paper, urging people to call authorities if he was seen, and family encouraged Graham to turn himself in. After an intense search, his mother was finally able to convince him to cooperate with the police. He called her on August 17 asking for food, she brought some to him, and then she helped him go to the police.

Graham insisted that his mother be present at the police ques-tioning. From the onset, she insisted that the bodies had been in the apartment prior to her son's moving in four years before. The police were not amused, and they revealed to her that all eight victims had been killed within the last year, some within two weeks. At this, Graham finally caved and admitted guilt. At first, he admitted to killing two by accident and denied any connection to the other victims. Finally, after a few days, he admitted to murdering at least seven women, but he claimed that it was an accident in each case. His claim was that he enjoyed sadomasochistic sex, choking his partner's airflow during the act. Police told him he was correct that the manner of death was strangulation, but they reminded Graham that some of the victims had been bound and gagged. Graham conceded they were right.

The police not only had Graham's confession, but they also acquired testimonies from friends to whom Graham sold drugs and from ex-girlfriends, saying that he was abusive and bragged of killing women. With this, they turned the evidence over to the prosecutor. At trial, however, Graham's public defender tried every means to have the trial thrown out or to declare Graham mentally ill. The judge, however, did not buy this. After five different experts evaluated Graham, he was declared sane and very aware of his actions.

The court also heard testimony from witnesses who made the claim that Graham was an abusive person and enjoyed threatening women. He had on occasion showed the dead bodies of his victims to women, telling them they would be next. One witness even testified that she had gone to police before Graham's arrest, but the police did not deem her credible because she was a known crack addict.

One witness also claimed that Graham had shown her a body of a woman he had killed prior to his first known victim. Police have been unable to locate any remains of the woman. This same witness also alleged that Graham confessed to her that he engaged in necrophilia with his victims. Because of this testimony, police have speculated he might be responsible for other deaths near the area.

After hearing the full testimony, the judge sentenced him to life in prison followed by a death sentence. Satisfied with the sentence, in uncanny fashion the defense attorney bragged that Graham had been given a fair and just sentence. However, in 1994 the State Supreme Court for Pennsylvania declared the sentence illegal. They argued that the more severe punishment should trump lesser punishments, which meant that a death warrant was to be signed. The execution was scheduled for December 7, 1994, but was later given a stay. The case was then delayed for over eight years until 2002. It was in that year that the U.S. Supreme Court banned the execution of mentally retarded people. Graham had an IQ of 63, a full seven points below the line of demarcation for retardation; his sentence was thus commuted to life.[22]

Currently, Graham is serving his sentence in a medium-security facility. Since his imprisonment he has supposedly become a minister, and he preaches to fellow inmates. This, however, should be taken lightly, because he alleged to be a devout Christian throughout his trial, claiming that he used the Bible as his guide and would never harm a soul.

Harrison Graham's victims
1. Unknown victim
2. Robin DeShazor, age 30
3. Valerie Jamison, age 25
4. Cynthia Brooks, age 28
5. Sandra Garvin, age 33
6. Patricia Franklin, age 24
7. Mary Jeter Mathis, age 35
8. Barbara Mahoney, age 22
9. Valerie Jamison, age 25

Vaughn Orrin Greenwood (The Skid Row Slasher)

The story of Vaughn Orrin Greenwood is one typical of many a black serial killer. Police profilers had him pegged as a white male, twenty to thirty years of age, with scraggly blond hair. He was suspected to be a loner by nature, shunned by society because of a traumatic life-changing event, and he took out his rage by slashing his victims violently. But upon his capture and subsequent confession, police realized that they had been led down the wrong path by the criminal profile on which they had relied.

Having grown up in Pennsylvania, Greenwood ran away from his foster parents' home at age fourteen and headed to California. Liking life on the road, he would continue this pattern of running the rails and hitchhiking between California and Chicago until his capture. Working as a migrant worker, he lived between bum camps and cheap motels for nearly two decades.

His first known murder occurred on November 13, 1964, in the infamous Skid Row District in Los Angeles. The victim was David Russell, an older transient man who did not have a chance; Greenwood sliced his throat before he could even fight back. In what would be his ritual, which seemed to be born out of voodoo, Greenwood would stab his victim repeatedly, cut cryptic unknown signs around some of the stab wounds, and finish by draining some of the victim's blood into a few small cups. After positioning the cups of blood near the body, he would then sprinkle salt around the outline of the head and finish by removing the victim's shoes and pointing them towards the body. According to police, it appeared that he even drank some of the blood. The day after Russell's murder, he repeated this pattern on his second victim, Benjamin Hornberg, in the restroom of a sleazy hotel.

Two years went by before Greenwood popped up again, this time for attempted murder in Chicago. He was reported to police and convicted, and he spent over five years in prison. After his release, he drifted back to California, eventually landing back where his murderous spree began. On the very spot where his first victim had been killed, he murdered his third victim, Charles Jackson, just over a decade later on December 1, 1974.

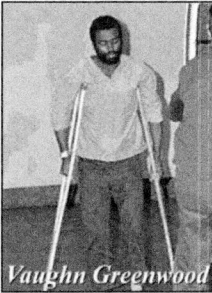
Vaughn Greenwood

Bloodthirsty, he did not hesitate taking three more victims in the month of December 1974. He murdered Moses Yakanac, Arthur Dahlstedt and David Perez, all killed in the same fashion and with the same ritual as his first three victims. By this time, police began to see a pattern, and they intensified their search for the killer whom the media dubbed the "Skid Row Slasher."

Not showing any signs of slowing, Greenwood continued slashing and killing through January 1975, taking the lives of five people. Casimir Strawinski, Robert Shannahan, and Samuel Suarez were his final victims in the Skid Row district before he made an abrupt change. Possibly having had a close brush with police, or perhaps fearing that he was drawing too much attention, he moved his operation to Hollywood, where he murdered George Friar and Clyde Hays.

It was at this time that two vital mistakes were made, one by police and one by Greenwood. Police had released the errant profile of the Skid Row Slasher, focusing all their efforts on a fictional white transient hippie. As for Greenwood, he picked the wrong target for his next victim.

He had grown arrogant in his brutal attacks, having had success in each attempt since his slip-up in Chicago. Feeling that he had the upper hand, he changed murder weapons, wielding a hatchet instead of a knife or bayonet. After attacking his next victim, he had the surprise of his life when the victim had a guest in his house who was not afraid of a man with a hatchet. The two wrestled for a bit before plunging through a large window, leaving Greenwood injured.

Confused and fleeing on foot, Greenwood tried breaking into the home of actor Burt Reynolds when he made another mistake. After he carelessly dropped a letter addressed to himself in Reynolds's driveway, police had found their man. Police arrested Greenwood on charges of burglary and assault, and they then searched his residence to find something they did not expect. On a table were the cufflinks of George Friar which, they had noted, were stolen just five days prior in his murder. Upon seeing the evidence, Greenwood confessed to the nine murders he committed after his release from prison. A jury later convicted him on these murders, but a mistrial was declared on his first two murders from 1964. He was sentenced to life in prison with no chance of parole.[23] Because of his transient nature, police suspect that he might have killed more people on his frequent trips riding the rails to Chicago.

Vaughn Greenwood's victims
1. David Russell, November 13, 1964
2. Benjamin Hornberg, age 67, November 14, 1964
3. Charles Jackson, age 46, December 1, 1974
4. Moses Yakanac, age 47, December 8, 1974
5. Arthur Dahlstedt, age 54, December 11, 1974
6. David Perez, age 42, December 22, 1974
7. Casimir Strawinski, age 58, January 9, 1975
8. Robert Shannahan, age 46, January 17, 1975
9. Samuel Suarez, age 49, January 1975
10. George Frias, age 45, January 29, 1975
11. Clyde Hays, age 34, January 31, 1975

Vincent Darrell Groves

The general perception of serial killers is that they either ex-perienced a horrible upbringing or had a traumatic experience at some point in their life to shape their sociopathic behavior. While this idea is well-founded, in some instances killers are raised in an environment that should propel people to a decent and successful future. Such is the case for Vincent Groves, who seemingly had an ideal early life.

Growing up in Denver as the son of a church deacon, he was one of the few blacks in his high school, but that did not impede him. As a member of the student council, he won numerous awards for scholarship, good citizenship, and musical ability, and he was well-known as a peacemaker who had a great outlook on life.

Standing at 6'5", he also was a standout forward on a basketball team for the '70-'72 seasons, whose cast featured a future NFL star, a future basketball coach, a future NBA player, and others who would later become prominent citizens of the community. His future looked bright, and as he went off to play basketball at Coe College in Iowa, his teammates thought this quiet star might have a possible future in the NBA.

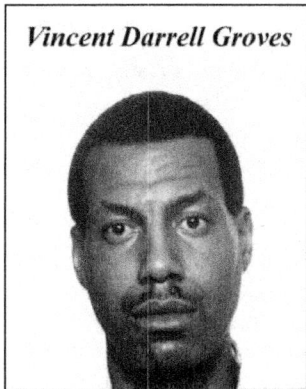

Vincent Darrell Groves

After two years of college ball, where he did see some success, he had a change of heart, turned his back on sports, and headed back home. Upon his return home, his friends and family noticed a change in his once-happy demeanor, noting that he seemed frustrated and was not the same person they had known.

While at Coe College, his teammates noticed that he began to dress flashy, which earned him the nickname "Superfly." Despite his style, he did not hang around the team but gave them the cold shoulder and had a noticeable bad attitude. His old friends in Denver noticed the same pattern of behavior, and even were threatened to "be taken care of" by Groves for things as simple as being aggressive while playing a pickup game of hoops.

By 1978, Groves had popped up on the police radar. Despite that he was married and was by his family's testimony a devout Christian, he had turned to a street-hustling lifestyle. As a pimp and drug dealer on Denver's infamous East Colfax Avenue, police questioned him in the violent death of one of his call-girls, Jeanette Louis Baca, who had been found lying dead in a ditch.

During the three-hour interview, the police caught Groves in numerous lies and suspected that he was the killer. Later, when the police interviewed his cousin, he almost implicated Groves when he told investigators that Groves had returned home with soot all over the front of his clothes. Police knew Ms. Baca's clothes had been burned in a park near where she had been found, but Groves denied the allegation he had soot and ashes on his clothes. Police had no other physical evidence and were forced to let him go.

Between July 1979 and April 1981, the bodies of six more of his girls had turned up in various parts of the city; all had died in the same manner as Ms. Baca, being strangled to death. Police were dumbfounded as to who might be responsible for the murders, but it was not uncommon to find dead hookers given their dangerous lifestyle. Therefore, police did not tie the murders together aside from noting that they all shared the same pimp, but that only slightly raised their interest.

In August of 1981, Groves slipped up. After peeling into the Lakewood Police Station at three in the morning with his young wife, he began to confess to the officer on duty of his drug problem, saying that he had made some horrible decisions in life. As the conversation went on for a while, the officer tried to give him advice. But after the officer was finished speaking, Groves changed the subject abruptly and informed the officer that there was a dead young woman in the back of his truck.

Alarmed, the officer went quickly to investigate and then began to question Groves. He swore that the young lady, Tammy Sue Woodrum, was a friend and co-worker's daughter who was also his girlfriend. He claimed that they had been snorting cocaine when she began to choke and bleed from the mouth. His wife validated his story, and from what the officer observed, her death seemed to fit the story.

Once the body was examined, the coroner read a different tale on the young woman's body. While there was cocaine present in the body, and while sexual intercourse had taken place, he noted that there were ligature strangulation marks on the neck. Moreover, the marks around her neck and on her body matched the unique stitching pattern on Groves' belt. Police arrested Groves on suspicion of murder; he was later sentenced on a second-degree murder charge and shipped off to prison for a fifteen-year sentence.

While in prison, he was reported to have been a model prisoner, studying hard, encouraging other inmates to finish their education, and swearing off a life of crime. He even swore that upon his release, he would make a difference by getting a decent job and working hard to support his wife.

During his prison stint, his wife had other thoughts, and she divorced him a few years before his parole. Soon thereafter, Groves began communicating with a female pen pal who shared his Christian convictions. According to Groves, she was even more devout than he was.

Due to a law that has since been repealed, Groves was given a mandatory early release after only (surprisingly) serving a five-year sentence. His first order of business was to marry his pen pal; his second order was to start hustling where he had left off.

Upon meeting his new wife, he determined that she was too pure for him to have sexual relations with her, so he took to visiting prostitutes. He would spend nights cruising on East Colfax Avenue, looking for the ideal lady and for new victims.

After roughing up numerous prostitutes, they became leery of him, and most in their trade steered clear of him. He was even stopped and questioned by police in 1987 after a few prostitutes reported him while being interviewed on a street corner. But since it was rumored in their enclave that he had killed other prostitutes, they refused to press any charges for fear that that he would kill them too. Perhaps they hoped that he would break down and confess his crimes, but as a hardened killer he knew how to lie and convince officers that he was innocent.

From April 1987 to August 1988, six more prostitutes in the area would be found dead in various places around the Denver area. Police noticed a pattern: the victims all worked East Colfax Avenue, were found partially nude, had been strangled, and were dumped in alleys or ditches. But police did not have any leads aside from Groves. In one case, there were witnesses who reported seeing a tall, thin black man dumping the victim, but they did not see his face. In five others, he was the last person reported to be seen with the women. But, as investigators noted, he had a connection to all six women, as he had with the eight women he was suspected of killing prior to 1982.

On September 1, 1988, police got their chance to interview Groves. He had been arrested while working a janitorial job for attempting to murder a prostitute at a motel. After his interview, police began questioning his family and friends, trying to obtain any information they could. His family, however, was indignant, alleging that their questioning was police harassment. As they had in his previous murder conviction, they stalwartly proclaimed his innocence.

Groves did not crack either, maintaining his innocence even in his murder conviction. While he went to trial for the attempted murder, police feverishly worked to find incriminating evidence to validate their theory that Groves had murdered at least fourteen prostitutes.

Family and friends launched a media campaign to portray Groves as a victim and an upstanding citizen of the community. They advanced the idea that Groves was only a bad guy in the eyes of the cops. They never hesitated to pull the race card, alleging that police were looking for the easy solution by pinning the crimes on a black man. The group ignored the evidence in his murder conviction as well as the testimony of numerous prostitutes who feared Groves. Partially as a result of their efforts, a jury acquitted Groves and he was set free.

By May of 1990, detectives had worked hard to put the pieces together, but they had a little help from DNA evidence. Two of his later victims, Juanita Lovato and Dianne Montoya Mancera, both had tested positive for having Groves' DNA in their body. Lab techs sampled the rest of the DNA from what had been preserved in the other murders;

however, due to the still somewhat primitive nature of the science in 1990, the results were deemed inconclusive. Despite this setback, Groves was arrested for the two murders.

During the trial his supporters again stood by his side, despite the physical and circumstantial evidence. His lawyers alleged that the DNA only proved that Groves had sexual relations with the women, not that he had killed them. They tried to paint Groves as an upstanding citizen who had been down on his luck and made a few bad choices which police had tried to exploit. The family even had pastors write letters proclaiming that Groves was not capable of committing murder, since he was such a nice and upstanding guy.

Prosecutors argued that in addition to the DNA evidence, witnesses had last seen the women with Groves. The jury was moved when a known drug dealer even took the stand and told a story of how Groves had admitted that he had to eliminate "Little Bit," the nick name of Ms. Lovato, because she had hit him. Their clincher was a pendant found in Groves' car that belonged to Ms. Lovato, for witnesses reported that she had worn it the last night she was alive.

Unmoved by Groves' defense, the jury found him guilty and recommended he receive two life sentences for the murders. Satisfied that their man was behind bars, the police stopped their investigation and listed Groves as the probable murderer of sixteen women.[24] In addition to this, they suspected that he might be responsible for up to twenty murders. Recently, police released information that his DNA was found on four more of the women he was suspected of killing in 1979.[25]

Soon after formal sentencing, Groves began to get ill with liver and pancreas problems, which were suspected to be brought on due to his severe drug and alcohol problem. After spending the next six years in and out of state hospitals, Vincent Groves died on October 31, 1996.[26] His family maintained his innocence to the end despite the overwhelming evidence against him, and they refused to give the detectives any information that might give closure to the families of his victims.

Vincent Darrell Grove's victims (and possible victims)
 1.   Jeanette Louise Baca, found on June 17, 1978

2. Emma Jenefor, age 25, found in May 1979
3. Joyce Ramey, age 23, found on July 4, 1979
4. Norma Jean Halford, age 21, found on August 24, 1979
5. Peggy Cuff, age 20, found in November 1979
6. Cynthia Boyd, age 19, found in February 1980
7. Juanita Mitchell, age 25, found in April 1981
8. Rhonda Fisher, age 30, found in April 1987
9. Karolyn Walker, age 18, found on July 5, 1987
10. Pamela Morgan, age 17, found on June 2, 1981
11. Tammy Sue Woodrum, age 17, found in August 1981
12. Zabra Ann Mason, age 19, found in September 1987
13. Faye M. Johnson, age 22, found on January 30, 1988
14. Juanita 'Becky' Lovato, age 19, found on April 29, 1988
15. Robin Nelson, age 25, found on June 12, 1988
16. Dianne Montoya Mancera, age 25, found on July 25, 1988
17. Carolyn Buchanan, age 35, found on August 12, 1988
18. Pamela Montgomery, age 35, found on August 14, 1988

Lester Harrison

A career criminal, Harrison had received his first prison sentence in 1945 for armed robbery in his hometown of Chicago, IL. He was sentenced to a term of five to ten years but got into more trouble while behind bars. In November of 1951, he killed another inmate, Norman Kimme, by beating him to death. However, instead of receiving more jail time, he was sent to a mental hospital after having been declared incompetent for trial.

After a short stint in the hospital, he was released only to continue his criminal endeavors. Racking up eight separate charges in a short time—larceny, battery, armed robbery, unlawful use of a weapon, and indecent exposure—he was sent back to the state hospital but was declared competent for trial. He was sentenced to eighteen months in prison in March 1972, but he was later relieved of his sentence by a judge because of the time he had spent in a state mental hospital.[27]

Though unknown to authorities, Harrison had committed a crime far worse than the crimes of which he was found guilty. On July 10, 1970, he attacked Agnes Lehman and Wilber McDonald in the peaceful and famous Grant Park. The two had been talking when Harrison ran up to them, knocking McDonald unconscious and turning his attention to Mrs. Lehman; he raped her and beat her to death. McDonald would later be convicted of the crime, despite his description of Harrison and details of the night. After serving two years, he was freed based upon Harrison's confession and intimate knowledge of the crime.

On Labor Day, September 5, 1972, Harrison struck again in Grant Park. His victim was Judith Bettelley, a twenty-four-year-old British woman. She was in the area working as an architect, and as she strolled in the park, he attacked her. After dragging her to some bushes, he raped her and then beat her to death, making her face unrecognizable.

Three weeks later he attempted to kill again. After knocking a woman out with a brick, he dragged her to a dark alley to kill again, but he was caught in the act. He was charged with the crime but was later released on $5,000 bond, which was unusually small considering the crime.

While his trial was pending for the assault, he murdered Irene Koutros in July 1973. After dragging her to a parking garage that flanked Grant Park, he raped her and stabbed her to death. Police had no suspects and added her name to the list of unsolved murders.

Just a few weeks later, on August 3, he attacked near the middle of the park. Lee Alexis Wilson was a twenty-three-year-old student from San Francisco visiting the art museum, and the young woman stood no chance at the hands of this hardened murderer. After he stabbed her, he wrestled her to some bushes where he raped the bleeding woman. When he was finished, he bashed her head in with a brick repeatedly, not stopping until her head was almost flat. He then embarked on an even darker path, even as citizens strolled in the park by him, and he ate part of the woman's body. With blood on his face and clothes, he fled the park.

Police were frantic to find the killer and suspected that the earlier deaths might be connected, given that the victims were all white females killed in close proximity and in a similar manner. Despite the connections, they had no suspects and were no closer to solving the crime. They needed a big break. On August 23, 1972, they got that break.

The Ott family was in from Seattle visiting family in the area. As the Otts enjoyed time in the park with their young son, Harrison spotted them and watched from a nearby public restroom. After some time, Judith Ott went into the restroom, and Harrison quietly slipped in behind her as the sun was setting. After he surprised her, she screamed, and he responded by stabbing her in the chest and face numerous times, killing her almost instantly and beating her face to a pulp. He wanted to rape her, but he felt nervous and decided to flee.

Fearing that others in the busy park might have heard her scream, Harrison tried to steal off into the night while carrying the bloody knife. Judith's husband David observed him running from the area of the scream, which prompted him to give chase. After tackling Harrison, he held him until police arrived, not knowing that his wife lay dead in the restroom.

Police arrived quickly and arrested Harrison for the murder of Judith Ott. While searching him for other weapons, they found a picture of Lee Wilson he had taken from her purse. Suspecting that he might be the killer they were trying to find, they promptly took him to the station for questioning.

After a few hours of confession, Harrison admitted to killing four women in Grant Park over the past few years, including Agnes Lehman in 1970. Police then asked him about the murder of Elizabeth Dawson, his next-door neighbor who was found murdered in a similar manner on August 27, 1972. He denied involvement, but police concluded that the evidence was overwhelming.

When questioned about his motivation, he said it was for a thrill. In each murder, he started off by watching a pornographic movie and drinking a few beers before hunting his victims. He said it was arousing to see women suffer, even after death. Cutting their bodies, removing hair for a souvenir, and even cannibalizing them (in the case of Ms. Wilson) were what he lived for.

Harrison stayed in custody for the next five years, bouncing from one psychiatric evaluation to the next so the court could determine if he was fit for trial. In March 1978, despite conflicting reports, the court acquitted Harrison of all charges on grounds of insanity. But fearing that he would murder again—as he had told police, he hated women and wanted them all dead—they used an old, rarely-used law in the Illinois books that allowed him to be jailed because he was a sexually dangerous menace to society. With this, the court sentenced him to serve life in psychiatric ward.

In 1986, Harrison was recovering from an acute infection in his spinal cord which for a short time had made him a quadriplegic. His attorney petitioned for his release because of his deteriorated condition. The court and his family disagreed. In a letter addressed to the court, his family lamented: "We feel that the crimes he is charged with are so heinous that they require his secure removal from society for the rest of his natural life. We fear that he is indeed capable of and likely to kill again if he has tasted human flesh. This very thought is abhorrent and repulsive. Yet it is a matter of public record. What assurance do we have that he will not continue to murder helpless people? . . . Our lives are in your hands."

The judge presiding over the petition for release agreed: "If Lester Harrison is physically able to move, I consider him dangerous." With that, Harrison was sent back to the ward where he lived out his final days.

Lester Harrison's victims
1. Norman Kimme
2. Agnes Lehman
3. Judith Bettelley
4. Elizabeth Dawson
5. Irene Koutros
6. Lee Alexis Wilson
7. Judith Ott

Calvin Jackson

Born in Buffalo, NY, Jackson was a drifter, well-known to police in his hometown as a small-time thief. After a failed attempt at a robbery in 1965, he was sentenced to serve a five-year prison sentence. Upon his release, he relocated to New York City, settling on West 77th street, an area with a high number of elderly widows, which was a favorite haunt of criminals seeking an easy score.

After relocation, Jackson rented a room at the low-income Park Plaza Hotel as one of the youngest tenants. After getting settled, he took a small job but quickly resumed robbing and mugging people for petty cash to support his drug habit. It would not take long for his crimes to take a turn for the worst.

On April 10, 1973, he broke into the apartment of Theresa Jordan, who at thirty-nine years was his youngest victim. After raping her, he suffocated her to death. But since he was scared to leave, he hung around for nearly an hour, pilfering the icebox for snacks. Satisfied that his victim was dead, he then raped her again before ransacking the room for valuables and fleeing the scene.

Next on his list was Kate Lewisohn, a sixty-five-year-old widow who lived in a small room and mostly kept to herself. He broke in on July 19, surprising the woman in her bed. After raping her, he strangled her and beat her head in. He then followed the regimen he established in the first murder: waiting, snacking on food, and raping the corpse. Before leaving, he ransacked the place again, looking for anything of value.

Police noted a similarity in the crimes but soon lost interest as Jackson took a nine-month furlough in his killings. It is speculated that the presence of police in the building made him nervous, making him wait until the trail grew cold.

Sensing that the police were not onto him, he struck again at the small apartment of Mable Hartmeyer. After sneaking into the sixty-year-old widow's room, he raped and strangled her before repeating his wicked postmortem ritual. Before leaving, however, he did not ransack the room; he took only a few valuable items to make the room seem untouched.

The trick worked. Both police and the medical examiner determined the cause of death to be old age. They did not notice the missing items until family members of Mrs. Hartmeyer reported numerous items missing. The police called for the medical examiner to re-evaluate the body, at which point it was discovered that she had been raped. Upon closer examination, bruising around the neck indicated strangulation. The police now had a homicide.

Four days later, as the police were just discovering the previous death to be a homicide, he sprung again, killing seventy-nine-year-old Yetta Vishnefsky. After surprising her in her apartment, he bound her with her nylon stockings and then raped her. When finished, he changed his routine up a bit, stabbing her in the back with a large butcher knife. He then pilfered the room before violating the woman's corpse.

Frantic, police were now positive that the two latest murders might have a connection to the previous murders, but they did not see a uniform pattern. While the victims all died in a similar manner and all four corpses had been raped, the pattern of burglary was different. The first two apartments had been torn apart, while only a few items were missing in the second two. They tried to find any incriminating clues, hoping he would not strike again before the case was solved.

He struck again after a month-and-a-half break, killing four times in the summer months and leaving residents in the hotel terrified for their lives. Police reeled as murder after murder was committed, the killer always one step ahead of them. First it was Winifred Miller on June 8, then Blanche Vincent on June 19. After waiting a few weeks, he struck again, taking the life of Martha Campbell on July 1. Police were frustrated due to the lack of leads, and then he struck again for the last time in the hotel, killing sixty-four-year-old Eleanor Pratt on August 30, 1974. While they had not narrowed down a list of suspects, they were determined that the killer was a resident of the hotel.

On September 12, he struck for the final time. Due to the increased pressure by police and the fear and trepidation of residents, he struck outside the hotel for the first time. In a neighboring building known to house wealthy residents, he murdered Pauline Spanierman in her twelfth-story suite. After killing Spanierman and meticulously performing his ritual, he fled the scene carrying a television. A witness spotted him and reported it to police, giving an adequate description of what he looked like.

Police immediately began searching the building for a tenant with a description fitting Mrs. Spanierman's murderer. After knocking on Jackson's door, they noticed the television similar to the one they were seeking, and they felt they had their man. He was arrested and taken to the station for questioning. Thinking he was just responsible for the one murder, the police were surprised when he confessed to the eight murders in his hotel and two attempted murders. During the three-hour interview, he accurately described each murder and the items he had taken. [28]

Police were more than satisfied that Jackson was the serial killer for whom they had been looking. When they asked why he had committed these crimes, he told them that he heard voices instructing him to rape and murder. When asked if he still heard voices, he said yes.

At trial, the judge sent Jackson to a psychological evaluation based off his continued claims of listening to evil spirits. The evaluation returned to say that he was schizophrenic and delusional. Upon this recommendation, the jury issued a lessened sentence of four twenty-five-year sentences, in addition to one life sentence.

Prior to the trial, Jackson's girlfriend wrote letters to the prosecuting attorney claiming that her boyfriend was framed. Her claim was based off a letter which Jackson sent to her, claiming that police had forced a testimony out of him. When pressed, her story changed, alleging that Jackson had confessed to keep a friend from getting the rap. While the court system was not impressed by her ploy, she did manage to get the story published in a few black newspapers, trying to garner support that Jackson was a victim of racist, incompetent cops.

Jackson is currently in the Elmira maximum-security prison in New York. Originally, his earliest parole was set to be in 2030, but now, for reasons unknown to me, he will be eligible for parole in March of 2013 at the age of sixty-five.

Calvin Jackson's victims
1. Theresa Jordan, age 39, on April 10, 1973
2. Kate Lewisohn, age 65, on July 19, 1973
3. Mable Hartmeyer, age 60, on April 24, 1974
4. Yetta Vishnefsky, age 79, on April, 28, 1974
5. Winifred Miller, age 47, on June 8, 1974
6. Blanche Vincent, age 71, on June 19, 1974
7. Martha Carpenter, age 69, on July 1, 1974
8. Eleanor Platt, age 64, on August 30, 1974
9. Pauline Spanierman, age 69, on September 12, 1974

Milton Johnson (A Summer of Terror)

During the summer of 1983, the national media had its eyes fixed on the town of Joliet, IL, dubbing it the "Town of Terror." Joliet was a quiet town with a population at that time around 73,000. But in a two-month period, this quiet town was rocked by a string of fourteen brutal murders and two attempted murders as police were scrambling to sort through the evidence.

Just prior to the first set of murders, Milton Johnson had finished serving a thirteen-year sentence for raping and robbing an eighteen-year-old woman in Joliet's Pilcher Park. The parole board believed that Johnson was ready to be assimilated back into society and that he no longer proved a serious threat. He was released on March 9, 1983, ready to make a fresh start.

On June 25, two elderly sisters, who were also next-door neighbors, were found dead by firefighters responding to a fire call. Their assailant had shot both of them in the home where they had been raised, and then he doused their bodies with some form of accelerant and lit them on fire. The victims' families described the women, Zita Blum and Honora Lahmann, as two sweethearts who would do anything to help their friends and family.

When investigators arrived, they found that the home of Ms. Blum had been broken into, and that she had probably been taken by force to her neighboring sister's home. Upon arriving at the sister's home, they speculated that the assailant had shot Ms. Blum, the more passive of the two, in the stomach. Turning his attention to her feisty sister, he struck her in the head with a hammer repeatedly and then raped her with a turkey baster before fatally shooting her. After searching the home for valuables, he torched the bodies, which were burned beyond recognition and had to be identified by dental records.

While police were still baffled at the monstrosity of the crime, they were rocked again on July 2 with another double murder. In Milton Township, they found the bodies of Terri Lynn Johnson and Kenneth Chacellor. Mrs. Johnson had been raped and both had been robbed before the killer dumped the bodies.

Forty miles up the road, Chicago was one of the murder capitals of the country, but in Will County, murders were not nearly as common—especially not two double homicides within one week. Police investigated them as possibly being committed by different killers, but they did not rule out the possibility that they had been committed by the same person.

Two weeks after the last double homicide, a couple was talking while parked along the side of a road. A black male approached and shot both of them, killing them instantly, and he proceeded to rob them. While he was robbing the deceased Cathleen Norwood and Richard Paulin, two auxiliary sheriff's deputies pulled up to check on the parked car to see if they needed assistance. The killer was standing near the car, and he told the deputies his battery needed a jump.

Milton Johnson

As the officers exited their vehicle, the killer sprang from in front of the parked car and shot both of them, instantly killing Steven Mayer and fatally wounding Denis Foley, who would succumb to his wounds a month later. After shooting the officers, the killer tried to escape, but officer Foley, who was still coherent, managed to flag down a passing car. But as the car slowed, the killer turned and shot the passengers, killing the driver George Kiehl and seriously wounding the female passenger by shooting her six times. The killer fled the scene, stealing Deputy Mayer's gun and wallet and the valuables from the other murder victims.

Deputy Foley, who had been shot in the neck and the mouth, tried to radio for help, but because of severe trauma to his mouth and several missing teeth, his communication was garbled. He turned his siren and lights on to alert other deputies to his location. After a nearby farmer heard the sirens, he called the police, who quickly made it to the scene. Upon arriving, authorities were dismayed at the carnage they found, which they would later call the Homer Township Ambush. Police had no suspects aside from the one survivor's story that a black man had been the killer. They had hoped that Denis Foley would recover and shed some light on the killer's identity, but his health gradually faded as he lay in the hospital, and he passed away on August 17.

The day after the massacre, police had yet another murder on their hands. Eighteen-year-old Anthony Hackett and his date were returning from a carnival, and they had stopped on the side of the road to rest before returning home. At 1:30 in the morning on July 17, the couple was awakened by someone rapping loudly on the driver's window. As Anthony began to roll the window down, he was shot in the chest with a .357 magnum multiple times, and he died instantly. His date had been asleep in the back seat and was awakened by the gunshots. The killer demanded their valuables, and she complied in an attempt to save her life.

Not satisfied, the killer took the female and demanded that she get into the front of his dark truck. As the killer drove down the road, he sexually assaulted the young woman despite her attempts to push him away. Not satisfied and wanting more, he pulled over and raped her in the truck. After finishing, he drove a bit longer before stopping and stabbing her in the chest with a steak knife, narrowly missing her heart. He then took her body and dumped it on some rocks along the side of the road, thinking she was dead. An hour later, at 5:30, a passing car with two hunters on their way to an early morning hunt found her without a pulse and rushed her to the hospital. After emergency surgery, the woman's life was spared.

Police were beginning to think that the series of murders which had left a trail of death and destruction might be related. The only evidence they had, though, was that witnesses described a black male at a few of the crime scenes.

A month later, on August 20, the killer struck again for the final time. At a local Joliet ceramics shop, four women were brutally murdered. The killer visited the shop just after 11 A.M., demanded money, and forced the women to the rear of the shop. After getting a small sum, he then stabbed each woman between seven and fifteen times, and he shot the oldest woman once in the stomach.

At 11:30, two frequent customers came in, surprised to see the doors wide open but no one at the counter. As they called out for a shop attendant, they noticed what appeared to be a body lying in a pool of blood in a hallway leading to the rear of the shop. Horrified that the killer was still in the building, they quietly found a phone and called the police. The police arrived at the scene to find the bodies of Marilyn Baers, Barbara Dunbar, Anna Agnes Ryan, and Pamela Ryan, with no evidence of sexual assault. Investigators noted that the stab wounds were similar to those in the survivor of the July 17 attack, and that Anna Ryan had been shot with a .357 magnum, the same caliber used in the July 17 attack.

Police suspected that the two attacks might be related to each other and possibly to the other three unsolved attacks. They searched frantically for clues, but the case was stalled until February of 1984. A young woman told police about a dark pickup truck that had followed her and passed her numerous times while she was driving in July near the scene of one of the crimes, but she had managed to give the truck the slip. Yet before she turned, her passenger had managed to get the license plate number as the truck passed them for the final time. Acting on the tip, police traced the vehicle to Johnson's stepfather.

Police approached the owner of the truck about searching the vehicle. After signing a consent form, he agreed to let them have a look. Inside, they found hair samples matching the woman who had survived his attack on July 17, 1983. They also found a bloody knife, blood stains, and a receipt for a Tasmanian devil doll from Anthony Hackett's wallet. Convinced that Johnson was the killer, they obtained a search warrant for the house, where they found .357 magnum shell casings matching those found at the crime scenes.

On March 9, Johnson participated in a police lineup after one of the surviving witnesses picked his photo out of police mug shot photos. She positively identified Johnson as the man who had attempted to kill her and who had killed Anthony Hackett. Not only was she positive that he was the killer then, but she told a prison review board nineteen years later: "I know he did this thing. . . . I saw him. I saw him open the door to the car. He didn't know I was in the car. . . . I saw him when he raped me. I saw him when he stabbed me right below the heart."[29]

After this, investigators found additional ties to the evidence from the other murders. At the scene of the Homer Township Ambush, a receipt belonging to his stepfather had blown out of Johnson's truck as he fled the scene. While at the ceramic shop massacre, Johnson's fingerprints were found both in the shop and on Pamela Ryan's pickup. Additionally, there were eyewitness reports that he had been seen harassing women in his stepfather's truck that summer. With this body of evidence, a jury of his peers sentenced him to death for the murder of Anthony Hackett and the ceramic shop murders. Prosecutors felt no need at that time to pursue charges in the other murders due to the sentence awarded.

In a huge blow to the families of the victims, in 2000, Governor George Ryan commuted his sentence in a political move to commute all serving on death row in Illinois to life in prison. While still upset about this, the families were dealt another blow in 2002. On January 1 of that year, the Illinois State Supreme Court reversed charges in part for the murder of Anthony Hackett and demanded that a new trial take place. They based their decision, not on the testimony of the survivor of this attack, nor on the physical evidence found, but on two technicalities. First, Johnson's public defender did not handle himself right and made poor choices in his representation of Johnson. Secondly, because a rape kit performed on the attack survivor had not been analyzed to see it Johnson was proven as the attacker, the court believed that Johnson's rights had been violated.

Despite subsequent appeals by the families and additional attempts by Will County prosecutors to bring him to trial in the additional murders, to this date their attempts have been unsuccessful. Johnson is currently serving a life sentence in general population for the ceramic shop murders. Police are positive that he is responsible for fourteen murders, and they have speculated that he might be responsible for two additional murders which occurred between his last known murder and his capture.

Milton Johnson's victims
1.   Zita Blum, age 66, on June 25, 1983
2.   Honora Blum Lahmann, age 67, on June 25, 1983
3.   Terri Lynn Johnson, age 19, on July 2, 1983
4.   Kenneth Chacellor, age 34, on July 2, 1983
5.   Steven Mayer, age 22, on July 16, 1983
6.   Cathleen Norwood, age 25, on July 16, 1983
7.   Richard Paulin, age 32, on July 16, 1983
8.   George Kiehl, on July 16, 1983
9.   Denis Foley, age 50, shot on July 16, 1983, died on August 17, 1983
10. Anthony Hackett, age 18, on July 17, 1983
11. Marilyn Baers, age 45, on August 20, 1983
12. Pamela Ryan, age 29, on August 20, 1983
13. Anna Agnes Ryan, age 75, on August 20, 1983
14. Barbara Dunbar, age 38, on August 20, 1983

Milton Johnson's possible victims
15. Ralph Dixon, age 40, on August 21, 1983
16. Crystal Knight, age 25, on August 21, 1983

Derrick Todd Lee (The Baton Rouge Serial Killer)

In the early part of the new millennium, one of the largest serial killer investigations in recent history took place in Baton Rouge, LA. It involved numerous city, state, and federal officials and was possibly the most extensive since the Green River murders of Seattle. Hundreds of potential suspects submitted DNA, and the police investigated hundreds of leads.

From the onset, the investigation was focused on a white suspect, for they had been convinced that most serial killers were white. However, when an eyewitness account described a black male, some dismissed this information while others explored the possibility. Talk of a black suspect faded away after a witness described a white male driving with what she presumed was an unconscious female near the drop spot where some of the bodies had been found. Police refocused their efforts on searching for a white serial killer, and billboards were placed around the Baton Rouge area with a composite sketch of a thirty-five-year-old white man as the chief suspect.

The police in the small town of Zachary, a suburb of Baton Rouge, had a different theory. They had known of Lee for a while, calling him the towns pervert, for he had been arrested numerous times for peeping through women's windows. There were two unsolved murders in their town in the area where Lee had been peeping, and they were committed in the same time frame. From the onset they were

Derrick Todd Lee

convinced that Lee was connected, but they could never build a solid case. With the cases cold and Lee spending time in and out of jail for burglary, theft, assault and other petty crimes, investigators had nowhere to turn.

From 2001 to 2003, the self-described ladies' man, who women reported as charming, would go on to commit six proven murders and five probable murders. He raped the women in many of the cases, and there is evidence of necrophilia in three of them. He posed the ladies he killed within their homes, as if he was having fun with them. He dumped others, disposing of them as if they were garbage.

Lee was very violent with each of his victims. For Randi MeBruer, he hit her head against the kitchen floor so hard that both contact lenses popped out of her eyes. Geralyn De Soto was hit in the head with a telephone and then stabbed three times in the neck. She fought back, getting a shotgun in an attempt to kill Lee, but he was able to wrestle it out of her hands and slice her throat from ear to ear. He stomped her body numerous times after she was dead.

In his most violent murder, he beat twenty-one-year-old Charlotte Murray Pace and then stabbed her over eighty times. Not satisfied that she was dead, he beat her with a clothes iron before cutting her throat and nearly decapitating her. The scene was so horrible that it made the stomachs of veteran investigators turn.

In July 2002, investigators in the Baton Rouge area were scrambling for answers and trying to find the killer. They had all chips bet on a thirty-five-year-old white male. Zachary police investigators disagreed. At a special investigative meeting, they presented their reasons why the murders of Warner and Mebreur were linked to the Baton Rouge murders and why they had Lee pegged as the killer. They were told to go home by the FBI, since everyone knew the killer was white.

With the FBI and Baton Rouge investigators wasting their time searching for white males in pickups, Lee was still killing. His final two victims, Trineisha Dene Colomb and Carrie Lynn Yoder, were killed in the same violent fashion as his previous victims. Colomb had her head bashed in by a large tree branch, while Yoder was hit with such force she suffered broken ribs and a lacerated liver. DNA evidence at the scene linked their killer to the other four Baton Rouge murders.

In April 2003, the Zachary police received complaints from a woman who was being stalked on her morning jogs. Near her window were size ten or eleven boot prints. They believed that their peeping Tom was up to his old tricks again.

Zachary investigators put together a timeline of the thirteen murders they believed were connected and compared it to Lee's prison sentences. They noticed that he was free during all the murders. In their minds, he was the most viable suspect walking the streets. They informed the State of Louisiana's Attorney General that they wanted a DNA sample from Lee. A court order was issued to obtain it in early May of 2003.

With surveillance set up at Lee's girlfriend's apartment and his wife's home, the Zachary police waited to find their slippery suspect. On May 5, he was spotted at his wife's home. They confronted Lee, showing him the court order to obtain a cheek swab for his DNA. Despite his reluctance, Lee agreed to consent. On May 25, 2003, the results came back. Lee's DNA was a 100% match for the six Baton Rouge murders that had linked DNA. They had their man.

Despite having an IQ of 65 and being recognized as mildly retarded, Lee was smart enough to get out of town. Two days later, though, investigators found him holed up in a motel room in Atlanta, GA.

To date, Lee has not admitted to an exact number of murders he committed. Investigators are therefore reluctant to pin all of the fourteen murders on him without DNA evidence or a full confession. His DNA has matched him to six murders in Baton Rouge, and physical evidence has him as the murderer in both Zachary murders. Police also found rings he had taken from a number of the victims, including the two Zachary cases. Aside from this, that all his victims except two were white females and that he exhibited overkill on each one are other indicators. Perhaps the biggest indicator is that after his capture, the violent murders ceased.

Currently, Lee is awaiting execution in Louisiana while serving a life sentence.[30] Amnesty advocates are demanding that his death sentence be commuted based on his low IQ. So far, the Louisiana judicial system has made the right call, recognizing that Lee was fully aware of his activities and various criminal exploits.

Derrick Todd Lee's victims
1. Connie Warner, a white woman, was bludgeoned to death with a hammer. Her body was found in a ditch on August 23, 1992.
2. Randi MeBruer, a white woman, was raped, beaten, and stabbed in her home, close to Warner's murder, on April 18, 1998.
3. Gina Wilson Green, a white woman, was raped and strangled at home on September 23, 2001.
4. Geralyn De Soto, a white woman, was severely beaten and stabbed on January 14, 2002.
5. Charlotte Mary Pace, a white woman, was raped and stabbed to death on May 31, 2002.
6. Pamela P. Kinamore, a white woman, was raped, beaten severely, and stabbed in the neck. Her body was dumped in a river on July 12, 2002.
7. Trineisha Dene Colomb, a black woman, was raped and bludgeoned with a large stick. Her body was dumped in a field on November 21, 2002.
8. Carrie Lynn Yoder, a white doctoral student, was strangled to death. Her body was dumped in a river, the same location as Kinamore's, on March 3, 2003.

Derrick Todd Lee's possible victims

1. Eugenie Boisfontaine died of a skull fracture on June 14, 1997. She lived on the same street as Pace and Green, known victims of Lee. Items taken from her were similar to his other totems from known murders.
2. Mary Ann Fowler, a white woman, disappeared on December 24, 2002. She was kidnapped outside a nail salon, and video surveillance showed a truck similar to Lee's speeding from the scene. Her body has never been found.
3. Lillian Robinson disappeared; her remains were found at the same spot as Kinamore's and Yoder's on January 1, 2002. Her method of death matched Lee's MO.
4. Melinda McGhee was a thirty-one-year-old white woman abducted from her home in Atmore, AL. Lee is considered a suspect based on eyewitness reports of a truck similar to his speeding away after the abduction and the similarity of the crime. Her body has never been found.
5. Christine Moore was a black student whose skeletal remains were found on May 24, 2002. No DNA evidence has been found, but investigators noted some similarities to Lee's known crimes.
6. Glenn Tankersley was an older white man who was a known acquaintance of Lee. He disappeared in December 2002, and foul play is suspected. Authorities speculate that he had connected Lee to the murders, or Lee had confided in him concerning his crimes. This, they believe, may have led Lee to eliminate Tankersley.

Eddie Lee Mosley (The Rape Man)

If there is news of some prolific white serial killer who has murdered twenty or more victims, any news of his apprehension makes nationwide media for days, with the killer's face splashed across every newspaper in America. Stories from surviving victims are later covered, documentaries detailing the story are made, and the killer's name is etched in the minds of countless people for generations. However, unlike the Ted Bundys and John Wayne Gacys of the world, the story of Eddie Lee Mosley did not even make the cover of his hometown newspaper; as a result, he is one of the most prolific serial killers whom no one has ever heard of.

Eddie grew up in a large family, and his mother knew that something was wrong with her son early on. He did not cry much, and he acted placid as an infant. He would later perform poorly in school, getting stuck in third grade and dropping out illiterate at age thirteen. Due to his mental ineptness, his family decided to care for him for him until he was arrested for the final time at the age of forty. What they did not know, though, was that this mildly retarded young boy in a hulking, large adult body had by 1971 begun to leave a path of destruction in neighborhoods across Ft. Lauderdale.

From 1971 to 1973, there were 150 reports of sexual assault from neighborhoods in the vicinity of Mosley's residence, and the reports were increasing in frequency. Many were almost identical accounts. A large black man with a limp, a cane, and a large scar on his left cheek would lure a young black woman into a house or field with alcohol and drugs. After getting her fix, the man would beat and then rape the woman, oftentimes attempting to strangle her.

On July 23, 1973, a detective was driving three victims of the rapes around the neighborhood, hoping that they could point out possible suspects. When one of them spotted Mosley walking on the sidewalk with his trademark silver cane and descriptive limp, the other ladies became visibly nervous and confirmed he was their attacker.

After turning around the car, the detective radioed for backup from Detective Doug Evans, who was one of the first black police officers hired by the department. Before Evans arrived, Mosley stole down an alley, and was hidden somewhere behind an abandoned house.

Eddie Lee Mosley

When Evans arrived, Mosley was then spotted sneaking out from behind the house wearing a pair of panties on his head, as a sort of mock disguise. Officers told Mosley to drop the cane and halt, but he hesitated and looked as if he was going to run. One of the officers fired a warning shot over his head, which prompted Mosley to lie down and surrender. Later the officer would say that he regretted not shooting Mosley instead.

Detective Evans put Mosley in a police lineup, where he was positively identified by over forty women as their rapist. Police knew they had their man, but they were curious if he might have more heinous baggage to be discovered.

In 1973, the bodies of two young women had been discovered in the same area Mosley had haunted. Both women had been raped, beaten, and then strangled to death—the same pattern Mosley was known to have. However, in those days, detailed forensic science was not yet available, and police had no way of positively tying Mosley to the murders beyond circumstantial evidence.

Mosley stood trial for the rapes, but due to a judicial failing, he was only convicted for three rapes despite conclusive evidence in over forty cases. More disappointingly, the court found him innocent on grounds of insanity and had him sent to a psychiatric hospital for five years of treatment.

Mosley was released in February 1979 and was supposed to be a changed man. Yet within a matter of weeks, more bodies began to turn up around his home, and more women claimed that they had been raped by a large black man. Four bodies would turn up from June to August, all murdered in a similar matter to the two in 1973. Mosley was immediately considered, and he was tailed by Detective Evans on a daily basis. After Evans requested to interview Mosley, his parents refused and sent him to Lakewood, FL, to stay with his grandfather until things settled down.

In Lakewood, Mosley felt no police pressure and fell back into his rut. Neighbors reported him as chasing black women and even beating one on another occasion. In addition, during the few months he was there, two black women disappeared and were found dead months after Mosley was gone. Police in Lakewood, not knowing anything about Mosley, did not even consider him as a suspect until years later.

After returning back to Ft. Lauderdale, in a strange twist of events, police lost interest in him after the arrest of Jerry Frank Townsend. During an interview, Townsend had confessed to the four murders in 1979 and the two in 1973. Despite inconsistencies in his story and the inability to provide any detail of the crimes, his confession was enough to prosecute him. He even mumbled to investigators that he thought it could be as high as twenty-three but was not very good with numbers. He was convicted of the murders and sent to prison on the six charges. With the heat off, Mosley began to roam the streets again.

Detective Evans, since meeting Mosley in 1973, was convinced that they had the wrong guy and that Mosley was the killer. He told other investigators that if Townsend was the murderer, the killings would stop, but if he was not, then they would increase in number.

After Townsend's arrest in September 1979, the killings began again as three more bodies turned up, all raped and strangled. Evans suspected Mosley; other police officers accused him of having either tunnel vision or a vendetta against Mosley.

In April 1980, Mosley was arrested for sexual battery for beating and raping a woman in a field. He was tried and sentenced to fifteen years in prison.

Despite his sentence, Mosley was sent back to the Broward County jail, where he went through a series of mental evaluations. After spending three and a half years in the county jail, where the jail officials had used his large size to break up fights, he was released from jail with the court satisfied that he had done his time.

One of the numerous people to interview Mosley was Dr. John Spencer, who worked in the jail. The interviews were off the record, not a part of Mosley's therapy, and they were conducted numerous times per week over a nine-month period. As a result, Dr. Spencer determined that Mosley was a sociopath and that it would not be wise for him to be released from prison. In a later interview, he said: "I believe that Eddie Lee Mosley, by his history and by his clinical profile and presentation, poses a significant risk to our society. I just mean that he happens along like a shark swimming through the water, and when he comes across something edible, he eats it." Unfortunately, Dr. Spencer was not allowed to be interviewed when the court was considering Mosley's release.

Within a month of his release, bodies again began to turn up. Evans was convinced that Mosley was their man, but he could not garner any support within the department for his theory. In April 1984, Mosley was again arrested for sexual battery. It was during this time that his nickname in the neighborhood, "The Rape Man," became more popular, as there were claims of his having raped almost 300 women.

A court-appointed psychiatrist gave his opinion during the trial: "This gentleman, if released, will be of danger to society in the future and most definitely will be prone to commit future acts of sexual battery." Despite this, Mosley was found not guilty, because the accuser was found to be a prostitute. He was free yet again.

Mosley took no time to continue his practice of raping and killing women while he scoured the city in search for bottles and junk to earn a living. After two more bodies surfaced, police finally admitted that they might have a serial killer on their hands; they called the FBI for assistance.

By this time, Detective Evans, who had known more about Mosley than anyone else on the force, had been transferred out of the homicide unit as he got closer to retirement. However, a savvy young detective found Evans's file on Mosley and began to believe that Mosley was their man.

During this time, the FBI profilers made a description of what they thought the serial killer would be like. They posited that he would be an unmarried, middle-aged black man living in the area of the murder. He would be streetwise, a school dropout with a history of mental illness and below-average intelligence. They believed he would be a loner who walked the streets with a fondness for alcohol and drugs, and he would have no military experience. They suspected that he may have been questioned before regarding the allegations, and he would have denied them. His motivation was that he was irritable and impulsive before committing each crime, but he would feign illness if caught. This profile was a dead ringer for Mosley.

After reading the profile, the young detective took the theory of Evans to the joint task force investigating the murders. After he explained his findings in conjunction with the body of evidence found by Evans, the task force believed that Mosley might be their man.

The department made it their mission to find Mosley, and they put together a procedural method for officers if they encountered him. Within days, on May 17, 1987, Mosley had been arrested. He had been caught with a shopping cart full of potted plants in the vicinity of a greenhouse that had reported the theft of numerous plants.

Police did not tread lightly with him in interviews, but went straight for the jugular. After the first interview, which lasted five hours, Mosley knew numerous things about the murders about which they questioned him—from the clothing the victims were wearing, to the manner of death, and even to the location where the bodies were found. Concluding the interview, Mosley leaned back, raised his large hands, and said, "Well, I guess they got me."

After spending time with his court-appointed lawyers, Mosley would change his tune: "They takin' advantage of me 'cause I ain't got no understandin' and I ain't got no education."

Because of Mosley's prior history of mental illness, the court appointed numerous psychiatrists to evaluate his mental health. Their opinions came back varied: some claimed he was able to stand trial, while others claimed he was incapable of understanding his crimes. All were in agreement that his IQ was low (from 44 to 63) and that he was either mildly retarded or close to retardation.

Taking these findings, the court moved to dismiss charges, for they felt that Mosley was unaware of any wrongdoing and was not mentally able to comprehend the gravity of his crimes. They argued that he did not know right from wrong and ordered him to be shipped to a mental hospital for further evaluation. Shockingly, the court said that if Mosley were found to improve after five years and if no further evidence were presented against him, he could be released.

With that, Mosley disappeared into the state's mental hospital, having barely made a blip on even the local media radar. When the Ft. Lauderdale *Sun-Sentinel* was asked why they did not run their story,

"The 15-Year Search for a Serial Killer," on the front page, they answered that they did not want to highlight another black man doing bad things. A fuzzy zoo animal made the cover instead, while Mosley's story made the middle of the paper. As a result, Mosley was unknown to the general public.

In 2001, while Mosley was still in the state mental hospital, his name would again resurface. Police had been trying to solve numerous cold-case murders, and they had matched his DNA to eight sets of remains they had tested, including three which other men had allegedly committed. Reeling from the find, Mosley's name made national headlines since two innocent men had been convicted of his crimes.

Despite the attention, the media gave but a snippet of Mosley's crimes, claiming that he was suspected in only a dozen murders. The truth, however, is that the police had tied him to at least twenty murders and suspected him in at least thirteen more, in addition to over 300 rapes.

Upon the results of the DNA tests, the State of Florida moved to release Jerry Frank Townsend for the murders to which he had confessed. Police took the blame for believing his testimony, of which Evans had been critical, based off the fact that Townsend functioned at the level of an eight-year-old child. In the years after his release, he was awarded a $4.4-million joint settlement for spending over two decades in jail as a result of sloppy police work.

Justice did not come quickly enough for Frank Lee Smith, who was wrongfully accused for Mosley's murder of an eight-year-old girl. Just a year before the DNA results, Smith had passed away from cancer while sitting on death row.

To date, DNA has solidly indicted Mosley on ten murders, while physical and circumstantial evidence has tied him to at least ten additional murders. Police believe, however, that he is guilty of thirty-three murders that occurred near his home. He is currently a permanent patient at the Florida State Hospital in Chattahoochee, FL, where he will probably remain the rest of his life without facing trial for any of his crimes.

Shortly before Detective Evans passed away in 2011, he did a series of interviews about his career and his role in Mosley's case. He told reporters, "Mosley was bigger than Gacy. Bigger than Bundy. But he wasn't doing college girls. And he wasn't hiding the corpses under his house. He was doing it in neighborhoods where nobody cared."[31] In his older age, Detective Evans became critical of the department, for he felt that the murders were ignored because they happened in black neighborhoods with black victims, many of whom were prostitutes. He also maintained to his death that he recognized Mosley was mental challenged, but he affirmed that Mosley knew full well what he had done—that he was putting on an act for the authorities.[32]

Eddie Lee Mosley's known victims
1. Naomi Gamble, age 15, in 1973
2. Thelma Jean Bell, age 20, in 1973
3. Vetta Turner, age 34, in 1973
4. Barbara Brown, age 21, on August 26, 1973
5. Terry Jean Cummings, age 19, on August 7, 1979
6. Ernestine German, age 23, on June 30, 1979
7. Sonjia Yvette Marion, age 13, on July 27, 1979
8. Cathy Lorraine Moore, age 24, found on August 2, 1979
9. Ida Ingles, age 22, in August 1979
10. Letha Mae Williams, age 21, in 1979
11. Susan Boynton, on December 24, 1979
12. Arnette Tukes, age 19, on February 22, 1980
13. Cynthia Maxwell, on March 10, 1980
14. Gloria Irving, age 16, in March 1980
15. Geraldine Barfield, age 35, on December 19, 1983
16. Emma Cook, age 54, on December 25, 1983
17. Loretta Young Brown, age 29, in November 1984
18. Teresa Giles, age 22, on December 18, 1984
19. Shandra Whitehead, age 8, on April 18, 1985
20. Santrail Lowe, age 24, on February 24, 1987

Cleophus Prince, Jr. (The Claremont Killer)

Having been discharged from the Navy in January of 1990, Prince quickly set out to kill his first known victim, twenty-year-old Tiffany Schultz, in her own apartment. In what would become his ritual, he tortured her, stabbed her numerous times, and traced a circle of blood around her breasts with his finger. Before leaving the scene, he took a piece of jewelry from the victim as his souvenir.

This same pattern was repeated five more times with white wo-men who lived in the same building as he did or, as in the case of his final two victims, with women he had seen at a health club. Each time he would stalk his victim without her knowing and detail her moves in a search for any weakness. Once he suspected that her guard was down, he broke into her home, grabbed a knife out of the kitchen, and swooped in for the kill.

These murders happened in a nine-month period and provoked the largest manhunt in Los Angeles history. Women in the vicinity of the killings were terrified as police scrambled to find the killer, but they searched in vain for a white suspect.

Cleophus Prince

After having a cooling-down period in which he committed over twenty burglaries, he made his last attempt at murder again. In February 1991, he attempted to break into the home of a woman he had followed from the health club. As she was about to step into the shower, she heard him trying to get in the door. She escaped through a window and called the police. Quick to the scene, police arrested him and asked him to come back to the station for questioning.

At the station, he consented to giving both blood and saliva sam-ples to compare to those found at the six murder sites. After a few days, the results came back conclusive that his DNA was present in his murder of Janene Weinhold, his only victim whom he also raped. Police were confident that he was the killer in all six of the cases based off the similarity of the crimes and their close proximity. Ironically, he had already been questioned after the death of the third woman, but police let him go thinking that he was not responsible.

After he was tried, it took the jury just one day of deliberation to recommend a death sentence. The family pled with the judge not to issue the death sentence but instead to grant him life. The judge disagreed and upheld the sentence.[33] Prince currently denies any wrongdoing but awaits his death in San Quinton.

Cleophus Prince, Jr's victims
1. Tiffany Shultz, age 20
2. Janene Weinhold, age 21
3. Holly Tarr, age 18
4. Elissa Keller
5. Pamela Clark, age 42
6. Amber Clark, age 18

George Waterfield Russell, Jr. (The Charmer, East Side Killer, or Bellevue Killer)

Russell is not stereotypical of black serial killers. He was raised in an affluent suburb of Seattle, WA, known for its upper-class Caucasian neighborhood. In school, he was a gifted student, known to have a higher-than-average IQ and a gift for persuasive speech. But, despite his seemingly good upbringing and home environment, his propensity for criminal behavior began at a young age. His first crimes begin in his formidable teen years and consisted of petty theft and breaking and entering. By age sixteen he had begun to dabble with both prescription and illegal drugs, having been caught numerous times by his stepfather and police.

By age seventeen, Russell began threatening kids he knew with a knife and "borrowing" their cars at knifepoint. Soon after his eighteenth birthday, he was charged with five connected felonies revolving around burglaries. After serving thirty-nine days in jail, he was set free.

From the ages of eighteen to twenty-eight, Russell spent his time burglarizing homes and stealing cars in the Seattle area. At this time he was also a police informant on numerous occasions, living out his dream of being a police officer by giving tips on drug dealers and other thieves. Notably, his white stepmother, whom he had tried to rape when he was sixteen, defended his thievery by blaming his behavior on his biological mother's leaving him when he was a teenager.

As a young man Russell had been shy towards females, not expressing interest in them. But at some point during his twenties, he began having sex with young children. In 1986, after a lengthy relationship with a fourteen-year-old girl in which they both spoke of being married forever, she became pregnant. Soon afterward, she had an abortion and Russell was arrested for theft and selling alcohol to minors.

After serving seven months in prison, Russell began his criminal activity again. He was hired by an arcade in 1988, but he was fired after it was found that he had skimmed over $23,000 from arcade machines. He later committed a string of over sixty burglaries in the Kirkland area and spent the next year in and out of trouble.

On June 22, 1990, he committed his first murder at the upscale Black Angus restaurant on Mercer Island. Mary Ann Pohlreich, a thirty-seven-year-old white woman, had been raped and then strangled outside the eatery. After engaging in necrophilia with the victim's body and beating it, he then posed the body. The authorities found the body nude and lying prone, with her arms crossed as if in a coffin and with a pinecone underneath her hands. A plastic top was placed over one eye, and one of her rings was kept as a totem. This symbolism has never been decoded or understood by authorities.

A little over a month later, Russell struck again. His victim was a thirty-five-year-old white woman, Carol Marie Beethe. He assaulted her, raped her, and killed her in her home as her two children slept. Her thirteen-year-old daughter discovered her body and called the police. Upon arrival, police determined that the manner of death was blunt trauma to her head. After killing her, Russell performed necrophilia, bit her several times on her arms, and kicked her torso numerous times. When police arrived on scene, they were horrified. They found the victim nude and lying on a bed with her head wrapped in plastic and covered with a pillow. Her legs were spread towards the door and a shotgun was shoved deep into her vagina in another one of Russell's hidden messages.

Police began to believe that the two murders were connected, but they did not have a suspect. Citizens of the tiny affluent island were terrified and hoped that they would not be the next victim.

On August 31, he struck again. This time, his victim was another white woman, twenty-seven-year-old Andrea Levine. After raping her, he killed her by stabbing her over 250 times. He then bashed her skull in and proceeded to perform his normal routine of necrophilia. He then posed the nude victim to be reading a book, *The Joy of Sex*, and shoved a sex toy into her mouth.

Thirteen days after the last murder, police had their man in custody. A DNA test was performed, and he was a positive match for the murders. In addition to this, police found several books and articles about Ted Bundy in his room. Despite the DNA evidence and what appeared to be a fascination with serial killing, Russell still denies any role in the murders.[34] Because of his crimes, he was sentenced to life without chance for parole.

George Waterfield Russell's victims
1. Mary Ann Pohlreich
2. Carol Marie Beethe
3. Andrea Levine

Lemuel Warren Smith

Born in 1941 in the sleepy town of Amsterdam, NY, to pro-fessing Christian parents, Smith seemed to have a good childhood. But all that would change at age ten, when something would snap in him. From the ages of ten to seventeen, he began stalking girls his age. On occasion he would kiss them, touch them, and even rape a few of them. Coinciding with these events was the emergence of what psychologists claim were two violent personalities separate from his normal happy-go-lucky personality.

On October 21, 1958, his chasing of girls took a turn for the worse. At the age of sixteen, he robbed Dorothy Waterstreet, a quiet, married mother of one, and then beat her to death near his home. Officials found the body the next day. The small town was in shock, as this sort of crime had never happened. Police were quick to round up Smith for questioning based off accounts that he was in the area at the time. Police were certain that he was the killer, but charges were dropped due to a technicality.

The daughter of Mrs. Waterstreet would later say, after Smith's confession of killing five white people, that had Smith been executed for her mother's death, four more lives would have been spared. The New York justice system failed the victims and their families, however, by letting Smith walk.

Following the dropped charges, he began a life of crime: raping and assaulting women, robbing homes and spending time in and out of prison. In 1959, he was sentenced to twenty years in prison for the assault of a white female. He would later admit that in prison he enjoyed homosexual activities to fulfill his violent sexual appetite.

Lemuel Warren Smith

After his release from a second stint in prison in 1976, he proved that the rehabilitation of violent criminals is a joke. Within a few weeks after his release, he struck again. On the day before Thanksgiving of 1976 in Albany, NY, in the back of a religious store, he killed the proprietor and his secretary in a brutal fashion. He slew Robert Hedderman and Margaret Byron, both well-respected citizens in their community. Police found hair, blood, and feces samples at the scene that would later prove to be vital evidence. Because of the proximity of Smith's job to the store, he was a suspect.

Police were still investigating the double homicide when he struck again on December 23, 1976. Police found the mutilated body of Joan Richburg, raped and mutilated in a fashion similar to the two murders one month prior. Police noted the kill pattern and the matching hair samples found on the body. Smith became their chief suspect, but he remained free pending the results of a formal investigation.

While investigators were still trying to pin the crimes on Smith, he struck again. On January 10, 1977, he tried to lure an attractive young woman out of a gift shop. When she refused, he held her grandmother hostage, threatening to shoot her in the head. Help arrived quickly, so he threw the elderly woman down and broke her hand by stomping on it before he fled the scene.

He would not strike again until summer. On July 21, 1976, he kidnapped, raped and then severely mutilated his fifth victim, Maralie Wilson, a shy and attractive young woman. The cause of death was strangulation; the mutilation occurred postmortem. Investigators noted that it was the worst mutilation they had ever seen in their town.

Within days, police were looking for Smith, who was the only suspect in their minds. Witnesses had seen a large black man who fit the description harassing Ms. Wilson prior to her death. Again, the hair and blood evidence from the scene matched the three prior Albany murders.

On August 19, 1977, police got their man. He had kidnapped an eighteen-year-old woman and had raped her severely. But instead of killing her, he had her drive him into Albany. A vigilant officer spotted the car and felt something was wrong. Upon seeing the condition of the young woman and after recognizing Smith, he arrested him without incident.

Police began comparing Smith's hair with hair samples found, and they had a match. Then they compared his bite pattern with bite marks found on two of his victim's faces. Again, they had a positive match. Smith still would not confess, though.

In their last attempt to break Smith, they took him and four other suspects to a nearby football field. After placing each suspect behind a cloth barrier, they let a trained dog get the scent of the killer from the feces-stained clothing found at the double homicide. Three separate times, the dog found Smith without even considering the other suspects. He finally broke, confessing to all four Albany murders and (to their surprise) to the murder of Mrs. Waterstreet in Amsterdam.

The trial was quick, but the conviction was far from adequate. Instead of seeking the death penalty on a first-degree murder charge for each crime, the court sought the more lenient second-degree murder charge, giving him a sentence of fifty years to life in prison for only four of his murders. The jury was convinced that the murders happened in the heat of the moment as a result of the assault, rather than being premeditated. This was in spite of evidence that he had stalked his victims for weeks in advance to learn their movements, and despite that he kept a murder weapon on him during the assault.

Smith's last murder occurred while in prison in 1981. He had been watching a white female prison guard, Donna Payant, for weeks as she did her job. On May 15, he attacked her in an isolated part of the prison, raped her, and then strangled her to death. He then mutilated her body almost beyond recognition and dumped it in a trash dumpster.

For this crime, Smith was sentenced to death on a charge of first-degree murder. This, however, would not stick. A year after his conviction, his appeals lawyer (who, during the trial, had concocted a faulty theory that Payant had instead lured him with offers of sex) also argued the state's death penalty law was unconstitutional. The appeals court, much to the chagrin of the victims' families and the three women he tried to kill, agreed and commuted his sentence to life in prison.[35] He is currently enjoying life at Five Fingers Correctional Facility in upstate New York, awaiting his eligibility for parole on February 19, 2029.

Lemuel Warren Smith's victims
1. Dorothy Waterstreet
2. Robert Hedderman
3. Margaret Byron
4. Joan Richburg
5. Maralie Wilson
6. Donna Payant

Anthony Edward Sowell (The Cleveland Strangler)

In 2009, the city of Cleveland was rocked by the discovery of two black serial killers who had lived just a few miles from one another but prowled the same streets. One of them, Joseph Harwell, was already behind bars for a murder he committed in 2007, but he would have an additional two murders (plus at least four others of which he is suspected) added to his tally. The other killer, Anthony Sowell, would eclipse Harwell's total and prove to be far more sinister in his crimes.

Having grown up in the Cleveland area, Anthony Sowell lived a normal life but complained of abuse by his mother. Tired of his rough home life, he signed up for the Marines at the young age of seventeen and was shipped off to boot camp soon afterward. After serving seven years, he was honorably discharged, having received numerous awards for his service.

His first serious conviction popped up in 1989. After inviting a three-months-pregnant friend over for some drinks, he overpowered her, bound her hands, and gagged her mouth. He then proceeded to rape her numerous times before trying to strangle her to death. Thankfully, his attempt was interrupted, sparing the woman's life. He was later convicted of the crimes, and served a prison sentence until his release in June 2005.

Anthony Sowell

After his release, a report evaluating his danger to society was performed to determine if he would likely be a repeat sexual offender. On September 1, 2005, officials concluded that it was unlikely that Sowell would commit further crimes.

In December 2008, Sowell invited a woman he had met at a corner store over to his home to have some drinks, but she declined. Sowell responded by punching her in the face, knocking her off her feet. He then dragged her back to his home and demanded that she strip off her clothes. The woman, however, escaped his house, ran down the street, and saw a police car. She alerted the officers as to what happened. Sowell was arrested that night on attempted rape and robbery charges, but the woman, fearing for her life, declined to press charges. In Sowell's later murder trial, she would confess that she saw the decapitated corpse of one of Sowell's victims in one of the rooms, but she was frightened for fear of her own life. She thought it best to forget what had happened.

On September 22, 2009, police had stopped by Sowell's home to make sure he was still living at the address listed on his sex offender rap sheet. Little did they know that events would unfold later to shed light on one of Cleveland's darkest secrets.

Later in the afternoon of the 22nd, Sowell invited over a woman he knew to drink four malted beverages and to smoke crack cocaine. After arriving at his home, he escorted her to a second-story room which was dark and empty except for a lone chair, a blanket, and an extension cord. She had a sick feeling in her stomach as the smell of death lingered in the air, but she shook it off as jittery nerves.

After finishing a few drinks, she said that Sowell became angered at her and punched her in the face. He then took the extension cord and began to strangle her at the same time he was raping her. She passed out but Sowell continued to ravage her lifeless body. When she awoke in the empty room, she feared that Sowell was going to kill her. She pled for her life, promising not to tell anyone what happened, even offering to pay money if he let her go. For reasons unknown, he decided to let her go.

The victim did not go straight to police, however; she waited for almost a month before telling them what happened. On October 29, 2009, police went to Sowell's home with a warrant for his arrest, but he was not home. Peering through the windows, they noticed two lifeless and deteriorated bodies in the living room. After gaining access, they called for investigators to come help scour for clues about the bodies.

When investigators arrived on the scene, they took to the task of going through the house, looking for any clues to the women's deaths. After searching further, they found the decayed remains of four additional women throughout the home, including one buried in a shallow grave in the basement and others in the crawlspace.

They located Sowell two days later, and he was arrested and charged with the deaths of six unidentified women. Within days, they found three more bodies buried in his backyard and the remains of a fourth. The last victim found was nothing more than a skull located in a bucket inside the house, which brought the tally up to eleven victims.

The remains were analyzed as police pored over missing person reports to determine the identity of Sowell's victims. By November 5, they started to make progress as two victims were identified; and over the next few months, police were able to identify all the victims. They were all black women from the area surrounding Sowell's home.

In August of 2011, Sowell's case went to trial. He at first denied any official involvement and proclaimed his innocence. Yet just after his arrest, when police asked him about the bodies, he told them, "I guess I did that." Despite his failure to remember his role in the murders, the evidence was stacked against him—as were the two chief witnesses, the women he had attempted to kill in 2008 and 2009.

After a short trial, the jury deliberated and recommended a sentence of death. Prior to their deliberation, the judge had allowed Sowell to take the stand for almost thirty minutes in an off-the-record talk about his childhood. Despite his insistence on having a rough childhood, and despite his attorney's pleas for the jury to be easy due to his service record, the jury and judge were unmoved. Sowell was sentenced to death with an execution date set in October of 2012.

The only words Sowell said concerning his crimes were revealed in his closing statements on the stand: "The only thing I wanna say is I'm sorry. I know that may not sound like much. But I am truly sorry from the bottom of my heart. I don't know what happened, it's not typical of me. I can't explain it, but I know it's not a lot, but it's all I can give you."[36]

On December 6, 2011, Anthony Sowell's home, known as the "House of Horrors," was demolished while the victims' families were gathered across the street to watch. Sounds of celebration were shouted as the machines made short work of Sowell's wicked halls of death.

Police in numerous states are currently investigating murders in areas where Sowell lived between prison sentences and after his military release. Also, Cleveland has forty-six unsolved murders from around Sowell's neighborhood with which he might possibly be connected. Like most serial killers, he has admitted only to whatever crimes for which evidence has condemned him; he has denied committing other murders, but that may change.

Anthony Sowell's victims
1. Crystal Dozier, age 38, in October 2007
2. Tishana Culver, age 31, in June 2008
3. Leshanda Long, age 25, in August 2008
4. Michelle Mason, age 45, in October 2008
5. Tonia Carmichael, age 52, in December 2008
6. Nancy Cobbs, age 43, in April 2009
7. Amelda Hunter, age 47, in April 2009
8. Telacia Fortson, age 31, in June 2009
9. Janice Webb, age 49, in June 2009
10. Kim Yvette Smith, age 44, in July 2009
11. Diane Turner, age 38, in September 2009

Edward Arthur Surratt (The Shotgun Killer)

The quiet farming communities that lie on both sides of the Ohio and Pennsylvania border, just on the outskirts of Pittsburgh, PA, were rocked by a series of violent murders in the late 1970s. In an area where farmers, miners, and steel workers were accustomed to leaving their doors unlocked, gun sales skyrocketed as people feared that they might be the next victim.

Edward Surratt

On September 20, 1977, the killer struck his first target. In the sleepy township of Beaver, just south of Youngstown, OH, the Hamilton family had turned in for the night. David, a young father of two, was up late watching television when Surratt knocked at the door just before 1 A.M. After answering the door to a man with a gun, David turned to run but was struck in the back of the head and each shoulder with a .38 caliber bullet. His children would find him dead the next morning. Awakened by the sound of gunshots, David's wife Linda ran into the kitchen and screamed at the sight of his dead body on the floor. Before she could react, Surratt grabbed her and stole off into the night with her as his hostage. Police responding the next day found no trace of her and assumed that she was David's killer. Nearly three decades later, Surratt would confess to murdering both victims and hiding Linda's body in a place he described as unrecoverable.

A week later, Surratt struck again forty-five miles away in Marshall Township, PA; his victim was Frank Ziegler. Ziegler had been taking milk from his farm to the local milk cooperative when he pulled over to the side of the road to take a nap. As he slept, Surratt opened the door of the truck and shot Ziegler point-blank in the head. Police suspected Linda Hamilton as the murderer, because the bullet matched those found in her husband. Police, however, quickly dismissed this theory when other crimes began happening in the area.

On September 30, Katherine Weinman was dressing a bedsore on her husband Joseph, who had been disabled in the Vietnam War. As Joseph lay on a cot, Surratt bolted through the door, surprising the Weinmans, and struck Joseph on the head with a five-pound sledgehammer to knock him out. Katherine ran, but she was caught by the faster Surratt. Joseph regained his consciousness and wheeled himself to a closet to grab a shotgun. Surratt got to him first and bashed his head in with multiple blows of the sledgehammer. Katherine ran outside, but Surratt caught her in the driveway, where he raped her. He then stabbed her eleven times in the face and chest with a butcher's knife, and for good measure he sliced her throat. Their children, who had hidden under a bed in fear of their lives, found them the next morning and called police.

Police were dismayed by the intensity of the Weinman murders; never had such brutality been seen in this quiet town. After interviewing neighbors in the area, they put together pieces that a prowler had been in the area peering into windows late at night. Horrified, neighbors kept their doors locked and were on edge.

It would be nearly a month later before the killer struck again, this time in the peaceful township of Findlay, about twenty miles southwest of Marshall. John Feeny, a seventeen-year-old student, had borrowed his parents' van to drive his fifteen-year-old girlfriend. Soon after they arrived at a desolate place in the country, Surratt surprised the young couple by opening the driver's door to the van. Young Feeny was shot in the chest with a 12 gauge shotgun, killing him instantly. His girlfriend, Ranee Ann Gregor, was then taken by Surratt to an unknown place to be raped and murdered. Her body has never been recovered.

It would be almost three weeks until the killer struck again on November 10, this time back in Beaver Township, which lay roughly fifty miles to the northwest of Findlay. John J. Davis had just awoken and was hoping to have a great day celebrating his sixty-fourth birthday with his wife. As they finished their morning coffee, a knock at the door changed their humble plans. After opening the door, John received a point-blank shotgun blast to his eye, killing him before he hit the floor. Surratt then chased his sixty-one-year-old wife Mary to the bedroom, where he stripped her and raped her on the couple's bed. He then shot her in the chest with his 12 gauge. Surratt then posed Mary's nude body to be spread eagle on the bed and shot the couple's dog. Before leaving, he doused the bodies with gasoline and lit the house on fire. After the fire was extinguished, only then did authorities realize that they had another horrific murder on their hands.

Just across the state line, the killer would strike in Beaver County on November 20. In the tiny borough of Fallston, Surratt surveyed the home of William Adams's family, looking for the right moment to strike. Finding his opportunity, he knocked on the family's door sometime in the middle of the night. Answering their door, William Adams was shot in the chest at close range with a 12 gauge shotgun. Surratt then kidnapped his wife Nancy. When police arrived, Nancy was gone with no trace of a struggle; her keys and purse were undisturbed. Fearing the worst, police began an intensive search for her and her captor. Her remains were found eight years later in a nearby park, where her killer had raped her before shooting her.

Just twenty miles south in the old town of Moon, PA, Surratt struck again on December 3rd. Police received a phone call by the young daughters of Richard and Donna Hyde, saying that something bad had happened to their parents. Upon arriving, police found the two scared girls huddled in the living room, their father dead on the kitchen floor from a shotgun blast. Their mother was missing, but the girls were positive that a black man had kidnapped her. Police later found her body under a patch of small pine trees, where she was nude from the waist down and had been beaten to death with a tree branch. There was no sign of rape; they theorized that barking dogs nearby had frightened the killer off.

At the Hyde residence, police found a spent shotgun shell which later matched the shell found at the Adamses' home. Police also suspected that other deaths in the area and in Ohio might be connected based on the similar patterns and manner of death. They began to label the killer as the "Shotgun Killer," after his favorite weapon of choice.

Things remained quiet for almost a month before the killer turned up in the unincorporated town of Breezewood, PA, known for decades as the town of motels just off the Pennsylvania Turnpike. On December 31, a couple noticed a black man peering in their window, but he fled upon being discovered. The couple did not feel it necessary to notify police, so they went back to their New Year's celebrations. Surratt then went to their neighbor's home, where the occupants did not take notice of him. After knocking on the door, Surratt shot Guy Mills point-blank with a shotgun in the chest. He then walked into the house, heading towards the sounds of Guy's wife Laura as she tried to hide in a back room. After finding her, he shot her in the chest, killing her instantly. But having not satisfied his thirst for death, Surratt then found Joel Drueger at a rest stop four miles away. While the weary traveler rested, Surratt shot him in the chest with a shotgun and fled the area.

Police in Bedford County were baffled at the three New Year's Eve murders, wondering what kind of monster had wrought this harm. Going off a tip, they ran the tag for a car which witnesses had noticed was parked among semi-trucks at an abandoned gas station. The car was owned by Edward A. Surratt of Aliquippa, PA; he instantly became their chief suspect.

After researching everything they could find on Surratt, they discovered that he was a long-distance truck driver and had been a garbage man for years. Every murder was either near a garbage dump or near a route that Surratt took on his trucking hauls. Police noticed the pattern and were convinced that Surratt was their man, but they needed more evidence. What little physical evidence they had from the crime scenes was a few hairs in the hands of one of his victims that matched a black man.

Bedford County learned that police investigating the other murders had drawn up a psychological profile of the killer. They suspected the killer of having combat experience, possibly a Vietnam veteran. They also surmised that he was of above-average intelligence, in his mid-thirties, white, and probably divorced. For an occupation, they reckoned that he was in the trucking business in some capacity. Surratt fit every bit of the profile except for the race, which was based on the fact that all victims had been white.

When considering his criminal record, it seemed to fit nicely with the profile and what they already knew of Surratt. Though he did not have a record of murder, he did have a lengthy record that included theft, loitering, assault, and rape. In 1973, soon after he had returned from Vietnam, he had been convicted of sodomizing a thirteen-year-old boy in Virginia Beach, VA. Serving three years, he was released just prior to committing his first murder. They suspected that he had developed murderous thoughts in prison and then carried his plans out after his release.

Police began an intensive search for Surratt, hoping he would not murder again. But on January 7, 1978, he did murder again, marking his first murder of the year. As John Shelkons watched TV in his quaint Baden, PA, home, Surratt snuck into the basement and up the stairs. Hearing the sound of footsteps, John opened the basement door to be met with a blast from a shotgun. His wife, who was asleep on the couch, was awakened by the commotion and saw a man with a bandana over his mouth. He told her to keep quiet and to come with him. She refused and ran for the phone, but he tackled her and began beating her and kicking her in the face, after which he stopped and ran. The couple's daughter had pulled into the driveway, which frightened the intruder away.

Confident that Surratt had committed this murder just outside his hometown, they questioned the badly beaten woman. She was in such shock from the attack that she could only remember bits and pieces and could not identify her attacker. When asked to describe him, she said she thought he might be a white guy. This deflated the detective's hopes of pinning it on Surratt; they were no closer to apprehending him.

Police looked for Surratt for the next three months, but the radar was quiet, not even giving a blip. Some investigators and the media were convinced that the unknown serial killer was a white man and not Surratt. Yet on March 27, 1978, he again showed up on their radar. After breaking into the home of seventy-year-old Katherine Flicky, he struck in a brutal fashion. Grabbing a skillet from the kitchen, he beat the elderly woman to death. After finishing, he removed her clothing and placed her body in a tub full of water, only to drain it a short time afterward.

After arriving on scene, police discovered that the killer was trying to destroy evidence from the murder. They began a detailed sweep of the crime scene, looking for any incriminating evidence. They found the hairs from a black male in the bathroom and in the kitchen. After speaking with the woman's friends and family, they discovered that she did not have any black friends. They also discovered that Surratt had been pulled over less than a mile from the house on the day of the murder for a traffic violation. The officer had not known Surratt was a suspect, so he let him go.

Police again began to think Surratt was the killer, and they continued the frantic search for him, but he disappeared. Police sought the help of his wife, explaining to her that they believed her husband was a killer responsible for most of the eighteen murders in the area over the last six months. She agreed to help.

On June 1, 1978, Luther Langford, a sixty-six-year-old retiree, was found murdered in his home in West Columbia, SC. He had been shot to death, and his wife, who was near death, had been bludgeoned with a heavy object. Police noticed their car was missing and put out an alert for the vehicle.

Just days later, Surratt's wife notified police that he had shown up with a car with South Carolina plates, and he felt it necessary to park it at the nearby steel mill to avoid suspicion. After running the plates, they realized that it was the missing car of Luther Langford, tying Surratt conclusively to the murder.

On June 6, deputies had been staked out at the steel mill, waiting for Surratt to return to retrieve the car. That night, they got their chance. After surprising Surratt, they told him to get on the ground, but instead he ran. After an intense chase, he lost them in the dark of the night. Officers were unclear as to which way he had gone; the one thing they knew is that Surratt was well-acquainted with the area, having grown up playing in the various tunnels and ditches. Despite differing theories over which way he had gone, the trail was cold; the police searched the night in vain. Some suggested that he had drowned in the river, and police searched the riverbanks the next day for his body.

Officers disagreed as to how long Surratt had stayed in the area, but they all agreed that he had eventually fled the area to parts unknown. Less than a month later, he popped up again, but far from the area—in sunny North Beach, FL. He had broken into the home and surprised the three occupants, a couple and their eighteen-year-old daughter. Wielding a 7mm Mauser rifle, he bound each person up with an electrical cord. After raping the man's wife and daughter repeatedly in front of the distraught man, Surratt downed a bottle of wine and smoked pot. In his drug-induced stupor, he passed out naked on the bed before he had a chance to kill his victims.

While Surratt slept, the man freed himself from his wraps and escaped with the rifle. He crept out to a neighbor's home to notify police. When police arrived, neighbors were holding the man, who wished to kill Surratt, preventing him from re-entering his home. Surratt was arrested without struggle and put into jail.

Surratt had finally been caught, but the Florida officers did not know who he was or understand the evil he had committed. After three days, they were able to identify him based on an FBI description of Surratt. They contacted officials in the states where Surratt was suspected of committing murders.

Surratt was tried in Florida for the rapes of the two women, where he was given a life sentence. For his crimes in South Carolina, he was given another life sentence to be fulfilled after his time in Florida. Despite the evidence tying him to the murders in Ohio and Pennsylvania, he steadfastly denied any knowledge of the murders. Police were positive that he was involved, but he was not talking.

It would be thirty years before he began to talk, in a plea to try to leave the Florida prison system for South Carolina. Over numerous interviews, he gave the details of the crimes, eventually confessing to a total of nineteen murders. When asked where the bodies of Linda Hamilton and Ranee Gregor were disposed, Surratt told the interviewer that the bodies were unrecoverable by anyone's standards. After this conversation, he closed up and refused to give any additional information unless he was transferred to South Carolina.

Surratt still sits in a Florida prison where he refuses to tell of the location of the two missing victims' bodies. He claims that if he gets transferred to South Carolina, he will give more information. Despite unsuccessful attempts to pin other murders on him from the time period, officials are still curious if there are additional murders to which he might eventually confess, ones he committed while he was on the road as a trucker.[37]

Arthur Edward Surratt's victims
1. David A. Hamilton, on September 20, 1977
2. Linda Hamilton, on September 20, 1977
3. Frank Ziegler, on September 27, 1977
4. Joseph Weinman, on September 30, 1977
5. Katherine Weinman, on September 30, 1977
6. Ranee Ann Gregor, on October 22, 1977
7. John Feeny, on October 22, 1977
8. John J. Davis, on November 10, 1977
9. Mary Davis, on November 10, 1977
10. William Adams, Jr., on November 20, 1977
11. Nancy Adams, on November 20, 1977
12. Richard Hyde, on December 3, 1977
13. Donna Hyde, on December 3, 1977
14. Guy Mills, on December 31, 1977
15. Laura Mills, on December 31, 1977
16. Joel Drueger, on December 31, 1977
17. John J. Shelkons, on January 7, 1978
18. Katherine Flicky, on March 27, 1978

19. Luther Langford, on June 1, 1978

John Floyd Thomas, Jr. (The Westside Rapist)

As yet another contender for the title of the most prolific serial killer in Los Angeles history, John Floyd Thomas is among the ranks of the other prolific killers—Lonnie David Franklin, Michael Hughes, and Brandon Tholmer. All of them were black males who killed within the same general area during roughly the same period, and each had possibly over thirty kills. Despite that the top five serial killers from the city were black; few have ever heard their names or the stories of their crimes.

Amongst these, Thomas' story, like that of Franklin's, is one of the more recently uncovered ones. With a murder spree that dates at least to 1972 and possibly as far back as the 1950s, he was arrested in 2009 after an accidental discovery. But his story is far from finished as police are still trying to put together the bits and pieces in their search for closure for the victims' families.

Thomas was known as a soft-spoken man and employed as an insurance claims specialist for years, so his neighbors were shocked when police arrested him. They had known him as friendly; some said he was a doll of a person. But police knew differently, and they had Thomas's rap sheet in hand to prove it.

The police got their big break in March of 2009. The previous October, detectives were having every paroled black rapist from L.A. submit a DNA sample to compare with the "Grim Sleeper" murders,

John Floyd Thomas

later pinned on Lonnie David Franklin. Thomas had been convicted of a 1978 rape and had served five years. His DNA came back negative for the Grim Sleeper case, but there was a positive hit for two murders, one in 1972 and another in 1976. This was significant, for it was the first big break in an old serial killer cold case known as the Westside Rapist.

From 1972 to 1978, the Westside Rapist had terrorized the Inglewood suburb of Los Angeles, leaving over twenty women dead and raping over two dozen more. Police had never had a serious crack in the case; all they knew was that he had a preference for single, elderly white women, and all reports were that he was a clean-cut black male in his twenties. Soon after the attacks began, police questioned Brandon Tholmer because of murders he had committed just north of Inglewood, but he was ruled out as a suspect along with fourteen other black men. The trail went cold, and the murders and rapes stopped in 1978—the same year Thomas was sentenced to prison.

On the other side of Los Angeles, another series of similar attacks began in 1983 around the town of Pomona, CA. Over a six-year span, over ten women were murdered, each fitting the same profile as the murders of the previous decade. Yet due to the distance between the crimes, not only geographically but also chronologically, the connection between the two was never made until Thomas was apprehended. After the police had Thomas in custody, his DNA also tested as a match for the 1986 murder of Adrienne Askew. Police found out after his release from prison that he relocated to the Pomona area but left in 1989 when he relocated to Glendale, CA.

Police studied the patterns and similarities between the crimes and noted that wherever Thomas was, elderly white women were raped and murdered. Yet, when he took his job as a state insurance worker in 1989, it appears that his murdering binge stopped. Police are not positive that it stopped, but they do note that there was not a surfacing of bodies in the Glendale area after 1989. It is possible that he could have traveled to other parts of the city to murder, but they have no evidence to support that theory, just the knowledge that serial killers have a difficult time shutting down their urge to kill. Yet they reason that possibly because he had a demanding job, in combination with his age being over fifty, he may have decided to hang it up.

In 2011, Thomas pled guilty to seven murders, six from his first go-round and one from his second. For these crimes, he received seven life sentences, for the prosecuting attorney considered that at his age (seventy-five at the time of the conviction), a death sentence would just further burden the tax payers, and he would likely pass away during the appeals process.

Police have thirty murders pegged on him, of which eighteen names have been released (see below). But because it often takes DNA evidence or a solid confession to get a murder conviction, they decided to press charges on the seven for which they had DNA evidence. They are currently looking into other murders he might have committed and think that thirty-nine is the upper limit to his mayhem, but they also admit that the figure might be low. They hope that he breaks down some day and confesses each of his crimes in full detail.

John Floyd Thomas, Jr.'s proven victims
1. Ethel Sokoloff in November 1972
2. Cora Perry in September 1975
3. Elizabeth McKeown in February 1976
4. Maybelle Hudson in April 1976
5. Miriam McKinley in June 1976
6. Evalyn Bunner in October 1976
7. Adrienne Askew in June 1986

John Floyd Thomas, Jr.'s probable victims
1. Mary Scialese, age 72, on November 7, 1974
2. Lucy Grant on, age 92, on November 8, 1974
3. Lillian Kramer, age 67, on November 14, 1974
4. Ramona Gartner, age 74, on December 4, 1974
5. Sylvia Vogel, age 71, on March 22 1975
6. Una Cartwright, age 78, on April 8, 1875
7. Olga Harper, age 75, on April 17, 1975
8. Effie Martin, age 76, on May 22, 1975
9. Leah Leshefsky, age 63, on October 28, 1975
10. Annette Weingarten, age 70, on November 19, 1975
11. Isabel Askew in 1983

Maury Troy Travis

At the beginning of the new millennium, police in the St. Louis area were faced with a string of homicides. Not wanting to alarm the public that a possible serial killer might be at work, they did not alert the media but instead kept their investigation under wraps. But no matter how much they denied it, the bodies kept turning up on both sides of the Mississippi River, and they had no clue as to who might be responsible.

Bodies began to turn up beginning in late 1999, and the story was always the same. A black prostitute had fallen victim to a killer who had strangled her and dumped her body in a field or ditch without a trace of who the killer might be. Oftentimes, only skeletal remains were found, so investigators had to use dental records to identify the victim.

In a city the size of St. Louis, with its crime-ridden neighborhood of East St. Louis, IL, across the river, finding a dead prostitute was not unusual. But there was a serious spike in prostitute deaths with over twenty unsolved murders for police to figure out, yet they lacked a clue as to how many might be connected. It was not until the killer slipped up that police were able to clear a large number of the homicides from their books.

On May 21, 2002, a letter was sent to the *Post-Dispatch* from a person who claimed to be the killer of numerous women in the St. Louis area. The envelope had its American flag stamp placed upside-down, and inside it was a map which the killer claimed would lead police to the body of victim number seventeen. Taking the letter seriously, the reporter contacted police.

Police acted on the tip and followed the map to a place in West Alton, MO. Roughly fifty yards from the "X," police found the skeletal remains of a woman which are still unidentified to this day. The law officers were familiar with this spot, as they had found the bodies of Verona Thompson and Teresa Wilson yards from there the year before. They wondered if perhaps the three murders had been related.

Maury Travis

They sought to determine if they could track who had sent the letter. They noticed that it had a return postmark of "I Thralldom, New York City, NY." After confirming that the address was bogus, a quick web search showed that "I Thralldom" was a website devoted to pornographic bondage and sexual torture. Slightly further investigation showed what the word "thralldom" itself meant: a condition of moral or mental servitude to one's master.

Stumped by the letter which they knew by the postmark had been sent in the St. Louis area, police attempted to track the origin of the map. Noting that the map matched the same format found on the Expedia.com website, the FBI, who had been called in to assist, subpoenaed Microsoft, the website's owner. Specifically, they were interested in any downloads of the map between May 18 and May 21, 2002.

On June 3, Microsoft reported that only one computer had requested that specific map in the three-day window, but instead of a name, all they had was an IP address of 65.227.106.78.

While this helped, the FBI did not know to whom this address belonged, so they turned to WorldCom for help. WorldCom was able to provide the necessary information quickly, saying that the "65" stood for the MSN network and the remaining number was a unique identifying number assigned to a man named Maury Travis on the day in question. Police believed they had their man.

Police began surveillance on the house where the map had been downloaded, and determined that thirty-six-year-old Maury Travis, a waiter by profession, lived there alone. On June 7, they swooped in for the arrest. At seven in the morning, two detectives and an FBI profiler rang Travis's door, rousing him from bed. When he answered the door, he asked, "Why are you here so early? It's 7 A.M." The officers answered, "You know why we're here." Travis nodded yes and let them in.

For the next two hours, the officers grilled Travis with questions only to have him pose the same questions in return, in an effort to redirect everything back to them. Police would later say that he wanted to control the conversation and was not budging an inch. While he never confessed to anything, he never denied any wrongdoings either. Frustrated, the investigators told him that they had a map which had been downloaded from his computer. Visibly upset, Travis cussed at his computer and said, "Damn Internet!" Taking this as an admission of guilt, police asked him to come back to the station for more questioning. Travis complied and told them, "I was born this way."

Back at the station, the FBI profiler spoke with Travis for three hours, trying to get him to confess his crimes or give a reason as to why he had killed. Travis, however, would not budge, and he continued his game of interrogating the interrogator. At some point in the interview, Travis was asked if his crimes (and the investigators were careful not to mention what type of crimes they were) were inherent or learned behavior. Travis peered into the investigators eyes, unmoved, and said: "You would never understand, I was born like this." He said he had been like this since he could remember.

During the interview, police had been searching Travis's home for additional clues. In the basement of the home, which had appeared well-kept and tidy, they found what appeared to be a torture room of sorts. They found sprays of blood on the walls and blood stains on the carpet. Further investigation revealed that there several layers of paint, with blood stains between the layers.

In one room they found homemade video tapes, over ten hours' worth, of Travis giving crack cocaine to women and having consensual sex with them. In some of the tapes, he was seen torturing, raping, and even killing his victims. In one disturbing tape labeled "My Wedding Day," he forced a woman he called "another crack-head ho" to repeatedly say, "You are the master. It pleases me to serve you." After some time in the video, the picture goes out of focus, and he is heard torturing the woman to death as she gasps her final breaths in agony.

Back in the interview, the investigators were told that there had been videotapes found of his murders and blood in his basement. When the investigator told Travis they had made a discovery in his basement, without remorse he replied, "Yeah, I knew you'd find it." At this, Travis dropped his head numerous times and told investigators that he was toast, begging them not to send him back to prison. Seeing that he was not revealing anything, they concluded the interview and held him on suspicion of murder.

The next day, he was interviewed for eight more hours as investigators continued searching his home and vehicles for clues. Travis again proved to be non-remorseful and continued to dodge questions by the interviewers. Frustrated, they tried a different approach.

The thick case file on the murders was brought before Travis to show him pictures of the women taken while they were still alive. As they asked him about each woman, he denied having ever seen any of the women. Exhausted, the investigators decided to continue their questions, trying to get him to confess. After about ten minutes of questions, Travis stopped them and said, "Let me see those pictures of the dead girls again." Investigators then stopped him and asked how he knew they were dead. Travis again hung his head low and said, "I'm toast".

After this, he agreed to cooperate with investigators and offered to drive them to the location of yet another body that he had left in East St. Louis. However, as they approached the bridge over the Mississippi, he clammed up and began loudly telling the officers that he did not want to go. He kept repeating, "Lock me up, I'm guilty." When asked if they could still go to get closure for the victim's family, he refused and claimed not to know anything. Frustrated, they turned around and took him back to the station.

After getting back to the station, they interviewed Travis again, but after nineteen minutes of questioning, Travis stopped the interviewers and told them that he wanted an attorney. He said, "I am not going back to prison."

Police decided to put Travis on suicide watch, and they shipped him back to his cell. But the next morning, the jailer found Travis dead: he had hanged himself with a makeshift noose made from bed sheets and covered his head with a pillowcase. On his bed lay a note, apologizing to his for hurting her. Nary was a word said about his crimes.

The next day, police were able to prove through DNA evidence conclusively that he murdered Brenda Beasley and Yvonne Crues. They were also able to confirm that a tire mark on the leg of Betty James matched tires on his car. After viewing the videos in depth, they were able to determine that Teresa Wilson and Betty James were on the films, but they have not been able to identify any additional victims from the tapes, primarily because the camera was at an odd angle and the picture was blurred at times.

Police now suspect Maury Travis to have committed between seventeen and twenty-two murders in the St. Louis area, with most investigators agreeing that twenty-two murders seem most likely. In addition to this, police in Atlanta, GA, think Travis might have committed a string of six unsolved murders during his time in college there from 1986 to 1988.

However, no matter how many murders Travis committed, he took any chance of a confession with him to the grave, and police may never know the exact number of victims he killed. The only thing of which they are positive is that he did kill at least twelve women.[38]

The last twist of Travis's story is that it helped investigators to track down another black serial killer in the East St. Louis area. Detectives were investigating four additional murders of bodies which were all dumped in the same vicinity; they at first attributed them to Travis. But after further investigation, they determined that they were instead victims of Donald E. Younge. However, after sitting in jail for nearly a decade, Younge was cleared of the murders, not because of the evidence that pointed towards him, but due to the sloppy police work. He is currently serving time in Utah for a murder committed in 1999.

Maury Troy Travis's victims
1. Mary Shields, age sixty-one, found on July 31, 2000
2. Cassandra R. Walker, age nineteen, found on March 24, 2001
3. Alysia Greenwade, age thirty-four, found on April 1, 2001
4. Teresa Wilson, age thirty-six, found on May 15, 2001
5. Betty James, age forty-six, found on May 23, 2001
6. Verona "Ronnie" Thompson, age thirty-six, found on June 29, 2001
7. Yvonne Crues, age fifty, found on August 25, 2001
8. Brenda Beasley, age thirty-three, found on October 8, 2001
9. Unidentified woman, found on January 30, 2002
10. Unidentified woman, found on March 11, 2002
11. Unidentified woman, found on March 28, 2002
12. Victim number seventeen from map, found on May 25, 2002

Chester Turner (Chester the Molester)

In the 1980s, the greater Los Angeles area was prowled by at least eight black serial killers who left police reeling to solve over 100 murders. Most of the murder victims were women, with many being black prostitutes. Complicating the issue was the constant supply of dead-end leads, false confessions, and decomposed bodies which left little if any tangible DNA evidence. Oftentimes police did not know if the murders were the result of one or two killers, or even a dozen. With time, though, and with improvements in DNA technology, police slowly were able to solve many of the murders.

From 1987 to 1998, police had found the bodies of fifteen women, including two who were pregnant, in a thirty-square-block area of South Los Angeles. Because the murders were spread over eleven years, and due to the high murder rate in the area, they did not suspect a serial killer to be responsible. In fact, when the bodies started turning up, they initially suspected one of their own, a veteran officer, in at least three of the deaths. After ballistic tests eliminated him as a suspect, the bodies continued to pile up without the emergence of any suspects.

Chester Turner

In 1992, the police thought they had solved four of the murders after a mentally handicapped janitor confessed to the crimes. He had been employed at a school near where the bodies were dumped, and, not understanding the gravity of the situation, answered that he had killed the women. As a result of his confession, he was convicted of the murders and sentenced to prison, where he served until police got an unexpected surprise.

On St. Patrick's Day of 2002, Chester Turner, who had grown up with the moniker "Chester the Molester," attacked and raped a woman. He was a security officer at a local homeless shelter, and he had attacked his victim in a shower. Fighting off her attacker, she ran to the nearby police station and told her story. At first, police were reluctant to believe her story, but following procedure, they sent her to the hospital to have her checked out. After determining she had been raped, police decided to move in on Chester, and they found him hiding fully clothed in one of the showers at the shelter. He was later found guilty of rape and sentenced to prison.

As with all rapists, his DNA was submitted to the California criminal database. During a random search, they found that his was positively connected to eleven of the murders via DNA. They were surprised, as they had not suspected that they might be dealing with a serial killer in the crimes.

When investigating Turner, all the pieces began to fit together. He was known in the neighborhood where the victims had been killed as a quiet guy who had a short fuse and would fly into violent rages with little provocation. They also found that he was known by the families of some of the victims. He had even attended the funeral of one of his victims and the backyard lunch reception, where guests noticed Turner overindulging on the food.

Besides this, police noted that each of the bodies was found in a similar manner, nude and dumped in an inconspicuous place. Some were dumped in alleys, others near abandoned homes, one in a school yard, and one in the backroom of a business. Each woman had been raped, strangled to death, and left partially nude. With this pattern established, in conjunction with the DNA evidence, police were confident that Turner was their man.

As a result of his DNA connections and the similar murder method for each victim, his conviction freed David Allen Jones, the man convicted in four of the murders. Turner received a death sentence for his crimes in 2007, and despite still denying any involvement, he was ushered off to prison.[39]

In 2011, police were able to connect Turner to four additional murders via DNA evidence. As with the others, he has denied any responsibility, but this has not stopped prosecutors from trying him again. He is due to go to trial sometime in 2012. Police think he might be connected to other murders, and they know that he was in Salt Lake City for a short time, where he may have committed murders as well. Currently he has been tied to the deaths of seventeen victims, two of whom were unborn children. Police suspect him in seven more murders for a total of twenty-four, making him one of the most prolific serial killers in Los Angeles history.

Chester Turner's victims
1. Diane Johnson, age 21, found partially nude and strangled on March 9, 1987
2. Elandra Bunn, age 33, found on June 5, 1987
3. Annette Ernest, age 26, found lying on a shoulder of a road in October 1987
4. Anita Fishman, age 31, strangled and left partially nude in an alley on January 10, 1989
5. Regina Washington, age 27, found on September 23, 1989; she was six months pregnant
6. Tammie Christmas, found on September 30, 1992
7. Debra Williams, age 32, found on November 16, 1992
8. Mary Edwards, age 41, found on December 16, 1992
9. Andrea Tripplett, age 29, was found on April 2, 1993; she was just over six months pregnant
10. Desarae Jones, age 29, found on May 16, 1993
11. Natalie Price, age 31, found on February 12, 1995
12. Mildred Beasley, age 45, found on November 6, 1996
13. Cynthia Annette Johnson, found on February 22, 1997
14. Paula Vance, age 24, found on February 3, 1998
15. Brenda Bries, age 39, found on April 6, 1998

Henry Louis Wallace (The Charlotte Strangler)

The image of a charming, confident serial killer who woos his victims with a smile and cleverly crafted words evokes fear in many women. Most times, this type of killer preys on women he has never met, presenting himself as a kind and helpful person interested in the well-being of the woman. On rare occasions, the killer has known some of his victims for a while before finding the right moment to pounce. This brand of killer is bloodthirsty, not caring for how close he was to his victims, counting them as sheep for the slaughter. Such is the case of

Henry Wallace, the man who was trusted and known by each of his victims.

In 1988, Wallace had been discharged from the navy for breaking and entering in Florida. His career having ended, he decided to head to his hometown of Barnwell, SC, with his young wife and her child. Once there, he landed a job and begin to fit into the small town.

On March 18, 1990, while driving down a city street, he noticed eighteen-year-old Tashanda Bethea walking by herself. She knew him, for, despite being six years older and married, he had made previous sexual advances on her, though she had always turned her down. He offered her a ride, which she gladly accepted. After driving her to a patch of woods on the outskirts of town, he demanded sex from her. She sternly refused, begging him to take her back to town. Angry, he pulled out a pistol, telling her not to resist. Fearing for her life, she allowed him to rape her in the backseat of the car. When finished, he asked if she would tell anyone, and she responded in the affirmative. Not satisfied with the answer, he choked her until he thought she was dead. Minutes later, when she regained consciousness, he again choked her until he thought she was dead. To make sure he did the job right, he took her out of the car and slit her wrists and throat, then threw her body in a nearby fishing pond. When her body was found two weeks later, the coroner would determine that she drowned while bleeding to death.

Henry Louis Wallace

Fearing for his life, he went immediately to a local carwash and detailed his car, vacuuming the back seat numerous times until he was satisfied that the seat held no clue to what he had done. He then resumed his life, acting as though nothing had ever happened.

After her body was recovered, Wallace became the prime suspect. When interviewed, he denied any knowledge of Ms. Bethea's death. Forensic investigators combed the back seat looking for any trace of evidence that might incriminate him. They found none and police decided to mark him off the list.

Just a few months later, he assaulted a young girl in the town, but she was able to alert her parents before he could rape her. He was arrested, but his attorney recommended a pretrial intervention program which would allow him to have the charges dropped and expunged from his record. He complied and completed the program to skate around the system.

He was arrested a year later after raping a seventeen-year-old girl in nearby Rock Hill, SC. The judge, who was days before retirement, released Wallace on his own accord without requesting bail. Somehow, the paperwork was lost and charges were never brought against him. Had Wallace been successfully charged, ten women's lives would have been spared.

Thinking he could get away from possible charges brought against him, he headed to Charlotte, NC, to be closer to his mother. Not long after getting there, he struck again. This time the victim was Sharon Nance, who was walking to meet friends late at night. It is not clear whether Wallace knew her or not, but regardless, he raped her and then bashed her head in with a large rock beside an old set of train tracks. Her body was found a few weeks later, but police had little to go on, thinking that perhaps she had gotten tangled with the wrong crowd.

Just a few weeks later, on June 15, 1992, he stole a key from his girlfriend which belonged to her best friend's apartment. After sneaking into her apartment, he hid in the bathroom, waiting for her to return home. When Carolin Love arrived, he demanded sex, but she told him to leave. Angered, he put her in a choke hold until she passed out; he then carried her to a bed and raped her. When she awoke while he was raping her, he choked her again with his hands, and when she resisted, he grabbed a curling iron to strangle her with the cord as he finished raping her. He wrapped her body in sheets and placed her in his trunk, to be deposited later that evening in a ditch. He went to the ditch two different times over the next few weeks, checking to make sure the body was decomposed. Police would not find her body's remains until Wallace led them to it two years later.

He would not strike again until February 19, 1993. After stopping by a friend's house, he chatted with her teen daughter Shawna D.

Hawk for over an hour until he got mad at something she had said. Incensed, he strangled her to death and then placed her body in a bathtub full of water. Her mother and boyfriend would discover her there later that night. When confessing this crime the next year, he admitted that he had no intention to kill her but got really angry with her. After her death, he attended the funeral and gave her grieving mother his condolences.

After cooling off for five months, he struck again, killing Audrey Ann Spain. On June 22, 1993, he called her to see if she wanted to smoke some marijuana. She agreed, and after finishing the joint with her, he pinned her to the ground, choking her until she went unconscious. He then dragged her to the bedroom and raped her. After she woke up, she begged for her life. He disagreed and choked her to death. For good measure, he tightly twisted a shirt and bra around her neck, and fled the scene with her credit cards.

A little over a month later, he stopped by a friend's house on August 9, 1993, to get advice from her about his love life. Trusting him, Valencia Jumper listened to his story and gave him advice. After some time speaking, Wallace asked Valencia to call his girlfriend and let her know that he would be home soon. But when she turned to grab the phone, he put her in a tight choke hold. She begged to be let go, offering to do anything if he would free her, and after he freed her, she allowed him to rape her. She was getting dressed afterward when he attacked from behind, strangling her to death with a towel. Not satisfied that she was dead, he poured rum over her body and lit her bed on fire. After firemen extinguished the fire, the coroner could not determine the exact cause of death and ruled it a natural death. It was not until Wallace later told the story of her death that police realized it was a homicide. Wallace would later claim that he regretted this murder the most, as she was like a little sister to him. He even attended her funeral, where he mourned alongside her family.

A month later, Wallace stopped by Michelle Denise Stinson's apartment, unannounced, at 11 P.M. He later claimed that his sole motivation for the visit was rape. After asking for a glass of water, he attacked her in the kitchen and then forced her to have sex with him, after which he committed his demented ritual. He strangled her with a towel, but he noticed that she made a great deal of noise. Wanting her to die more quickly, he stabbed her in the back four times with a large kitchen knife. He then left her dead body on the floor as her two children slept in the back room.

By this time, Charlotte police began suspecting that some of the murders might be connected. Due to the size of the city and the random frequency of the murders, they had been investigating each murder individually. But with a fifth murder on their hands in the same vicinity of others fitting the same description, they began paying closer attention.

While police scrambled to find a pattern, Wallace killed again on February 20, 1994. He showed up at the house of Vanessa Little Mack, desiring to rob her to support his drug habit, and possibly to rape her. He carried a pillowcase in his pocket to incapacitate her and to carry the loot from her apartment. After asking Vanessa for a soda, he put the pillowcase around her neck and asked for her credit cards and valuables. Once she gave these over, he demanded sex from her, at which she consented, fearing for her life. She tried to get away from him after he was finished, but he overpowered her and strangled her to death with the pillowcase. Police believed that Vanessa's murder was tied to the other murders, but they still had not had a big break yet. The media by this time had labeled the killer as the "Charlotte Strangler."

During the second week of March, things began to heat up, and Wallace made some blunders that would later haunt him. On March 8, 1994, he stopped by the apartment of Betty Jean Baucom and asked to use her phone. Trusting him, she let him in. He did not need to use the phone, though, but had come over to get the keys to the safe of the restaurant at which she was a supervisor. When Betty gave him the phone, he pretended to be making calls in an attempt to lose her attention. Once she turned her back, he attacked her and demanded that she remove her clothes. After she was naked, he raped her with his hands around her throat while telling her to be quiet. When he was finished, he told her to give over her keys and any money or jewelry she had. Once she consented, he strangled her to death with a towel. Before leaving her apartment, he stole her television and stereo equipment.

After leaving her apartment, he went a few doors down to the apartment of Brandi Henderson, another woman he knew. She was the girlfriend of one of his best friends, so she trusted him completely. He claimed that he needed to drop a few things off for his friend, so she gladly let him in. But once she turned her back, he grabbed her in a bear hug and demanded her money. It was not quite the haul he expected; he netted only fifteen dollars and some loose change. Not satisfied, he forced her to perform oral sex and then raped her. Once he had finished torturing the woman, she began to sob and knelt down, praying out loud to God. Trying to reassure her, he said, "I'm not going to hurt you." She gave him a hug in response, genuinely believing him. But as she hugged him, he choked her with a towel until her heart stopped. He grabbed his clothes to leave when the woman's ten-month-old child began to cry. Wallace did his best to comfort the baby, but the infant still cried. Frustrated, he put a towel tightly around the baby's neck, only allowing him enough air to breathe, but not enough to cry. The baby's father would find his child near death and his girlfriend murdered less than a half hour later.

With this last series of murders, police had a chief suspect. After poring over each victim's case, they noticed a common connection: each one had known Wallace. They put out an APB on him and on car he had stolen from Betty Baucom. Investigators were desperate to catch him before he struck again.

Police located the stolen car within days. After scouring it for physical evidence, they lifted fingerprints from the trunk that were a dead match for Wallace. They had their man, but they were not quick enough to save his last victim.

While police scoured the city in search for Wallace, he stopped by the apartment of Debra Slaughter on the 11th, asking her if she wanted to buy some cocaine with him. She told him she did not have the money, which infuriated him. After punching her repeatedly, he forced his way into her apartment, and then grabbed her in his customary choke hold. Debra proved a better fighter than his other victims, making this usually easy task difficult. She even told him that she had suspected him for months to have been the Charlotte Strangler! He denied the allegation and reached his arm back to strike her again. Sensing an opportunity to get away, she lunged away and grabbed her purse, searching for a small knife she kept. When she found the knife, she tried to stab Wallace, but he proved too quick and grabbed her arm, forcing the knife from her hand. He then grabbed her again and stabbed her over twenty times, bringing her nearly to death. To finish the deed, he grabbed a small white linen and strangled her to death.

The next day, police found him while staking out his home and places he often frequented. At 5 P.M., he was stopping into a friend's home for a visit when police caught sight of him and arrested him without incident. They reported that he was cool and collected, cooperating with them in a courteous manner.

When they returned to the station, they asked him to confess his crimes, though they had suspected him only in seven murders. After a prayer with the investigators, he began to talk, eventually confessing to a total of ten murders in the Charlotte area. With each confession, he provided gory details of each crime, filling in pieces that the police had not known before.[40] They had their man.

Before the trial, Wallace finally admitted to the murder of Tashanda Bethea four years earlier in South Carolina. He said that it had haunted him and drove him nearly to suicide on numerous occasions. Police in the area also suspected that he had murdered another young woman outside Barnwell, SC; based on the manner of death and his relationship with her. To this day he still denies the murder, but police are 100% positive that he is the killer.

At trial, Wallace claimed that the confession had been drawn out of him and that he was innocent, but the judge and jury did not buy it. After considering the confession, Wallace's DNA, and physical evidence that placed him at each crime, the jury had a short deliberation. They recommended a death sentence. The judge gave him nine death sentences and recommended that he be executed quickly to remove any additional burden on the state. He currently still sits on death row, awaiting his execution.

Henry Louis Wallace's victims
1. Tashanda Bethea
2. Unidentified woman
3. Sharon Nance
4. Carolin Love

5. Shawna D. Hawk
6. Audrey Ann Spain
7. Valencia Jumper
8. Michelle Denise Stinson's
9. Vanessa Little Mack
10. Betty Jean Baucom
11. Brandi Henderson
12. Debra Slaughter

Carl "Coral" Eugene Watts (The Sunday Morning Slasher)

Watts stands alone among notorious serial killers, yet he is one of the least frequently mentioned when top serial killers are discussed. When comparing him to the body count of the top white serial killers, few come close to the path of destruction he left, yet his story has almost been forgotten. Thankfully it has been mentioned briefly in a few serial killer books, and a detailed book has even been written about his crimes. But despite this effort, little is known about the vast majority of his crimes.

Investigators in Michigan believe he committed his first murder in 1972, just after graduating high school at the age of nineteen. He then attended college sporadically and attempted to hold down several small jobs. Since none ever panned out, he eventually dropped out of school, lived from job to job, took to stealing what he could lay hands on, and murdered women he had never met.

Carl Watts

Over the next decade, he put together a series of murders that no one has successfully solved to this day. Most investigators believe the number is at least forty-four but agree that eighty is a conservative estimate. Watts usually gave a range of 80 to 100 murders, but on at least one occasion he hinted at possibly as many as 120. Unlike other serial killers who have claimed lofty numbers only to later recant or have no proof to back up their claims, Watts never failed to prove his story. Yet, after he was imprisoned, he never let on to the specifics of his crimes, aside from the admissions that landed him in jail in the first place.

His victim selection tied his murders together. Among the known victims, and according to his testimony, he favored killing white women, killing a black woman only once. His motivation was different from most black serial killers who stalk white ladies; it was not rape. Instead, he insisted that the women he killed had evil eyes, and his goal was to eliminate them. He even went to the extent of burning their clothes or belongings to release their evil spirit from the world.

From 1972 to 1981, police in the vicinity of Detroit, MI, have tied at least sixteen murders to him, all of which are listed at the end of this biography. Yet, they could never pin any of the murders on him while he was in Michigan, and he constantly shook them from his tail to commit more murders.

Early on, his tactics had been simple. For his earliest kills, he would spot a potential victim at Western Michigan University and follow her back to her dorm. He would then knock at her door and ask if Charles was home. After having the woman tell him that there was no Charles at that residence, he would leave for a spell and come back to repeat this routine. He was able to express a sense of urgency in his tone that made the women feel he was genuinely looking for someone. In almost every situation, he would suggest he leave a note for the imaginary person, to which the women would agree. While in the process of writing the note, he would force his way into their domicile and make his kill.

During his formative years of murdering, he was not always successful. There were times when the phone rang in the middle of his murder session or when someone showed up unexpected at the door. Other times, the woman would scream as he raped her, and he would run fearing his capture. It is believed that three women escaped his clutches in the first few years of his killing.

After being caught stealing plywood from the college on repeated occasions, he was interviewed about the rapes, assaults, and murders. He then changed his tactics, taking to the streets. Part of this could have also been due to his getting married. His wife would later tell police that after sex, he would act angry and leave for hours, sometimes coming back with ash or even traces of blood on his clothing.

He spent hours prowling the streets of the Detroit metro area, ranging as far as Ann Arbor to the west and Windsor to the east. Once he spotted a potential victim, he would follow her until he felt the opportunity was right. Then, when he suspected no one was looking, he would pounce and leave his victim dead. There was no more talking with the victims, as he had done earlier, nor was there time for rape. His tactic was to make the kill and flee.

It was during this next phase in his killing that he explored new killing methods. While he had relied on strangulation earlier, he progressed to beating and stabbing; he also occasionally shot and drowned a few victims. As he later told investigators, he was always trying new techniques to release the evil spirits. It was this tactic, in combination with his wide hunting area in Michigan, which kept detectives off his trail for years. They knew that there were numerous unsolved murders, but they did not connect them due to the varied killing methods and distance between kills.

After some time, the police in Michigan did catch up to him. They noticed that dead bodies turned up wherever he was. For instance, every time his car crossed the border into Canada, the border patrol recorded his tag number and the time of the crossing. With every crossing, bodies turned up soon afterward. In one case, he left a woman near death with extensive injuries from a butcher's knife, and she was able to identify him years later as her attacker.

But despite suspicions and the circumstantial evidence, police were never able to get him to crack. They brought him in for questioning on numerous occasions, only to spend hours having him dodge their interrogation by questioning them. The police noted that he had a low IQ (near seventy according to his school records), yet they said he was the most deceptive person they had ever interviewed. He was able to slither away from every accusation unscathed, without revealing any of his dark secrets.

Frustrated, police decided to try another tactic. The lead detective in the case took to tailing Watts' every move. When Watts left for work in the morning, police were waiting by his car to tell him good morning. After work they were always there, whether he stopped at a convenience store, the bank, or his home, to ask how he was doing and if he had any information about the numerous unsolved murders in the area.

After some time of this cat-and-mouse game, they could sense Watts' frustration, and they noticed that no new murders had popped up in the area. Watts was down though, having not killed in some time, so he decided to leave the area. After bumping into the detective at the courthouse, where Watts had been on trial for other charges, he became visibly aggravated and decided to make a change. Making sure that the police did not notice, he fled to West Virginia to visit his mother that same day.

While at his mother's, Watts saved up money to move to Houston, TX, to stay with a friend he had met in Michigan. Police speculate that he committed a few of the unsolved murders during his brief stay. However, when asked about them, Watts always denied any knowledge of them.

After leaving his mother's, Watts flew to Houston and was able to land a job working with his friend. Police in Michigan were furious at his departure, and they had been unable to track Watts until his name popped up via a letter forwarded to Houston. The police felt they had to do something, so they sent a copy of Watts' file to the Houston police, informing them that Watts was a suspected serial killer who might have killed dozens of women and telling them to expect bodies to begin turning up in their area.

At first the Houston police took things seriously and assigned an unmarked car to follow Watts, seeing if he had any habits or patterns which would lead them to believe he was a serial killer. After not noticing anything out of the ordinary, due to budget restraints they pulled off the detail just a few days into its duty. Watts took notice and slowly resumed his murderous habits.

Over the next eight months, from late 1981 to mid-1982, he killed at least twelve women and attempted to kill at least three more. In his last day walking free, he overdid it, even for a seasoned serial killer such as himself.

After killing Michelle Maday on May 23 by drowning her in her bathtub, his thirst for blood was still strong. He headed to a nearby apartment complex and noticed a young woman headed towards her apartment. After overpowering her while she was unlocking her door, he noticed that she had a female roommate who was home. Moving with fervent speed, he knocked the first woman out, tied the hands of the roommate with a clothes hanger, and then knocked her unconscious.

He took the first woman into the bathroom and filled the tub with water to murder her by his new favorite method. But the sound of the running water woke her roommate, and she realized that she had to get out of the apartment. She struggled to free her hands, but it was no use. While she tried to work free, she heard Watts coming to check on her, so she acted as though she were still passed out. Satisfied, he went back to the task of drowning his first victim, whistling a cheerful-sounding tune in the process.

In a remarkable struggle to survive, the roommate made it to the patio door of the apartment, but she was unable to get the door open with her hands tied behind her back. She tried to unlock the door and open it, but her petite frame and lack of feeling in her hands kept her from budging the door. Finally, after what seemed to be an eternity, she was able to open the door just enough for her to squeeze through. Then she faced an even bigger problem: they lived in a second-story apartment. With no other choice, she flung herself over the guard rail and landed fifteen feet below on her feet, but she rolled as if landing with a parachute and was able to escape injury. Quickly getting to her feet, she ran to a neighbor's apartment and frantically told her to call the police, saying that there was a black man killing her friend.

Thankfully, an officer was just around the corner, and he arrived in a flash. And as if by divine intervention, upon his arrival, Watts ran out of the apartment and almost into his squad car. After a short chase, the officer had Watts on the ground and in cuffs. The officer's partner ran into the apartment, hoping that it was not too late to save the victim.

Upon his first sight of the victim, she looked dead. Her color was gone, and her face floated just beneath the surface of the water. Not discouraged, though, the officer pulled her out of the water and initiated CPR. An ambulance arrived within minutes to help with the task of trying to revive the young woman. It did not take long before they were able to get the woman breathing again. She was later able to identify Watts as her attacker.

With Watts in custody, a few of the detectives saw his name and remembered being warned about him as a possible serial killer. Now they were convinced that they should have made a stronger commitment in keeping tabs on him.

Progress was slow at first. They knew that Watts had committed one murder and attempted two others on the same day, but aside from that they had nothing on him. Watts denied the murder, but despite denying the attempted murders, he knew the police had him on that. The police and district attorney chose a bold and controversial tactic to get Watts to budge. They offered Watts a plea bargain such that if he told them everything, they would not pursue any murder charge against him, but instead would prosecute him on a lesser burglary charge, based on a crime of which he was suspected. Watts took the offer.

Watts told the entire story of his murders in Houston and, to their surprise, admitted to twelve kills and three attempted murders. Police suspect that he killed a few more, but twelve were all that Watts was ever able to remember. He even led them to the burial spot of a few of the victims. When asked why he did it, he kept telling them about the evil eyes of his victims. But when asked about how many women he killed in total, Watts insisted that twelve was only the tip of the iceberg. He once said that it was more than all the fingers and toes of everyone in the room, when there were five men, including him, present at the time.

Satisfied that Watts had confessed to most if not all of his Houston murders, the detectives asked him to tell them about what he did in Michigan. He almost opened up, and he told the investigators that that was a long story. He also alluded to many more victims whom he had killed in Houston. But before he said much more, he remembered some advice he had received from a paralegal he had been dating at the time.

Watts sensed that what he said about any murders in Michigan would indict him and make him liable to get shipped to Michigan to stand trial. After remembering what to say and not to say, he clammed up and spoke not another word.

Police from Michigan flew to Houston to interview him, but he would not budge. He told the Houston DA that if they wanted him to talk, they needed to offer him immunity as well. They refused the offer and flew back to Michigan, frustrated that they could not pin Watts to the numerous murders and missing women they suspected him of killing.

Watts was eventually sent to prison on a charge of first-degree burglary with a sixty-year sentence. Citizens of Houston following the story were appalled, but they were happy that the killer would be in prison for most likely the rest of his life.

Things changed, however, over the next twenty years. As a result of crowded prisons and Watts' good behavior, the State of Texas decided that Watts was eligible for parole. He went before six parole boards, each time with the families of his victims petitioning the board to refuse his parole. Yet, because of an obscure law, Watts was facing a mandatory parole in 2006, and there was nothing the families could do to keep him in jail after that time. They knew something had to be done.

The mother of one of his Houston victims, who had been one of the most vocal in garnering support for him to be denied parole, flew to Michigan. She let the district attorney know about the situation and pleaded with him to extradite Watts and put him on trial for at least some of the murders in Michigan. He told her that he knew Watts was connected to numerous homicides, but in a court of law he could connect him only on two.

When Watts had been arrested in 1982, his face made a brief flash on national television. A man in Michigan, while eating his dinner, felt his heart skip a beat when he saw Watts' face on the screen. He had witnessed the murder of Helen Mae Dutcher on December 1, 1979, and he exchanged a long look with Watts after the murder. Watts seemed unconcerned that he had been seen, and he hopped back in his car to leave in no big hurry. This man had told his story to police, but up until that fateful day in 1982, he had never seen Watts' face again. He was happy that Watts would be behind bars for the rest of his life.

In 2004, this same man was watching TV when he saw Watts' face again, this time in a story talking about him being denied parole again. He did not just sit on the information this time, but went to the police. He told them the complete story of the events that night: the car he saw Watts get in, the clothes he was wearing, and the manner in which Dutcher had died. It was a perfect match for Watts on all counts, from the car to the clothes.

It was with this information that the district attorney in Detroit felt he had a viable case. He submitted the proper paperwork and within a few months had Watts in a Michigan jail awaiting trial. After the trial, Watts was sentenced to life in prison for the murder of Mrs. Dutcher, and he was considered the chief suspect in many other murders.

Watts denied his involvement in the murder even after the trial. He died in 2007 of pancreatic cancer, and despite attempts by police to get him to tell the full story, he never again opened up to tell of his crimes. Aside from the murders in Detroit and Texas, he is thought to have killed in Illinois, Missouri, Oklahoma, Kansas, Ohio, and West Virginia. Despite the efforts of law enforcement in those states to get him to confess, he took his secrets to his grave. Some effort was put into trying to recover DNA from evidence in the murders, but in every case, either the evidence had not been stored correctly to preserve the DNA, or there was no evidence left at all. We will probably never know the true number of murders. Below are the twenty-eight murders to which he is connected, but because of lack of information, I have yet to find the names of any of the other women he is suspected in killing.[41]

Carl Eugene Watts's known murders
1. Linda Katherine Tilley, age 26, drowned in Eagle Lake, TX, on September 5, 1981
2. Elizabeth Ann Montgomery, age 25, stabbed with a sliced throat in Houston, TX, on September 13, 1981
3. Susan Wolf, age 22, stabbed nine times in Houston, TX, on September 13, 1981
4. Phyllis Ellen Tamm, age 27, strangled and hanged in Houston, TX, on January 4, 1982

5. Margaret Everson Fossi, age 25, suffered a blow to her throat in Houston, TX, on January 17, 1982
6. Elena Semander, age 21, strangled in Houston, TX, on February 7, 1982
7. Emily Elizabeth LaQua, age 14, strangled in Brookshire, TX, on March 20, 1982
8. Edith Ann Ledet, age 34, stabbed seventeen times in Houston, TX, on March 27, 1982
9. Yolanda Garcia, age 22, stabbed four times in Houston, TX, on September 28, 1981
10. Carrie Mae Jefferson, age 32, stabbed twice in Houston, TX, on April 16, 1982
11. Suzanne Searles, age 25, strangled in Houston, TX, on April 24, 1982
12. Michelle Maday, age 20, drowned in Houston, TX, on May 23, 1982

Carl Eugene Watts's suspected murders
1. Zenaida Tomes, stabbed in Taylor, MI, in 1972
2. Gloria Steele, age 19, stabbed thirty-three times in Kalamazoo, MI, on October 30, 1974. Watts was convicted.
3. Peggy Pochmara, age 22, strangled in Detroit, MI, on October 8, 1979.
4. Dawn Jerome, strangled in Taylor, MI, on October 2, 1979.
5. Jeanne Clyne, age 44, stabbed thirteen times in Grosse Pointe Farms, MI, on October 31, 1979. Watts confessed.
6. Helen Mae Dutcher, age 36, stabbed twelve times in Ferndale, MI, on December 1, 1979. Watts was convicted.
7. Malak "Mimi" Haddad, age 32, decapitated in Detroit, MI, on September 21, 1979.
8. Hazel Conniff, age 23, strangled with body posed in Detroit, MI, on March 10, 1980.
9. Denise Dunmore, age 26, strangled in Detroit, MI, on March 31, 1980
10. Shirley Small, age 17, stabbed with face sliced in Ann Arbor, MI, on April 20, 1980
11. Linda Monterio, age 27, strangled in Detroit, MI, on May 31, 1980
12. Glenda Richmond, age 26, stabbed twenty-eight times with a screwdriver, Ann Arbor, MI, on July 13, 1980
13. Lilli Marlene Dunn, age 28, kidnapped by car like Watts's, but body not found, in Wyandotte, MI, on July 31, 1980
14. Rebecca Greer Huff, age 20, stabbed fifty-four times with a screwdriver in Ann Arbor, MI, on September 14, 1980. Her school notebook was found in his car.
15. Lena Joyce Bennett, age 63, hanged and raped in Harper Woods, MI, on November 6, 1980
16. Connie Sue Thompson, age 19, strangled and stabbed in Toledo, OH, on January 17, 1981

ENDNOTES

[1] Rothrock, Millicent, *Serial Killer Admits to Two More Killings, News & Record, Greensboro, NC*, September 4, 1998.

[2] Braun, Bill, *Jury Hears of Suspect's Confession*, Tulsa World, October 23, 2008.

[3] Askari, Emilia & Schaefeer, Jim, *Suspect Charged with 2 Slayings- Police say man Kept Bodies in His Basement, Detroit Free Press*, January 17, 2002.

[4] Schaefer, Jim, *Victim's Kin Upset as Killer Skips Sentencing*, Detroit Free Press, September 24, 2002.

[5] Swickard, Joe, *Serial Killer Dies 4 years into 11 Life Sentences*, Detroit Free Press, October 11, 1997.

[6] For more about Benjamin check out: Bradley, Alan, *The Benjamin Atkins Story: America's Most Prolific Serial Kille*r, Kindle Edition, 2013, 27 pages.

[7] Associated Press, *Axe-Swinging Jake Bird Admits 44 Murders—Police Confirm 11*, Eugene Register-Guard, January 15, 1948.

[8] Associated Press, *Bird Rapped by Attorney*, Tri-City Herald, December 8, 1947.

[9] Associated Press, *Indiana Man Sentenced to 245 Years in Prison for murders of 3 Women, Rape*, Fox News, November 4, 2006.

[10] Hansen, Ronald, J, *Man Charged in 7 Prostitute Deaths—Prosecutor says Suspect in String of Slayings Projected Anger Toward Mom onto His Victims*, The Detroit News, August 40, 2006.

[11] Staff Writer, *DNA Tests Could Solve 15 Slayings*, Fort Worth Star-Telegram, May 27, 2005.

[12] Shephard, Joseph, *Stolen Trinkets Led to Catoe's Undoing*, Afro-American Newspaper, September 6, 1941, p. 8.

[13] Ressler, Robert K., Douglas, John E., Burgess, Ann W., & Burgess, Allen G., *Crime Classification Manual: A Standard System for Investigating and Classifying Violent Crimes.*, 2011.

[14] Excellent timeline found in 2011: http://www.timetoast.com/timelines/26746

[15]Hillard, Terry G, & Jurkanin, Thomas Joseph, *Chicago Police: An Inside View-The Story of Superintendent Terry G. Hillard*, 2006, page 132.

[16] Associated Press, *Taxi Cab Driver Charged in Serial Killings*, Sarasota Herald-Tribune, June 17, 2003.

[17] Rosen, Fred, *Body Dump*, 2002.

[18] Spencer, Buffy, *Convicted Serial Killer, Alfred Gaynor, Admits Killing Another Springfield Woman and Leaving her Infant Daughter to Die*, The Republican, December 2, 2008.

[19] Lambe, Joe, *Lawyers Sum Up Gilyard Case, After Closing Arguments, Judge Says He Will Return Verdicts Thursday in Seven Slayings*, Kansas City Star, March 14, 2007.

[20] Kiefer, Michael, *Baseline Killer Sentenced to Death*, the Arizona Republic, November 30, 2011.

[21] Warrick, Joe, *Gruesome Crimes Dog City of Brotherly 'Love'*, Schenectady Gazette, August 15, 1987.

[22] Caruso, David B., *Citing Court Ruling, Retarded Man Being Taken Off Death Row*, Beaver County Times, July 4, 2002.

[23] Farr, William, *Greenwood Gets 9 Life Terms in Slasher Slayings*, Los Angeles Times, January 19, 1977.

[24] Guitierrez, Hector, *Groves Gets life in Slaying*, Rocky Mountain News, May 26, 1990.

[25] Mitchell, Kirk, *Deceased Serial Killer Linked to Murders of 4 Colorado Women*, Denver Post, March 7, 2012.

[26] Ensslin, John C., *Crimes Go To Grave With Dead Murderer*, Rocky Mountain News, November 4, 1996.

[27] Wattley, Phillip, *How Red Tape Tied Law's Hands, Freed Harrison*, Chicago Tribune, August 19, 1973.

[28] McFadden, Robert, *Ex-Convict Gives Details of Seven West Side Murders*, New York Times, September 15, 1974.

[29] Staff Writer, *Sniper Spree is Reminder of Milton Johnson*, The Herald News-Joliet, IL, October 187, 2002

[30] Staff Writer, *LA Jury Recommends Death for Twice-Convicted Killer*, USA Today, October 14, 2004.

[31] King, Jonathon, *Remembering the Dead Obsessed with Justice*, The Broward Bulldog, November 20, 2009.

[32] King, Jonathon, *The 15-Year Hunt for a Serial Killer*, South Florida Sun, October 30, 1988.

[33] Associated Press, *Family Urges jury to Spare Prince's Life*, times Daily, August 6, 1993.

[34] Associated Press, *Three Deaths Were Work of Serial Killer*, Moscow-Pullman Daily News, March 5, 1991.

[35] Associated Press, *Lemuel Smith resentences 25-to-Life for Payant Murder*, Schenectady Gazette, March 27, 1985.

[36] Seewer, John, *Jury Recommends death for Ohio Killer*, Boston Globe, August 11, 2011. This apology was given in his unsworn court testimony and can be viewed in full in several places on the internet.

[37] Swint, Jack, *Who Killed...? Pittsburgh, PA,* 2007

[38] Staff Writer, *Internet Used to Find Man Who is Charged in 2 of 10 Killings*, New York Times, June 11, 2002.

[39] Spano, John, *Killer is Sentenced to Death*, Los Angeles Times, July 11, 2007.

[40] Staff Writer, *Investigator: Prayer Led to Wallace Confession*, Charlotte Observer, April 4, 1995

[41] For the complete story on Carl Watts, see: Mitchell, Corey, *Evil Eyes: The Most Insatiable Serial Killer Ever,* 2006.

Chapter 7

Individual Black Serial Killers

Ables, Tony A (1954 -)
YEARS ACTIVE: 1971, 1983-
1990
VICTIMS: 4+
RACE OF VICTIMS: White
AREA: St. Petersburg, FL
KILL METHODS: Suffocation
RAPE: Yes
NOTES: A repeat offender who
after release murdered and
raped three more victims.
Police now suspect many
more.

Adams, Keith (1971 -)
YEARS ACTIVE: 2001, 2005
VICTIMS: 3
RACE OF VICTIMS: White
AREA: Ft. Lauderdale, FL
KILL METHODS: Shooting,
Stabbing
RAPE: No
NOTES: From FL Prison
website.

Agee, Derrick (1979 -)
YEARS ACTIVE: 1997-2000
VICTIMS: 3
RACE OF VICTIMS: Black
AREA: Atlanta, GA
KILL METHODS: Shooting
RAPE: No
NOTES: From GA Prison
website.

Aiken, Ian Orville (1967 -)
YEARS ACTIVE: 1992-1995
VICTIMS: 5-15
RACE OF VICTIMS: Varied
AREA: FL, NY
KILL METHODS: Shooting
RAPE: No
NOTES: A member of a gang called
the Moscow Posse. He is connected
to numerous homicides in at least
two states.

Alexander, Billy (1969 -)
YEARS ACTIVE: 1991
VICTIMS: 3
RACE OF VICTIMS: Black
AREA: Miami, FL
KILL METHODS: Shooting
RAPE: No
NOTES: All victims were Haitian
immigrants.

Alix, Franklin DeWayne
(1975 - 2010)
YEARS ACTIVE: 1997-1998
VICTIMS: 4
RACE OF VICTIMS: Varied
AREA: Houston, TX
KILL METHODS: Shooting
RAPE: Yes
NOTES: After his arrest in connec-
tion to the death of a man, he
confessed to killing three more

men, raping two women, kidnapping four women, attempting two murders, and committing nine robberies. He was executed.

Allen, Bill (? - 1882)
YEARS ACTIVE: 1882
VICTIMS: 4
RACE OF VICTIMS: Varied
AREA: Chicago, IL
KILL METHODS: Shooting
RAPE: Yes
NOTES: Led police on one of the biggest manhunts in Chicago history. A 10,000+ mob of whites and blacks hunted him along with police. He was killed in battle, and his body was displayed over a three-day period in a store window. Over 300,000 people came to see the body, and police said that a noticeable drop in crime over the next few years occurred as a result of displaying the body.

Allen, Howard Arthur (1949 -)
YEARS ACTIVE: 1974 & 1987
VICTIMS: 3
RACE OF VICTIMS: White
AREA: Indianapolis, IN
KILL METHODS: Beating, strangulation, stabbing
RAPE: Yes
NOTES: Victims were elderly women. One attempted and up to eleven rapes of elderly women.

Allen, James, F (1950 -)
YEARS ACTIVE: 1969, 1986
VICTIMS: 3-4

RACE OF VICTIMS: White
AREA: Chicago, IL
KILL METHODS: Shooting
RAPE: No
NOTES: Murdered a Chicago police officer in 1969, served time and after release murdered at least two more. He's suspected in additional murders.

Allen, Quincy Jovan (1979 -)
NICKNAME: Weird Man
YEARS ACTIVE: 2002
VICTIMS: 4
RACE OF VICTIMS: White
AREA: NC, SC, OH
KILL METHODS: Shooting
RAPE: No
NOTES: One attempted. He recorded his murders in a tape recorder and before he started killing, called himself "Weird Man."

Allen, Wanda Jean (1959 - 2001)
YEARS ACTIVE: 1981, 1988
VICTIMS: 2
RACE OF VICTIMS: Varied
AREA: Oklahoma City, OK
KILL METHODS: Shooting
RAPE: No
NOTES: Both victims were her lesbian lovers. She was the first black woman executed after the ban on executions was lifted.

Allridge, Ronald Keith
(1969 - 1995)
YEARS ACTIVE: 1977, 1984
VICTIMS: 2
RACE OF VICTIMS: White
AREA: Houston, TX
KILL METHODS: Shooting
RAPE: No

NOTES: A repeat offender. He was executed for his crimes.

Alston, Robert Sylvester
(1970 -)
YEARS ACTIVE: 1991-1993
VICTIMS: 4
RACE OF VICTIMS: Black
AREA: Greensboro, NC
KILL METHODS:
Strangulation, decapitation, mutilation
RAPE: Yes
NOTES: See Chapter 6 for info.

Anderson, Darryl (1988 -)
YEARS ACTIVE: 2012
VICTIMS: 3-5
RACE OF VICTIMS: Varied
AREA: Baltimore, MD
KILL METHODS: Shooting
RAPE: No
NOTES: He committed at least three murders over a 4 month span, and is suspected in others.

Anderson, Dickie Edgar
(1970 -)
YEARS ACTIVE: 1997-1998
VICTIMS: 2
RACE OF VICTIMS: White
AREA: New London, CT
KILL METHODS: Shooting
RAPE: Yes
NOTES: Possible others.

Anderson, Emmanuel (1902 -)
YEARS ACTIVE: 1934-1936
VICTIMS: 3
RACE OF VICTIMS: Varied
AREA: Chicago, IL

KILL METHODS: Stabbing, shooting
RAPE: Yes
NOTES: Killed one white woman with ice pick and two black women by shooting.

Anderson, Joshua Julius
(1984 -)
YEARS ACTIVE: 2006-2007
VICTIMS: 5-7
RACE OF VICTIMS: Varied
AREA: Tulsa, OK
KILL METHODS: Shooting, Torture
RAPE: Yes
NOTES: See Chapter 6 for info.

Anderson, Robert (? -)
NICKNAME: Tampa Killer
YEARS ACTIVE: 1912
VICTIMS: 3
RACE OF VICTIMS: White
AREA: Tampa, FL
KILL METHODS: Shooting
RAPE: Yes
NOTES: Three dead whites and three wounded mulattos in a two-month period.

Anthony, Antwan Andre (1982 -)
YEARS ACTIVE: 2012
VICTIMS: 5
RACE OF VICTIMS: Varied
AREA: Farmville, NC
KILL METHODS: Shooting
RAPE: No
NOTES: Killed in two separate events, possibly additional murders.

Anthony, Michael Lee (1948 -)
YEARS ACTIVE: 2000
VICTIMS: 2

RACE OF VICTIMS: Black
AREA: Detroit, MI
KILL METHODS: Strangulation
RAPE: Yes
NOTES: Stored bodies in his
bedroom for a year.

Arnold, Jermarr Carlos
(1958 - 2002)
YEARS ACTIVE: 1983, 1990
VICTIMS: 2
RACE OF VICTIMS: Varied
AREA: Corpus Christi, TX
KILL METHODS: Shooting,
Stabbing
RAPE: No
NOTES: Executed.

Arrington, Marie Dean (1933-)
YEARS ACTIVE: 1964 &1968
VICTIMS: 2
RACE OF VICTIMS: Varied
AREA: Florida
KILL METHODS:
Strangulation, Shooting, Running
over
RAPE: No
NOTES: Killed her husband,
then years later kidnapped and
killed a woman.

Askins, Robert Ellwood
(1919 - 2010)
NICKNAME: Freeway Phantom
YEARS ACTIVE: 1938, 1955,
1971-1973
VICTIMS: 3-9
RACE OF VICTIMS: Black
AREA: Washington, D.C.
KILL METHODS: Shooting,
strangulation, poison
RAPE: Yes

NOTES: One of the most enigmatic
killers in the twentieth century, all
indicators pointed to him being a
killer, but things always fell apart.
In 1938, he poisoned five
prostitutes because he wanted to rid
the world of their kind. One died,
and two days later he stabbed
another prostitute to death. He told
police he once caught a venereal
disease from a prostitute and had
bitterness towards them. The trial
fell apart as the surviving women
would not testify against him. In
1955, he killed another prostitute
and raped two more and was found
guilty. In 1958, he was freed from
prison on a technicality. He worked
as a computer scientist in the D.C.
area. From 1971 to 1973, six young
black women were killed by an unknown killer called the "Freeway
Phantom." After raping and
attempting to kill a woman, police
questioned him about the killings.
He denied any connection, but he
kept using the word "tantamount,"
and his co-workers confirmed that
it was his buzzword. In the pants of
one of the victims was a note with
one word on it, "tantamount." In
his 1955 killing, he had left a similar note. The case was never
solved, despite extensive
investigation of his residence. The
one physical clue linking the six
deaths together was matching green
carpet fiber found on all the bodies.
By the time police obtained a
search warrant for Askins's home,
he had new carpet and told
investigators that he never had
green carpet. He died in prison,

where he had been since 1974 serving for two rapes and attempted murders. Most investigators are convinced that he was the Freeway Phantom.

Atkins, Benjamin Tony (1968 - 1997)
NICKNAME: West Corridor Killer
YEARS ACTIVE: 1991-1992
VICTIMS: 11
RACE OF VICTIMS: Black
AREA: Detroit, MI
KILL METHODS: Strangulation
RAPE: Yes
NOTES: See Chapter 6 for info.

Ausby, John Milton (1950 -)
YEARS ACTIVE: 1971
VICTIMS: 3
RACE OF VICTIMS: White
AREA: Washington, DC
KILL METHODS: Shooting
RAPE: Yes
NOTES: Was a tall devotee to Islam who called himself "Goliath" and dressed in a toga. He raped and killed two Australian young women working in D.C., then a month later killed and raped another young woman in her apartment. He said his religion excused him from his crimes, because it was honorable.

Azmoe, Ricky Allen (1964 -)
YEARS ACTIVE: 1987, 1990-1991
VICTIMS: 3
RACE OF VICTIMS: Unknown
AREA: Miami, FL

KILL METHODS: Shooting
RAPE: No
NOTES: From FL Prison website.

Baker, Edward (1860 -)
NICKNAME: Nigger
YEARS ACTIVE: 1888-1891
VICTIMS: 6
RACE OF VICTIMS: Varied
AREA: NM, NY, TX
KILL METHODS: Beating, Shooting
RAPE: No
NOTES: His father was a career criminal, as were his brothers. He confessed to his crimes in full, telling of the numerous robberies, attempted murders, rapes, and assaults. His story filled a half page of the *Spokesman Review* on March 29, 1903.

Balaam, Anthony (1965 -)
NICKNAME: Trenton Strangler
YEARS ACTIVE: 1994-1996
VICTIMS: 4-5
RACE OF VICTIMS: Varied
AREA: Trenton, NJ
KILL METHODS: Strangulation
RAPE: Yes
NOTES: Killed prostitutes and was described by police to be one of the most respectful criminals they ever interviewed. He confessed all of his crimes in full.

Bankston, Jr., Clinton (1971 -)
YEARS ACTIVE: 1987
VICTIMS: 5
RACE OF VICTIMS: White
AREA: Athens, GA
KILL METHODS: Axe
RAPE: Yes

NOTES: Killed a couple in April and then later killed three women in their home. Police described the second murder as the biggest bloodbath in Athens's history.

Barnwell, Lamar (1967 -)
YEARS ACTIVE: 1988-1992
VICTIMS: 7
RACE OF VICTIMS: Black
AREA: Los Angeles, CA
KILL METHODS: Shooting
RAPE: No
NOTES: Was caught in the act of committing his last two murders by police. He was later tied to three additional murders after witnesses felt it was safe to come forward with their testimony.

Barnes, James Antonio (1944 -)
YEARS ACTIVE: 1988
VICTIMS: 4-7
RACE OF VICTIMS: Black
AREA: Memphis, TN
KILL METHODS: Shooting
RAPE: No
NOTES: Victims were women. Attempted two additional murders, and implicated in at least four more.

Barr, Charles (1901 - 1926)
YEARS ACTIVE: 1923-1924
VICTIMS: 3-6
RACE OF VICTIMS: White
AREA: Memphis, TN
KILL METHODS: Shooting
RAPE: Yes

NOTES: All killed in a section of Memphis known as Lover's Lane. He was connected to three of the six murders over a one-year period, all of which happened around midnight. He was suspected in the other three murders and was later executed.

Barrett, Jerome Sydney (1947 -)
YEARS ACTIVE: 1975
VICTIMS: 4
RACE OF VICTIMS: White
AREA: Nashville, TN
KILL METHODS: Strangulation
RAPE: Yes
NOTES: Killed women and girls. He bragged to fellow inmates that he had killed "four blue-eyed bitches." Police think he might be tied to additional homicides.

Baskin, Jr., Lamar (1961 -)
YEARS ACTIVE: 1990, 2002
VICTIMS: 3
RACE OF VICTIMS: White
AREA: Houston, TX
KILL METHODS: Shooting
RAPE: Yes
NOTES: Killed women in robberies. He was serving time for a 2002 murder when DNA connected him to two murders in 1990. Police suspect he might be responsible for other murders.

Bates, Anthony (1973 -)
YEARS ACTIVE: 1995-1996
VICTIMS: 3
RACE OF VICTIMS: Unknown
AREA: Atlanta, GA
KILL METHODS: Shooting
RAPE: No

NOTES: Said in court, "If I had a chance to do it again, I can't say that I wouldn't."

Battle, Anthony George (1963 -)
YEARS ACTIVE: 1987, 1997
VICTIMS: 2
RACE OF VICTIMS: Black
AREA: NC, GA
KILL METHODS: Stabbing, Hammer
RAPE: No
NOTES: Killed his wife by stabbing. While in prison, he pulverized a prison guard's skull with a hammer.

Baxter, Patrick (1969 -)
YEARS ACTIVE: 1987-1990
VICTIMS: 3
RACE OF VICTIMS: Black
AREA: Hudson Valley, NY
KILL METHODS: Suffocation, strangulation
RAPE: Yes
NOTES: Was later convicted because of DNA when police were investigating cold cases.

Belcher, Howard Milton (1979 -)
YEARS ACTIVE: 2002
VICTIMS: 4
RACE OF VICTIMS: Black
AREA: Atlanta, GA
KILL METHODS: Strangulation
RAPE: Yes
NOTES: He worked as a prostitute, and all victims were homosexual men.

Bell, Michael Bernard (1970 -)
YEARS ACTIVE: 1989-1993
VICTIMS: 5
RACE OF VICTIMS: Black
AREA: Jacksonville, FL
KILL METHODS: shooting
RAPE: No
NOTES: After his brother was shot in a drive-by shooting, he hunted down all he thought were responsible. In the process he murdered numerous people who had no connection and wounded almost a dozen others.

Bellamy, Shiquan (1991 -)
YEARS ACTIVE: 2010
VICTIMS: 5
RACE OF VICTIMS: Black
AREA: Jersey City, NJ
KILL METHODS: Shooting
RAPE: No
NOTES: Happened over a five-month period.

Bennett, Bob (? -)
YEARS ACTIVE: 1913-1914
VICTIMS: 4
RACE OF VICTIMS: Varied
AREA: Atlanta, GA
KILL METHODS: Stabbing
RAPE: No
NOTES: Apprehended in 1914 after stabbing Mandy Gordon to death, confessed to three additional murders.

Bennett, Daniel Ray (1969 -)
NICKNAME: Lump
YEARS ACTIVE: 1988-1995
VICTIMS: 2-5
RACE OF VICTIMS: Varied
AREA: Las Vegas, NV

KILL METHODS: Shooting,
Beating
RAPE: No
NOTES: Hit man tied to two
  murders but suspected in five.

Bernard, Norman (1951 -)
YEARS ACTIVE: 1983
VICTIMS: 3-4
RACE OF VICTIMS: White
AREA: Los Angeles, CA
KILL METHODS: Shooting
RAPE: No
NOTES: One attempted in North
  Carolina, where he severed the
  penis from a man and shot
  him.

Berryhill, Cedrick (1995 -)
YEARS ACTIVE: 2010
VICTIMS: 4
RACE OF VICTIMS: Varied
AREA: New Orleans, LA
KILL METHODS: Shooting
RAPE: No
NOTES: Went on a deadly
  rampage on 12/23/2010,
  killing three. On the 27th he
  killed again. Earlier in
  December he tried to kill
  others and raped a woman.

Best, Alton Alonzo (1956 -)
YEARS ACTIVE: 1986-1987
VICTIMS: 5-6
RACE OF VICTIMS: Black
AREA: Washington, DC
KILL METHODS: Strangulation
RAPE: Yes
NOTES: Light skinned black
  women in their 20s. Parolled
  2008.

Best, Jason (1976 -)
NICKNAME: J-Boo
YEARS ACTIVE: 1993-1999
VICTIMS: 3-4
RACE OF VICTIMS: Black
AREA: Gary, IN
KILL METHODS: Shooting
RAPE: No
NOTES: Was the leader of a gang
  called the Bronx Brothers.

Bethell, Brian Ricardo (1965 -)
YEARS ACTIVE: 2006
VICTIMS: 3
RACE OF VICTIMS: White
AREA: Broward County, FL
KILL METHODS: Shooting
RAPE: No
NOTES: Desperate for money, he
  killed and robbed each victim.

Bey, Marko (1965 -)
YEARS ACTIVE: 1983-1984
VICTIMS: 2
RACE OF VICTIMS: White
AREA: NJ, Monmouth County
KILL METHODS: strangling
RAPE: Yes
NOTES: He was seventeen in the first
  murder and eighteen in the second.
  He fully confessed his crimes.

Bigoms, Tony (1960 -)
YEARS ACTIVE: 2006-2012
VICTIMS: 2+
RACE OF VICTIMS: White
AREA: Chatanooga, TN
KILL METHODS: Strangulation,
Stabbing
RAPE: Yes
NOTES: Two known victims, others
  suspected. His last he victim was
  stabbed, and then strangled to

death. Her body was dismembered before being dumped in the woods.

Billingslea, Darrell Bernard (1971 -)
YEARS ACTIVE: 1990, 2008
VICTIMS: 3
RACE OF VICTIMS: Varied
AREA: Dallas, TX
KILL METHODS: Shooting, Stabbing
RAPE: No
NOTES: Was on release from prison when he killed his girlfriend.

Bird, Jake (1902 - 1949)
NICKNAME: Tacoma Axe Killer
YEARS ACTIVE: 1923-1947
VICTIMS: 44
RACE OF VICTIMS: White
AREA: 16 states
KILL METHODS: Axe, stabbing, hatchet, shooting
RAPE: Yes
NOTES: See Chapter 6 for info.

Bixler, Rodney Troy (1968 -)
YEARS ACTIVE: 2000
VICTIMS: 3
RACE OF VICTIMS: White
AREA: Lawrenceburg, KY
KILL METHODS: Strangulation
RAPE: Yes
NOTES: His first two victims were found strangled in their bathtubs. The last victim was dumped in a river. He also raped three women.

Blacknell III, Joe (1989 -)

YEARS ACTIVE: 2009
VICTIMS: 4+
RACE OF VICTIMS: Black
AREA: Richmond, CA
KILL METHODS: Shooting
RAPE: No
NOTES: Was a member of a street gang and was possibly involved in other murders.

Blair, Terry A (1961 -)
YEARS ACTIVE: 2003-2004
VICTIMS: 8
RACE OF VICTIMS: Black
AREA: Kansas City, MO
KILL METHODS: Strangulation
RAPE: Yes
NOTES: One attempted. All bodies were found in an eighteen-square block area over an eleven-month period. All victims were women.

Blair, Mitchelle (1980 -)
YEARS ACTIVE: 2012-2013
VICTIMS: 2
RACE OF VICTIMS: Black
AREA: Detroit, MI
KILL METHODS: Strangulation, suffocation, beating
RAPE: No
NOTES: Both victims were her children, killed 9 months apart. The first was her 9 year old son, who she severely tortured for 2 weeks prior to his death. The second was her 14 year old daughter, who complained about her mom killing her brother. Both victims were found in deep freezers.

Bolder, Martsay L (1957 - 1993)
YEARS ACTIVE: 1973, 1979
VICTIMS: 2

RACE OF VICTIMS: Varied
AREA: Missouri
KILL METHODS: Stabbing
RAPE: No
NOTES: Victims were men.

Bomar, Arthur Jerome
(1959 -)
YEARS ACTIVE: 1996
VICTIMS: 4
RACE OF VICTIMS: Varied
AREA: Philadelphia and NV
KILL METHODS: Shooting
RAPE: No
NOTES: The NV murder was
    over a parking space, for
    which he only served twelve
    years.

Bonner, Willie (1974 -)
YEARS ACTIVE: 1992, 1998
VICTIMS: 2-3
RACE OF VICTIMS: White
AREA: Miami, FL
KILL METHODS: Shooting
RAPE: No
NOTES: Was released from
    prison. After seeing the
    arresting officer who originally
    caught him, he thanked him for
    leading him out of a life of
    crime. The next day he killed
    again and is suspected in
    another murder.

Borders, Donald Eugene
(1959 -)
YEARS ACTIVE: 2003
VICTIMS: 3
RACE OF VICTIMS: White
AREA: North Carolina
KILL METHODS: Beating
RAPE: Yes

NOTES: Killed elderly women. It
    took five years for police to
    consider him a suspect. At first he
    was a wintess in one of the
    murders, but after a DNA test
    pointed to him, he was arrested.

Bosket, Willie James (1962 -)
YEARS ACTIVE: 1978
VICTIMS: 2
RACE OF VICTIMS: White
AREA: New York
KILL METHODS: shooting
RAPE: Yes
NOTES: Murders were when he was
    fifteen years old.

Boswell, Rufus (1942 - 2010)
YEARS ACTIVE: 1987, 1992
VICTIMS: 2
RACE OF VICTIMS: Unknown
AREA: Miami, FL
KILL METHODS: Shooting
RAPE: No
NOTES: One attempted. Died in
    Prison

Bowman, Renee (1965 -)
YEARS ACTIVE: 2007-2008
VICTIMS: 2
RACE OF VICTIMS: Black
AREA: Rockville, MD
KILL METHODS: Strangulation,
beating
RAPE: No
NOTES: Both were her adopted
    daughters. She also attempted to
    murder one more.

Boyd, Charles Anthony
(1959 - 1999)
NICKNAME: Bathroom Slayer
YEARS ACTIVE: 1986-1987

VICTIMS: 3
RACE OF VICTIMS: White
AREA: Dallas, TX
KILL METHODS: Stabbing,
drowning
RAPE: Yes
NOTES: His victims were young
women whom he robbed. He
was caught after pawning
jewelry from each of the
women. As he was being
executed, he still maintained
his innocence despite the
evidence against him.

Boyd, Lucious (1959 -)
NICKNAME: Lady Killer
YEARS ACTIVE: 1998-1999
VICTIMS: 3-13
RACE OF VICTIMS: Black
AREA: Ft. Lauderdale, FL
KILL METHODS: Strangling
RAPE: Yes
NOTES: Victims were young
women. The first was driving
home from church when she
ran out of gas, and he stopped;
instead of helping, he raped
and murdered her. He is
suspected in at least ten more
unsolved murders.

Bradford, Wilford (1944-2005)
YEARS ACTIVE: 1976, 1990
VICTIMS: 2
RACE OF VICTIMS: Black
AREA: Florida
KILL METHODS: Stabbing
RAPE: No
NOTES: From FL Prison
website.

Braxton, Michael Jerome (1973-)
YEARS ACTIVE: 1992-1996
VICTIMS: 3
RACE OF VICTIMS: Black
AREA: North Carolina
KILL METHODS: Shooting,
Strangulation
RAPE: No
NOTES: One murder and also a
double homicide.

Breedlove, McArthur
(1947 - 2010)
YEARS ACTIVE: 1974-1978
VICTIMS: 2
RACE OF VICTIMS: White
AREA: Miami, FL
KILL METHODS: Stabbing
RAPE: No
NOTES: Died in prison.

Brewer, James D. (1956 -)
YEARS ACTIVE: 1977-1977
VICTIMS: 2
RACE OF VICTIMS: White
AREA: Indianapolis, IN
KILL METHODS: beating and
shooting
RAPE: Yes
NOTES: Posed as a police officer at
white male's home. Molested as a
child.

Brice, Jr., Gregory (1974 -)
YEARS ACTIVE: 1992-2000
VICTIMS: 4
RACE OF VICTIMS: Black
AREA: Washington, DC
KILL METHODS: Shooting
RAPE: No
NOTES: Was also a drug dealer.

Bridges, Tyrone (1958 - 1987)

YEARS ACTIVE: 1987
VICTIMS: 2
RACE OF VICTIMS: White
AREA: New Orleans, LA
KILL METHODS: Shooting
RAPE: No
NOTES: Two attempted. He died
    in a police shoot out.

Brinkley, Sidney Rufus
(1955 -)
NICKNAME: City Line Stalker
YEARS ACTIVE: 1979
VICTIMS: 4
RACE OF VICTIMS: Varied
AREA: Pennsylvania
KILL METHODS:
Strangulation, Bludgeoning,
Stabbing
RAPE: Yes
NOTES: He killed women on
    both sides of Pennsylvania and
    committed necrophilia with
    their bodies. He had planned to
    kill five people at his trial,
    including the judge, and was
    caught with six razor blades in
    jail, after which he confessed
    his plan in full.

Brisbon, Henry (1956 -)
NICKNAME: I-57 Killer
YEARS ACTIVE: 1973, 1979
VICTIMS: 4
RACE OF VICTIMS: Black
AREA: Illinois
KILL METHODS: Shooting
RAPE: No
NOTES: Killed a husband and
    wife in a robbery, then another
    inmate in prison. Listed as a
    serial killer due to his outbursts
    in court where he claimed he

was a killer and would kill again.
Famous for stabbing John Wayne
Gacy in prison too.

Brisbon, Jr, Ronald T. (1975 -)
YEARS ACTIVE: 1994-2000
VICTIMS: 7
RACE OF VICTIMS: Black
AREA: Washington, D.C.
KILL METHODS: Shooting
RAPE: No
NOTES: Was in jail for murder and
    decided to confess the previous
    murders.

Britt, L. J. (1976 -)
NICKNAME: Capone
YEARS ACTIVE: 1988-1999
VICTIMS: 3
RACE OF VICTIMS: Varied
AREA: Ft. Worth, TX
KILL METHODS: Shooting
RAPE: No
NOTES: All murders were drug
    related.

Britt, Eugene Victor (1957 -)
YEARS ACTIVE: 1995
VICTIMS: 11
RACE OF VICTIMS: Black
AREA: Gary, IN
KILL METHODS: Strangulation,
Beating
RAPE: Yes
NOTES: See Chapter 6 for info.

Broady, Clarence (1973 -)
NICKNAME: Killer
YEARS ACTIVE: 2000's
VICTIMS: 3-6
RACE OF VICTIMS: Black
AREA: Memphis, TN
KILL METHODS: Shooting

RAPE: No
NOTES: Was a hit man for the
    Craig Pettis Drug organization,
    and claims to have killed three
    men and to have assisted in
    three additional murders.
    Suspected of additional
    murders.

Brogsdale, Ricky Henry
(1963 -)
Peeping Tom Killer
YEARS ACTIVE: 1987
VICTIMS: 4
RACE OF VICTIMS: Black
AREA: Washington, DC
KILL METHODS: shooting,
strangling
RAPE: Yes
NOTES: Killed his victims with
    a .22 caliber pistol.

Brooks, Donald (1992 -)
NICKNAME: Crip
YEARS ACTIVE: 2012
VICTIMS: 3-4
RACE OF VICTIMS: Black
AREA: New Orleans, LA
KILL METHODS: Shooting
RAPE: No
NOTES: Was the trigger man in
    a series of drug related
    murders in January 2012.
    Police put the number at three
    to four.

Brooks, Grady (1914 - 1933)
YEARS ACTIVE: 1931-1933
VICTIMS: 19-20
RACE OF VICTIMS: Varied
AREA: Georgia
KILL METHODS:
Strangulation, Knife, Axe

RAPE: Yes
NOTES: Confessed just prior to his
    electrocution. Was able to recall the
    names of eleven victims plus vivid
    details unknown to police about
    eight of the murders.

Brooks, John (1966 -)
YEARS ACTIVE: 1986
VICTIMS: 9
RACE OF VICTIMS: Varied
AREA: New Orleans, LA
KILL METHODS: Shooting
RAPE: No
NOTES: Two attempted murders.
    The murders were over a five-
    month span.

Brooks, Shelly Andre (1969 -)
YEARS ACTIVE: 1999-2006
VICTIMS: 7-14
RACE OF VICTIMS: Black
AREA: Detroit, MI
KILL METHODS: Strangulation
RAPE: Yes
NOTES: See Chapter 6 for info.

Brown, Ali Muhammad (1985-)
YEARS ACTIVE: 2014
VICTIMS: 4
RACE OF VICTIMS: Varied
AREA: Washington and New Jersey
KILL METHODS: Shooting
RAPE: No
NOTES: Over a 2 ½ span, he claimed
    it was his jihad against infidels.

Brown, Charles (1939 - 2007)
YEARS ACTIVE: 1961-1964
VICTIMS: 2
RACE OF VICTIMS: Unknown
AREA: Lakeland, FL
KILL METHODS: unknown

RAPE: No
NOTES: One attempted. Died in
prison.

Brown, Curtis Don (1958 -)
YEARS ACTIVE: 1984-1986
VICTIMS: 3-18
RACE OF VICTIMS: Varied
AREA: Ft. Worth, TX
KILL METHODS: Shooting,
Strangulation
RAPE: Yes
NOTES: See Chapter 6 for info.

Brown, James Cornelius
(1989 -)
NICKNAME: Escort Killer
YEARS ACTIVE: 2011
VICTIMS: 4
RACE OF VICTIMS: Black
AREA: Detroit, MI
KILL METHODS: Strangulation
RAPE: Yes
NOTES: Vicitims were
prostitutes that he killed in
pairs in late 2011. He put their
bodies in the trunk of cars,
then lit the car on fire. His
DNA and confession linked
him to the murders.

Brown, John Henry (1924 -)
YEARS ACTIVE: 1963, 1986
VICTIMS: 2
RACE OF VICTIMS: Unknown
AREA: Georgia
KILL METHODS: Shooting
RAPE: No
NOTES: A repeat offender.

Brown, Vernon (1953 - 2005)
YEARS ACTIVE: 1985-1987
VICTIMS: 5

RACE OF VICTIMS: Black
AREA: IN, MO, TX
KILL METHODS: Strangulation,
stabbing
RAPE: Yes
NOTES: Victims were girls and
women. Had one additional
murder. Executed.

Brown, Vincent William
(1966 -)
YEARS ACTIVE: 2003-2008
VICTIMS: 5
RACE OF VICTIMS: Black
AREA: Baltimore, MD
KILL METHODS: Beating,
Strangulation
RAPE: Yes
NOTES: DNA connected him to his
crimes. He also had one attempted
murder and numerous rapes.

Brown, Willie (1948 -)
YEARS ACTIVE: 1968-1971
VICTIMS: 2
RACE OF VICTIMS: Unknown
AREA: Michigan
KILL METHODS:
RAPE: No
NOTES: A repeat offender.

Brown, Willie A. (1956 -)
YEARS ACTIVE: 1979, 1999
VICTIMS: 3-5
RACE OF VICTIMS: Black
AREA: Detroit, MI
KILL METHODS: Strangulation
RAPE: Yes
NOTES: Worked as a prostitute and
killed at least three gay men. Police
think he killed at least two more,
but the number could be higher.

Broxton, Eugene Alvin (1955 -)
YEARS ACTIVE: 1991
VICTIMS: 5-6
RACE OF VICTIMS: Varied
AREA: Houston, TX
KILL METHODS: Shooting
RAPE: No
NOTES: Two attempted murders
and numerous burglaries over
a seven-week period. He
previously had attempted to
kill two police officers.

Bruce, David Lance (1963 -)
YEARS ACTIVE: 2000-2005
VICTIMS: 6-32
RACE OF VICTIMS: Black
AREA: Lancaster, OH
KILL METHODS: Stabbing
RAPE: Yes
NOTES: Victims were women
left in newly constructed
homes, ditches, fields, and
woods. Suspected in up to 32
more deaths.

Bryant-Bey, Gregory L
(1955 - 2008)
YEARS ACTIVE: 1992
VICTIMS: 2
RACE OF VICTIMS: White
AREA: Toledo, OH
KILL METHODS: Stabbing
RAPE: No
NOTES: Victims were all men.
He removed their pants and
placed them next to the bodies
with their shoes. Executed.

Bryant, Philip Michael (1988-)
YEARS ACTIVE: 2009-2010
VICTIMS: 3

RACE OF VICTIMS: Varied
AREA: Virginia, New York
KILL METHODS: Shooting
RAPE: No
NOTES: Murdered a parole officer in
June 2009 in New York. Murdered
again in November 2009, and then
dismembered the body with an axe
and disposed of it in a trash
dumpster. Last murder was in
March 2010.

Buari, Calvin (1971 -)
YEARS ACTIVE: 1992-1993
VICTIMS: 3-8
RACE OF VICTIMS: Black
AREA: Bronx, NY
KILL METHODS: Shooting
RAPE: No
NOTES: Had the people in his
neighborhood convinced that he
knew black magic and that they
would disappear in the night. He is
charged with 3 murders, but police
believe this number is low.

Bullock, David (1960 -)
YEARS ACTIVE: 1981-1982
VICTIMS: 6
RACE OF VICTIMS: Varied
AREA: New York City, NY
KILL METHODS: shooting
RAPE: No
NOTES: He worked as a gay
prostitute and killed five men and
one woman. The woman was a
prostitute with whom he was
friends. After he told her about his
first murder, she laughed at him.
Enraged, he smothered her with a
pillow. When asked about the
murders, he told police it amused

him. Police think he might
have additional murders.

Bullock, Joseph (1967 -)
YEARS ACTIVE: 1993-1994
VICTIMS: 4-7
RACE OF VICTIMS: Black
AREA: Richmond, VA
KILL METHODS: Shooting
RAPE: No
NOTES: Was the triggerman for
a small drug gang.

Burchart, Leslie Leon
(1950 - 2002)
NICKNAME: Golden Years
Killer
YEARS ACTIVE: 1990-1996
VICTIMS: 7-14
RACE OF VICTIMS: White
AREA: Richmond, VA
KILL METHODS: Strangulation
RAPE: Yes
NOTES: Dubbed the "Golden
Years Killer" because all of his
victims were elderly women.
Police have confirmed he
killed 7, but suspect him in all
14 murders.

Burgess, Jermaine Derrick
(1971 -)
YEARS ACTIVE: 2001-2008
VICTIMS: 4
RACE OF VICTIMS: White
AREA: Philadelphia, PA
KILL METHODS: Strangulation
RAPE: Yes
NOTES: Two attempted
murders. Arrested on another
charge, DNA linked him as the
killer in two cases. Afterwards
he confessed to wo more. All
victims were elderly.

Burkett, Nathan (1950 -)
YEARS ACTIVE: 1978-2002
VICTIMS: 5-6
RACE OF VICTIMS: Varied
AREA: Las Vegas, NV; Mississippi
KILL METHODS: Strangulation
RAPE: Yes
NOTES: All victims were women.
At least four of his victims were
murdered in Las Vegas, all had
been raped. He murdered his
mother in 1982 in MS, and buried
her body in her yard. Suspected in
other murders in both states.

Burks, Adrian Wayne (1971 -)
YEARS ACTIVE: 2005-2009
VICTIMS: 5-6
RACE OF VICTIMS: White
AREA: KS, CA
KILL METHODS: Shooting
RAPE: No
NOTES: He killed four people in
Kansas City execution-style on
June 22, 2009. After arrest, police
connected him to a few murders in
Southern California.

Burns, Keith (1973 -)
YEARS ACTIVE: 1988-1995
VICTIMS: 7+
RACE OF VICTIMS: Black
AREA: Detroit, MI
KILL METHODS: Strangulation
RAPE: Yes
NOTES: Convicted of a 1995 murder,
in 2007 DNA linked him to two
additional murders, and implicated
him in at least four more. Police
have now tied him to all seven

murders, and think he may be responsible for more.

Burton, Harry M (1980 -)
YEARS ACTIVE: 2003
VICTIMS: 3
RACE OF VICTIMS: Varied
AREA: Baltimore, MD
KILL METHODS: Shooting
RAPE: No
NOTES: Leader of the Latrobe organization, a small drug ring.

Burton, Pat (1871 - 1899)
YEARS ACTIVE: 1897-1899
VICTIMS: 7
RACE OF VICTIMS: White
AREA: Texas
KILL METHODS: Shooting
RAPE: No
NOTES: Captured in 1899 after murdering a man, his wife, and their child, he confessed to four additional murders. He was executed on March 24, 1899.

Butler, Jerome (1936 - 1990)
YEARS ACTIVE: 1974, 1986
VICTIMS: 2
RACE OF VICTIMS: Black
AREA: Houston, TX
KILL METHODS: Shooting
RAPE: No
NOTES: A repeat offender who was executed.

Butler, Robert Joe
(1930 - 1997)
YEARS ACTIVE: 1955, 1971, 1992
VICTIMS: 3
RACE OF VICTIMS: White

AREA: TX, KS
KILL METHODS: Stabbing
RAPE: No
NOTES: Was a repeat offender who murdered twice and was paroled twice. His last murder was for stabbing his wife.

Byrd, Maurice Oscar
(1954 - 1991)
YEARS ACTIVE: 1980-1981
VICTIMS: 5
RACE OF VICTIMS: Varied
AREA: St. Louis, MO
KILL METHODS: shooting
RAPE: No
NOTES: Victims of robberies, both male and female.

Calhoun, Vincent (1962 - 1908)
YEARS ACTIVE: 2004-2006
VICTIMS: 2-3
RACE OF VICTIMS: Varied
AREA: Detroit, MI
KILL METHODS: Shooting
RAPE: No
NOTES: Three attempted, he was killed in shootout

Camel, Percy (1990 -)
YEARS ACTIVE: 2009
VICTIMS: 2
RACE OF VICTIMS: Varied
AREA: Stockton CA
KILL METHODS: Shooting
RAPE: No
NOTES: Victims were men.

Campbell, Joseph (1895 -)
NICKNAME: Chicken Joe
YEARS ACTIVE: 1913, 1915
VICTIMS: 2
RACE OF VICTIMS: Varied

AREA: Joliet, IL
KILL METHODS: Beating
RAPE: Yes
NOTES: One victim was the
prison warden's wife.

Campbell, Chester Wheeler
(1931 -)
YEARS ACTIVE: 1955-1980's
VICTIMS: 30+
RACE OF VICTIMS: Varied
AREA: Nationwide
KILL METHODS: Shooting
RAPE: No
NOTES: Was a professional hit
man for Detroit drug dealers.
Most of his hits were in
Detroit, but he was known to
make out-of-town kills. When
arrested, he had a list with over
300 names, many of which
were victims in unsolved
homicides. Police connected at
least thirty of the murders to
him, but suspect many more.

Cantrell, Rufus (? -)
YEARS ACTIVE: 1900-1903
VICTIMS: 6
RACE OF VICTIMS: White
AREA: Indianapolis, IN
KILL METHODS: Shooting
RAPE: No
NOTES: Grave robber as well,
robbed 100 graves to supply
skeletons to a medical supply
company. When they
complained about needing
fresher specimens, he began
killing.

Caple, Patrick Ohara (1964 -)
YEARS ACTIVE: 1994

VICTIMS: 4
RACE OF VICTIMS: Black
AREA: Atlanta, GA
KILL METHODS: Shooting
RAPE: No
NOTES: Killed victims of robberies.

Carrington, Celeste Simone (1962-)
YEARS ACTIVE: 1992
VICTIMS: 2
RACE OF VICTIMS: White
AREA: San Carlos, CA
KILL METHODS: Shooting
RAPE: No
NOTES: Robbery victims. One
attempted

Carter, Charles Lendelle
(1968 -)
YEARS ACTIVE: 2005-2006
VICTIMS: 6
RACE OF VICTIMS: Black
AREA: Atlanta, GA
KILL METHODS: Shooting,
Stabbing, Strangulation
RAPE: Yes
NOTES: Claims to have hunted
Atlantians for 15 years, and is
being investigated for connections
to other murders.

Carter, Clarence (1962 - 2011)
YEARS ACTIVE: 1980
VICTIMS: 2
RACE OF VICTIMS: Varied
AREA: Cleveland, OH
KILL METHODS: Beating
RAPE: No
NOTES: Hit man.

Carter, Robert Anthony
(1964 - 1998)
YEARS ACTIVE: 1981

VICTIMS: 2
RACE OF VICTIMS: White
AREA: Houston, TX
KILL METHODS: shooting
RAPE: No
NOTES: Executed.

Carter, Stephen Nathaniel
(1878 -)
YEARS ACTIVE: 1920
VICTIMS: 2
RACE OF VICTIMS: White
AREA: OH, HI
KILL METHODS: Shooting
RAPE: No
NOTES: Admitted killing a
person while stationed at Pearl
Harbor. Later that year after
leaving the navy, he murdered
in Ohio.

Carter, Samuel (1961 -)
A.K.A. Chin
YEARS ACTIVE: 1989-1996
VICTIMS: 9-13
RACE OF VICTIMS: Varied
AREA: Washington, DC
KILL METHODS: Shooting
RAPE: No
NOTES: Hit man for a drug
organization.

Carter, Shan Edward (1974 -)
YEARS ACTIVE: 1996-1997
VICTIMS: 3
RACE OF VICTIMS: Black
AREA: Wilmington, NC
KILL METHODS: Shooting
RAPE: No
NOTES: Victims were men.

**Catoe, Jarvis Theodore
Roosevelt** (1905 - 1943)

YEARS ACTIVE: 1941-1942
VICTIMS: 13
RACE OF VICTIMS: Varied
AREA: DC, NY
KILL METHODS: Strangulation,
mutilation,
RAPE: Yes
NOTES: See Chapter 6 for info.

Chapple, Damon Lopez
(1960 -)
YEARS ACTIVE: 1984, 1988
VICTIMS: 2
RACE OF VICTIMS: White
AREA: Spokane, WA
KILL METHODS: Beating,
Strangulation, Stabbing
RAPE: Yes
NOTES: A semi-pro body builder
and amateur boxer, he squeezed
one man to death, then stomped his
head flat. Two months later he
raped and beat an elderly woman to
death. He had two more attempted
murders.

Charles, Levi (? - 1901)
A.K.A. George Peters
YEARS ACTIVE: 1895-1900
VICTIMS: 9
RACE OF VICTIMS: Varied
AREA: LA, MS
KILL METHODS: Shooting
RAPE: No
NOTES: After killing two police
officers in New Orleans in 1900, he
incited blacks to riot. The ensuing
riot lasted three days, leaving ten
people killed and another thirty
wounded. He admitted to killing
one woman in the riot. Police
thought they had killed him in the
riot, but that later turned out to be a

case of mistaken identity. In 1901 he contracted smallpox while working in a lumber camp, and made a full confession of his crimes. He admitted to killing the two officers and woman in New Orleans, as well as four men and two women under an alias.

Charleston, Shavonda (1979 -)
YEARS ACTIVE: 2000
VICTIMS: 4
RACE OF VICTIMS: Black
AREA: Louisville, KY
KILL METHODS: Suffocation
RAPE: No
NOTES: Killed her daughters over a five-month period.

Chase, Xavier Demark (1963 -)
YEARS ACTIVE: 1991, 2007
VICTIMS: 3
RACE OF VICTIMS: Black
AREA: Michigan
KILL METHODS: Shooting
RAPE: No
NOTES: A repeat offender

Chatman, Stanley Brent
(1987 -)
YEARS ACTIVE: 2005-2013
VICTIMS: 4
RACE OF VICTIMS: Black
AREA: Birmingham, AL
KILL METHODS: Shooting
RAPE: No
NOTES: Served 7 years for a 2005 murder, killed again soon after release. While out on bond and awaiting trial he murdered a pair of 17 year old

twins and criticially injured their mother.

Cheatham, Phillip Delbert (1973 -)
YEARS ACTIVE: 1994-2003
VICTIMS: 3-4
RACE OF VICTIMS: Black
AREA: Topeka, KS
KILL METHODS: Shooting
RAPE: No
NOTES: Was convicted of manslaughter in 1994 and served a short sentence. In 2003 he killed two women and attempted to kill another as they sat in their car. He is suspected in one additional murder.

Cherry, Ervin E. (1966 -)
YEARS ACTIVE: 1993-1994
VICTIMS: 3
RACE OF VICTIMS: Black
AREA: Florida
KILL METHODS: Strangulation
RAPE: Yes
NOTES: Victims were women.

Chester, Elroy (1969 - 2013)
YEARS ACTIVE: 1997-1998
VICTIMS: 5
RACE OF VICTIMS: White
AREA: Port Arthur, TX
KILL METHODS: Strangulation, Beating, Shooting
RAPE: Yes
NOTES: Admitted to killing three men and two women over a six-month period. His last victim had caught him trying to rape two young girls and was killed.

Chinn III, Sam (1960 -)

YEARS ACTIVE: 1989
VICTIMS: 3
RACE OF VICTIMS: White
AREA: NY, TX
KILL METHODS: Strangulation
RAPE: Yes
NOTES: Killed women. He was a transient who traveled the rails abroad. Police in numerous states where he popped up are investigating cold cases to see if he is connected.

Chisolm, Donsurvi (1980 -)
YEARS ACTIVE: 2007-2010
VICTIMS: 2+
RACE OF VICTIMS: Black
AREA: South Carolina
KILL METHODS: Shooting
RAPE: No
NOTES: Murdered a man in 2007, was released on bond. While awaiting his trial he murdered his nephew and attempted two additional murders.

Choyce, William Jennings (1954 -)
YEARS ACTIVE: 1988-1997
VICTIMS: 3
RACE OF VICTIMS: Black
AREA: Stockton, CA
KILL METHODS: Strangulation
RAPE: Yes
NOTES: Shot women in the head and posed their nude bodies where he dumped them.

Christopher, Leonard (1951 -)
NICKNAME: Frankford Slasher
YEARS ACTIVE: 1985-1990

VICTIMS: 7-9
RACE OF VICTIMS: White
AREA: Philadelphia, PA
KILL METHODS: stabbed with screw driver
RAPE: Yes
NOTES: Was convicted on one count of first- degree murder, and is suspected in up to eight more deaths. Some internet sites list these crimes as unsolved, but the killings stopped after Christopher's arrest, and police consider him the only suspect.

Clark, John (? -)
YEARS ACTIVE: 1908-1924
VICTIMS: 8
RACE OF VICTIMS: Varied
AREA: AL, TN, VA, IL, OH
KILL METHODS: Axe and hammer
RAPE: Yes
NOTES: When caught in 1924 he mumbled, "I'm a murderer, all right and now I'm ready to die." He gave his full confession and told how he had escaped from prison in 1910 in Tennessee to begin a fourteen-year crime spree.

Clark, Tom (- 1902)
YEARS ACTIVE: 1900-1902
VICTIMS: 3
RACE OF VICTIMS: White
AREA: Mississippi
KILL METHODS: Stabbing
RAPE: Yes
NOTES: After the body of Carrie Whitfield was found in Corinth, MS, raped and mutilated, with her head almost severed, police began their hunt. Tom's wife was afraid of him and after a drinking binge

decided to go to the police. When the police arrived he confessed to the crime, and admitted killing two men at different times elsewhere in MS. He was publically executed in Corinth, MS, drawing a crowd in excess of 5,000 people.

Clark, Vernon Lee (1956 -)
YEARS ACTIVE: 1979-1989
VICTIMS: 5-7
RACE OF VICTIMS: White
AREA: White
KILL METHODS:
Strangulation, stabbing
RAPE: Yes
NOTES: All victims were
  female, except one male. The
  five known victims were aged
  23, 61, 68, 70, and 81, he did
  yard work for all. The two
  murders he is suspected in are
  a couple aged 66 and 70 from
  1979. Suspected in additional
  murders.

Clepper, Gregory (1968 -)
YEARS ACTIVE: 1991-1996
VICTIMS: 8-14
RACE OF VICTIMS: Black
AREA: Chicago, IL
KILL METHODS: Strangulation
RAPE: Yes
NOTES: Killed women. Claimed
  40 murders to police, but
  police have been unable to
  verify this.

Clisby, Willie (1947 - 1995)
YEARS ACTIVE: 1978-1979
VICTIMS: 2

RACE OF VICTIMS: White
AREA: Birmingham, AL
KILL METHODS: Axe, Knife
RAPE: No
NOTES: Executed.

Code Jr, Nathaniel R. (1956 -)
YEARS ACTIVE: 1984-1987
VICTIMS: 12
RACE OF VICTIMS: Black
AREA: Louisiana
KILL METHODS: Stabbing,
mutilation, shooting
RAPE: Yes
NOTES: See Chapter 6 for info.

Colbert, Techumseh (1984 -)
YEARS ACTIVE: 2004
VICTIMS: 2
RACE OF VICTIMS: White
AREA: San Diego, CA
KILL METHODS: Shooting
RAPE: No
NOTES: Victims were men.

Collins, Darnell (1962 - 1995)
YEARS ACTIVE: 1995
VICTIMS: 7
RACE OF VICTIMS: Varied
AREA: NY/NJ
KILL METHODS: Stabbing
RAPE: Yes
NOTES: Over a week-long period, he
  killed his girlfriend and six other
  people after failing a drug test. He
  was killed by police.

Collins, Fred (1895 - 1932)
YEARS ACTIVE: 1931-1932
VICTIMS: 2
RACE OF VICTIMS: White
AREA: Pennsylvania

KILL METHODS: Strangulation and stabbing
RAPE: Yes
NOTES: He was serving time for a previous murder. While visiting the prison doctor's home as part of the work release program, he raped and killed the doctor's daughter. At his execution, he smiled and said he was glad he did it.

Collins, Jim (? - 1913)
YEARS ACTIVE: 1900-1913
VICTIMS: 5-7
RACE OF VICTIMS: White
AREA: NY/NJ
KILL METHODS: Stabbing, Shooting
RAPE: No
NOTES: He ran from Arkansas where he was wanted for 3-5 murders. After ending up in Montana, the sheriff wanted to question him about his role in petty crimes. He killed the sheriff and one deputy. He was later lynched by townsfolk.

Colvin, Delmus Charles (1959 -)
YEARS ACTIVE: 2000-2005
VICTIMS: 6
RACE OF VICTIMS: White
AREA: OH, NY
KILL METHODS: Strangulation
RAPE: Yes
NOTES: Was a truck driver and thought to have killed others across the country

Cook, Michael (1974 -)
YEARS ACTIVE: 1998

VICTIMS: 2
RACE OF VICTIMS: White
AREA: Cathedral City, CA
KILL METHODS: Burned to death
RAPE: Yes
NOTES: Killed eldery women.

Cooper, Carl Derrick (1970 -)
YEARS ACTIVE: 1993-1997
VICTIMS: 4
RACE OF VICTIMS: White
AREA: Washington, DC
KILL METHODS: Shooting
RAPE: No
NOTES: Two attempted murders and numerous burglaries.

Cooper, David (1970 -)
YEARS ACTIVE: 1995
VICTIMS: 2
RACE OF VICTIMS: Black
AREA: New Jersey
KILL METHODS: Strangulation
RAPE: Yes
NOTES: Victims were children.

Cooper, Samuel James (1977 -)
YEARS ACTIVE: 2006-2007
VICTIMS: 5
RACE OF VICTIMS: Varied
AREA: Raleigh, NC
KILL METHODS: Shooting
RAPE: No
NOTES: Numerous robberies.

Copeland, Herbert (? - 1925)
YEARS ACTIVE: 1909-1918
VICTIMS: 12
RACE OF VICTIMS: White
AREA: DC., IL, TX, NC
KILL METHODS: Shooting
RAPE: No

NOTES: He was hanged for killing two police officers and a deputy sheriff. Days before his hanging, he confessed to killing another police officer and eight more people. He was able to name most of the names and all of the places and dates of the murders.

Cosby, Keith (1959 -)
YEARS ACTIVE: 1985
VICTIMS: 2
RACE OF VICTIMS: White
AREA: El Cajon, CA
KILL METHODS: Shooting
RAPE: No
NOTES: Killed his robbery victims. One was stabbed 37 times.

Cotton, Walter (? - 1900)
YEARS ACTIVE: 1900
VICTIMS: 4
RACE OF VICTIMS: White
AREA: Virginia
KILL METHODS: Shooting
RAPE: No
NOTES: Had been found guilty of two murders and sentenced to death, but he escaped from jail. While being apprehended, he killed two sheriff's deputies. Angered that he had escaped and killed again, the town lynched him.

Cousar, Bernard (1979 -)
YEARS ACTIVE: 1999
VICTIMS: 2
RACE OF VICTIMS: Black
AREA: Philadelphia, PA
KILL METHODS: Shooting

RAPE: No
NOTES: Victims were men.

Cousins, Clifton (1968 -)
A.K.A. Abdullah Jihad Al-Malik
YEARS ACTIVE: 1988-1989
VICTIMS: 3
RACE OF VICTIMS: Black
AREA: Cleveland, OH
KILL METHODS: Stabbing, shooting
RAPE: Yes
NOTES: Killed two women and one man.

Cousins, Perry Elton (1986 -)
YEARS ACTIVE: 2002-2007
VICTIMS: 2-4
RACE OF VICTIMS: Black
AREA: Newport News VA
KILL METHODS: Shooting
RAPE: No
NOTES: A gang member who took pleasure in killing rivals.

Covington, Juan (1962 -)
YEARS ACTIVE: 1998-2005
VICTIMS: 3
RACE OF VICTIMS: White
AREA: Philadelphia, PA
KILL METHODS: Shooting
RAPE: No
NOTES: Two more attempted.

Cox, Dexter (1990-)
YEARS ACTIVE: 2007
VICTIMS: 3
RACE OF VICTIMS: White
AREA: Memphis, TN
KILL METHODS: Shooting
RAPE: No
NOTES: All murders took place over atwo month span. He had one

attempted murder as well, but the victim survived to testify against him.

Cox, Frederick Pete (1953 -)
YEARS ACTIVE: 1997
VICTIMS: 3
RACE OF VICTIMS: Varied
AREA: Orange County, FL
KILL METHODS: Shooting
RAPE: Yes
NOTES: Two attempted. The Miami news media was not ashamed to call him a serial killer.

Craig, Donald Lavell (1960 -)
NICKNAME: Donnie
YEARS ACTIVE: 1995, 1996
VICTIMS: 2-3
RACE OF VICTIMS: White
AREA: Summit County, Ohio
KILL METHODS: Strangulation
RAPE: Yes
NOTES: Killed girls aged 12-13.

Craine, Louis (1975 - 1989)
YEARS ACTIVE: 1984-1987
VICTIMS: 5
RACE OF VICTIMS: Black
AREA: Los Angeles, CA
KILL METHODS: strangling
RAPE: Yes
NOTES: One of the serial killers stalking LA in the eighties, killing women. His family turned him in and testified against him in court. He was sentenced to death, but he died four months into his sentence.

Crawford, Andre (1962 -)
YEARS ACTIVE: 1994-1999

VICTIMS: 11
RACE OF VICTIMS: Varied
AREA: Chicago, IL
KILL METHODS: Strangulation, beating
RAPE: Yes
NOTES: See Chapter 6 for info.

Crawford, Davon (1976 -)
YEARS ACTIVE: 1995, 2009
VICTIMS: 4
RACE OF VICTIMS: Black
AREA: Cleveland, OH
KILL METHODS: Shooting
RAPE: No
NOTES: Convicted in a 1995 murder, he was released and started a family. In 2009 he murdered his wife and two children.

Crawford, Lucious (1952 -)
YEARS ACTIVE: 1993-2013
VICTIMS: 3
RACE OF VICTIMS: Varied
AREA: SC, NY
KILL METHODS: Stabbing
RAPE: No
NOTES: A man with a history of violence against women, he once stabbed five women in a five day span in 1973. In the 80's he stabbed a woman almost to death, but she survived. In 1993 he stabbed two women in separate incidents, and crushed the skull of one. He was later arrested and served time for assaulting his girlfriend. After being parolled he skipped out on his parole officer, and police found the body of his third victim in his apartment in 2013. He is suspected in other murders in New York.

1975 murder and died in prison.

Crawley, DeWitt (1952 -)
YEARS ACTIVE: 1971 & 1983
VICTIMS: 4
RACE OF VICTIMS: Black
AREA: Philadelphia, PA
KILL METHODS: Stabbing
RAPE: Yes
NOTES: Victims were nieces
and two men

Crockham, Jahmell W. (1992-)
YEARS ACTIVE: 2010
VICTIMS: 2
RACE OF VICTIMS: Varied
AREA: Lakewood, NJ
KILL METHODS: Shooting
RAPE: No
NOTES: One victim was shot 5
times in the chest, the other
was a cop murdered three
months later.

Cromwell, James M. (1938 -)
YEARS ACTIVE: 1987
VICTIMS: 2
RACE OF VICTIMS: White
AREA: Wichita, KS
KILL METHODS: Strangulation
RAPE: Yes
NOTES: Other rapes and
robberies.

Crowson, James (1942 -)
NICKNAME: Smiley
YEARS ACTIVE: 1957, 1975
VICTIMS: 3-4
RACE OF VICTIMS: White
AREA: Philadelphia, PA
KILL METHODS: Shooting
RAPE: No
NOTES: Served two 'life
sentences', was convicted in a

Crump, Michael Wayne
(1960 -)
YEARS ACTIVE: 1985-1986
VICTIMS: 2
RACE OF VICTIMS: Black
AREA: FL, Hillsborough
KILL METHODS: strangling
RAPE: Yes
NOTES: Killed victims of robbery.

Cruz, Jason Andre (1982 -)
YEARS ACTIVE: 2006-2008
VICTIMS: 2
RACE OF VICTIMS: Black
AREA: Wichita, KS
KILL METHODS: Shooting
RAPE: No
NOTES: Committed other assaults
and attempted murder. Might have
committed additional murders.

Cummings, Edward Lee (1941 -)
YEARS ACTIVE: 1983, 1985
VICTIMS: 2
RACE OF VICTIMS: Black
AREA: Raleigh, NC
KILL METHODS: Stabbing
RAPE: Yes
NOTES: Killed two sisters, two years
apart.

Cunningham, Daniel Allen (1960-)
YEARS ACTIVE: 1975, 1981
VICTIMS: 3-6
RACE OF VICTIMS: Black
AREA: Memphis, TN
KILL METHODS: Shooting
RAPE: No
NOTES: Was a hit man for the Craig
Pettis Drug organization, and
claims to have killed three men and

to have assisted in three additional murders. Suspected of additional murders.

Curry, Alva (1969 - 2003)
YEARS ACTIVE: 1991
VICTIMS: 2
RACE OF VICTIMS: White
AREA: Austin, TX
KILL METHODS: Shooting
RAPE: No
NOTES: Killed robbery victims.

Damon, Marvin (1965-)
YEARS ACTIVE: 1993-1994
VICTIMS: 3+
RACE OF VICTIMS: Black
AREA: Richmond, VA
KILL METHODS: Shooting
RAPE: No
NOTES: Was part of a drug enterprise and was the hit man for the group.

Daniels, James Edward (1938 - 1984)
YEARS ACTIVE: 1964, 1979-1984
VICTIMS: 4-7
RACE OF VICTIMS: White
AREA: NY, NJ
KILL METHODS: Shooting
RAPE: No
NOTES: Was a paroled murderer wanted for three murders in NYC. He shot a police officer, then died in a car crash an hour later. He was a member of the New Black Panther Party.

Daughtrey, Earl Llewellyn (1949-)

YEARS ACTIVE: 1971-1980
VICTIMS: 3-4
RACE OF VICTIMS: White
AREA: Georgia
KILL METHODS: Strangulation
RAPE: Yes
NOTES: Four attempted murders. The evidence was suppressed in each of his crimes, and he was never convicted. He later died of Diabetes.

Davidson, Latine Marie Gordon (1965 -)
YEARS ACTIVE: 1983-1985
VICTIMS: 2
RACE OF VICTIMS: Black
AREA: Jeffersonville, IN
KILL METHODS: strangling, drowning
RAPE: No
NOTES: Killed her children.

Davis, Ali Elijah (1987 -)
YEARS ACTIVE: 2007
VICTIMS: 4
RACE OF VICTIMS: Black
AREA: Allentown, PA
KILL METHODS: Shooting
RAPE: No
NOTES: One was a triple murder.

Davis, Bernice (1929 - 1952)
NICKNAME: Bernie
YEARS ACTIVE: 1949-1950
VICTIMS: 3
RACE OF VICTIMS: White
AREA: Chicago, IL
KILL METHODS: Shooting
RAPE: No
NOTES: Killed one man and two police officers.

Davis, Cecil Emile (1959 -)
YEARS ACTIVE: 1997
VICTIMS: 3
RACE OF VICTIMS: Varied
AREA: Tacoma WA
KILL METHODS: Drowning,
suffocation
RAPE: Yes
NOTES: Victims were all
women.

Davis, Curt (1972 -)
YEARS ACTIVE: 1989, 2012
VICTIMS: 4
RACE OF VICTIMS: Black
AREA: Chicago, IL
KILL METHODS: Shooting
RAPE: No
NOTES: Served 18 years of a 40
year sentence for 1st murder,
triple murder 18 years later.

Davis, Daron Duane (1968 -)
YEARS ACTIVE: 1994, 2010
VICTIMS: 2
RACE OF VICTIMS: Black
AREA: South Carolina
KILL METHODS: Child Abuse
RAPE: No
NOTES: Killed two daughters,
sixteen years apart.

Davis, Edward (1985 -)
NICKNAME: Cabbage
YEARS ACTIVE: 2006-2007
VICTIMS: 2-3
RACE OF VICTIMS: Black
AREA: Norfolk, VA
KILL METHODS: Shooting
RAPE: No
NOTES: Gang member shooting
rivals.

Davis, Girvies L (1958 - 1995)
YEARS ACTIVE: 1978-1980
VICTIMS: 4
RACE OF VICTIMS: White
AREA: East St. Louis, IL
KILL METHODS: Shooting
RAPE: No
NOTES: Confessed to the murders,
one of which was of an elderly man
in a wheelchair, he was later
executed.

Davis, Gregory (1965 -)
YEARS ACTIVE: 1986-1987
VICTIMS: 4
RACE OF VICTIMS: White
AREA: MS, GA
KILL METHODS: Strangling,
beating, bludgeoning
RAPE: Yes
NOTES: Victims were elderly
widows. One attempted.

Davis, Johnny (1976 -)
YEARS ACTIVE: 2001
VICTIMS: 4
RACE OF VICTIMS: Black
AREA: New Orleans, LA
KILL METHODS: Shooting
RAPE: No
NOTES: Killed men and women. He
was already serving a life sentence
for murder when in 2009 police
connected him to other murders.

Davis, Larry (1989 -)
YEARS ACTIVE: 2010-2012
VICTIMS: 2
RACE OF VICTIMS: Black
AREA: Harlem, NY
KILL METHODS: Strangulation
RAPE: No

NOTES: Murdered his transvestite lover in 2010, then a year later he murdered his grandmother. He stuffed his grandmother's body in a closet and had a drug fueled party with a prostitute in the bedroom just feet away from the body. Family walked in on his romp two days later, and found the body after smelling rotting flesh.

Davis, Rader (1907 - 1933)
YEARS ACTIVE: 1933
VICTIMS: 2
RACE OF VICTIMS: White
AREA: Atlanta, GA
KILL METHODS: Bludgeoning
RAPE: No
NOTES: Was later executed.

Davis, Robert E. (1966 -)
YEARS ACTIVE: 1985, 2011
VICTIMS: 2
RACE OF VICTIMS: Black
AREA: IL, IN
KILL METHODS: Shooting
RAPE: No
NOTES: Served 13 years and killed again soon after release.

Davis, Von Clark (1946 -)
YEARS ACTIVE: 1970, 1983
VICTIMS: 2
RACE OF VICTIMS: Black
AREA: Hamilton, OH
KILL METHODS: Stabbing, Shooting
RAPE: No
NOTES: Killed his wife and girlfriend.

Davis, William (?-)
YEARS ACTIVE: 1929
VICTIMS: 3
RACE OF VICTIMS: Varied
AREA: South Carolina, New Jersey
KILL METHODS: Shooting, Stabbing
RAPE: No
NOTES: First to murders were in Asheville, SC, the third was a police officer in New Jersey.

Davis, William Howard (1942 -)
YEARS ACTIVE: 1986, 2007
VICTIMS: 6
RACE OF VICTIMS: Black
AREA: Atlanta, GA
KILL METHODS: Shooting
RAPE: No
NOTES: Served time for a manslaughter charge in 1986. After his release, he committed three murders in 2007. Police noticed the murder weapon was the same one used in additional murders in 1986-87 involving people Davis knew. Police now suspect him in those murders as well.

Dawson, Timothy Carl (1961 -)
YEARS ACTIVE: 1998
VICTIMS: 5
RACE OF VICTIMS: Black
AREA: Atlanta, GA
KILL METHODS: Shooting
RAPE: No
NOTES: All happened in October 1998, and he was found guilty of other assaults and rapes.

Dean, Michael (1988 -)
YEARS ACTIVE: 2011-2012

VICTIMS: 4
RACE OF VICTIMS: Black
AREA: Memphis, TN
KILL METHODS: Shooting
RAPE: No
NOTES: Had his girlfriend lure
men with sex. Once the men
agreed and had their guard
down, he would show up and
kill them.

DeCastro, Eugene T. (1965 -)
YEARS ACTIVE: 1982, 1992
VICTIMS: 3
RACE OF VICTIMS: White
AREA: North Carolina
KILL METHODS: Stabbing
RAPE: No
NOTES: His last murder was of
an elderly couple.

Degrafeed, Tony (1964 -)
YEARS ACTIVE: 1994, 2014
VICTIMS: 2
RACE OF VICTIMS: Black
AREA: Indianapolis
KILL METHODS: Stabbing
RAPE: No
NOTES: Both victims were
married to him, each killed 20
years apart.

Demps, Bennie Eddie
(1950 - 2000)
YEARS ACTIVE: 1971-1976
VICTIMS: 3
RACE OF VICTIMS: Black
AREA: Florida
KILL METHODS: Stabbing
RAPE: No
NOTES: One double murder and
one prison murder.

Dennis, Jerome (1966 -)
YEARS ACTIVE: 1991-1992
VICTIMS: 5
RACE OF VICTIMS: Black
AREA: New Jersey
KILL METHODS: Strangling
RAPE: Yes
NOTES: Had been paroled for a rape,
and within a month of his release
he was murdering and raping.

Denton, Omar (1984 -)
YEARS ACTIVE: 2004-2013
VICTIMS: 2-3
RACE OF VICTIMS: Black
AREA: Boston, MA
KILL METHODS: Shooting
RAPE: No
NOTES: First murder was thrown out
of court because of sloppy police
work.

Dickerson, Dashon (1975 -)
YEARS ACTIVE: 1995
VICTIMS: 3
RACE OF VICTIMS: Black
AREA: Youngstown, OH
KILL METHODS: Shooting
RAPE: No
NOTES: A gang member shooting
rivals and innocent people.

Dixon, Emile (1971 -)
YEARS ACTIVE: 1988-2002
VICTIMS: 2-3
RACE OF VICTIMS: Black
AREA: New York City, NY
KILL METHODS: Shooting
RAPE: No
NOTES: Was the leader of the Patio
Crew Gang.

Donnelly, Mike (1882 - 1963)
YEARS ACTIVE: 1911, 1923
VICTIMS: 3
RACE OF VICTIMS: Varied
AREA: WA, ID
KILL METHODS: shooting
RAPE: No
NOTES: A repeat offender. Died in prison.

Dorner, Christopher (1980-2013)
YEARS ACTIVE: 2013
VICTIMS: 4
RACE OF VICTIMS: Varied
AREA: Southern California
KILL METHODS: Shooting
RAPE: No
NOTES: Was a disgruntled ex-LA cop who killed four over a two week span, two of which were police officers. Lead police on one of the largest manhunts in California history, murdered self in remote cabin.

Dorris, Damien Lamont (1979-)
YEARS ACTIVE: 1993-2005
VICTIMS: 5
RACE OF VICTIMS: Varied
AREA: Detroit, MI
KILL METHODS: Shooting
RAPE: No
NOTES: Started his murdering spree at age fourteen as a gang member.

Dorsey IV, Leon David (1995 - 2008)
YEARS ACTIVE: 1994
VICTIMS: 3
RACE OF VICTIMS: White
AREA: Dallas, TX

KILL METHODS: Shooting
RAPE: No
NOTES: Was executed.

Dotson, Jessie (1974 -)
YEARS ACTIVE: 1994, 2008
VICTIMS: 7
RACE OF VICTIMS: Black
AREA: Nashville, TN
KILL METHODS: Shooting, Stabbing
RAPE: No
NOTES: Was paroled for a murder. A few months later he murdered six of his family members.

Drane, Ronnie D (1973 -)
YEARS ACTIVE: 2002-2003
VICTIMS: 4
RACE OF VICTIMS: Black
AREA: IN, KY
KILL METHODS: Shooting
RAPE: No
NOTES: Killed his cousin, another man, and a couple.

Durousseau, Paul (1970 -)
Nicknames: The Killer Cabbie, Jacksonville Serial Killer
YEARS ACTIVE: 1997-2003
VICTIMS: 9-11
RACE OF VICTIMS: Black
AREA: SE US
KILL METHODS: Strangulation
RAPE: Yes
NOTES: See Chapter 6 for info.

Duffy, Charles Lee (1976 -)
YEARS ACTIVE: 1997
VICTIMS: 6
RACE OF VICTIMS: Black
AREA: Atlanta, GA

KILL METHODS: shooting
RAPE: Yes
NOTES: Victims were all
women. In an e-mail interview,
when asked what he would do
tomorrow if released, he
responded, "Find me a pistol."
Yet he denies his crimes.

Dukes, Glen (1967-)
YEARS ACTIVE: 2012
VICTIMS: 2-4
RACE OF VICTIMS: Varied
AREA: San Antonio, TX
KILL METHODS: Shooting,
Strangulation
RAPE: Yes
NOTES: Arrested for two
murders, he is currently the
leading suspect in two
additional murders from 2012.
May have prior murders.

Dunbar, Jerry Lee (1961 -)
YEARS ACTIVE: 1989
VICTIMS: 2
RACE OF VICTIMS: Black
AREA: VA,Fairfax
KILL METHODS: strangling
RAPE: Yes
NOTES: Stashed the bodies
under motel beds.

Dunnham, Dave (1906 -)
YEARS ACTIVE: 1930-1931
VICTIMS: 3
RACE OF VICTIMS: Black
AREA: Maryland
KILL METHODS: Shooting
RAPE: No
NOTES: While serving for one
murder, he admitted to killing
a woman and her son.

Dunnigan, Ahmond (1968 -)
YEARS ACTIVE: 1993
VICTIMS: 2-3
RACE OF VICTIMS: Black
AREA: Atlanta, GA
KILL METHODS: Extreme torture
RAPE: Yes
NOTES: From GA Prison website.

Dye, Ernest (? -)
YEARS ACTIVE: 1906, 1911
VICTIMS: 2
RACE OF VICTIMS: White
AREA: TX, NC
KILL METHODS: Shooting
RAPE: No
NOTES: Killed a soldier and a police
officer.

Easley, Ike (1962-)
YEARS ACTIVE: 1982, 1989
VICTIMS: 2
RACE OF VICTIMS: White
AREA: Joilet, IL
KILL METHODS: Stabbing
RAPE: No
NOTES: One victim was a well
known school superintendent

Ebron, Joseph (1979 -)
YEARS ACTIVE: 1994-2005
VICTIMS: 3
RACE OF VICTIMS: White
AREA: CO, TX
KILL METHODS: Stabbing
RAPE: No
NOTES: First murder at fifteen,
second at seventeen, and third in
prison.

Edeline, Tommy (1968 -)
YEARS ACTIVE: 1992-1998

VICTIMS: 4-14
RACE OF VICTIMS: Varied
AREA: Washington, DC
KILL METHODS: Shooting
RAPE: No
NOTES: Helped his dad preach against drugs and street violence. But he ran the 1-5 Mob, a drug ring in which he took out competitors.

Edwards, Delroy (1959 -)
NICKNAME: Uzi
YEARS ACTIVE: 1984 -1988
VICTIMS: 6
RACE OF VICTIMS: Black
AREA: Brooklyn, NY
KILL METHODS: beaten and shot
RAPE: No
NOTES: Operated a drug ring and was also convicted of seventeen assaults.

Ellis, Walter E. (1951 - 2013)
NICKNAME: Northside Strangler
YEARS ACTIVE: 1986-2007
VICTIMS: 9
RACE OF VICTIMS: Varied
AREA: Milwaukee, WI
KILL METHODS: beating, strangled, shooting, and stabbed
RAPE: Yes
NOTES: Killed women over a twenty-one-year span. Investigators took his DNA from his toothbrush while searching his apartment, and found that it matched that of the nine known victims. He might have additional murders.

Ellis, Will (? -)
A.K.A. Elliot Gardner
YEARS ACTIVE: 1903-1905
VICTIMS: 6
RACE OF VICTIMS: Black
AREA: KY, MS, AL, GA
KILL METHODS: Stabbing
RAPE: No
NOTES: Last victim was a police officer.

Elton, Dwayne W. (1954 -)
YEARS ACTIVE: 1984
VICTIMS: 2
RACE OF VICTIMS: Black
AREA: Washington
KILL METHODS: shooting, strangled, and slit throat
RAPE: Yes
NOTES: Both victims were found at Ft. Lewis, where he was serving in the army. One was twenty-two, another fourteen.

Engram, Andrew R. (1954 -)
YEARS ACTIVE: 1976, 1997
VICTIMS: 2
RACE OF VICTIMS: White
AREA: Arkansas
KILL METHODS: Strangulation
RAPE: Yes
NOTES: A repeat offender for murder. He killed again after his release. On June 6, 1997, at a mall in Little Rock, AR, he raped, beat, and then hanged Laura White with a cord. The crime was listed as one of the most heinous in city history, but typical with media blackouts of blacks hanging whites, the coverage outside of Little Rock was nonexistent.

Essex, Mark James Robert
(1949 - 1973)
YEARS ACTIVE: 1972-1973
VICTIMS: 9-10
RACE OF VICTIMS: White
AREA: New Orleans, LA
KILL METHODS: Shooting
RAPE: No
NOTES: Also wounded thirteen, and was killed by SWAT team after a one-day standoff.

Evins, Fredrick Antonio (1968-)
YEARS ACTIVE: 2002-2003
VICTIMS: 2
RACE OF VICTIMS: White
AREA: Spartanburg, SC
KILL METHODS: Shooting
RAPE: Yes
NOTES: Both victims were females that were raped. One was 55, the other 32.

Ewell, John Wesley (1957 -)
NICKNAME: Grim Creeper
YEARS ACTIVE: 2005-2010
VICTIMS: 4
RACE OF VICTIMS: White
AREA: Los Angeles, CA
KILL METHODS: Shooting
RAPE: No
NOTES: Was a copycat to the Grim Sleeper serial killer. Used the ATM cards of his victims without covering his face for the camera, which led to his identification.

Faison, Stanley (1942 -)
YEARS ACTIVE: 1966, 1987
VICTIMS: 2
RACE OF VICTIMS: Black
AREA: Detroit, MI

KILL METHODS: Beating, Shooting
RAPE: No
NOTES: A repeat offender.

Fayne, Lorenzo (1971 -)
YEARS ACTIVE: 1980s-1990s
VICTIMS: 6
RACE OF VICTIMS: Black
AREA: IL, WI
KILL METHODS: stabbing, strangling
RAPE: Yes
NOTES: Killed five children and one woman.

Ferguson, John Errol
(1948 - 2013)
YEARS ACTIVE: 1977-1978
VICTIMS: 8-10
RACE OF VICTIMS: White
AREA: Miami, FL
KILL METHODS: beating, shooting
RAPE: Yes
NOTES: Five attempted murders, numerous rapes, and burglaries. Six of his victims died in a mass execution.

Ferrell, Jack Dempsey (1940 -)
YEARS ACTIVE: 1981-1992
VICTIMS: 2
RACE OF VICTIMS: Black
AREA: Orlando, FL
KILL METHODS: shooting
RAPE: Yes
NOTES: A repeat offender who killed his girlfriend.

Fields, Stephen Lamar (? -)
YEARS ACTIVE: 1974 & 1978
VICTIMS: 2
RACE OF VICTIMS: Black
AREA: Los Angeles, CA

KILL METHODS: Bludgeoning, stabbing
RAPE: Yes
NOTES: Killed one friend and one woman. Two attempted.

Fisher, Ronald Leo (1981 -)
YEARS ACTIVE: 2005-2009
VICTIMS: 2-3
RACE OF VICTIMS: Black
AREA: Atlanta, GA
KILL METHODS: Shooting
RAPE: No
NOTES: Received life in prison for his first murder.

Fitzgerald, Young (1850 -)
YEARS ACTIVE: 1865-1867
VICTIMS: 5
RACE OF VICTIMS: Varied
AREA: TN, MS
KILL METHODS: Stabbing, Axe
RAPE: No
NOTES: Killed three white men and two black. It is not known what happened to him, but it is suggested his black neighbors helped the sheriff lynch him.

Fletcher, John Bill (1957 -)
YEARS ACTIVE: 1987
VICTIMS: 2
RACE OF VICTIMS: White
AREA: Yakima, WA
KILL METHODS: Stabbing
RAPE: Yes
NOTES: Killed women. Six additional rapes.

Foggy, Henry Lee (1935 - 2014)
YEARS ACTIVE: 1964, 1995
VICTIMS: 2+

RACE OF VICTIMS: Black
AREA: Arizona, Nevada
KILL METHODS: Shooting
RAPE: No
NOTES: After raping a woman in 1964, he went home and returned to kill her boyfriend. After release he was suspected in one additional murder, and murdered again in 1995.

Foster, James (1926 - 1995)
YEARS ACTIVE: 1963
VICTIMS: 4
RACE OF VICTIMS: Black
AREA: New York City, NY
KILL METHODS: Strangulation
RAPE: Yes
NOTES: Admitted to killing a 15 year old girl in his mother's home, and three others in hotels. Was caught checking into a hotel with a young lady he'd planned to make his 5th victim.

Florence, Henry Antawon (1976 -)
YEARS ACTIVE: 1998-1999
VICTIMS: 2
RACE OF VICTIMS: Unknown
AREA: Fort Meyers, FL
KILL METHODS: Shooting
RAPE: No
NOTES: From FL prison website.

Ford, Robert (1892 - 1924)
A.K.A. Noah Arnold
YEARS ACTIVE: 1915-1923
VICTIMS: 5
RACE OF VICTIMS: Varied
AREA: ID, WA
KILL METHODS: Shooting
RAPE: Yes

NOTES: Confessed to five murders and one attempted.

Forte, Linwood Earl (1965 -)
NICKNAME: Nightstalker
YEARS ACTIVE: 1990
VICTIMS: 3
RACE OF VICTIMS: White
AREA: Goldsbourough, NC
KILL METHODS:
Strangulation, Arson, Suffocation
RAPE: Yes
NOTES: Killed elderly women.

Francois, Kendall (1971 - 2014)
YEARS ACTIVE: 1996-1998
VICTIMS: 8-10
RACE OF VICTIMS: White
AREA: Poughkeepsie, NY
KILL METHODS: Strangulation
RAPE: Yes
NOTES: See Chapter 6 for info.

Franklin, Jr., Lonnie David
(1953 -)
NICKNAME: Grim Sleeper
YEARS ACTIVE: 1970-1990
VICTIMS: 17-68
RACE OF VICTIMS: Black
AREA: Los Angeles, CA
KILL METHODS:
Strangulation, shooting
RAPE: Yes
NOTES: See Chapter 6 for info.

Franklin, Quawn Moses
(1977 -)
YEARS ACTIVE: 2001
VICTIMS: 2
RACE OF VICTIMS: White
AREA: Orlando, FL
KILL METHODS: Shooting
RAPE: No

NOTES: Two attempted.

Franklin, Zackery Cody(1991-)
YEARS ACTIVE: 2007-2011
VICTIMS: 4
RACE OF VICTIMS: Black
AREA: New Haven, CT
KILL METHODS: Shooting
RAPE: No
NOTES: All victims were men. One was murdered for his gold chain, another for his three wheeled bike.

Freeney, Ray MacArthur
(1973 -)
YEARS ACTIVE: 2002
VICTIMS: 2
RACE OF VICTIMS: Black
AREA: Houston, TX
KILL METHODS: Stabbing,
Strangulation
RAPE: Yes
NOTES: Three attempted.

Gaffney, Marquel (1993 -)
YEARS ACTIVE: 2007-2014
VICTIMS: 2
RACE OF VICTIMS: Black
AREA: Baltimore, MD
KILL METHODS: Shooting
RAPE: No
NOTES: Convicted of murder in 2007, he served a few years then killed at least one additional time. Other possible murders.

Gary, Carlton Michael (1952 -)
NICKNAME: Stocking Strangler
YEARS ACTIVE: 1970-1978
VICTIMS: 9
RACE OF VICTIMS: White
AREA: NY, GA

KILL METHODS: Strangulation
RAPE: Yes
NOTES: All victims were white women. He had 3 attempted that survived. Despite DNA matching his in some of the cases, surviving eyewitness' that described him, a bite-mark that matched his, and him having processions from some of the dead victims; in 2014 lawyers appealed the state of Georgia proclaiming his innocence.

Gaskin, Louis Bernard (1967 -)
NICKNAME: Ninja Killer
YEARS ACTIVE: 1986 & 1989
VICTIMS: 8
RACE OF VICTIMS: White
AREA: Palm Coast, FL
KILL METHODS: Shooting
RAPE: No
NOTES: Thought that he was a ninja who could turn invisible to escape capture.

Gay, Andre Cleveland (1974 -)
YEARS ACTIVE: 1990, 2014
VICTIMS: 4
RACE OF VICTIMS: Black
AREA: Atlanta, GA
KILL METHODS: Shooting
RAPE: No
NOTES: After serving a 22 year prison sentence, he murdered two more victims he was holding for ransom just months after his release.

Gaynor, Alfred J. (1965 -)
A.K.A. Big Al

YEARS ACTIVE: 1996-1998
VICTIMS: 10
RACE OF VICTIMS: Varied
AREA: Maryland
KILL METHODS: Strangulation
RAPE: Yes
NOTES: See Chapter 6 for info.

Geralds, Jr., Hubert (1964 -)
YEARS ACTIVE: 1995
VICTIMS: 7
RACE OF VICTIMS: Black
AREA: Chicago, IL
KILL METHODS: Strangulation
RAPE: Yes
NOTES: Admitted to killing six women, but the evidence ties him to one additional murder.

Gibbs, Amin (1978-)
YEARS ACTIVE: 1995, 2012
VICTIMS: 2
RACE OF VICTIMS: Varied
AREA: Philadelphia, PA
KILL METHODS: Shooting
RAPE: No
NOTES: One victim was during a robbery, another was gunned down at a party.

Gibson, Gregory Devon (1978 - 1998)
YEARS ACTIVE: 1992, 1997
VICTIMS: 2
RACE OF VICTIMS: White
AREA: Durham, NC
KILL METHODS: Hammer
RAPE: No
NOTES: Hanged himself in jail.

Gibson, Moses (? - 1920)
YEARS ACTIVE: 1908-1920
VICTIMS: 7

RACE OF VICTIMS: White
AREA: LA, AZ, CA
KILL METHODS: Hammer
RAPE: No
NOTES: Was sentenced to die
for the killing of a rancher,
Roy Trapp. After his trial he
confessed to murdering six
others with a hammer, and
provided the names and places
of the murders.

Gilyard, Lorenzo J. (1950 -)
YEARS ACTIVE: 1977-1993
VICTIMS: 13
RACE OF VICTIMS: Varied
AREA: Kansas City, MO
KILL METHODS: Strangulation
RAPE: Yes
NOTES: See Chapter 6 for info.

Glenn, Freddie (1957 -)
YEARS ACTIVE: 1975
VICTIMS: 3
RACE OF VICTIMS: White
AREA: Colorado Springs, CO
KILL METHODS: Stabbing
RAPE: Yes
NOTES: Kelsey Grammer's
sister was a victim.

Gordon, John (? - 1897)
A.K.A. Lewis Nelson
YEARS ACTIVE: 1895-1897
VICTIMS: 3
RACE OF VICTIMS: White
AREA: Vicksburg, MS
KILL METHODS: Beating
RAPE: No
NOTES: Beat a man to death
with a gun barrel and was
caught. Confessed two other
murders. After verifying the

information, the town came
together and hanged him from a
pecan tree.

Gorman, Michael L. (1960 -)
YEARS ACTIVE: 1988, 1989
VICTIMS: 2
RACE OF VICTIMS: Black
AREA: Kansas City, MO
KILL METHODS: unknown
RAPE: Yes
NOTES: Victims were women. DNA
incriminated him in 2003.

Gosnell, Kermit (1941 -)
YEARS ACTIVE: 2012
VICTIMS: 7+
RACE OF VICTIMS: Varied
AREA: Philadelpia, PA
KILL METHODS: Strangulation
RAPE: No
NOTES: Was an abortion doctor that
delievered full term babies alive,
then killed them by slicing their
spines a few minutes after birth.
Police speculate some could have
been alive for up to an hour after
birth, and seven may be a low
number.

Goudeau, Mark (1964 -)
NICKNAME: Baseline Killer
YEARS ACTIVE: 2005-2006
VICTIMS: 9
RACE OF VICTIMS: Varied
AREA: Valley of the Sun, AZ
KILL METHODS: Shooting
RAPE: Yes
NOTES: See Chapter 6 for info.

Graham, Harrison F (1958 -)
Nicknames: Marty, The Corpse
Collector

YEARS ACTIVE: 1987
VICTIMS: 9
RACE OF VICTIMS: Black
AREA: Philadelphia, PA
KILL METHODS: Strangulation
RAPE: Yes
NOTES: See Chapter 6 for info.

Grant, Freddie (1961 -)
YEARS ACTIVE: 2010-2012
VICTIMS: 3
RACE OF VICTIMS: Black
AREA: Columbia, SC
KILL METHODS: Shooting
RAPE: Yes
NOTES: Yougest victim was 14,
   all victims were females.

Grant, Sam (? - 1876)
YEARS ACTIVE: 1870-1876
VICTIMS: 20-50
RACE OF VICTIMS: Varied
AREA: West US
KILL METHODS: Shooting
RAPE: No
NOTES: Was a hired killer.
   Killed by John "Liver Eating"
   Johnston with a tomahawk in
   the northern plains. Killed in
   battle.

Granviel, Kenneth
(1950 - 1996)
YEARS ACTIVE: 1974
VICTIMS: 7
RACE OF VICTIMS: Black
AREA: Ft. Worth, TX
KILL METHODS: Stabbing
RAPE: Yes
NOTES: Killed a family of five
   and also killed two friends.
   Executed

Gray, Coleman Wayne
(1961 - 1991)
YEARS ACTIVE: 1984-1985
VICTIMS: 3
RACE OF VICTIMS: White
AREA: Virginia
KILL METHODS: shooting
RAPE: No
NOTES: Killed a mother and
   daughter and one man. Executed.

Gray, Josephine Virginia
(1946 -)
YEARS ACTIVE: 1974-1996
VICTIMS: 3
RACE OF VICTIMS: Black
AREA: Washington, DC
KILL METHODS: Shooting
RAPE: No
NOTES: All victims were husbands.

Gray, Ronald Adrian (1966 -)
YEARS ACTIVE: 1986-1987
VICTIMS: 4
RACE OF VICTIMS: White
AREA: North Carolina
KILL METHODS: Shooting
RAPE: Yes
NOTES: Killed women. Four more
   women were raped but survived.

Green, Andra Gabriel (1988 -)
YEARS ACTIVE: 2007-2009
VICTIMS: 2-3
RACE OF VICTIMS: Black
AREA: Hampton, VA
KILL METHODS: Shooting
RAPE: No
NOTES: Motivation was to steal
   drugs.

Green III, Cleo Joel (1957 - 1993)

NICKNAME: Red Demon
YEARS ACTIVE: 1983
VICTIMS: 3
RACE OF VICTIMS: Black
AREA: Louisville NY
KILL METHODS:
Strangulation, Beating
RAPE: Yes
NOTES: Killed women. He
attempted one more.

Greene, Dwayne (1976 -)
YEARS ACTIVE: 2012
VICTIMS: 2
RACE OF VICTIMS: Black
AREA: Savannah, GA
KILL METHODS: Shooting
RAPE: No
NOTES: 1 attempted, all drug
related.

Greenwood, Vaughn Orrin
(1943 -)
NICKNAME: The Skid Row
Slasher
YEARS ACTIVE: 1964, 1974-
1975
VICTIMS: 11
RACE OF VICTIMS: White
AREA: Los Angeles, CA
KILL METHODS: Stabbing,
Beating
RAPE: Yes
NOTES: See Chapter 6 for info.

Griffin, Geoffrey (1970 -)
NICKNAME: Roseland Killer
YEARS ACTIVE: 2000
VICTIMS: 7-8
RACE OF VICTIMS: Black
AREA: Chicago, IL
KILL METHODS: Strangulation
RAPE: Yes

NOTES: All victims were women. He
stashed their bodies in abandoned
homes, and some weren't found
until weeks after the murder.

Griffin, Kenneth (1945 -)
YEARS ACTIVE: 1968, 1975
VICTIMS: 3
RACE OF VICTIMS: White
AREA: Gainesville, FL
KILL METHODS: Shooting
RAPE: No
NOTES: A repeat offender. Was
released from prison in 2008

Grissom, Jr., Richard (1960 -)
YEARS ACTIVE: 1989
VICTIMS: 4
RACE OF VICTIMS: White
AREA: KS, MO
KILL METHODS: Strangulation
RAPE: Yes
NOTES: Killed women. Two more
possible murders.

Groves, Vincent Darrell
(1954 - 1996)
YEARS ACTIVE: 1978-1988
VICTIMS: 18-20
RACE OF VICTIMS: White
AREA: Denver, CO
KILL METHODS: Strangulation
RAPE: Yes
NOTES: See Chapter 6 for info.

Guillory, Jeffery Lee (1966 -)
YEARS ACTIVE: 1999-2002
VICTIMS: 8
RACE OF VICTIMS: Black
AREA: Baton Rouge, LA
KILL METHODS: beating
RAPE: Yes
NOTES: Suspected in more.

Guzman, Matthew (1989 -)
YEARS ACTIVE: 2010
VICTIMS: 2
RACE OF VICTIMS: White
AREA: Miami, FL
KILL METHODS: Shooting
RAPE: No
NOTES: Victims were men.

Hager, Thomas Morroco
(1973 -)
YEARS ACTIVE: 1992-1997
VICTIMS: 7-12
RACE OF VICTIMS: Varied
AREA: DC, VA
KILL METHODS: Stabbing,
shooting
RAPE: No
NOTES: A ruthless killer who
also sold drugs. One victim
was stabbed eighty-two times.
Others were shot.

Hall, Eric (1981 -)
YEARS ACTIVE: 1996-2003
VICTIMS: 4-6
RACE OF VICTIMS: Varied
AREA: Baltimore, MD
KILL METHODS: Shooting
RAPE: No
NOTES: Was the hit man for the
Rice Drug Organization.

Hall, Dewain (1964 - 2005)
YEARS ACTIVE: 1989
VICTIMS: 2
RACE OF VICTIMS: Black
AREA: Oakland, CA
KILL METHODS: Hanging,
beating, and shooting
RAPE: Yes
NOTES: Suspected in more.

Hammond, Lloyd W (1986 -)
YEARS ACTIVE: 2006
VICTIMS: 3-4
RACE OF VICTIMS: Black
AREA: Louisville, KY
KILL METHODS: Shooting
RAPE: No
NOTES: Victims were men.

Hammond, Tevin (1992 -)
YEARS ACTIVE: 2013
VICTIMS: 6
RACE OF VICTIMS: Varied
AREA: Philadelphia, PA
KILL METHODS: Shooting
RAPE: No
NOTES: All were murders were
robbery related, but according to
his accomplice he didn't have to
kill the victim, but started because
he lusted for blood.

Hampton, Thomas J. (? - 1901)
YEARS ACTIVE: 1887-1901
VICTIMS: 7
RACE OF VICTIMS: Varied
AREA: FL, SC, GA
KILL METHODS: Beating, stabbing
RAPE: No
NOTES: Was to be executed for a
double murder in Florida. Just
before execution he admitted to the
five other murders. While at the
gallows, he smiled while smoking a
cigar. He was noted to have a
chipper attitude, even joking with
the executioner as the black hood
was placed over his head. Some
consider this proof his consience
was clear and he was ready for
death.

Hampton, Kevin L. (1961 -)
YEARS ACTIVE: 2000
VICTIMS: 3
RACE OF VICTIMS: White
AREA: Terre Haute, IN
KILL METHODS: Strangulation
RAPE: Yes
NOTES: Victims were women.
Two additional rapes.

Hance, William Henry
(1945 - 1994)
YEARS ACTIVE: 1978
VICTIMS: 4
RACE OF VICTIMS: Black
AREA: Ft. Benning, GA
KILL METHODS: Strangulation
RAPE: Yes
NOTES: Sent a letter to police
claiming to be a group of white
supremacists who loved killing
black women. He was later
executed.

Hankerson, Larry Shannon
(1973 -)
YEARS ACTIVE: 1994
VICTIMS: 3
RACE OF VICTIMS: Black
AREA: Atlanta, GA
KILL METHODS: Shooting
RAPE: No
NOTES: Victims were men.

Hankton, Telly (1975 -)
YEARS ACTIVE: 2008-2012
VICTIMS: 4+
RACE OF VICTIMS: Black
AREA: New Orleans, LA
KILL METHODS: Shooting
RAPE: No

NOTES: All were murders were drug
related. Suspected in additional
murders.

Hardaway, John Coleman (1966-)
YEARS ACTIVE: 1996, 2011
VICTIMS: 2
RACE OF VICTIMS: White
AREA: Portland, OR
KILL METHODS: Beating
RAPE: No
NOTES: Both murders were
girlfriends, parolled for first murder

Hardy, Jr., Melvin Jay (1978 -)
YEARS ACTIVE: 1995-1997
VICTIMS: 2
RACE OF VICTIMS: Varied
AREA: Charlotte, NC
KILL METHODS: Shooting
RAPE: No
NOTES: Robbed victims.

Hargrove, Demetrius Ramar
(1973 -)
YEARS ACTIVE: 1998
VICTIMS: 3-4
RACE OF VICTIMS: Varied
AREA: Leavenworth, KS
KILL METHODS: Shooting
RAPE: No
NOTES: Killed for revenge and
because of a small debt owed to
him.

Harrington, Paul (1946 -)
YEARS ACTIVE: 1975, 1999
VICTIMS: 5
RACE OF VICTIMS: Black
AREA: Detroit, MI
KILL METHODS: Shooting
RAPE: No

NOTES: In 1975, killed his wife and kids. In 1999, repeated this with new wife and child.

Harris, Carl (1934 -)
YEARS ACTIVE: 1993
VICTIMS: 3
RACE OF VICTIMS: Black
AREA: Brunswick GA
KILL METHODS: Shooting
RAPE: No
NOTES: Killed two women and one infant.

Harris, Earl Carl (1902 -)
YEARS ACTIVE: 1936-1936
VICTIMS: 5
RACE OF VICTIMS: Black
AREA: MO, MI
KILL METHODS: Stabbing, bludgeoning
RAPE: Yes
NOTES: Victims were black women he wooed with his voodoo charm.

Harris, DeWayne Lee (1964 -)
YEARS ACTIVE: 1998
VICTIMS: 3
RACE OF VICTIMS: White
AREA: Seattle, WA
KILL METHODS: Strangulation
RAPE: Yes
NOTES: Killed women. Bound victims with their shoelaces, gagged them with their underpants, strangled them, and left them in vacant city lots.

Harris, Joseph M.
(1956 - 1996)
YEARS ACTIVE: 1990-1991

VICTIMS: 4
RACE OF VICTIMS: White
AREA: New Jersey
KILL METHODS: Shooting, Stabbing
RAPE: Yes
NOTES: First victim was shot, his wife and young daughters raped by Joseph. A year later he broke into his boss's home and decapitated her with a sword and shot her boyfriend. The same day he shot and killed two mail clerks at the post office. Before being caught, he attempted to blow up police with explosives.

Harris, Michael Darnell
(1963 -)
YEARS ACTIVE: 1983
VICTIMS: 2
RACE OF VICTIMS: Varied
AREA: Detroit, MI
KILL METHODS: Strangling
RAPE: Yes
NOTES: Killed elderly women.

Harris, Ralph (1972 -)
NICKNAME: Pill Hill Rapist
YEARS ACTIVE: 1992-1995
VICTIMS: 6
RACE OF VICTIMS: White
AREA: Chicago, IL
KILL METHODS: Shooting
RAPE: Yes
NOTES: Committed thirteen armed robberies and six sexual assaults.

Harris, Robert Wayne
(1972 - 2012)
YEARS ACTIVE: 1999-2000
VICTIMS: 6
RACE OF VICTIMS: Varied

AREA: Dallas, TX
KILL METHODS: Shooting
RAPE: No
NOTES: Kidnapped and murdered a woman in November 1999. In March 2000 he was fired for exposing himself to female co-workers. Disgruntled he borrowed a car three days later, and surprised everyone at the carwash he had worked at. After shooting seven former co-workers, five died from their wounds. On the day of his arrest a few days later he was on his way to murder his ex-girlfriend. Executed in 2012.

Harrison, Lester (1933 -)
YEARS ACTIVE: 1951-1973
VICTIMS: 7
RACE OF VICTIMS: White
AREA: Grant Park, IL
KILL METHODS: Strangulation, stabbing, beating
RAPE: Yes
NOTES: See Chapter 6 for info.

Hartley, Kenneth (1967 -)
YEARS ACTIVE: 1987, 1991
VICTIMS: 2-2
RACE OF VICTIMS: Black
AREA: Tampa, FL
KILL METHODS: Shooting
RAPE: No
NOTES: Killed girlfriend and friend.

Harvard, William Gary
(1957 - 2005)
YEARS ACTIVE: 1978, 1986
VICTIMS: 2

RACE OF VICTIMS: White
AREA: Miami, FL
KILL METHODS: Shooting
RAPE: No
NOTES: A repeat offender. Died in prison.

Harwell, Joseph (1960 -)
YEARS ACTIVE: 1989-1997
VICTIMS: 6
RACE OF VICTIMS: Black
AREA: Cleveland OH
KILL METHODS: Strangling
RAPE: Yes
NOTES: Was already serving time in prison for a murder when police tied his DNA to five other victims. He lived in the same neighborhood as Anthony Sowell, and they were investigating murders from the area to see if Sowell was their killer when the evidence pointing to Harwell was found.

Hauser, Melvin (1953 -)
YEARS ACTIVE: 1967-1990
VICTIMS: 3
RACE OF VICTIMS: Black
AREA: Pittsburgh, PA
KILL METHODS: Shooting
RAPE: No
NOTES: Repeat offender.

Hawkins, Charles C.
(1940 - 2000)
YEARS ACTIVE: 1966
VICTIMS: 3
RACE OF VICTIMS: White
AREA: Ocala, FL
KILL METHODS: Shooting
RAPE: No
NOTES: Died in prison.

Hawkins, Samuel (1943 - 1995)
NICKNAME: Traveling Rapist
YEARS ACTIVE: 1976-1977
VICTIMS: 2
RACE OF VICTIMS: Black
AREA: Amarillo, TX
KILL METHODS: Stabbing
RAPE: Yes
NOTES: Killed one girl and one woman. Confessed to over forty rapes in CO, OK, and TX.

Hawkins, Timothy Andrew (1970 -)
YEARS ACTIVE: 1998, 2001
VICTIMS: 3
RACE OF VICTIMS: Black
AREA: Baltimore, MD
KILL METHODS: Strangulation
RAPE: Yes
NOTES: Killed two women and a twelve-year-old boy. DNA tied him to the women's deaths years later.

Hawkins, Jr., Thomas William (1963 - 1994)
YEARS ACTIVE: 1980, 1996
VICTIMS: 3
RACE OF VICTIMS: Varied
AREA: Norristown, PA
KILL METHODS: Strangulation, stabbing
RAPE: Yes
NOTES: Three girls. Suspected in more. Executed.

Hawkins, Jr., James David (1944 -)
YEARS ACTIVE: 1983-1984
VICTIMS: 3
RACE OF VICTIMS: Varied

AREA: Watts, CA
KILL METHODS: Shooting
RAPE: No
NOTES: A gang member who robbed and killed aside from his gang.

Hayward, Steven Douglas (1969 -)
YEARS ACTIVE: 1988 & 2004
VICTIMS: 2-3
RACE OF VICTIMS: White
AREA: Port St. Lucie, FL
KILL METHODS: Shooting
RAPE: No
NOTES: A repeat offender.

Henderson, Thomas A (1952 -)
YEARS ACTIVE: 1996-1998
VICTIMS: 5
RACE OF VICTIMS: Black
AREA: Georgia
KILL METHODS: Shooting
RAPE: No
NOTES: Killed men and women.

Henry, John Ruthell (1951 -)
YEARS ACTIVE: 1975 & 1985
VICTIMS: 3
RACE OF VICTIMS: Black
AREA: Florida
KILL METHODS: Stabbing
RAPE: No
NOTES: Killed both of his wives and one step child.

Herring, William Morgan (1959 -)
YEARS ACTIVE: 1994
VICTIMS: 2
RACE OF VICTIMS: White
AREA: Raleigh, NC
KILL METHODS: Unknown
RAPE: Yes
NOTES: From NC prison website.

Herron, Ronald Raheem (1983-)
NICKNAME: Ra Diggs
YEARS ACTIVE: 2001-2009
VICTIMS: 3
RACE OF VICTIMS: Black
AREA: New York City, NY
KILL METHODS: Shooting
RAPE: No
NOTES: In 2001 he was found innocent in a court of law for murder. In 2010, while serving a federal prison sentence for drugs, he posted to his Twitter account about beating the system in 2001 and about two other murders in 2008 and 2009.

Hickson, Monroe (1909 - 1967)
NICKNAME: Blue Boy
YEARS ACTIVE: 1946-1957
VICTIMS: 4
RACE OF VICTIMS: Varied
AREA: South Carolina
KILL METHODS: Shooting
RAPE: No
NOTES: Arrested for larceny in 1957, he astounded the police by confessing to a string of crimes dating back to 1946 that included four murders.

Hill, Clarence (1908 - 1973)
NICKNAME: Duck Island Killer
YEARS ACTIVE: 1939-1942
VICTIMS: 6
RACE OF VICTIMS: White
AREA: New Jersey
KILL METHODS: Shooting
RAPE: No
NOTES: Victims were three pairs of lover's lane couples.

Recently there has been an abundance of blogs proclaiming he was framed, but this contradicts the evidence and his confession.

Hill, DdeAngelo (1998 -)
YEARS ACTIVE: 2014
VICTIMS: 2
RACE OF VICTIMS: Black
AREA: Indianapolis, IN
KILL METHODS: Shooting
RAPE: No
NOTES: Both victims killed a week apart.

Hill, Donetta (1966 -)
YEARS ACTIVE: 1990
VICTIMS: 2
RACE OF VICTIMS: Varied
AREA: Philadelphia, PA
KILL METHODS: Hammer
RAPE: No
NOTES: She was a prostitute who killed customers because of a crack addicition.

Hill, Ivan Jerome (1961 -)
NICKNAME: 60 Freeway Slayer
YEARS ACTIVE: 1986-1994
VICTIMS: 8
RACE OF VICTIMS: Varied
AREA: Los Angeles, CA
KILL METHODS: Strangulation
RAPE: Yes
NOTES: Earned his nickname because the murders were all within close proximity to the Ponoma 60 Freeway. He freely admitted his crimes, but like many serial killers, he admitted to the murders about which police asked him and no more. He first confessed to the six murders on

which he was questioned. In 2009 he was connected to two additional murders and confessed to both.

Hill, Theodis (1967 -)
YEARS ACTIVE: <2010
VICTIMS: 4
RACE OF VICTIMS: Varied
AREA: MO, AR
KILL METHODS: Strangulation
RAPE: Yes
NOTES: Killed women. Suspected in additional murders.

Hill, Walter (1937 - 1997)
YEARS ACTIVE: 1951, 1977
VICTIMS: 5
RACE OF VICTIMS: Black
AREA: GA, AL
KILL METHODS: Shooting
RAPE: No
NOTES: On Jan. 7, 1977, ex-convict Hill fatally shot Willie Mae Hammock, 60 (who refused to allow him to marry her 13-year-old daughter, Toni), Miss Hammock's stepbrother, John Tatum Jr., 36, and his wife, Lois Jean Tatum, 34. The three of them were shot. Hill was executed.

Hill, Warren Lee (1960 -)
YEARS ACTIVE: 1985, 1990
VICTIMS: 2
RACE OF VICTIMS: Varied
AREA: Georgia
KILL METHODS: Shooting, Beating
RAPE: No

NOTES: First murder was his girlfriend; the second was a prison murder.

Hines, Douglas (1949 -)
YEARS ACTIVE: 1973-1991
VICTIMS: 2
RACE OF VICTIMS: White
AREA: TX/CA
KILL METHODS: stabbing
RAPE: Yes
NOTES: Victims were women.

Hinton, Ronald (1972 -)
YEARS ACTIVE: 1996-1999
VICTIMS: 3
RACE OF VICTIMS: White
AREA: Chicago, IL
KILL METHODS: Strangulation
RAPE: Yes
NOTES: Killed with accomplices. His third-grade daughter saw a police composite sketch on a media broadcast and told her teacher that her daddy was on TV.

Hipps, Anthony Jerome (1949 -)
YEARS ACTIVE: 1978, 1995
VICTIMS: 2
RACE OF VICTIMS: Black
AREA: Spencer, NC
KILL METHODS: Stabbing, bludgeoning
RAPE: No
NOTES: A repeat offender.

Hodges, Willie James (1960 -)
YEARS ACTIVE: 2001-2003
VICTIMS: 3
RACE OF VICTIMS: White
AREA: FL, AL, OH
KILL METHODS: Hammer, stabbing

RAPE: Yes
NOTES: Suspected in more.

Holland, Phillip Dylan
(1958 - 2009)
YEARS ACTIVE: 1981, 1988
VICTIMS: 2
RACE OF VICTIMS: Unknown
AREA: Ft. Lauderdale, FL
KILL METHODS: Unknown
RAPE: No
NOTES: Killed one woman and
one inmate.

Holmes, Darryl Lamont
(1974 -)
YEARS ACTIVE: 1996
VICTIMS: 2
RACE OF VICTIMS: White
AREA: Greenville, SC
KILL METHODS: Shooting
RAPE: No
NOTES: Robbed victims.

Holmes, Willie James (1943 -)
YEARS ACTIVE: 1978-1979
VICTIMS: 4
RACE OF VICTIMS: Black
AREA: Pittsburgh, PA
KILL METHODS: Shooting,
strangulation, stabbing
RAPE: No
NOTES: Was a contractor who
knew the victims and even
attended church with a few of
them. After killing them, he
robbed their homes. He was
caught after the wife of his last
victim shook her bindings off
her wrists and escaped to tell
police. He later died in prison.

Holstem, Leon Cornelius
(1950 -)
YEARS ACTIVE: 1966
VICTIMS: 3
RACE OF VICTIMS: White
AREA: Ft. Lauderdale, FL
KILL METHODS: Stabbing
RAPE: Yes
NOTES: Killed three white boys.
Raped. One more knifed.

Hooper, Murry (1946 -)
YEARS ACTIVE: 1980-1981
VICTIMS: 5
RACE OF VICTIMS: Varied
AREA: AZ, IL
KILL METHODS: Shooting
RAPE: No
NOTES: Hit man.

Hopewell, Raymond (1971 -)
NICKNAME: Money
YEARS ACTIVE: 2004-2005
VICTIMS: 5
RACE OF VICTIMS: White
AREA: West Baltimore, MD
KILL METHODS: Strangulation
RAPE: Yes
NOTES: One additional rape and four
assaults. Was released from a
halfway house in 2004 and soon
began his killing spree.

Horton II, James F (? -)
YEARS ACTIVE: 1973, 1984
VICTIMS: 2
RACE OF VICTIMS: White
AREA: IL, CA
KILL METHODS: Shooting, hammer
RAPE: No
NOTES: Released, see chapter 5 for
more info.

Howard, Angelo (1976 -)
YEARS ACTIVE: 2003-2005
VICTIMS: 5
RACE OF VICTIMS: Black
AREA: Cincinnati, OH
KILL METHODS: Shooting
RAPE: No
NOTES: Had possible accomplices.

Howard, Ronnie (1958 - 1999)
YEARS ACTIVE: 1985
VICTIMS: 2
RACE OF VICTIMS: Varied
AREA: South Carolina
KILL METHODS: Suffocation
RAPE: Yes
NOTES: Kidnapping and numerous robberies.

Howze, Gene (1942 -)
YEARS ACTIVE: 1970, 1972
VICTIMS: 2
RACE OF VICTIMS: Unknown
AREA: Jacksonville, FL
KILL METHODS: Shooting
RAPE: No
NOTES: One attempted.

Hubbard, Arenza Douglas
(1972 -)
YEARS ACTIVE: 2003, 2007
VICTIMS: 2
RACE OF VICTIMS: Black
AREA: Battle Creek, MI
KILL METHODS: Shooting, vehicle
RAPE: No
NOTES: One victim was his girlfriend, whom he killed by running her over with a car.

Hudson, Vincent (1972 -)
YEARS ACTIVE: 2007
VICTIMS: 3
RACE OF VICTIMS: Black
AREA: Chicago, IL
KILL METHODS: Beating
RAPE: Yes
NOTES: Four rapes and attempted murders

Hughes, Michael (1957 -)
NICKNAME: Southside Slayer
YEARS ACTIVE: 1986-1993
VICTIMS: 12-44
RACE OF VICTIMS: Black
AREA: Los Angeles, CA
KILL METHODS: Strangulation
RAPE: Yes
NOTES: Possibly one of the most prolific serial killers in US history, but police do not have a firm grasp of his crimes. He has been tied to twelve murders conclusively and suspected in others. He enjoyed posing his victims in various sexual and graphic poses to shock the police. They are investigating other homicides in the LA area and their connection to him, and they are investigating other murders from when he was stationed in the navy around various bases in the US. Police put the upper end of his crimes at 44, but think the number could climb if he is connected to out-of-state homicides.

Hunter, Richard Louis (1955 -)
YEARS ACTIVE: 1986
VICTIMS: 4
RACE OF VICTIMS: Black
AREA: Atlanta, GA
KILL METHODS: Suffocation

RAPE: Yes
NOTES: All victims were elderly
  women. Possibly other
  murders.

Hunter, Lendell (1953 -)
YEARS ACTIVE: 1970-1974
VICTIMS: 2-3
RACE OF VICTIMS: Varied
AREA: Augusta, GA
KILL METHODS: Bludgeoning
RAPE: Yes
NOTES: Killed women.
  Numerous rapes, suspected in
  more deaths.

Ivery, Samuel Lee (1957 - 2005)
NICKNAME: Ninja of God
YEARS ACTIVE: 1992
VICTIMS: 4
RACE OF VICTIMS: Varied
AREA: CA, AZ, IL, AL
KILL METHODS: Beating, axe,
machete
RAPE: Yes
NOTES: Suspected in more.
  Victims decapitated.

Jacks, Banita (1974 -)
YEARS ACTIVE: 2007
VICTIMS: 4
RACE OF VICTIMS: Black
AREA: Washington, DC
KILL METHODS: Suffocation,
Beating, Stabbing
RAPE: No
NOTES: Killed children over a
  one-month period.

Jackson, Anthony J. (1939 -)
YEARS ACTIVE: 1972-1973
VICTIMS: 8
RACE OF VICTIMS: White

AREA: Cambridge, MA
KILL METHODS: Beating,
strangulation, and stabbing
RAPE: Yes
NOTES: All victims were women
  ages 18-22 who were killed away
  from their home. He was arrested
  after a high-speed chase and
  shootout with police. After his
  arrest they discovered evidence
  linking him to the murders.

Jackson, Anthony L (1964 -)
YEARS ACTIVE: 1984-1985
VICTIMS: 2-3
RACE OF VICTIMS: Varied
AREA: Lakeland, FL
KILL METHODS: Beating shooting
RAPE: No
NOTES: Killed one sixty-two-year-
old man and one seventeen-year-old
pregnant girl. He confessed after
feeling convicted while attending a
church service.

Jackson, Calvin (1948 -)
YEARS ACTIVE: 1973-1974
VICTIMS: 9-11
RACE OF VICTIMS: Varied
AREA: New York City, NY
KILL METHODS: Suffication,
stabbing
RAPE: Yes
NOTES: See Chapter 6 for info.

Jackson, Charles Junior
(1933 - 2002)
YEARS ACTIVE: 1975-1982
VICTIMS: 9+
RACE OF VICTIMS: White
AREA: Oakland, CA
KILL METHODS: Strangulation,
beating, suffocation

RAPE: Yes
NOTES: He was linked to the murder of one girl and eight women via DNA in 2005. Because of the large time period between the murders and his capture, police suspect that he has additional murders.

Jackson, Earl Lloyd (1956 -)
YEARS ACTIVE: 1977
VICTIMS: 2-3
RACE OF VICTIMS: White
AREA: Long Beach, CA
KILL METHODS: Beating
RAPE: Yes
NOTES: Killed elderly neighbors.

Jackson, Elton Manning
(1956 -)
NICKNAME: Hampton Roads Killer
YEARS ACTIVE: 1990's
VICTIMS: 12
RACE OF VICTIMS: Varied
AREA: Norfolk, VA
KILL METHODS: Strangulation
RAPE: Yes
NOTES: His victims were gay men. Originally he was connected to one murder of twelve unsolved murders in the area. But after investigation police are convinced that he is guilty of all twelve.

Jackson, Jr., Leroy (1926 -)
YEARS ACTIVE: 1953-1954
VICTIMS: 2
RACE OF VICTIMS: White
AREA: Chicago, IL
KILL METHODS: Beating

RAPE: Yes
NOTES: Both victims were men, but he had over 100 rapes of men and women.

Jackson, Patricia Ann Thomas
(1949 -)
YEARS ACTIVE: 1966-1981
VICTIMS: 2
RACE OF VICTIMS: Black
AREA: Tuscaloosa, AL
KILL METHODS: Stabbing
RAPE: No
NOTES: Both victims were women.

Jackson, Ray Shawn (1968 -)
NICKNAME: Gilham Park Strangler
YEARS ACTIVE: 1989-1990
VICTIMS: 6
RACE OF VICTIMS: Black
AREA: Kansas City, MO
KILL METHODS: Strangulation
RAPE: Yes
NOTES: Admitted to killing the women in Gilham Park. The night before he was arrested he attempted to murder a seventh woman, who survived and told police.

Jackson, Richard Hilliard (1939-)
YEARS ACTIVE: 1969-1976
VICTIMS: 2
RACE OF VICTIMS: Black
AREA: Maryland
KILL METHODS: Beating, strangulation
RAPE: Yes
NOTES: Murdered his infant stepson, and served only 23 months in a half-way house. After his release he murdered an elderly female.

James, Edward (1959 -)
YEARS ACTIVE: 1996
VICTIMS: 3
RACE OF VICTIMS: Varied
AREA: Las Vegas NV
KILL METHODS: Shooting
RAPE: No
NOTES: Stuffed one victim in a suitcase, and hid another under a hotel bed. He is suspected in more murders.

James, Eugene H. (1917 - 1949)
YEARS ACTIVE: 1948
VICTIMS: 2
RACE OF VICTIMS: White
AREA: MD, DC
KILL METHODS: Stabbing
RAPE: Yes
NOTES: Sliced throats of two young girls and raped them. Executed.

Jameswhite, Richard (1973 -)
NICKNAME: Babyface
YEARS ACTIVE: 1990's
VICTIMS: 15
RACE OF VICTIMS: Black
AREA: NY, GA
KILL METHODS: Stabbing, shooting
RAPE: No
NOTES: Believed he could turn invisible in part to a witch doctor's spell.

Jefferson, Steven (1959 -)
YEARS ACTIVE: 1991, 2009
VICTIMS: 2
RACE OF VICTIMS: Black
AREA: Nashville, TN
KILL METHODS: Bludgeoning
RAPE: Yes

NOTES: After serving 13 years for murdering a woman, he murdered another woman by bashing her skull in.

Jenkins, Cecil C (1966 -)
YEARS ACTIVE: 1996-1998
VICTIMS: 4-5
RACE OF VICTIMS: Varied
AREA: Indianapolis, IN
KILL METHODS: Strangulation
RAPE: No
NOTES: Used drugs to lure his victims, then he raped and murdered them.

Jenkins, John Cornelius
(1960 -)
YEARS ACTIVE: 1980, 1990
VICTIMS: 13
RACE OF VICTIMS: Black
AREA: Detroit, MI
KILL METHODS: Shooting
RAPE: No
NOTES: A repeat offender. He was released after a six-year sentence and committed at least twelve more murders.

Jenkins, Nikko A. (1986 -)
YEARS ACTIVE: 2013
VICTIMS: 4
RACE OF VICTIMS: Varied
AREA:Omaha, NB
KILL METHODS: Shooting
RAPE: No
NOTES: After being released from prison, the killer killed 4 people over a 10 day period. He claimed demons and a snake god commanded him to kill.

Jenkins, Tyree (1987 -)
YEARS ACTIVE: 2006-2008
VICTIMS: 3
RACE OF VICTIMS: Varied
AREA: Dade City, FL
KILL METHODS: Shooting
RAPE: No
NOTES: Two victims were
   teenagers executed on a
   desolate stretch of road. The
   last victim was at a sandwich
   shop.

Jennings, Wilbur Lee (1941 -)
NICKNAME: Ditchbank killer
YEARS ACTIVE: 1983-1984
VICTIMS: 6
RACE OF VICTIMS: Varied
AREA: Fresno and Sacramento,
CA
KILL METHODS: Strangulation
RAPE: Yes
NOTES: Nine other possible
   murders.

Jett, Andrew (1960 -)
YEARS ACTIVE: 1992, 2012
VICTIMS: 2
RACE OF VICTIMS: Black
AREA: Providence, RI
KILL METHODS: Beating
RAPE: No
NOTES: Both victims were his
   girlfriends. He served 18 years
   for the first murder, and had
   killed within months after
   release.

Johns, Kevin Gregory
(1982 - 2009)
YEARS ACTIVE: 2002-2005
VICTIMS: 3
RACE OF VICTIMS: Black

AREA: Maryland
KILL METHODS: Strangulation,
knife
RAPE: No
NOTES: Died in prison.

Johns, Ronnie (1973 -)
NICKNAME: 44-caliber killer
YEARS ACTIVE: 1991
VICTIMS: 4
RACE OF VICTIMS: White
AREA: Flint, MI
KILL METHODS: Shooting
RAPE: No
NOTES: Four attempted.

Johnson, Alvin (1941 -)
YEARS ACTIVE: 1973 & 1983
VICTIMS: 3
RACE OF VICTIMS: White
AREA: UT, OR, CA
KILL METHODS: Strangulation
RAPE: Yes
NOTES: Killed one woman and two
   men.

Johnson, Brandon (1988 -)
YEARS ACTIVE: 2008-2009
VICTIMS: 3
RACE OF VICTIMS: White
AREA: Little Rock, AR
KILL METHODS: Shooting
RAPE: No
NOTES: Shot two men and one
   woman over a thirty-day period
   with a .38 special pistol.

Johnson, Clarence (1989-)
NICKNAME: Burger
YEARS ACTIVE: 2011-2012
VICTIMS: 3-4
RACE OF VICTIMS: Black
AREA: Annapolis, MD

KILL METHODS: Shooting
RAPE: No
NOTES: Suspected in other
  murders, at least one was drug
  related. The others appear to
  be out of cold blood

Johnson, David Lee (1960 -)
YEARS ACTIVE: 1978, 1994
VICTIMS: 2-2
RACE OF VICTIMS: Unknown
AREA: Battle Creek, MI
KILL METHODS: Unknown
RAPE: No
NOTES: From MI prison
  website.

Johnson, Eddie James
(1952 - 1997)
YEARS ACTIVE: 1975, 1987
VICTIMS: 4
RACE OF VICTIMS: White
AREA: IL, TX
KILL METHODS: Shooting
RAPE: Yes
NOTES: A repeat offender.

Johnson, Emanuel (1963 -)
YEARS ACTIVE: 1988
VICTIMS: 2
RACE OF VICTIMS: White
AREA: FL, Sarasota County
KILL METHODS: stabbing
RAPE: Yes
NOTES: Gave full confession to
  police. Admitted to beating
  one victim, raping her, and
  stabbing her twenty-four times.

Johnson, James Earl
(1947 - 2008)
YEARS ACTIVE: 1992-1993
VICTIMS: 2

RACE OF VICTIMS: White
AREA: Worcester, MA
KILL METHODS: Strangulation
RAPE: Yes
NOTES: Two attempted and possible
  other murders.

Johnson, Jay Thomas (1967 -)
YEARS ACTIVE: 1991
VICTIMS: 2
RACE OF VICTIMS: White
AREA: Minneapolis MN
KILL METHODS: Shooting
RAPE: Yes
NOTES: One attempted.

Johnson, Johnny Ray
(1957 - 2009)
YEARS ACTIVE: 1995
VICTIMS: 5
RACE OF VICTIMS: Black
AREA: Houston, TX
KILL METHODS: Beating,
strangulation
RAPE: Yes
NOTES: Victims were women. He
  performed necrophila. Later
  executed.

Johnson, Matthew Steven (1963 -)
YEARS ACTIVE: 2000-2001
VICTIMS: 3
RACE OF VICTIMS: Varied
AREA: Hartford, CT
KILL METHODS: Strangulation,
beating
RAPE: Yes
NOTES: Victims were prostitutes.

Johnson, Michael A. (1986 -)
YEARS ACTIVE: 2008-2010
VICTIMS: 3-4
RACE OF VICTIMS: Black

AREA: Chicago, IL
KILL METHODS: Strangulation
RAPE: Yes
NOTES: Victims were all women. He attempted one more.

Johnson, Melvin (1958 - 2003)
YEARS ACTIVE: 1984
VICTIMS: 4
RACE OF VICTIMS: Varied
AREA: Decatur, IL
KILL METHODS:
Strangulation, stabbing
RAPE: Yes
NOTES: All victims were young girls.

Johnson, Milton (1950 -)
YEARS ACTIVE: 1983
VICTIMS: 14-17
RACE OF VICTIMS: White
AREA: Joliet, IL
KILL METHODS: Shooting
RAPE: Yes
NOTES: See Chapter 6 for info.

Johnson, Montell (1966-)
YEARS ACTIVE: 1990-1994
VICTIMS: 4+
RACE OF VICTIMS: Black
AREA: California, Illinois
KILL METHODS: Shooting
RAPE: No
NOTES: Convicted of three separate murders in California, he's now serving time for a fourth murder in Illinois. During his last trial, he claimed to have killed at least 30, but there was no proof provided to validate his claim.

Johnson, Patrick (? - 1987)
YEARS ACTIVE: 1980's
VICTIMS: 2-10
RACE OF VICTIMS: Black
AREA: Detroit, MI
KILL METHODS: Shooting
RAPE: No
NOTES: Hit man, murdered on the streets.

Johnson, Raymond Eugene (1974 -)
YEARS ACTIVE: 1995, 2009
VICTIMS: 3
RACE OF VICTIMS: Black
AREA: Tulsa, OK
KILL METHODS: Shooting, hammer.
RAPE: No
NOTES: Murdered a man and served one short prison term. After release he beat a woman and her young child to death, and then burned their bodies.

Johnson, Roderick Andre (1976 -)
YEARS ACTIVE: 1992, 1996
VICTIMS: 3-4
RACE OF VICTIMS: Varied
AREA: Richardson, TX, PA
KILL METHODS: Shooting
RAPE: No
NOTES: Was the leader of a gang set called the Street Disciplez Souljas.

Johnson, Ronnie (1961 -)
YEARS ACTIVE: 1989
VICTIMS: 2
RACE OF VICTIMS: Varied
AREA: Miami, FL
KILL METHODS: Shooting
RAPE: No
NOTES: Three attempted.

Johnson, Steve (1948 - 2004)
YEARS ACTIVE: 1963
VICTIMS: 3
RACE OF VICTIMS: White
AREA: St. Petersburg, FL
KILL METHODS: Strangulation
RAPE: Yes
NOTES: Victims were all elderly women. Two attempted. Died in prison.

Johnson, Tivan (1970 -)
YEARS ACTIVE: 1991
VICTIMS: 3
RACE OF VICTIMS: White
AREA: Miami, FL
KILL METHODS: Shooting
RAPE: No
NOTES: Victims of robberies.

Johnson, Thomas (1943 -)
NICKNAME: Hucklebuck
YEARS ACTIVE: 1987, 1993
VICTIMS: 2
RACE OF VICTIMS: Unknown
AREA: Clewiston, FL
KILL METHODS: Shooting
RAPE: No
NOTES: From FL prison website.

Johnson, Vincent (1969 -)
NICKNAME: Brooklyn Strangler
YEARS ACTIVE: 1999-2000
VICTIMS: 6
RACE OF VICTIMS: Varied
AREA: Brooklyn, NY
KILL METHODS: Strangulation
RAPE: Yes

NOTES: Necrophilia in at least one case, but suspected in his other murders.

Johnston, John (1877 - 1904)
YEARS ACTIVE: 1895-1904
VICTIMS: 5
RACE OF VICTIMS: Varied
AREA: PA, VA, GA
KILL METHODS: Beating, shooting, knife
RAPE: No
NOTES: Executed.

Joiner, Anthony (1959 -)
NICKNAME: Elderly Home of Horrors
YEARS ACTIVE: 1980's
VICTIMS: 7+
RACE OF VICTIMS: Varied
AREA: Philadelphia, PA
KILL METHODS: Suffoctation, strangulation
RAPE: Yes
NOTES: Worked in a nursing home and murdered elderly women. He is suspected in numerous rapes and other murders.

Jones, Alton (1993 -)
YEARS ACTIVE: 2012
VICTIMS: 2-3
RACE OF VICTIMS: Black
AREA: Trenton, NJ
KILL METHODS: Shooting
RAPE: No
NOTES: Suspected in more deaths. The first two were one month apart.

Jones, Bryan Maurice (1957 -)
The Dumpster Killer
YEARS ACTIVE: 1985-1986
VICTIMS: 4

RACE OF VICTIMS: Black
AREA: San Diego, CA
KILL METHODS:
Strangulation, stabbing, burning
RAPE: Yes
NOTES: Served twenty-two
    years for rape. After his
    release, committed the murders
    and other rapes.

Jones, Daniel O. (1969 -)
YEARS ACTIVE: 2001-2002
VICTIMS: 4-5
RACE OF VICTIMS: Black
AREA: Kansas City, MO
KILL METHODS: Stabbing
RAPE: Yes
NOTES: Victims were women.

Jones, Henry Lee (1963 -)
NICKNAME: Bam
YEARS ACTIVE: 2002-2003
VICTIMS: 4
RACE OF VICTIMS: White
AREA: TN, FL
KILL METHODS: Shooting
RAPE: Yes
NOTES: Couple killed in
    Memphis, two men in Florida.

Jones, Ja'Mari (1993 -)
YEARS ACTIVE: 2008-2012
VICTIMS: 2
RACE OF VICTIMS: Black
AREA: Seattle, WA
KILL METHODS: Shooting
RAPE: No
NOTES: Both victims were men.

Jones, Jeffery Gerald (1960 -)
YEARS ACTIVE: 1985
VICTIMS: 4
RACE OF VICTIMS: White

AREA: Sacramento, CA
KILL METHODS: Hammer
RAPE: No
NOTES: Victims were men.

Jones, Jesse (1924 -)
YEARS ACTIVE: 1942
VICTIMS: 4
RACE OF VICTIMS: White
AREA: Spartenburg County, SC
KILL METHODS: Axe
RAPE: No
NOTES: Killed two elderly couples.

Jones, Joe Willie (1915 -)
YEARS ACTIVE: 1947, 1980
VICTIMS: 2
RACE OF VICTIMS: White
AREA: LA, KS
KILL METHODS: Shooting
RAPE: No
NOTES: A repeat offender.

Jones, Martin (1966 - 2007)
YEARS ACTIVE: 1985-1987
VICTIMS: 2-3
RACE OF VICTIMS: White
AREA: Buffalo, NY
KILL METHODS: Hammer, stabbing
RAPE: No
NOTES: He robbed his victims. In
    one murder he got $5.

Jones, Peter J. (1967 -)
YEARS ACTIVE: 1997, 2006, 2014
VICTIMS: 3
RACE OF VICTIMS: White
AREA: Michigan, Florida
KILL METHODS: Shooting
RAPE: No
NOTES: He served only 6 years for
    his first two murders, and killed
    only one year after his release.

Jones, Stephen Anthony
(1969 -)
YEARS ACTIVE: 2003-2004
VICTIMS: 2
RACE OF VICTIMS: Varied
AREA: Los Angeles, CA
KILL METHODS: Beating
RAPE: No
NOTES: Killed one man and one woman, but confessed to four attempted and numerous rapes.

Jones, Sydney (? - 1915)
YEARS ACTIVE: 1900
VICTIMS: 13
RACE OF VICTIMS: Varied
AREA: Alabama
KILL METHODS: Shooting, Strangulation
RAPE: No
NOTES: Gave a full confession of his crimes just prior to being executed. Killed eight black men, one Chinese, one Mexican, one Indian, and two whites.

Jordan, Keydrick Deon (1972-)
YEARS ACTIVE: 1991-1992
VICTIMS: 2
RACE OF VICTIMS: White
AREA: Orlando, FL
KILL METHODS: Shooting
RAPE: Yes
NOTES: Killed elderly women. In the last case he dressed the victim and placed her body sitting in a chair before setting her house on fire. He grew up in a household where voodoo was practiced and saw his father murdered.

Joyner, Anthony (1959 -)
YEARS ACTIVE: 1983
VICTIMS: 6
RACE OF VICTIMS: White
AREA: Philadelphia, PA
KILL METHODS: Drowning, suffocation, strangulation
RAPE: Yes
NOTES: Killed women in a nursing home.

Julius, Arthur James
(1946 - 1989)
YEARS ACTIVE: 1972, 1978
VICTIMS: 2
RACE OF VICTIMS: Black
AREA: Alabama
KILL METHODS: Shooting, strangulation
RAPE: Yes
NOTES: Possible others. He was later executed.

Kee, Arhon Malik (1973 -)
YEARS ACTIVE: 1991-1998
VICTIMS: 3
RACE OF VICTIMS: Black
AREA: Harlem, NY
KILL METHODS: Suffocation, stabbing, burning
RAPE: Yes
NOTES: All victims were girls of ages 13-17. He raped four others of ages 13-15. One girl was burned alive on a rooftop, another was suffocated, and another was stabbed to death.

Keeling, Melvin M.
(1962 - 2005)
YEARS ACTIVE: 2005
VICTIMS: 3
RACE OF VICTIMS: White

AREA: OH, IN
KILL METHODS: Shooting
RAPE: Yes
NOTES: Killed a female teen
and two adults. Committed
suicide.

Kelly, Horace Edward (1959 -)
YEARS ACTIVE: 1984
VICTIMS: 3
RACE OF VICTIMS: White
AREA: San Bernadino, CA
KILL METHODS: Shooting
RAPE: Yes
NOTES: Killed women. One
attempted.

Kelly, Ricky (1972 -)
YEARS ACTIVE: 1996-2005
VICTIMS: 10
RACE OF VICTIMS: Black
AREA: Louisville, KY
KILL METHODS: Shooting
RAPE: No
NOTES: Was a hit man for a
large drug operation. He was
initially charged with 8 of the
10 murders he confessed too.
But as part of a plea agreement
to net the other members of the
drug enterprise, the murder
charges were dropped. He
received only a 30 year
sentence on racketeering.

Kennedy, Edward Dean
(1945 - 1992)
YEARS ACTIVE: 1978-1981
VICTIMS: 3
RACE OF VICTIMS: White
AREA: Miami, FL
KILL METHODS: Shooting
RAPE: No

NOTES: Killed one woman and two
men. He was later executed.

Kidd, Leonard (1961 -)
YEARS ACTIVE: 1980, 1984
VICTIMS: 14
RACE OF VICTIMS: Black
AREA: Chicago, IL
KILL METHODS: Shooting, arson
RAPE: No
NOTES: Burned an apartment
knowing it was full of people,
killing ten. He also helped execute
four people in 1984.

Kilgore, Dean (1950 -)
YEARS ACTIVE: 1977-1989
VICTIMS: 2
RACE OF VICTIMS: Varied
AREA: Lakeland, FL
KILL METHODS: Stabbing, beating
RAPE: Yes
NOTES: Victims were men.

Kimbrough, Petrie (1887 - 1920)
A.K.A. Will Lockett
YEARS ACTIVE: 1912-1919
VICTIMS: 4
RACE OF VICTIMS: White
AREA: Lexington, KY
KILL METHODS: Strangulation,
bludgeoning
RAPE: Yes
NOTES: Killed three women and one
girl. Executed.

King, Carolyn Ann
(1965 - 1994)
YEARS ACTIVE: 1993
VICTIMS: 3
RACE OF VICTIMS: White
AREA: PA, ND, NV
KILL METHODS: Shooting

RAPE: No
NOTES: The only instance of a black and white serial killing duo, King enlisted her white boyfriend to help her brutally kill at least two people, and possibly a third in two different states.

King, Darell Steven (1983 -)
NICKNAME: Juice
YEARS ACTIVE: 1998, 2007
VICTIMS: 2
RACE OF VICTIMS: Black
AREA: Tulsa, OK
KILL METHODS: Shooting
RAPE: No
NOTES: A repeat offender.

King, James Donald (1944 -)
YEARS ACTIVE: 1967, 1988
VICTIMS: 2
RACE OF VICTIMS: Black
AREA: Greensboro, NC
KILL METHODS: Shooting
RAPE: No
NOTES: Both victims were his wives.

Kirkland, Anthony Wayne
(1968 -)
YEARS ACTIVE: 2002-2006
VICTIMS: 5
RACE OF VICTIMS: Varied
AREA: Cincinnati, OH
KILL METHODS: Burning, strangulation, beating
RAPE: Yes
NOTES: Killed women and one thirteen-year-old girl.

Kline, Donald (1956 -)
YEARS ACTIVE: 1985, 1998

VICTIMS: 3
RACE OF VICTIMS: Varied
AREA: Detroit, MI
KILL METHODS: Stabbing, strangulation
RAPE: Yes
NOTES: Overkill.

Knight, Thomas Otis (1951 - 2014)
NICKNAME: Askari Abdullah Muhammad
YEARS ACTIVE: 1974, 1980
VICTIMS: 3
RACE OF VICTIMS: White
AREA: Miami, FL
KILL METHODS: Shooting, stabbing
RAPE: No
NOTES: Killed a couple and a prison guard.

Ladson, Frank (1910 - 1940
YEARS ACTIVE: 1939-1940
VICTIMS: 5
RACE OF VICTIMS: Varied
AREA: SC, FL
KILL METHODS: Ax
RAPE: No
NOTES: Murdered his last victim in 1940 in South Carolina. He then surprised police by confessing to 4 murders in SC and FL. Executed in 1940. (Some reports have his name as Frank Lansing).

Lagrone, Edward Lewis
(1957 - 2004)
YEARS ACTIVE: 1977, 1991
VICTIMS: 4
RACE OF VICTIMS: Black
AREA: Ft. Worth, TX
KILL METHODS: Shooting
RAPE: No

NOTES: His first murder was of a man. His last was of two of his aunts and one ten-year-old niece he had impregnated. Also one attempted. Executed.

Lamar, Keith (1969 -)
YEARS ACTIVE: 1989, 1993
VICTIMS: 5
RACE OF VICTIMS: White
AREA: Ohio
KILL METHODS: Stabbing
RAPE: No
NOTES: Was a convicted murderer who killed four inmates in 1993.

Lang, Donald (1945 -)
YEARS ACTIVE: 1965-1972
VICTIMS: 2+
RACE OF VICTIMS: Black
AREA: Chicago, IL
KILL METHODS: Stabbing
RAPE: Yes
NOTES: The only deaf serial killer on record. Police noticed that wherever he lived, dead prostitutes were found. They suspect him in other murders.

Laskey, Jr., Posteal
(1937 - 2007)
NICKNAME: Cincinnati Strangler
YEARS ACTIVE: 1965-1966
VICTIMS: 7
RACE OF VICTIMS: White
AREA: Cincinnati, OH
KILL METHODS: Stabbing, strangulation
RAPE: Yes
NOTES: Was a laborer who stalked and killed his elderly victims. He raped at least five and may be responsible for more rapes. He also committed a few armed robberies and later died in prison.

Laurent, Kylan M
(1989 - 2011)
YEARS ACTIVE: 2011
VICTIMS: 2-22
RACE OF VICTIMS: Black
AREA: LA, TX
KILL METHODS: Strangulation
RAPE: Yes
NOTES: Police have confirmation that he killed two women and kept their cell phones as souvenirs. After leading police on a chase, he committed suicide by jumping into the Mississippi River. Police found twenty-two cell phones and some purses in his car, and are investigating to see if they are merely stolen or taken from murder victims.

Lawson, Bennie L (1969 - 1994)
YEARS ACTIVE: 1993-1994
VICTIMS: 6
RACE OF VICTIMS: Varied
AREA: Washington, DC
KILL METHODS: Shooting
RAPE: No
NOTES: Police wanted to question him about three murders whose evidence all pointed to him. He showed up to the police station for questioning, but started shooting instead. In the end, three officers were dead and he committed suicide at the scene.

Lear, Tuhran A (1959 -)
YEARS ACTIVE: 1974, 1988

VICTIMS: 3
RACE OF VICTIMS: Varied
AREA: Illinois
KILL METHODS: Shooting
RAPE: No
NOTES: Robbed his victims,
   then shot them.

Lee, Derrick Todd (1968 -)
NICKNAME: Baton Rouge
Serial Killer
YEARS ACTIVE: 1992-2003
VICTIMS: 8-14
RACE OF VICTIMS: White
AREA: Baton Rouge, LA
KILL METHODS: Beating,
stabbing, hammer, strangulation
RAPE: Yes
NOTES: See Chapter 6 for info.

Lee, Donald Edward (1955 -)
YEARS ACTIVE: 1987-1988
VICTIMS: 2
RACE OF VICTIMS: Unknown
AREA: Jacksonville, FL
KILL METHODS: Unknown
RAPE: No
NOTES: From FL prison
   website.

Lee, Tobias Chano (1976 -)
YEARS ACTIVE: 2004
VICTIMS: 2
RACE OF VICTIMS: Black
AREA: SC, GA, East Point
KILL METHODS: Shooting
RAPE: Yes
NOTES: Killed men. Raped one
   woman.

LeGrand, Deveron
(1924 - 2006)
NICKNAME: Bishop

YEARS ACTIVE: 1968-1975
VICTIMS: 4-6
RACE OF VICTIMS: Black
AREA: New York City, NY
KILL METHODS: Beating, shooting,
strangulation
RAPE: No
NOTES: Had eleven "nuns" in his
   church with whom he had forty-
   seven children total.

LeGrand, Steven (1956 -)
YEARS ACTIVE: 1963-1975
VICTIMS: 2
RACE OF VICTIMS: Black
AREA: Sullivan County NY
KILL METHODS: Beating
RAPE: Yes
NOTES: Killed his sisters. In what is
   an obvious perversion of justice, he
   was deported to England after
   proving that he was an English
   citizen. He had served years in a
   US prison prior to this. England
   refused to imprison him and even
   offered to put him on public
   assistance until he could get back
   on his feet.

Lewis, Tyrone (1986-)
YEARS ACTIVE: 2005-2012
VICTIMS: 3
RACE OF VICTIMS: Black
AREA: Maryland
KILL METHODS: Shooting
RAPE: No
NOTES: Both victims were males,
   one was the famous community
   activist Lenny Harris.

Lewis, William Charles
(1959 -)
YEARS ACTIVE: 2001

VICTIMS: 2
RACE OF VICTIMS: Black
AREA: Atlanta, GA
KILL METHODS: Shooting
RAPE: No
NOTES: Two attempted.

Little, Keith D. (1963 -)
YEARS ACTIVE: 2003, 2012
VICTIMS: 2
RACE OF VICTIMS: Black
AREA: Maryland
KILL METHODS: Stabbing
RAPE: No
NOTES: Both victims were co-
workers. The first case was
thrown out on a technicality. In
the second he stabbed his boss
seventy times.

Little, Sam (1941 -)
YEARS ACTIVE: 1977-1980's
VICTIMS: 6-20+
RACE OF VICTIMS: Varied
AREA: CA, MS, FL
KILL METHODS: Stabbing,
Strangulation
RAPE: Yes
NOTES: Arrested in 2013 after
DNA evidence tied him to at
least three unsolved murders
from Los Angeles from the
1980s. While in jail his DNA
was also linked to unsolved
murders in Mississippi and
Florida. Police are currently
cross referencing his DNA and
murder clues against other
unsolved cases from across
America, and suspect the
number may exceed 20
murders.

Lofton, Jr. , Franklin D. (1985 -)
YEARS ACTIVE: 2006-2007
VICTIMS: 2
RACE OF VICTIMS: Black
AREA: Rockford, IL
KILL METHODS: Shooting
RAPE: No
NOTES: Victims were both men he
knew.

Lott, Ronald Carole (1960 - 2013)
YEARS ACTIVE: 1986
VICTIMS: 2
RACE OF VICTIMS: White
AREA: Oklahoma City, OK
KILL METHODS: Strangulation
RAPE: Yes
NOTES: Killed elderly women. Had
two additional rapes. Executed.

Louding, Michael (1992 -)
YEARS ACTIVE: 2009
VICTIMS: 6
RACE OF VICTIMS: Black
AREA: Baton Rouge, LA
KILL METHODS: Shooting
RAPE: No
NOTES: Was only seventeen when
the murders were committed.

Lovette, Laurence Alvin
(1991 -)
YEARS ACTIVE: 2008
VICTIMS: 2
RACE OF VICTIMS: White
AREA: Raleigh, NC
KILL METHODS: Shooting
RAPE: No
NOTES: Was seventeen when he
committed the murders. One was
an engineering student on
1/18/2008; the other was Eve
Carson on 3/5/2008.

Lynch, Franklin (1955 -)
NICKNAME: Daytime Stalker
YEARS ACTIVE: 1981-1987
VICTIMS: 3-13
RACE OF VICTIMS: White
AREA: San Francisco, CA
KILL METHODS: Unknown
RAPE: Yes
NOTES: His victims were
  elderly women. Police suspect
  him in all thirteen murders, but
  he was only tried in three. He
  has sat on death row since his
  trial.

Mack, Ulysses (1900 - 1932)
YEARS ACTIVE: 1929
VICTIMS: 3
RACE OF VICTIMS: White
AREA: Gary, In
KILL METHODS: Axe
RAPE: Yes
NOTES: Killed two girls and one
  man.

Mack, Gillis (1901 -)
YEARS ACTIVE: 1929
VICTIMS: 3
RACE OF VICTIMS: White
AREA: Indiana
KILL METHODS: Axe
RAPE: Yes
NOTES: Victims were women.

Mack, Daryl Linnie
(1958 - 2006)
YEARS ACTIVE: 1988-1999
VICTIMS: 2
RACE OF VICTIMS: Varied
AREA: Nevada
KILL METHODS: Strangulation

RAPE: Yes
NOTES: Executed.

Macon, Ronald (1964 -)
YEARS ACTIVE: 1999
VICTIMS: 3
RACE OF VICTIMS: Varied
AREA: Chicago, IL
KILL METHODS: Shooting
RAPE: Yes
NOTES: Suspected in more.

Macon, Matthew Emmanuel
(1979-)
YEARS ACTIVE: 2004
VICTIMS: 6-7
RACE OF VICTIMS: White
AREA: Lansing, MI
KILL METHODS: Torture, beating
RAPE: Yes
NOTES: A career criminal and
  registered sex offender. He killed
  elderly women and then robbed
  their homes. In all cases, they were
  brutally raped and beaten, leaving
  numerous fractured bones. Some
  died from their beatings. Others
  were strangled.

Madison, Michael (1978 -)
YEARS ACTIVE: 2013
VICTIMS: 3
RACE OF VICTIMS: Black
AREA: Cleveland, OH
KILL METHODS: Shooting
RAPE: Yes
NOTES: Possibly more victims,
  inspired by Anthony Sowell.

Madonda, Muziwokuthula
(1978-)
YEARS ACTIVE: 2009-2011
VICTIMS: 4

RACE OF VICTIMS: White
AREA: OH, NM
KILL METHODS: Shooting
RAPE: No
NOTES: A native of South
Africa. He was in the US
studying theology at a
seminary.

Malone, Victor King (1947 -)
YEARS ACTIVE: 1973-1985
VICTIMS: 11
RACE OF VICTIMS: Black
AREA: Detroit, MI
KILL METHODS: Shooting
RAPE: Yes
NOTES: All victims were
prostitutes. He was convicted
on three cases, but evidence
tied him to eleven murders.

Malone, Joe (1875 - 1898)
NICKNAME: Dobie
YEARS ACTIVE: 1890-1898
VICTIMS: 6
RACE OF VICTIMS: White
AREA: Texas
KILL METHODS: Shooting
RAPE: Yes
NOTES: Killed women, all of
whom were raped. He had four
additional rapes. Executed.

Mann, Arthur (1967 -)
YEARS ACTIVE: 1991, 2007
VICTIMS: 2
RACE OF VICTIMS: Unknown
AREA: FL, GA
KILL METHODS: Shooting
RAPE: No
NOTES: Numerous robberies
and rapes.

Mann, Andy (1882 -)
YEARS ACTIVE: 1929-1930
VICTIMS: 3
RACE OF VICTIMS: White
AREA: Minnesota
KILL METHODS: Stabbing, burning
RAPE: Yes
NOTES: Killed one boy, one girl, and
one man.

Manning, Willie Jerome
(1968 -)
YEARS ACTIVE: 1992-1993
VICTIMS: 4
RACE OF VICTIMS: Varied
AREA: Oktibbeha County, MS
KILL METHODS: Shooting, beating,
stabbing
RAPE: No
NOTES: Killed two students and two
elderly women.

Manuel, Keith Devon (1977 -)
YEARS ACTIVE: 2006-2009
VICTIMS: 2
RACE OF VICTIMS: Black
AREA: GA, NC
KILL METHODS: Stabbing
RAPE: Yes
NOTES: Killed women. One was his
girlfriend.

Marbley, Odell (1955 -)
YEARS ACTIVE: 1977-1980
VICTIMS: 2
RACE OF VICTIMS: Black
AREA: Indianapolis, IN
KILL METHODS: Biting, beating
RAPE: No
NOTES: Both victims were children
of his girlfriends. One he kicked,
bit, and punched repeatedly in the
stomach, causing failure of vital

organs and the severing of the intestines.

Marcus, Jerry (1951 -)
NICKNAME: Tuskegee Strangler
YEARS ACTIVE: 1970-1987
VICTIMS: 7-15
RACE OF VICTIMS: Black
AREA: Tuskegee, MS
KILL METHODS: Strangulation
RAPE: Yes
NOTES: He admitted to seven murders, but police are positive he committed at least eight more.

Marshall, Lamont Waldron (1954-)
NICKNAME: Heritage Hill Murders
YEARS ACTIVE: 1970-1975
VICTIMS: 2-7
RACE OF VICTIMS: White
AREA: Grand Rapids, MI
KILL METHODS: Strangulation
RAPE: Yes
NOTES: Convicted of two murders, he is suspected in five others and one attempted from the same timeframe. Each murder was almost identical, but no DNA evidence remains to connect Lamont except in two cases. He denies any involvement in any of the murders, despite the DNA evidence.

Martin, Arthur James (1969 -)
YEARS ACTIVE: 1997, 2009
VICTIMS: 2
RACE OF VICTIMS: Black
AREA: Jacksonville, FL
KILL METHODS: Shooting
RAPE: No
NOTES: He served a ten year sentence for his first murder, and murdered again within 5 months of his release.

Martin, Derrick (1973 -)
YEARS ACTIVE: 1992, 2007
VICTIMS: 2
RACE OF VICTIMS: White
AREA: Indianapolis, IN
KILL METHODS: Bludgeoning
RAPE: Yes
NOTES: Two known victims. There might be others.

Martin, Curtis (1971 -)
YEARS ACTIVE: 1994, 2009
VICTIMS: 4
RACE OF VICTIMS: Black
AREA: Oakland, CA
KILL METHODS: Shooting, Blugeoning
RAPE: Yes
NOTES: Two of the victims were toddlers, one was a young mother of one of the children, and one victim was a witness to the first murder. He served only six years for the first brutal murder.

Martin, Willie Wash (? - 1926)
YEARS ACTIVE: 1920-1925
VICTIMS: 7
RACE OF VICTIMS: White
AREA: Arkansas
KILL METHODS: Bludgeoning
RAPE: Yes
NOTES: His victims were all attractive women who walked past a swamp where he spent a good deal of time. After dragging them

into the swamp, he raped them and then beat them to death with rocks, tree branches, or pipes. He was later executed by electrocution.

Martinez, Alberto (1966 -)
NICKNAME: Alpo
YEARS ACTIVE: 1987-1991
VICTIMS: 14
RACE OF VICTIMS: Varied
AREA: New York City, NY
KILL METHODS: Shooting
RAPE: No
NOTES: He was one of the largest cocaine dealers in Harlem and Washington, D.C. After being caught, he confessed to fourteen murders but received a plea bargain for becoming a government witness. He was released from prison in 2008.

Mason, Michael Baraka
(1976 -)
YEARS ACTIVE: 2005-2007
VICTIMS: 3
RACE OF VICTIMS: Black
AREA: San Diego, CA
KILL METHODS: Shooting
RAPE: No
NOTES: Committed first murder in 2005. The other two were in a home invasion, he attempted three other murders.

Mason, Morris Odell
(1954 - 1985)
YEARS ACTIVE: 1978
VICTIMS: 2
RACE OF VICTIMS: White
AREA: Richmond, VA

KILL METHODS: Stabbing, axe, arson
RAPE: Yes
NOTES: Raped two eldery women. Killed two teens in a two-week crime spree. Nailed one's hands to a chair before setting her house on fire. Executed.

Mathis, Ben T. (? -)
YEARS ACTIVE: 1963-1964
VICTIMS: 3
RACE OF VICTIMS: Varied
AREA: Alabama
KILL METHODS: Strangulation, mutilation
RAPE: No
NOTES: Killed one black woman and one white couple.

Matthew, Jesse Lee
(1982 -)
YEARS ACTIVE: 1999-2000
VICTIMS: 2+
RACE OF VICTIMS: White
AREA: Virginia
KILL METHODS: Strangulation
RAPE: Yes
NOTES: Victims were women. Attempted additional murder and rape, and is suspected in other murders.

Matthews, Ynobe Katron
(1976 - 2004)
YEARS ACTIVE: 1999-2000
VICTIMS: 2
RACE OF VICTIMS: White
AREA: College Station, TX
KILL METHODS: Strangulation
RAPE: Yes
NOTES: Victims were women. Was later executed.

Maxwell, Bobby Joe (1945 -)
NICKNAME: Skid Row Stabber
YEARS ACTIVE: 1978-1979
VICTIMS: 10-11
RACE OF VICTIMS: Varied
AREA: Los Angeles, CA
KILL METHODS: Stabbing
RAPE: No
NOTES: Was originally
convicted on two of the
murders in 1984, but the
sentence was overturned in
2010 as a result of faulty
testimony of a jailhouse snitch.
He was never released because
the overwhelming evidence
that he was the Skid Row
Stabber. In 2013 he was
brought up on charges on three
murders he wasn't originally
tried on.

McCarthy, Kimberly Lagayle
(1961 - 2013)
YEARS ACTIVE: 1988 & 1997
VICTIMS: 3
RACE OF VICTIMS: White
AREA: Dallas, TX
KILL METHODS: Stabbing
RAPE: No
NOTES: Victims were female
patients to whom she provided
in-home care. Executed.

McCaskill, Boyd (1950 -)
YEARS ACTIVE: 1971, 1983

VICTIMS: 2+
RACE OF VICTIMS: Unknown
AREA: Florida
KILL METHODS: Unknown
RAPE: No

NOTES: From the Florida prison
system website.

McCloud, Larkin (? -)
A.K.A. Charles Smith
YEARS ACTIVE: 1916-1917
VICTIMS: 4
RACE OF VICTIMS: White
AREA: Nebraska
KILL METHODS: Stabbing, beating,
mutilation
RAPE: No
NOTES: Received a life sentence for
murdering a woman and a police
officer. There were two other
deaths where he was the only
suspect, but he was never tried for
the murders. He screamed and
threw a fit when the judge read the
verdict.

McCollum, Henry L (1965 -)
YEARS ACTIVE: 1983, 1991
VICTIMS: 2
RACE OF VICTIMS: Black
AREA: North Carolina
KILL METHODS: Strangulation
RAPE: Yes
NOTES: In the last case after raping
the girl, he stuffed her panties
down her throat and strangled her
to death. Her nude body was found
in a field.

McCoy, Ricky Bernard
(1966 -)
YEARS ACTIVE: 1994-1995
VICTIMS: 5
RACE OF VICTIMS: Black
AREA: Atlanta, GA
KILL METHODS: Shooting
RAPE: No
NOTES: All victims of robberies.

McCray, Jeremiah (1933 -)
YEARS ACTIVE: 1956-1958
VICTIMS: 5
RACE OF VICTIMS: White
AREA: VA, OH, GA, AL
KILL METHODS: Beating
RAPE: Yes
NOTES: One attempted.

McDowell, Robert Henry
(1951 -)
YEARS ACTIVE: 1972, 1979
VICTIMS: 2
RACE OF VICTIMS: White
AREA: Smithfield, NC
KILL METHODS: Stabbing,
machete
RAPE: No
NOTES: A repeat offender.

McFadden, Reginald (1953 -)
YEARS ACTIVE: 1969-1984
VICTIMS: 3-4
RACE OF VICTIMS: Varied
AREA: NY/PA, Nassau County
KILL METHODS: Stabbing and
strangling
RAPE: Yes
NOTES: Despite his confession
and daring a judge to sentence
him to 1,000 years, he received
a sentence only of twenty-five
years to life.

McFadden, Vincent (1980 -)
YEARS ACTIVE: 2001-2002
VICTIMS: 2-3
RACE OF VICTIMS: Black
AREA: Missouri
KILL METHODS: Shooting
RAPE: No

NOTES: Leader of the 6 Deuces
gang.

McGregor, Edward George
(1973 -)
YEARS ACTIVE: 1990-2005
VICTIMS: 4
RACE OF VICTIMS: White
AREA: Houston, TX
KILL METHODS: Stabbing,
strangulation
RAPE: Yes
NOTES: Possible murders in other
states.

McKelton, Calvin (1975 -)
YEARS ACTIVE: 2008-2009
VICTIMS: 2
RACE OF VICTIMS: Black
AREA: Cincinnati, OH
KILL METHODS: Strangulation
RAPE: Yes
NOTES: Killed his girlfriend and
friend.

McKinnon, Crandall (1968 -)
YEARS ACTIVE: 1994
VICTIMS: 2-3
RACE OF VICTIMS: Black
AREA: Banning, CA
KILL METHODS: Shooting
RAPE: No
NOTES: Was a gang member who
killed members of other gangs.

McKnight, Anthony (1954 -)
NICKNAME: East Bay Serial Killer
YEARS ACTIVE: 1984-1986
VICTIMS: 8
RACE OF VICTIMS: Black
AREA: Oakland, CA
KILL METHODS: Stabbing

RAPE: Yes
NOTES: Dismembered his
victims. All were females he
had raped.

McKnight, Gregory (1976 -)
YEARS ACTIVE: 1993, 2000
VICTIMS: 3
RACE OF VICTIMS: White
AREA: Vinton County, OH
KILL METHODS: Shooting
RAPE: Yes
NOTES: A repeat offender.

McKoy, Lamon J. (1988 -)
YEARS ACTIVE: 2003
VICTIMS: 2
RACE OF VICTIMS: Black
AREA: Geneva, NY
KILL METHODS: Strangulation
RAPE: Yes
NOTES: One victim was his
cousin; the other a stranger. He
is suspected in more.

McLain, Jr., Stephon (1990 -)
YEARS ACTIVE: 2012-2013
VICTIMS: 2
RACE OF VICTIMS: Black
AREA: Conway, SC
KILL METHODS: Shooting
RAPE: No
NOTES: Arrested for murder in
2013, DNA connected him to
an additional murder in 2012.

McLaughlin, Elton Odell
(1951 -)
YEARS ACTIVE: 1974, 1984
VICTIMS: 4
RACE OF VICTIMS: Black
AREA: Elizabethtown, NC
KILL METHODS: Shooting

RAPE: No
NOTES: A repeat offender.

McLean, Ralph (1966 - 1995)
NICKNAME: Cop Killer
YEARS ACTIVE: 1995
VICTIMS: 2
RACE OF VICTIMS: White
AREA: DC, MD
KILL METHODS: Shooting
RAPE: No
NOTES: Wrote his own gangster rap
song with cop-killing lyrics. Loved
gangster rap.

McNeil, Leroy (1941 - 2008)
YEARS ACTIVE: 1977, 1982
VICTIMS: 4-6
RACE OF VICTIMS: White
AREA: North Carolina
KILL METHODS: Shooting
RAPE: No
NOTES: Died in prison.

McTier, James (1982 -)
YEARS ACTIVE: 2000-2002
VICTIMS: 3-5
RACE OF VICTIMS: Black
AREA: Brooklyn, NY
KILL METHODS: Shooting
RAPE: No
NOTES: A gang member who killed
other gang members and innocent
bystanders.

McWilliams, LeMarques Devon
(1975 -)
NICKNAME: Four Acres Homes
Killer
YEARS ACTIVE: 2006-2009
VICTIMS: 2-10
RACE OF VICTIMS: Black
AREA: Houston, TX

KILL METHODS: Strangulation
RAPE: Yes
NOTES: Police have tied him to two murders so far, but these deaths closely resemble seven other murders. He is also suspected in numerous rapes.

Mealey, James (? - 1903)
A.K.A. Will Jones
YEARS ACTIVE: 1900-1903
VICTIMS: 3-4
RACE OF VICTIMS: White
AREA: VA, MD, NC
KILL METHODS: Unknown
RAPE: No
NOTES: Executed for his crimes.

Means, Leon (1954 -)
YEARS ACTIVE: 1989, 2014
VICTIMS: 4
RACE OF VICTIMS: Varied
AREA: Muskegon, MI
KILL METHODS: Unknown
RAPE: No
NOTES: After escaping prison in 1989 he committed his first two murders, his wife and mother-in-law. After being released from prison, he murdered two women, and stole their car. After confessing to the the last two murders, he confessed to the other murders from 1989.

Meeks, Douglas Ray (1953 -)
YEARS ACTIVE: 1974
VICTIMS: 2
RACE OF VICTIMS: White
AREA: FL, Taylor County
KILL METHODS: Stabbing, shooting
RAPE: No

NOTES: Killed victims during the course of robberies.

Melton, Antonio Lebaron
(1972 -)
YEARS ACTIVE: 1990-1991
VICTIMS: 2
RACE OF VICTIMS: White
AREA: Pensacola, FL
KILL METHODS: Shooting
RAPE: No
NOTES: Killed his victims while robbing them.

Melvin, Michael (1980 -)
YEARS ACTIVE: 2004-2008
VICTIMS: 6
RACE OF VICTIMS: Black
AREA: Newark, NJ
KILL METHODS: Shooting
RAPE: No
NOTES: Despite the evidence against him and his confession, he only received a sixteen-year sentence and will likely be paroled in the next few years.

Mengel, Alex (1955 - 1985)
YEARS ACTIVE: 1985
VICTIMS: 2
RACE OF VICTIMS: White
AREA: New York
KILL METHODS: Shooting
RAPE: No
NOTES: A native of Guyana. His second victim was a police officer.

Mercer, Kevin Jermaine
(1977 -)
YEARS ACTIVE: 2000-2002
VICTIMS: 2
RACE OF VICTIMS: White
AREA: Columbia, SC

KILL METHODS: Shooting
RAPE: No
NOTES: Both victims were
   males.

Meredith, Henry
(1981 -)
YEARS ACTIVE: 1996
VICTIMS: 2
RACE OF VICTIMS: Black
AREA: New Orleans, LA
KILL METHODS: Shooting
RAPE: No
NOTES: Both victims were
   males, possibly conencted to
   gangs.

Middleton, David Stephen
(1961 -)
NICKNAME: The Cable Guy,
Big Dave
YEARS ACTIVE: 1994-1995
VICTIMS: 3-4
RACE OF VICTIMS: White
AREA: NV & Norwood, CO
KILL METHODS: Shooting
RAPE: No
NOTES: Made tapes of himself
   with prostitutes. Charged with
   raping a sixteen-year-old girl.
   Was a former police officer.

Miller, Joseph Lewis (1937-)
VICTIMS: 2
RACE OF VICTIMS: White
AREA: Harrisbury, PA
KILL METHODS: Shooting
RAPE: No
NOTES: First victim and his
   wife was shot, but she
   survived. After release from
   prison he murdered again, but

hid under an alias in Texas for 34
years before being caught.

Mills, David (1974 -)
YEARS ACTIVE: 1997-2005
VICTIMS: 4
RACE OF VICTIMS: Varied
AREA: Oakland, CA
KILL METHODS: Shooting
RAPE: No
NOTES: Murdered one victim in
   1997 and committed a triple
   homicide in 2005.

Minley, Kevin Eric (1957 -)
YEARS ACTIVE: 1987-1988
VICTIMS: 2-4
RACE OF VICTIMS: Varied
AREA: Detroit, MI
KILL METHODS: Shooting
RAPE: No
NOTES: Was the hit man for a drug
   ring.

Mitchell, John Allen
(1944 - 2003)
YEARS ACTIVE: 1970
VICTIMS: 2-3
RACE OF VICTIMS: White
AREA: Miami, FL
KILL METHODS: Shooting
RAPE: No
NOTES: Shot during robberies.

Mitchell, William Gerald (1950-)
YEARS ACTIVE: 1974, 1998
VICTIMS: 2
RACE OF VICTIMS: White
AREA: Mississippi
KILL METHODS: Beating,
strangulation, car
RAPE: Yes
NOTES: Three attempted.

Mitchell, Tony Garrett
(1979 -)
YEARS ACTIVE: 2002
VICTIMS: 2
RACE OF VICTIMS: White
AREA: Tennessee
KILL METHODS: Shooting
RAPE: Yes
NOTES: Killed women. One
attempted.

Mitchell, Roy (1892 - 1923)
YEARS ACTIVE: 1922-1923
VICTIMS: 6-8
RACE OF VICTIMS: White
AREA: Waco, TX
KILL METHODS: Shooting
RAPE: Yes
NOTES: Suspected of murder.
Police found the gun used in
five murders and a watch of
one of his victims in his home.
He later confessed to six
murders, but police put the
number at eight.

Moffett, Jessie Ray (1958 -
1998)
YEARS ACTIVE: 1979-1987
VICTIMS: 2
RACE OF VICTIMS: White
AREA: Los Angeles, CA
KILL METHODS: Beating,
shooting
RAPE: Yes
NOTES: Killed a man and
woman.

Monroe, Kasey Jack (1963 -)
YEARS ACTIVE: 1995
VICTIMS: 2
RACE OF VICTIMS: White
AREA: Scotland, NC

KILL METHODS: Shooting
RAPE: Yes
NOTES: Killed women.

Moore, Todd (1972 -)
YEARS ACTIVE: 1992-1994
VICTIMS: 4-5
RACE OF VICTIMS: Black
AREA: NY, VA
KILL METHODS: Shooting
RAPE: No
NOTES: Two double murders. One
was his pregnant girlfriend.

Moore, Thomas James (1973 -)
YEARS ACTIVE: 1990-1993
VICTIMS: 2
RACE OF VICTIMS: White
AREA: Jacksonville, FL
KILL METHODS: Shooting
RAPE: No
NOTES: DNA convicted him on the
second count in 2010.

Morgan, Arsenio (1991 -)
YEARS ACTIVE: 2007-2009
VICTIMS: 4
RACE OF VICTIMS: White
AREA: Los Angeles, CA
KILL METHODS: Shooting
RAPE: No
NOTES: Leader of a gang set. Two
murders were gang initiates; the
other two were hate crimes
targeting whites.

Morgan, James Lewis (1955 -)
YEARS ACTIVE: 1976, 1997
VICTIMS: 2
RACE OF VICTIMS: Black
AREA: Ashville, NC
KILL METHODS: Stabbing
RAPE: Yes

NOTES: Two attempted.

Morgan, Letisha (1976 -)
YEARS ACTIVE: 2010
VICTIMS: 2
RACE OF VICTIMS: White
AREA: South Dakota, Texas
KILL METHODS: Shooting,
Stabbing
RAPE: No
NOTES: First victim was shot
   multiple times in Texas. She
   fled to South Dakota where six
   months later she killed her
   second victim by stabbing him
   37 times.

Morris, Dontae Rashawn
(1985 -)
YEARS ACTIVE: 2010
VICTIMS: 5
RACE OF VICTIMS: Varied
AREA: Tampa, FL
KILL METHODS: Shooting
RAPE: No
NOTES: All victims killed over a
   40 day period. He had an
   extensive record, but made
   parole early and began his
   murdering career.

Morris, Cory Deonn (1978 -)
NICKNAME: Crackhead Killer
YEARS ACTIVE: 2002-2003
VICTIMS: 7-11
RACE OF VICTIMS: Varied
AREA: AZ, OK
KILL METHODS: Strangulation
RAPE: Yes
NOTES: His victims were
   women with whom he smoked
   crack. He stored some of the
   bodies in his RV and others in

an empty neighboring lot. He is
suspected of killing four women in
Oklahoma. He performed
necrophilia on some of his victims.

Moseley, Eddie Lee (1947 -)
NICKNAME: Rape Man
YEARS ACTIVE: 1973-1987
VICTIMS: 25-33
RACE OF VICTIMS: Black
AREA: Ft. Lauderdale, FL
KILL METHODS: Strangulation
RAPE: Yes
NOTES: See Chapter 6 for info.

Moseley, Winston (1935 -)
YEARS ACTIVE: <1964
VICTIMS: 3
RACE OF VICTIMS: White
AREA: New York City, NY
KILL METHODS: Shooting
RAPE: Yes
NOTES: Performed necrophilia.
   Escaped by beating a guard nearly
   to death. Held five people hostage
   and raped one woman in front of
   her husband. Participated in Attica
   Prison Riots. Up for parole in 2011.

Moses, Errol Duke (1972 -)
YEARS ACTIVE: 1995-1996
VICTIMS: 2
RACE OF VICTIMS: Black
AREA: Winston-Salem, NC
KILL METHODS: Shooting
RAPE: No
NOTES: His pager number was
   found in both victims' pockets. He
   confessed his crimes.

Mosley, Barry Wendell
(1959 -)
YEARS ACTIVE: 1999-2000

VICTIMS: 3
RACE OF VICTIMS: Black
AREA: Los Angeles, CA
KILL METHODS: Strangulation
RAPE: Yes
NOTES: Killed two women and
  one teenage girl.

Moss, Joseph Eli (1973 -)
YEARS ACTIVE: 2001, 2007
VICTIMS: 2
RACE OF VICTIMS: Varied
AREA: Pennsylvania
KILL METHODS: Shooting,
Stabbing
RAPE: No
NOTES: He was acquitted of the
  first murder on a technicality,
  and murdered again in 2007.

Mullins, Michael (1961 -)
YEARS ACTIVE: 1999-2012
VICTIMS: 4-5
RACE OF VICTIMS: Black
AREA: Memphis, TN
KILL METHODS:
Strangulation, stabbing
RAPE: Yes
NOTES: After being caught
  murdering his last victim in
  2012 his DNA was a match for
  at least three additional
  murders dating back to 1999.
  All victims were homeless
  women, and he is suspected in
  at least one additional murder
  and numerous rapes. Police
  suspect him in additional
  murders.

Mu'Min, Dawud Majid
(1953 - 1997)
(David Michael Allen)

YEARS ACTIVE: 1973, 1988
VICTIMS: 2
RACE OF VICTIMS: White
AREA: Virginia
KILL METHODS: Stabbing with
screwdriver
RAPE: Yes
NOTES: While serving time for a
  previous murder, he was working
  on a road crew. At a lunch break,
  he slipped away to rape and stab
  one women sixteen times in her
  neck with a screwdriver and stole
  four dollars from her. He was
  executed.

Murphy, Donald (1944 -)
YEARS ACTIVE: 1980
VICTIMS: 6-12
RACE OF VICTIMS: Varied
AREA: Detroit, MI
KILL METHODS: stabbing
RAPE: Yes
NOTES: Killed women. Confessed to
  six murders, but suspected in six
  more.

Murray, John (1953 -)
YEARS ACTIVE: 1978, 2012
VICTIMS: 2+
RACE OF VICTIMS: Varied
AREA: New York
KILL METHODS: Shooting
RAPE: No
NOTES: First victim was in 1978.
  After release from prison in 2011
  he killed again just a few months
  later. Suspected of numerous prison
  murders.

Murray, Floyd (1962 -)
YEARS ACTIVE: 1987, 2013
VICTIMS: 2+

RACE OF VICTIMS: Black
AREA: Dallas, TX
KILL METHODS: Shooting
RAPE: No
NOTES: First victim was in 1987. After release from prison he killed a woman in 2013. Suspected in other murders.

Myers, Henry Carlton (1974 -)
YEARS ACTIVE: 2005
VICTIMS: 2
RACE OF VICTIMS: Black
AREA: Jacksonville, FL
KILL METHODS: Stabbing, beating, shooting
RAPE: No
NOTES: Victims were men.

Nealy, Eddie (1957 -)
YEARS ACTIVE: 1985-1991
VICTIMS: 2+
RACE OF VICTIMS: White
AREA: Fresno, CA
KILL METHODS: Strangulation, stabbing, beating
RAPE: Yes
NOTES: The first victim was a 14 year old girl whose body was found by a canal. The murder went unsolved until DNA pointed to Nealy in 2006. He's connected to at least one additional murder, possible others, and numerous rapes.

Neverson, Andre (1965 -)
YEARS ACTIVE: 2002
VICTIMS: 3
RACE OF VICTIMS: Black
AREA: New York City, NY

KILL METHODS: Shooting
RAPE: No
NOTES: Killed women over a three-day period. A resident of Trinidad who snuck into US after being deported for attempted murder.

Newton, Huey P. (1942 - 1989)
YEARS ACTIVE: 1967-1974
VICTIMS: 2-4
RACE OF VICTIMS: White
AREA: Oakland, CA
KILL METHODS: Shooting
RAPE: No
NOTES: Co-founder of the Black Panthers.

Nixon, Robert (1920 - 1939)
A.K.A. Thomas Crosby
YEARS ACTIVE: 1936-1938
VICTIMS: 7
RACE OF VICTIMS: White
AREA: IL, CA
KILL METHODS: Bludgeoning with a brick
RAPE: Yes
NOTES: After caught, he confessed to two murders but later gave the details of five other murders.

Noble, Sherman (1952 -)
YEARS ACTIVE: 1987
VICTIMS: 4
RACE OF VICTIMS: Black
AREA: Kentucky
KILL METHODS: Beating
RAPE: No
NOTES: Victims were men.

Nolan, Jr., Dempsey (1967 -)
YEARS ACTIVE: 1996-1997
VICTIMS: 5
RACE OF VICTIMS: White

AREA: IN, CA
KILL METHODS: Shooting
RAPE: No
NOTES: He was convicted on three counts, but investigators tied five murders to him.

Nolden, Thomas (1908 -)
YEARS ACTIVE: 1945
VICTIMS: 2
RACE OF VICTIMS: Varied
AREA: Milwukee, WI
KILL METHODS: Bludgeoning
RAPE: No
NOTES: Was caught after pawning jewelry from his victims.

Norris, Michael Wayne (1958-)
YEARS ACTIVE: 1979, 1986
VICTIMS: 3
RACE OF VICTIMS: Black
AREA: LA, TX
KILL METHODS: Shooting
RAPE: No
NOTES: A repeat offender.

Nunnery, Eugene (1979 -)
YEARS ACTIVE: 2006
VICTIMS: 3
RACE OF VICTIMS: Varied
AREA: Las Vegas, NV
KILL METHODS: Shooting
RAPE: No
NOTES: Killed over a one-month period. He attempted eleven more murders and numerous armed robberies. When asked if he was remorseful, he said, "I'd do it all over again."

Oliver, Louis (1938 - 2008)

YEARS ACTIVE: 1962, 1981
VICTIMS: 2
RACE OF VICTIMS: Unknown
AREA: Florida
KILL METHODS: Unknown
RAPE: No
NOTES: A repeat offender. Died in prison.

Owens, Freddie Eugene (1978 -)
YEARS ACTIVE: 1997, 1999
VICTIMS: 2
RACE OF VICTIMS: Varied
AREA: Greenville, SC
KILL METHODS: Shooting, Strangulation, Beating
RAPE: No
NOTES: The first murder was during the course of the robbery. The second was during his trial in jail, the victim was a young man serving a 90 day sentence for a traffic violation. The latter murder victim was beaten, stomped, had a pen shoved through his nose into his brain, and was finally strangled. Information was obtained from correspondence with officer who had escorted Owens to the holding facility the day prior to the second murder.

Pace, Lyndon Fitzgerald (1964 -)
YEARS ACTIVE: 1988-1991
VICTIMS: 5
RACE OF VICTIMS: White
AREA: Atlanta, GA
KILL METHODS: Strangulation
RAPE: Yes

NOTES: Maintains his innocence, but his DNA has been found in each case.

Page, Ivan L. (1969 -)
YEARS ACTIVE: 2001
VICTIMS: 3
RACE OF VICTIMS: Black
AREA: Flint, MI
KILL METHODS: Strangulation
RAPE: Yes
NOTES: Women

Palmer, Antonio (1989 -)
YEARS ACTIVE: 2012
VICTIMS: 2+
RACE OF VICTIMS: Varied
AREA: Minnesota
KILL METHODS: Hammer, Strangulation
RAPE: Yes
NOTES: He attempted three murders in Georgia, and now is suspected in additional murders. His victims were prostitutes he picked up online, and raped, then beat before killing them and stuffing them into trunks of abandoned cars.

Paris, Lamont Daunelle
(1976 -)
NICKNAME: L-L Boogey Man
YEARS ACTIVE: 2000s
VICTIMS: 4-30
RACE OF VICTIMS: Black
AREA: Nationwide
KILL METHODS: Shooting
RAPE: No
NOTES: Was a hit man for various drug organizations in Detroit. Police know he killed four, but suspect him in at least thirty murders in Detroit and the East Coast. He was a member of a gang called the Connecticut Boys.

Parker, Gerald (1955 -)
NICKNAME: The Bedroom Basher
YEARS ACTIVE: 1978-1979
VICTIMS: 6-8
RACE OF VICTIMS: White
AREA: Los Angeles, CA
KILL METHODS: Bludgeoning
RAPE: Yes
NOTES: Raped women in a one-year span. When finished, he beat them to death by bashing their heads in. In one instance, he bashed a woman against a toilet until dead. Investigators did not pin the murders on him until seventeen years later when DNA connected him to the crimes.

Parker, Lodrick (1959 -)
YEARS ACTIVE: 1980-1992
VICTIMS: 7-30
RACE OF VICTIMS: Varied
AREA: Detroit, MI
KILL METHODS: Shooting
RAPE: No
NOTES: A dangerous hit man in Detroit. He is suspected of killing infamous druglord Maserati Richard Cater, and guilty of at least six more murders. Police put the conservative number of his kills at thirty but believe it is much more.

Parker, Kenneth (1979 -)
YEARS ACTIVE: 2000-2001
VICTIMS: 3
RACE OF VICTIMS: Black
AREA: Louisville, KY
KILL METHODS: Shooting

RAPE: No
NOTES: Victims were all men.

Parker, Jr., Norman (1944 -)
YEARS ACTIVE: 1966-1978
VICTIMS: 6
RACE OF VICTIMS: Varied
AREA: FL, DC
KILL METHODS: Shooting
RAPE: Yes
NOTES: Some of the murders
were related to drug sales.

Parker, Robert Lee (1972 -)
a.k.a Robert White
YEARS ACTIVE: 1995-1996
VICTIMS: 4
RACE OF VICTIMS: Varied
AREA: WA, GA
KILL METHODS: Burning,
shooting
RAPE: Yes
NOTES: Killed three women and
one man.

Parker, Willie J. (1982 -)
YEARS ACTIVE: 2009
VICTIMS: 2
RACE OF VICTIMS: White
AREA: Salina, KS
KILL METHODS: Shooting
RAPE: No
NOTES: Both victims killed in
the same month.

Payne, Alfred B. (1926 -)
YEARS ACTIVE: 1947-1948
VICTIMS: 3
RACE OF VICTIMS: Varied
AREA: VA, NJ
KILL METHODS: Shooting
RAPE: No

NOTES: Killed one farmer and two
friends.

Payne, Edjuan (1970 -)
YEARS ACTIVE: 1987, 2010
VICTIMS: 2
RACE OF VICTIMS: Black
AREA: Peoria, IL
KILL METHODS: Shooting
RAPE: No
NOTES: Served 15 years of a 25
year sentence for his first murder.

Peeler, Jr., Russell (1972 -)
YEARS ACTIVE: 1999-2000
VICTIMS: 3
RACE OF VICTIMS: Black
AREA: Bridgeport, CT
KILL METHODS: Shooting
RAPE: No
NOTES: Killed one man, one
woman, and her eight-year-old son.

Perkins, Mary (1922 -)
YEARS ACTIVE: 1955-1956
VICTIMS: 3-10
RACE OF VICTIMS: Black
AREA: Alabama
KILL METHODS: Strangulation,
poison
RAPE: Yes
NOTES: Killed her husband, her
friend, and a young girl.
Perkins, Reginald Wendell
(1955 - 2009)
YEARS ACTIVE: 1980, 1991, 2000
VICTIMS: 4-6
RACE OF VICTIMS: Black
AREA: OH, TX
KILL METHODS: Strangulation
RAPE: Yes
NOTES: One murder in Ohio in
1980. Double homicide in 1991 in

Ft. Worth. Killed stepmother in 2000 in Ft. Worth. Suspected in the murder of the mother and father of a girl he raped. Numerous sexual assaults in Ohio. Executed.

Perry, George L. O. (? - 1902)
YEARS ACTIVE: 1902
VICTIMS: 2-6
RACE OF VICTIMS: White
AREA: Cambridge, MA
KILL METHODS: Beating
RAPE: No
NOTES: Died of typhoid fever.

Perry, Raymond (1966 -)
YEARS ACTIVE: 1989, 2009
VICTIMS: 2
RACE OF VICTIMS: White
AREA: New Jersey
KILL METHODS: Shooting
RAPE: No
NOTES: A repeat offender.

Peterson, Christopher Dewayne (1969 -)
A.K.A. Obadyah Ben Yisrael,
NICKNAME: Shotgun Killer
YEARS ACTIVE: 1990
VICTIMS: 7
RACE OF VICTIMS: Varied
AREA: Indiana
KILL METHODS: Shooting
RAPE: Yes
NOTES: Three attempted.

Phillips, Clifford X
(1934 - 1993)
YEARS ACTIVE: 1972, 1982
VICTIMS: 2
RACE OF VICTIMS: White
AREA: NY, TX

KILL METHODS: Strangulation
RAPE: No
NOTES: A repeat offender.

Pierce, Sonny (1987 -)
YEARS ACTIVE: 2010-2011
VICTIMS: 3
RACE OF VICTIMS: Black
AREA: Chicago, IL
KILL METHODS: Beating
RAPE: Yes
NOTES: Lured at least three teen girls (ages 15-18) from online chatrooms to meet him, then he killed them.

Pinder, Andre R. (1969 -)
YEARS ACTIVE: 1991-1992
VICTIMS: 2+
RACE OF VICTIMS: Black
AREA: Miami, FL
KILL METHODS: Shooting
RAPE: No
NOTES: A career criminal, he's escaped from prison twice, and is suspected in more deaths. Considered one of the most violent offenders in Florida.

Pittman, Antwan Maurice
(1978 -)
YEARS ACTIVE: 2002-2009
VICTIMS: 8-10
RACE OF VICTIMS: Black
AREA: Rocky Mount, NC
KILL METHODS: Stabbing, mutilation, beating
RAPE: Yes
NOTES: Killed women.

Player, Michael (1971 - 1987)

A.K.A. Marcus Nisby
NICKNAME: Skidrow Slayer
YEARS ACTIVE: 1986-1987
VICTIMS: 10
RACE OF VICTIMS: Varied
AREA: South Carolina
KILL METHODS: Shooting
RAPE: No
NOTES: He attempted four more
  murders before killing himself.
  He used a .38 revolver in each
  murder.

Pless, Wallace (1899 -)
YEARS ACTIVE: 1917, 1956,
1964
VICTIMS: 5
RACE OF VICTIMS: Varied
AREA: Tallahassee, FL
KILL METHODS: Shooting
RAPE: No
NOTES: A repeat offender.

Pough, James Edward
(1948 - 1990)
YEARS ACTIVE: 1971, 1990
VICTIMS: 12
RACE OF VICTIMS: White
AREA: Jacksonville, FL
KILL METHODS: Shooting
RAPE: No
NOTES: Killed one friend in
  1971 and eleven others in 1990
  at a GMAC finance office. He
  committed suicide in the latter
  massacre.

Powell, Jeremy (1990 - 2013)
YEARS ACTIVE: 2012-2013
VICTIMS: 2
RACE OF VICTIMS: Black
AREA: Jackson, MS
KILL METHODS: Shooting

RAPE: No
NOTES: While be interviewed for
  his parcipation in another murder,
  he shot and killed the police
  detective. He then turned the gun
  on himself.

Powell, Jim (- 1910)
YEARS ACTIVE: 1907-1909
VICTIMS: 7+
RACE OF VICTIMS: Varied
AREA: Birmingham, AL
KILL METHODS: Stabbing
RAPE: No
NOTES: After caught in his last
  murder, he confessed to six
  additional. Was executed.

Powell, Reginald D (1956 -)
YEARS ACTIVE: 1984, 2011
VICTIMS: 2
RACE OF VICTIMS: White
AREA: White Plains, NY
KILL METHODS: Shooting
RAPE: Yes
NOTES: A repeat offender.

Poyner, Syvasky L. (1957 -)
YEARS ACTIVE: 1984
VICTIMS: 5
RACE OF VICTIMS: Black
AREA: Newport News VA
KILL METHODS: Shooting
RAPE: No
NOTES: Over a two-week period he
  killed his victims for no motivation
  other than murder. All murders
  were during the lunch hour.

Pratt, Steven (1968 -)
YEARS ACTIVE: 1984, 2014
VICTIMS: 2
RACE OF VICTIMS: Black

AREA: Atlantic City, NJ
KILL METHODS: Shooting,
Blunt Trauma
RAPE: No
NOTES: At 15 he killed a man
by beating him unconscious
with a lead pipe, then shooting
him. 2 days after serving a 30
year sentence, he beat his
mother to death.

Prejean, Dalton (1959 - 1990)
YEARS ACTIVE: 1974-1977
VICTIMS: 2
RACE OF VICTIMS: Black
AREA: Louisiana
KILL METHODS: Shooting
RAPE: No
NOTES: Victims were males. He
was later executed.

Presley, Aeman (1981 -)
YEARS ACTIVE: 2014
VICTIMS: 4
RACE OF VICTIMS: Varied
AREA: Atlanta, GA
KILL METHODS: Shooting
RAPE: No
NOTES: Killed the first victim in
a robbery. Decided he loved
the thrill of killing, and
decided to kill again.

Pressley, Marcus Dewayne
(1969 -)
YEARS ACTIVE: 1996
VICTIMS: 2
RACE OF VICTIMS: White
AREA: Alabama
KILL METHODS: Shooting
RAPE: No
NOTES: Victims were men.

Pretlow, Bilal (1970 - 1992)
YEARS ACTIVE: 1987-1989
VICTIMS: 3-7
RACE OF VICTIMS: Black
AREA: New York City, NY
KILL METHODS: Shooting
RAPE: No
NOTES: Ran a drug ring and killed
competitors or those who owed him
money. He hanged himself in jail.

Price, Craig Chandler (1974 -)
NICKNAME: Slasher of Warwick
YEARS ACTIVE: 1987-1989
VICTIMS: 4
RACE OF VICTIMS: White
AREA: Warwick, RI
KILL METHODS: Stabbing
RAPE: No
NOTES: Overkill with every murder.
He was almost set free, and he will
most likely be paroled while young
enough to kill again. Read more
about him on page 109 and 181.

Prince, Jr., Cleophus (1967 -)
Clairemont Killer
YEARS ACTIVE: 1990
VICTIMS: 6
RACE OF VICTIMS: White
AREA: San Diego, CA
KILL METHODS: Stabbing,
strangulation
RAPE: Yes
NOTES: Killed women in the
apartment complex he lived. He
was described as a smart, charming
lady's man. He was tied to the
murders by his DNA from a rape
victim who escaped before he
could kill her.

Profit, Mark Antonio

(1963 - 2001)
YEARS ACTIVE: 1996
VICTIMS: 4
RACE OF VICTIMS: Black
AREA: Minneapolis MN
KILL METHODS:
Strangulation, burning
RAPE: Yes
NOTES: Victims were
   prostitutes. He died in prison.

Ragan, Jr., Anthawn
(1994 -)
YEARS ACTIVE: 2013
VICTIMS: 2
RACE OF VICTIMS: Varied
AREA: Miami, FL
KILL METHODS: Shooting
RAPE: No
NOTES: Killed at least two
   people in in December 2013.
   Police are checking to see if he
   is connected to other murders.

Rahman, Yusef Abdullah
(1969 -)
YEARS ACTIVE: 1987
VICTIMS: 4-5
RACE OF VICTIMS: White
AREA: KS, NY
KILL METHODS: Shooting
RAPE: No
NOTES: Sniped people with a
   .22 rifle. Two attempted
   murders.

Ray, Quan John (1972 -)
YEARS ACTIVE: 1995
VICTIMS: 2-3
RACE OF VICTIMS: Black
AREA: Chicago, IL
KILL METHODS: Shooting
RAPE: No

NOTES: Was a member of the
   Gangster Disciples and was the hit
   man for his local set.

Ray, Clifton L. (1959 -)
YEARS ACTIVE: 1987-1994
VICTIMS: 3-9
RACE OF VICTIMS: Black
AREA: MO, Kansas City
KILL METHODS: Strangulation
RAPE: No
NOTES: Was due to be paroled in
   2007, but DNA evidence from two
   previous murders pointed to him as
   the killer. Police think he
   committed two more murders but
   have not been able to prove it.

Rector, Charles Henry
(1954 - 1999)
YEARS ACTIVE: 1974, 1982
VICTIMS: 2
RACE OF VICTIMS: White
AREA: Austin, TX
KILL METHODS: Shooting,
drowning
RAPE: Yes
NOTES: A repeat offender. Executed.

Reed, Walter D (1939 -)
YEARS ACTIVE: 1970, 1982
VICTIMS: 2
RACE OF VICTIMS: Unknown
AREA: Florida
KILL METHODS:
RAPE: No
NOTES: One attempted.

Reed, Willie (1917 - 1937)
YEARS ACTIVE: 1937
VICTIMS: 2
RACE OF VICTIMS: White

AREA: Alabama
KILL METHODS: Hacksaw
RAPE: Yes
NOTES: Killed women. Was
  dragged to death and burned
  by angry townfolk.

Reid, Anthony (1967 -)
NICKNAME: Tone
YEARS ACTIVE: 1988-1989
VICTIMS: 4
RACE OF VICTIMS: Varied
AREA: Philadelphia
KILL METHODS: Shooting
RAPE: No
NOTES: Was a member of the
  Junior Black Mafia. Possibly
  tied to other murders.

Reid, Michael (1975 -)
YEARS ACTIVE: 2010-2012
VICTIMS: 3+
RACE OF VICTIMS: Black
AREA: Chicago, IL
KILL METHODS: Shooting
RAPE: No
NOTES: Killed at least three,
  suspected in additional
  murders.

Respus, Asbury (1873 - 1932)
A.K.A. Will Moore
YEARS ACTIVE: 1912-1930
VICTIMS: 9
RACE OF VICTIMS: White
AREA: North Carolina
KILL METHODS: Beating
RAPE: No
NOTES: After being convicted
  for killing a young girl, he
  confessed to eight other
  murders.

Reynolds, Jeremy (1986 -)
YEARS ACTIVE: 2003, 2013
VICTIMS: 2+
RACE OF VICTIMS: Black
AREA: Chattanooga, TN
KILL METHODS: Shooting
RAPE: Yes
NOTES: After his release from
  prison he murdered again and is
  suspected in additional murders.

Rhoiney, Eugene (1950 -)
YEARS ACTIVE: 1969, 1988
VICTIMS: 2+
RACE OF VICTIMS: Unknown
AREA: Chicago, IL
KILL METHODS: Shooting
RAPE: No
NOTES: Soon after release for a
  murder in 1969 he killed again.
  Suspected in additional murders.

Richards, Antonio (? - 1898)
A.K.A. Pierre, A.K.A. Richard
Creole
YEARS ACTIVE: 1884-1898
VICTIMS: 11
RACE OF VICTIMS: White
AREA: Lousiana
KILL METHODS: Unknown
RAPE: No
NOTES: Confessed to murdering ten
  Italians and one black woman.
  Executed.

Richey, Frederick A. (1953 -)
YEARS ACTIVE: 1984
VICTIMS: 2
RACE OF VICTIMS: White
AREA: Oregon
KILL METHODS: Beating, stabbing
RAPE: Yes

NOTES: He was convicted of one murder in 1984. Later told another inmate that he committed a second murder. It was not until 2011 that DNA proved a connection between him and the second murder.

Richmond, Earl J (1961 - 2005)
YEARS ACTIVE: 1991
VICTIMS: 5
RACE OF VICTIMS: Black
AREA: NC, NJ
KILL METHODS: Strangulation
RAPE: Yes
NOTES: Convicted of two murders one year apart. Later confessed to five murders. He also raped a twelve-year-old girl. Executed.

Riggins, Reginald Reonard (1977 -)
YEARS ACTIVE: 2009-2011
VICTIMS: 2
RACE OF VICTIMS: White
AREA: Port St. Lucie, FL
KILL METHODS: Suffocation
RAPE: Yes
NOTES: Killed women.

Riveira, Raymondeze (1978 -)
YEARS ACTIVE: 2006
VICTIMS: 2+
RACE OF VICTIMS: Black
AREA: Anderson, SC
KILL METHODS: Strangulation
RAPE: No
NOTES: Was paid to kill two different women. Suspected in other deaths.

Robbins, Steven J (1947 -)

YEARS ACTIVE: 1968, 1975, 1980, 2001
VICTIMS: 4
RACE OF VICTIMS: Black
AREA: IL, IN
KILL METHODS: Shooting
RAPE: No
NOTES: A repeat offender.

Roberts, David James (1944 -)
YEARS ACTIVE: 1975 & 1977
VICTIMS: 4
RACE OF VICTIMS: White
AREA: Whiteland, IN
KILL METHODS: Unknown
RAPE: Yes
NOTES: Killed a family of three and one infant.

Robinson, Alfred Lee (1962 -)
YEARS ACTIVE: <1991
VICTIMS: 4-5
RACE OF VICTIMS: Black
AREA: Daytona Beach, FL
KILL METHODS: Shooting, strangulation
RAPE: Yes
NOTES: Killed women, one of whom was pregnant.

Robinson, Alexander (1953 -)
YEARS ACTIVE: 1974-1981
VICTIMS: 3
RACE OF VICTIMS: White
AREA: St. Petersburg, FL
KILL METHODS: Shooting
RAPE: No
NOTES: His first murder was dismissed by a judge on a minor technicality. He was retried and found guilty, but was released only to murder again four months later.

He was released from prison in 2007 for the second time.

Robinson, Alonzo (1895 - 1935)
A.K.A. James H. Coyner
YEARS ACTIVE: 1926-1934
VICTIMS: 6
RACE OF VICTIMS: White
AREA: MS/MI/MA
KILL METHODS: Axe
RAPE: Yes
NOTES: Killed one couple and four women , decapitating one. Robbed graves

Robinson, Julius Omar
(1977 -)
NICKNAME: Scarface
YEARS ACTIVE: 1998-1999
VICTIMS: 3
RACE OF VICTIMS: Varied
AREA: Ft. Worth, TX
KILL METHODS: Shooting
RAPE: No
NOTES: Thought he was killing a man who caused him to lose money, but killed the wrong man. He also killed rival drug dealers.

Robinson, Linnell (1928 -)
YEARS ACTIVE: 1951, 1958
VICTIMS: 2
RACE OF VICTIMS: Black
AREA: Alabama
KILL METHODS: Stabbing
RAPE: No
NOTES: Killed men.

Robinson, Quincy (1958 - 1982)
YEARS ACTIVE: 1974-1978
VICTIMS: 9-20
RACE OF VICTIMS: Varied

AREA: Detroit, MI
KILL METHODS: Shooting
RAPE: No
NOTES: Murdered in prison.

Rodgers, Theodore (1940 -)
YEARS ACTIVE: 1978 and 2001
VICTIMS: 2
RACE OF VICTIMS: Unknown
AREA: Orlando, FL
KILL METHODS:
RAPE: Yes
NOTES: Killed girlfriend and wife.

Rodriguez, Antonio (1980 -)
NICKNAME: Kensington Strangler
YEARS ACTIVE: 2010
VICTIMS: 3
RACE OF VICTIMS: White
AREA: Philadelphia, PA
KILL METHODS: Strangulation
RAPE: Yes
NOTES: Victims were all women. There might be others. He attempted at least one more.

Rogers, Irvin Cornnel (1966 -)
YEARS ACTIVE: 1987 & 1991
VICTIMS: 2
RACE OF VICTIMS: Black
AREA: Orlando, FL
KILL METHODS: Beating
RAPE: No
NOTES: Killed two stepchildren.

Rollack, Peter (1974 -)
NICKNAME: Pistol Pete
YEARS ACTIVE: 1990s
VICTIMS: 8
RACE OF VICTIMS: Black
AREA: New York City, NY
KILL METHODS: Shooting
RAPE: No

NOTES: Head of a gang set called Sex, Money, and Murder. He killed rivals and anyone that got into his way. He has been memorialized in rap songs and is a hero to countless gang members.

Rouzan, Seth Joseph (1985 -)
YEARS ACTIVE: 2005-2006
VICTIMS: 2+
RACE OF VICTIMS: Varied
AREA: Augusta, GA
KILL METHODS: Stabbed, Shot
RAPE: No
NOTES: Possibly connected to additional murders.

Royal, Marcus Edward
(1982 -)
YEARS ACTIVE: 2011-2012
VICTIMS: 2+
RACE OF VICTIMS: Black
AREA: Florida
KILL METHODS: Strangled
RAPE: No
NOTES: Victims were elderly women, possibly more.

Roye, Norman (1937 -)
YEARS ACTIVE: 1954
VICTIMS: 3
RACE OF VICTIMS: Black
AREA: New York
KILL METHODS: Strangled
RAPE: Yes
NOTES: Killed women.

Rozier, Robert Earnest
(1955 -)
A.K.A. Neariah Israel
YEARS ACTIVE: 1985

VICTIMS: 7
RACE OF VICTIMS: White
AREA: FL, NY, MD
KILL METHODS: Unknown
RAPE: Yes
NOTES: Ex-NFL player who joined the Yahweh Cult. He served only ten years in prison but is doing twenty-five to life after committing another felony.

Ruffin, Antiono (1971 -)
YEARS ACTIVE: 1991, 1999, 2009
VICTIMS: 3
RACE OF VICTIMS: White
AREA: Augusta, GA
KILL METHODS: Shooting, Stabbing
RAPE: No
NOTES: A repeat offender. His last murder was a prison inmate.

Russell, Jr, George Waterfield
(1958 -)
NICKNAME: The Bellevue Killer, The Charmer, Eastside Serial Killer
YEARS ACTIVE: 1990
VICTIMS: 3
RACE OF VICTIMS: White
AREA: Mercer Island, WA
KILL METHODS: Torture, stabbing, strangulation
RAPE: Yes
NOTES: See Chapter 6 for info.

Sakai, Stephen (1975 -)
YEARS ACTIVE: 2005-2006
VICTIMS: 4
RACE OF VICTIMS: Varied
AREA: New York City, NY
KILL METHODS: Shooting
RAPE: No

NOTES: Was a bouncer who killed men in cold blood.

Sanford, Arthur Lee (1953 -)
YEARS ACTIVE: 1983, 2003
VICTIMS: 2
RACE OF VICTIMS: Black
AREA: Newport News VA
KILL METHODS: Stabbing
RAPE: No
NOTES: Both victims were girlfriends. For the first murder he was parolled and re-murdered one year after release.

Sappington, Marc Vincent (1960 -)
NICKNAME: Kansas City Vampire
YEARS ACTIVE: 2001
VICTIMS: 4
RACE OF VICTIMS: Black
AREA: Kansas
KILL METHODS: Stabbing
RAPE: No
NOTES: Killed his young male victims, drank their blood, and ate parts of three of them.

Sattiewhite, Vernon Lamar (1955 - 1995)
YEARS ACTIVE: 1977, 1986
VICTIMS: 2
RACE OF VICTIMS: Black
AREA: San Antonio, TX
KILL METHODS: Shooting
RAPE: No
NOTES: A repeat offender.

Scarver, Christopher J (1969 -)

YEARS ACTIVE: 1990, 1994
VICTIMS: 3
RACE OF VICTIMS: Varied
AREA: Wisconsin
KILL METHODS:
RAPE: No
NOTES: Killed men, including Jeffrey Dahmer.

Scheanette, Dale Devon (1974 - 2009)
NICKNAME: Bathtub Killer
YEARS ACTIVE: 1996
VICTIMS: 2
RACE OF VICTIMS: Black
AREA: Dallas, TX
KILL METHODS: Strangulation, drowning
RAPE: Yes
NOTES: Executed.

Scott, Kody Dejohn (1963 -)
A.K.A. Sanyika Shakur
NICKNAME: Monster
YEARS ACTIVE: 1976-1984
VICTIMS: 12
RACE OF VICTIMS: Varied
AREA: Los Angeles, CA
KILL METHODS: Shooting
RAPE: No
NOTES: One of the most famous gang members from Los Angeles. His murders have been memorialized in songs and a few books. He was sent to prison on a variety of charges, but none of them were for murder.

Scott, Jason Thomas (1983 -)
YEARS ACTIVE: 2010
VICTIMS: 4-5
RACE OF VICTIMS: Black
AREA: Prince Georges County, MD

KILL METHODS: Shooting, burning
RAPE: No
NOTES: Killed two mother-daughter pairs and another victim. He used his UPS job to track victims and his degree in criminology to hide evidence.

Sears, Charles (1949 - 1985)
YEARS ACTIVE: 1981
VICTIMS: 2
RACE OF VICTIMS: White
AREA: New York City, NY
KILL METHODS: Slicing throats
RAPE: No
NOTES: Thirteen attempted.

Seay, Martez (1984 -)
YEARS ACTIVE: 2008-2009
VICTIMS: 5
RACE OF VICTIMS: Black
AREA: Birmingham, AL
KILL METHODS: Shooting
RAPE: No
NOTES: Had help from brothers Demarius and Cortez. His mother Yolanda planned the murders. One more woman was shot and paralyzed.

Sharif, Omar (1982 -)
YEARS ACTIVE: 2008
VICTIMS: 2
RACE OF VICTIMS: Varies
AREA: Doylestown, PA
KILL METHODS: Shooting
RAPE: Yes
NOTES: Killed a teenager and killed another man over two weeks later. He also kidnapped the latter man's girlfriend,

raped her three times, and attempted to kill her.

Shaw, De'Merius (1993 -)
YEARS ACTIVE: 2011-2012
VICTIMS: 2
RACE OF VICTIMS: Black
AREA: Indianapolis, IN
KILL METHODS: Shooting
RAPE: No
NOTES: Was already wanted for one murder when he killed a woman.

Shields, Darryl (1987 -)
NICKNAME: Snook
YEARS ACTIVE: 2005-2007
VICTIMS: 2-3
RACE OF VICTIMS: Black
AREA: New Orleans, LA
KILL METHODS: Shooting
RAPE: No
NOTES: Was a member of the Josephine Dog pound.

Simmons, Beoria Abraham (1954 -)
YEARS ACTIVE: 1981-1983
VICTIMS: 3
RACE OF VICTIMS: White
AREA: Kentucky
KILL METHODS: Beating, shooting
RAPE: Yes
NOTES: Killed women. One attempted.

Simmons, Lamar (1978 -)
YEARS ACTIVE: 2004-2011
VICTIMS: 3
RACE OF VICTIMS: Varied
AREA: Cincinatti, OH
KILL METHODS: Shooting
RAPE: No

NOTES: Suspected in other murders, Lamar murdered a friend and his girlfriend on separate occasions.

Simmons, Willie (1964 -)
YEARS ACTIVE: 1987
VICTIMS: 2
RACE OF VICTIMS: Black
AREA: St. Louis, MO
KILL METHODS: Shooting
RAPE: No
NOTES: Several wounded in two different shootouts.

Sims, Ray Dell (1935 -)
YEARS ACTIVE: 1970's
VICTIMS: 5
RACE OF VICTIMS: Varied
AREA: Fresno, CA
KILL METHODS: Strangulation
RAPE: Yes
NOTES: Killed teenage girls.

Sims, Zeno Eugene (1966 -)
YEARS ACTIVE: 1990s, 2000
VICTIMS: 2
RACE OF VICTIMS: Black
AREA: Kansas City, KS
KILL METHODS: Shooting
RAPE: No
NOTES: Sent to prison for eight years for the murder of a twenty-four-year-old man. Released on parole in Kansas City. He then murdered DeAntreia L Ashley, a fifteen-year-old-girl, after a minor traffic accident.

Sinegal, Gary (1965 -)
YEARS ACTIVE: 2005
VICTIMS: 5-6

RACE OF VICTIMS: White
AREA: Port Arthur, TX
KILL METHODS: Beating, strangulation
RAPE: Yes
NOTES: Killed elderly women during the course of robberies. He raped at least two more whom he did not kill, and attempted one more.

Skinner, Antony (1993 -)
YEARS ACTIVE: 2009-2010
VICTIMS: 2
RACE OF VICTIMS: Black
AREA: Buffalo, NY
KILL METHODS: Shooting
RAPE: No
NOTES: He had 5 more attempted murders.

Sloan, III, Warren Herman (1971 -)
YEARS ACTIVE: 2012
VICTIMS: 2
RACE OF VICTIMS: White
AREA: Fairfield, CA
KILL METHODS: Shooting
RAPE: No
NOTES: Murdered his first victim, Clarence James in the victim's driveway. Just over three weeks later he stabbed a 19 year old woman to death in her backyard.

Smallwood, Jr., Robert Franklin (1974 -)
YEARS ACTIVE: 1999-2006
VICTIMS: 3
RACE OF VICTIMS: Black
AREA: Lexington, KY
KILL METHODS: Strangulation
RAPE: Yes
NOTES: Victims were women.

Smith, Alvin (1960 -)
YEARS ACTIVE: 1994-1995
VICTIMS: 4
RACE OF VICTIMS: Unknown
AREA: Atlanta, GA
KILL METHODS: Shooting
RAPE: No
NOTES: Victims of robberies.

Smith, Anthony Wayne (1965-)
YEARS ACTIVE: 1999-2008
VICTIMS: 4-8
RACE OF VICTIMS: Black
AREA: Los Angeles, CA
KILL METHODS: Shooting,
Beating
RAPE: No
NOTES: A former NFL player
    for eight seasons, he murdered
    at least eight men. One was
    beaten to death, and had his
    head stomped almost flat.

Smith Jr., Clyde (1973 - 2006)
YEARS ACTIVE: 1992
VICTIMS: 2
RACE OF VICTIMS: White
AREA: Houston, TX
KILL METHODS: Shooting
RAPE: No
NOTES: Victims were men. He
    was later executed.

Smith, Howard L (1960 -)
YEARS ACTIVE: 1977, 1987
VICTIMS: 2
RACE OF VICTIMS: Varied
AREA: Washington, DC
KILL METHODS: Stabbing
RAPE: No
NOTES: Killed one man and one
    inmate.

Smith, Lemuel Warren (1941 -)
YEARS ACTIVE: 1958, 1976-1978,
1981
VICTIMS: 6
RACE OF VICTIMS: White
AREA: New York
KILL METHODS: Beating
RAPE: Yes
NOTES: See Chapter 6 for info.

Smith, Reginald (1968 -)
YEARS ACTIVE: 1994
VICTIMS: 3
RACE OF VICTIMS: White
AREA: Miami, FL
KILL METHODS: Beating, stabbing
RAPE: No
NOTES: One attempted.

Smith, Roy Gene (1958 -)
YEARS ACTIVE: 1988
VICTIMS: 2
RACE OF VICTIMS: White
AREA: Houston, TX
KILL METHODS: Shooting
RAPE: No
NOTES: Victims were women.
Smith, Samuel D (1960 - 2001)
YEARS ACTIVE: 1978, 1987
VICTIMS: 2
RACE OF VICTIMS: Black
AREA: Missouri
KILL METHODS: Shooting,
stabbing
RAPE: No
NOTES: Executed.

Smith, Wilbert James (1981-)
YEARS ACTIVE: 2000, 2008
VICTIMS: 3
RACE OF VICTIMS: Black
AREA: Huntsville, AL

KILL METHODS: Shooting
RAPE: No
NOTES: Convicted for a murder
  in 2000, he committed a
  gruesome double homocide in
  2008 after his release.

Smothers, Vincent (1979 -)
YEARS ACTIVE: 2006
VICTIMS: 8-9
RACE OF VICTIMS: Black
AREA: Detroit, MI
KILL METHODS: Shooting
RAPE: No
NOTES: Hit man who killed for
  a wealthy drug ring, but was
  caught after a cop hired him to
  kill his wife.

Smyth, Evan David (1963 -)
YEARS ACTIVE: 2003
VICTIMS: 4
RACE OF VICTIMS: Varied
AREA: Wheaton, MD
KILL METHODS: Beating,
strangulation, stabbing
RAPE: Yes
NOTES: A contractor who killed
  women.

Snyder, Leroy (1931 - 2001)
YEARS ACTIVE: 1969
VICTIMS: 7
RACE OF VICTIMS: Black
AREA: Camden, NJ
KILL METHODS: Beating,
stabbing
RAPE: Yes
NOTES: He killed close friends
  to rob them.

Solomon, Jr., Morris (1944 -)
YEARS ACTIVE: 1986-1987

VICTIMS: 7
RACE OF VICTIMS: Black
AREA: Sacramento, CA
KILL METHODS: Unknown
RAPE: Yes
NOTES: Killed prostitutes and might
  be guilty of other murders. While
  in prison, he raped a female prison
  guard.

Sowell, Anthony Edward
(1969 -)
YEARS ACTIVE: 2007-2009
VICTIMS: 11
RACE OF VICTIMS: Black
AREA: Cleveland, OH
KILL METHODS: Strangulation,
torture
RAPE: Yes
NOTES: See Chapter 6 for info.

Spells, Lonnie Victor (1962 - 2000)
NICKNAME: Trucker Murderer
YEARS ACTIVE: 1976-1992
VICTIMS: 12-17
RACE OF VICTIMS: Varied
AREA: OH, TN, IN, PA
KILL METHODS: Strangulation
RAPE: Yes
NOTES: He is suspected of
  murdering in at least nine states,
  and investigators feel he murdered
  far more than 17 women. In each
  case the woman was raped, and
  then strangled, suffocated, or
  beaten to death. Victim's bodies
  were transported in the sleeper of
  his semi-truck and dumped far
  from where they were picked up.

Spencer, Anthony (1947 -)
YEARS ACTIVE: 1963-1964
VICTIMS: 2

RACE OF VICTIMS: Black
AREA: New York City, NY
KILL METHODS: Unknown
RAPE: Yes
NOTES: Also convicted of
fourteen rapes.

Spencer, Timothy Wilson
(1963 - 1994)
NICKNAME: Southside
Strangler
YEARS ACTIVE: 1984-1987
VICTIMS: 5
RACE OF VICTIMS: White
AREA: Richmond, VA
KILL METHODS: Strangulation
RAPE: Yes
NOTES: Victims were women.
He was later executed. The
name "Southside Strangler"
has become a pop icon in
Virginia, yet few people knew
he was black.

Spraggins, Jerry Jerome
(1954 -)
YEARS ACTIVE: 1981-1983
VICTIMS: 3
RACE OF VICTIMS: White
AREA: New Jersey
KILL METHODS: Shooting,
strangulation
RAPE: Yes
NOTES: Killed women. Because
of a technicality his sentence
was reduced to thirty years to
life. He will probably be
paroled soon.

Spruill, Eugen (1945 -)
YEARS ACTIVE: 1972-1973

VICTIMS: 3-6
RACE OF VICTIMS: Varied
AREA: Pittsburgh, PA
KILL METHODS: Shooting,
strangulation, stabbing, arson
RAPE: No
NOTES: Was awaiting trial for a
1972 murder when he escaped and
committed at least two more
murders. Police also list him as the
killer of a woman and accuse him
of firebombing of a home to kill
two other people.

Steenburgh, Sam (1834 - 1878)
YEARS ACTIVE: 1870s
VICTIMS: 11
RACE OF VICTIMS: White
AREA: New York
KILL METHODS: Unknown
RAPE: Yes
NOTES: After being convicted of one
murder, he agreed to confess his
crimes for the large sum of $100
($3,000 in 2012 funds). After being
paid by the sheriff, he gave the
illicit details of ten other murders
and numerous other crimes. The
twenty-two-page confession was
later sold by the county for a
quarter, and sold over 5,000 copies.
He was executed, and his $100 was
given to a daughter he had not seen
in years.

Stephens, Jason D. (1974 -)
YEARS ACTIVE: 1996, 1997
VICTIMS: 2
RACE OF VICTIMS: Black
AREA: Jacksonville, FL
KILL METHODS: Shooting,
strangulation
RAPE: No

NOTES: One attempted.

Stephens, Lee Edward (1979 -)
YEARS ACTIVE: 1990s, 2006
VICTIMS: 2-3
RACE OF VICTIMS: Varied
AREA: Maryland
KILL METHODS: Shooting,
stabbing
RAPE: No
NOTES: He was in prison for
  previous murders when he
  stabbed a prison guard over
  seventy times.

Sterling, Gary Lynn
(1967 - 2005)
YEARS ACTIVE: 1988
VICTIMS: 4
RACE OF VICTIMS: White
AREA: Texas
KILL METHODS: Shooting,
bludgeoning with a car jack
RAPE: Yes
NOTES: The murders were
  committed over a one-week
  period. Executed.

Stevens, Charles Arnett
(1969 -)
YEARS ACTIVE: 1989
VICTIMS: 4
RACE OF VICTIMS: White
AREA: Oakland, CA
KILL METHODS: Stabbing
RAPE: Yes
NOTES: Six attempted.

Stewart, Adrian (1973 -)
YEARS ACTIVE: 2005-2009
VICTIMS: 2
RACE OF VICTIMS: Black
AREA: Montgomery, AL

KILL METHODS: Shooting
RAPE: No
NOTES: Both victims were male.

Stewart, Raymond Lee
(1952 - 1996)
YEARS ACTIVE: 1981
VICTIMS: 6
RACE OF VICTIMS: White
AREA: Illinois
KILL METHODS: Shooting
RAPE: No
NOTES: Most were victims of
  robbery. He was later executed.

Stewart, Tommy Lee (1949 -)
YEARS ACTIVE: 1971, 1986
VICTIMS: 3
RACE OF VICTIMS: Black
AREA: Texas
KILL METHODS: Strangulation
RAPE: Yes
NOTES: A repeat offender.

Stokes, Winford Lavern
(1951 - 1990)
YEARS ACTIVE: 1969, 1978
VICTIMS: 3
RACE OF VICTIMS: White
AREA: MO, AR
KILL METHODS: Stabbing,
strangulation
RAPE: Yes
NOTES: Killed women. Was found
  insane on first two murders and
  released. Killed again and was later
  executed.

Stuard, James William
(1937 - 2004)
NICKNAME: Senior Citizen Killer
YEARS ACTIVE: 1989-1990
VICTIMS: 3

RACE OF VICTIMS: White
AREA: Arizona
KILL METHODS: Unknown
RAPE: Yes
NOTES: Killed elderly women.
One more attempted. Died in
prison.

Surratt, Edward Arthur
(1941 -)
NICKNAME: The Shotgun
Killer
YEARS ACTIVE: 1977-1978
VICTIMS: 19
RACE OF VICTIMS: White
AREA: FL, OH, PA, SC
KILL METHODS: Shooting,
beating
RAPE: Yes
NOTES: See Chapter 6 for info.

Swann, James Edward
(1964 -)
NICKNAME: Shotgun Stalker
YEARS ACTIVE: 1993
VICTIMS: 4
RACE OF VICTIMS: Black
AREA: Washington, DC
KILL METHODS: Shooting
RAPE: No
NOTES: Claimed that the ghost
of Malcolm X told him to
avenge his death and killed
four people.

Sweet, William Earl (1967 -)
YEARS ACTIVE: 1990
VICTIMS: 2
RACE OF VICTIMS: Black
AREA: Jacksonville, FL
KILL METHODS: Shooting

RAPE: No
NOTES: Victims were robbed.

Tate, Deangleo D. (1983 -)
YEARS ACTIVE: 2008-2009
VICTIMS: 2
RACE OF VICTIMS: Black
AREA: St. Louis, MO
KILL METHODS: Shooting
RAPE: No
NOTES: Was out on bond for the
first murder when he killed again.

Taylor, Alvin (1948 -)
YEARS ACTIVE: 1985-1988
VICTIMS: 4
RACE OF VICTIMS: White
AREA: Rural Wisconsin
KILL METHODS: Shooting,
Stabbing
RAPE: No
NOTES: Confessed to killing four of
his friends, including his college
roommate. Spent 25 years in a
mental institution, petitioned to be
paroled in 2013 but was denied.
Currently serving in mental
hospital in Madison, WI.

Taylor, Kevin (1974 -)
YEARS ACTIVE: 2001
VICTIMS: 4
RACE OF VICTIMS: Black
AREA: Chicago, IL
KILL METHODS: Strangling
RAPE: Yes
NOTES: One attempted.

Taylor, John Henry (? - 1900)
YEARS ACTIVE: 1899
VICTIMS: 4
RACE OF VICTIMS: Varied
AREA: VA, NC

KILL METHODS: Shooting
RAPE: No
NOTES: Executed.

Taylor, Michael (1979 -)
YEARS ACTIVE: 1995, 1999
VICTIMS: 2
RACE OF VICTIMS: Black
AREA: Missouri
KILL METHODS: Shooting,
strangulation
RAPE: Yes
NOTES: Killed one woman and
an inmate.

Taylor, Norris Carlton
(1945 - 2006)
YEARS ACTIVE: 1979
VICTIMS: 3-4
RACE OF VICTIMS: White
AREA: NC, VA
KILL METHODS: Shooting
RAPE: Yes
NOTES: Died in prison.

Taylor, Ronald T (1979 -)
YEARS ACTIVE: 2003-2011
VICTIMS: 3
RACE OF VICTIMS: Black
AREA: Kansas City, MO
KILL METHODS: Shooting
RAPE: No
NOTES: He also had two
assaults.

Terry, Benjamin (1950 -)
YEARS ACTIVE: 1971, 1979
VICTIMS: 4
RACE OF VICTIMS: Varied
AREA: Pennsylvania
KILL METHODS: Baseball bat,
arson
RAPE: No

NOTES: Killed one family and one
prison guard.

Terry, Michael (1979 - 2003)
YEARS ACTIVE: 1997, 1999
VICTIMS: 2
RACE OF VICTIMS: Varied
AREA: Missouri
KILL METHODS: Strangulation,
beating
RAPE: Yes
NOTES: Killed one woman and one
cellmate. Executed.

Terry, Michael Devern
(1960 -)
YEARS ACTIVE: 1985-1986
VICTIMS: 6
RACE OF VICTIMS: Black
AREA: Atlanta, GA
KILL METHODS: Unknown
RAPE: No
NOTES: Was a gay prostitute who
killed his customers.

Tholmer, Brandon (1949 -)
YEARS ACTIVE: 1981-1984
VICTIMS: 12-34
RACE OF VICTIMS: Black
AREA: Los Angeles, CA
KILL METHODS: Strangulation
RAPE: Yes
NOTES: He was convicted in the
deaths of twelve women, but has
connections to possibly thirty-four.
He admitted at least forty murders
to police, but they were never able
to validate every detail of his story.

Thomas, Alex D. (1963-)
YEARS ACTIVE: 1978, 1985, 1997
VICTIMS: 3
RACE OF VICTIMS: White
AREA: California

KILL METHODS: Shooting, strangulation, beating, stabbing
RAPE: Yes
NOTES: First murder was as a teenager for shooting a man. He murdered again in prison by slicing an inmates throat. After parole he was working as a subsitute janitor in a school and brutally raped an 18 year old student, then bashed her head in with a crowbar and sliced her throat.

Thomas, Andre (1977 -)
YEARS ACTIVE: 2003-2005
VICTIMS: 2-5
RACE OF VICTIMS: Black
AREA: Cincinnati, OH
KILL METHODS:
RAPE: No
NOTES: Robberies and kidnapping charges also.

Thomas, Daniel M. (1949 - 1986)
YEARS ACTIVE: 1976-1977
VICTIMS: 2-3
RACE OF VICTIMS: White
AREA: Bartow, FL
KILL METHODS: Shooting
RAPE: Yes
NOTES: Leader of the Ski Mask Gang. Killed victims of robberies.

Thomas, Dante (1985 -)
YEARS ACTIVE: 2015
VICTIMS: 2
RACE OF VICTIMS: mixed
AREA: Houston, TX
KILL METHODS: Shooting, stabbing

RAPE: No
NOTES: Killed his girlfriend by stabbing her. A month later he shot his aunt, killing her. He attempted to kill his cousin as well.

Thomas, Gus (1884 -)
A.K.A. Gus Young
YEARS ACTIVE: 1909-1910
VICTIMS: 4
RACE OF VICTIMS: White
AREA: Kansas
KILL METHODS: Stabbing
RAPE: Yes
NOTES: Killed one family and one man.

Thomas, Jr., John Floyd (1936 -)
NICKNAME: West Side Rapist
YEARS ACTIVE: 1970-1990
VICTIMS: 30-39
RACE OF VICTIMS: White
AREA: Los Angeles, CA
KILL METHODS: Strangulation, shooting
RAPE: Yes
NOTES: See Chapter 6 for info.

Thomas, Markquice (1986 -)
NICKNAME: Tank
YEARS ACTIVE: 2012-2014
VICTIMS: 2
RACE OF VICTIMS: Black
AREA: Trenton, NJ
KILL METHODS: Strangulation, shooting
RAPE: Yes
NOTES: Both victims were show in broad daylight, and were possibly gang related.

Thomas, Regis Deon (1970 -)

YEARS ACTIVE: 1992-1993
VICTIMS: 3-4
RACE OF VICTIMS: Varied
AREA: Compton, CA
KILL METHODS: Shooting
RAPE: No
NOTES: Killed two cops and one
   gang member. One other
   possible.

Thomas, Renard Carlos
(1961 -)
YEARS ACTIVE: 1981-1998
VICTIMS: 3
RACE OF VICTIMS: Black
AREA: Georgia
KILL METHODS: Shooting
RAPE: No
NOTES: He stalked his victims
   and kidnapped them before
   murdering them.

Thomas, Shareef (1965 -)
NICKNAME: Sug
YEARS ACTIVE: 2004-2008
VICTIMS: 2-6
RACE OF VICTIMS: Black
AREA: Newark, NJ
KILL METHODS: Shooting
RAPE: No
NOTES: Leader of a gang, he
   murdered at least two people
   and is suspected in the deaths
   of four other witnesses in a
   mass murder to silence them.

Thomas, Robert Lee
(1945 -)
YEARS ACTIVE: 1962
VICTIMS: 2
RACE OF VICTIMS: White
AREA: North Carolina

KILL METHODS: Shooting
RAPE: Yes
NOTES: Was only 17 at the time of
   the murders,

Thomas III, Troy Tyrone
(1965 -)
YEARS ACTIVE: 1981, 2008
VICTIMS: 2
RACE OF VICTIMS: Black
AREA: San Francisco, CA
KILL METHODS: Shooting
RAPE: No
NOTES: First murder was as a
   teenager. After serving time, he
   was released and later murdered a
   college professor.

Thompson, Earl A (1946 -)
YEARS ACTIVE: 1979, 1992
VICTIMS: 3
RACE OF VICTIMS: Unknown
AREA: Miami, FL
KILL METHODS: Shooting
RAPE: No
NOTES: A repeat offender.

Thompson, Scottie (1972 -)
YEARS ACTIVE: 1989, 2013
VICTIMS: 2
RACE OF VICTIMS: White
AREA: Centreville, MO
KILL METHODS: Shooting, Beating
RAPE: No
NOTES: His first murder was an
   elderly woman he was employed
   by. After being released in
   February 2013, he beat a 20 year
   old to death in August 2013.

Tisdale, Jason (1980 -)
YEARS ACTIVE: 1998-2004
VICTIMS: 3-4

RACE OF VICTIMS: Black
AREA: Wichita, KS
KILL METHODS: Shooting
RAPE: No
NOTES: Was a member of a
    Crips set. Also had two
    attempted murders.

Toney, Twdarryl (1982 -)
YEARS ACTIVE: 2003-2004
VICTIMS: 3
RACE OF VICTIMS: Black
AREA: New Orleans, LA
KILL METHODS: Shooting
RAPE: No
NOTES: Killed his friend. Killed
    two as a hit man.

Townser, Anthony (1975 -)
YEARS ACTIVE: 1993
VICTIMS: 3
RACE OF VICTIMS: White
AREA: St. Louis, MO, IL
KILL METHODS: Strangulation
RAPE: Yes
NOTES: Killed elderly people.

Travis, Maury Troy
(1949 - 2002)
YEARS ACTIVE: 2000-2002
VICTIMS: 17-22
RACE OF VICTIMS: Black
AREA: St. Louis, MO
KILL METHODS:
Strangulation, beating, torture
RAPE: Yes
NOTES: See Chapter 6 for info.

Trevillion, John (1984 -)
YEARS ACTIVE: 2005-2013
VICTIMS: 2-3
RACE OF VICTIMS: Black
AREA: St. Louis, MO

KILL METHODS: Shooting
RAPE: No
NOTES: He had a prior murder
    conviction, and killed again soon
    after release.

Trotter, Clarence (1959 -)
YEARS ACTIVE: 1981, 1986
VICTIMS: 2
RACE OF VICTIMS: White
AREA: Chicago, IL
KILL METHODS: Drowning,
suffocation.
RAPE: Yes
NOTES: He was in prison for the
    1981 murder when in 2007 his
    DNA pointed to the other in 1986.
    Police are investigating other cold
    case files to see if there is a
    connection.

Tucker, Emerson (1957 -)
A.K.A. John Turner
YEARS ACTIVE: 2003
VICTIMS: 3
RACE OF VICTIMS: Varied
AREA: NY, IL
KILL METHODS: Strangulation
RAPE: Yes
NOTES: Killed women. Police are
    investigating other murders in other
    states to which he might be tied.

Tucker, Russell (1967 -)
YEARS ACTIVE: 1994
VICTIMS: 2
RACE OF VICTIMS: Black
AREA: Winston-Salem, NC
KILL METHODS: Shooting
RAPE: No
NOTES: Stuffed one victim into a
    suitcase.

Tuggle, Debra Sue (1958 -)
YEARS ACTIVE: 1974-1982
VICTIMS: 6
RACE OF VICTIMS: Black
AREA: Little Rock, AR
KILL METHODS: Suffocation
RAPE: No
NOTES: Killed four of her kids
and two more people.

Turner, Chester Dewayne
(1966 -)
NICKNAME: Chester the
Molester
YEARS ACTIVE: 1987-1998
VICTIMS: 17-24
RACE OF VICTIMS: Black
AREA: Los Angeles, CA
KILL METHODS: Strangulation
RAPE: Yes
NOTES: See Chapter 6 for info

Turner, Darryl Donnell
(1964 -)
YEARS ACTIVE: 1994-1997
VICTIMS: 4
RACE OF VICTIMS: Black
AREA: Washington, DC
KILL METHODS: Strangulation
RAPE: Yes
NOTES: His DNA was originally
linked to just two women, but
police later found it on two
more.

Unnamed Youth (1892 -)
YEARS ACTIVE: 1896-1897
VICTIMS: 3
RACE OF VICTIMS: Black
AREA: Lacrosse, FL
KILL METHODS: Burning,
shooting, stabbing
RAPE: No

NOTES: Killed three siblings while
under five years old. When I first
found this killer, I thought it was a
media misprint, but after further
investigation I found the story to be
true. The parents told the sheriff
that he killed his sister while four
by pouring kerosene on her and
lighting her on fire. The next year,
he stabbed his older brother to
death twelve times. His last murder
was of an older brother whom he
shot with a pistol. He also killed
pets and other animals. The sheriff
suspected the father at first, but
after neighbors corroborated the
story, the boy was shipped off to a
mental hospital. The killings
stopped and no more of his siblings
died. As far as can be told, the boy
either died in the hosptial or was
locked away for life, both of which
were common practice in 1900.

Usher, Sr., Frank Lee (1942 -)
Big Frank Nitty
YEARS ACTIVE: 1970's-1980s
VICTIMS: 11-14
RACE OF VICTIMS: Black
AREA: Detroit, MI
KILL METHODS: Shooting,
beheading
RAPE: No
NOTES: Hit man.

Vann, Darren Deon (1971 -)
YEARS ACTIVE: 2013-2014
VICTIMS: 7+
RACE OF VICTIMS: Mixed
AREA: Gary, IN
KILL METHODS: Strangulation,
beating
RAPE: Yes

NOTES: Served 4 years for a rape sentence, then killed at least 7 women after release. Authorities are investigating cold case files in Texas, and Indiana for further murders.

Vernon, Michael (1973 -)
YEARS ACTIVE: 1993-1995
VICTIMS: 6-7
RACE OF VICTIMS: White
AREA: Bronx, NY
KILL METHODS: Shooting
RAPE: No
NOTES: Killed one to two cab drivers, and five more in a shoe store.

Victor, Clarence (1932 -)
YEARS ACTIVE: 1964-1987
VICTIMS: 3
RACE OF VICTIMS: White
AREA: Nebraska
KILL METHODS: Strangulation
RAPE: Yes
NOTES: Killed women.

Victorianne, Javier William (1977 -)
YEARS ACTIVE: 1999-2000
VICTIMS: 3
RACE OF VICTIMS: White
AREA: Riverside County, CA
KILL METHODS: Beating, strangulation, hanging
RAPE: Yes
NOTES: He hanged two of the victims in classic lynching style. The other victim was a mentally handicapped woman whom he killed and left in an abandoned car in the desert. Read more on page 149.

Wade, Dione Andre (1989 -)
YEARS ACTIVE: 2009- 2012
VICTIMS: 3-4
RACE OF VICTIMS: Varied
AREA: Dayton, OH
KILL METHODS: Shooting
RAPE: No
NOTES: Hunted down Arab looking people out of hatred and to steal their money. Suspected in other deaths.

Wadsworth, Anthony L (1993 -)
YEARS ACTIVE: 2012
VICTIMS: 2
RACE OF VICTIMS: White
AREA: Columbus, OH
KILL METHODS: Shooting
RAPE: No
NOTES: Both victims were men.

Walker, Clarence (1929 -)
A.K.A. Clyde W. Haynes, A.K.A. James Darnell
YEARS ACTIVE: 1945-1966
VICTIMS: 19
RACE OF VICTIMS: Varied
AREA: TN, IL, OH, MI
KILL METHODS: Beating, stabbing
RAPE: Yes
NOTES: While serving a 320-year sentence in an Illinois prison for numerous rapes, police connected him to eighteen unsolved murders. He had committed a murder in 1945 and was out of prison by 1963. The eighteen latter murders were over a three-year span from 1963-1966. He was tried and had time added to his sentence which was already longer than life.

Walker, Darick Demorris
(1973 - 2010)
YEARS ACTIVE: 1996, 1997
VICTIMS: 2
RACE OF VICTIMS: Black
AREA: Richmond, VA
KILL METHODS: Shooting
RAPE: No
NOTES: In both instances,
  kicked the door into the
  victim's house and shot them
  in front of their family.
  Executed.

Walker, Maurice (1968 -)
YEARS ACTIVE: 1984, 1996
VICTIMS: 2
RACE OF VICTIMS: White
AREA: Albany, NY
KILL METHODS: Shooting
RAPE: No
NOTES: A repeat offender.

Walker, Tony (1966 - 2002)
YEARS ACTIVE: 1978, 1992
VICTIMS: 3
RACE OF VICTIMS: Black
AREA: Dallas, TX
KILL METHODS: Shooting
RAPE: Yes
NOTES: A repeat offender.

Walker, Tyrone (1965 -)
YEARS ACTIVE: 1989, 2011
VICTIMS: 2+
RACE OF VICTIMS: Black
AREA: Kansas
KILL METHODS: Shooting
RAPE: No
NOTES: Murdered in 1989 and
was in prison until February
2011. In June 2011 he murdered
a woman by beating her, then

strangling her with her shoelaces.
Other possible murders.

Walker, Tyrone (1969 -)
YEARS ACTIVE: 1993-1996
VICTIMS: 3
RACE OF VICTIMS: White
AREA: New York
KILL METHODS: Shooting
RAPE: No
NOTES: Was already wanted for two
  murders when he killed a forty-
  two-year-old woman.

Wallace, Henry Louis (1965 -)
NICKNAME: The Charlotte
Strangler
YEARS ACTIVE: 1990-1994
VICTIMS: 12
RACE OF VICTIMS: Black
AREA: Charlotte, NC
KILL METHODS: Strangulation
RAPE: Yes
NOTES: See Chapter 6 for info.

Walton, Edward (? - 1908)
A.K.A. Frank Johnson
YEARS ACTIVE: 1896-1908
VICTIMS: 5
RACE OF VICTIMS: Black
AREA: IL/PA/OH/WV/AL
KILL METHODS: Shooting
RAPE: No
NOTES: Executed by hanging.

Ward, Lucky (1965 -)
A.K.A. Lawayne Jackson
YEARS ACTIVE: 2010
VICTIMS: 5
RACE OF VICTIMS: Varied
AREA: Houston, TX
KILL METHODS: Strangulation
RAPE: Yes

NOTES: Victims were male and female and were all active in the Houston homosexual scene.

Ward, Carmen Lee (1960 -)
YEARS ACTIVE: 1987-1988
VICTIMS: 2
RACE OF VICTIMS: Black
AREA: Los Angeles, CA
KILL METHODS: Shooting
RAPE: No
NOTES: Was a member of the Ghost Town Crips and shot two fellow Crips members.

Ware, Pearison (1938 - 2011)
YEARS ACTIVE: 1966, 1990
VICTIMS: 2
RACE OF VICTIMS: Black
AREA: Miami, FL
KILL METHODS: Stabbing
RAPE: No
NOTES: A repeat offender.

Washington, Annette J
(1959 -)
YEARS ACTIVE: 1985-1986
VICTIMS: 2
RACE OF VICTIMS: Black
AREA: New York City, NY
KILL METHODS: Stabbing
RAPE: No
NOTES: Was an in-home health care provider. She killed two elderly women and robbed their apartments. The first victim had her throat sliced with a kitchen knife. The last victim was stabbed over ninety times with a large butcher knife.

Washington, Charles Edward
(1960 -)
YEARS ACTIVE: 1977, 1985
VICTIMS: 3
RACE OF VICTIMS: Unknown
AREA: Jacksonville, FL
KILL METHODS:
RAPE: No
NOTES: A repeat offender.

Washington, David L
(1949 - 1984)
YEARS ACTIVE: 1976
VICTIMS: 3
RACE OF VICTIMS: White
AREA: Miami, FL
KILL METHODS: Shooting
RAPE: No
NOTES: Killed a pastor, an elderly woman, and a male student in a two-week period in September.

Washington, Jr., Steven
(1948 - 2004)
YEARS ACTIVE: 1963
VICTIMS: 3-5
RACE OF VICTIMS: White
AREA: Tampa, FL
KILL METHODS: Strangulation
RAPE: Yes
NOTES: Killed elderly women. Two more rapes and attempted murders. Died in prison.

Watkins, Johnny (1960 -)
YEARS ACTIVE: 1983
VICTIMS: 2
RACE OF VICTIMS: White
AREA: Virginia
KILL METHODS: shooting
RAPE: No

NOTES: Murders were over a two-week span.

Watson, Jr., Alexander Wayne
(1970 -)
YEARS ACTIVE: 1986-1993
VICTIMS: 4
RACE OF VICTIMS: Black
AREA: Maryland
KILL METHODS: Beating, strangulation, stabbing
RAPE: Yes
NOTES: Killed three women and one girl.

Watts, Carlton Eugene
(1953 - 2007)
NICKNAME: Coral, Sunday Slasher
YEARS ACTIVE: 1972-1982
VICTIMS: 44-100
RACE OF VICTIMS: White
AREA: TX, MI, Midwest
KILL METHODS: Strangulation, drowning, stabbing, shooting, beating
RAPE: Yes
NOTES: See Chapter 6 for info.

Watts, Robert Austin
(1922 - 1951)
YEARS ACTIVE: 1947
VICTIMS: 5
RACE OF VICTIMS: White
AREA: Indianapolis, IN
KILL METHODS: Stabbing, shooting
RAPE: Yes
NOTES: While a delivery truck driver, he killed his female victims. Was later executed.

Webb, Willis (? - 1913)

YEARS ACTIVE: 1911-1913
VICTIMS: 4
RACE OF VICTIMS: Black
AREA: AR, MO
KILL METHODS: Shooting
RAPE: No
NOTES: Killed two black men and two black women. Was lynched by an all-black mob.

Webb, Emmanuel Lovell
(1966 -)
YEARS ACTIVE: 1980-1990
VICTIMS: 6+
RACE OF VICTIMS: Black
AREA: Bridgeport, CT
KILL METHODS: Strangled
RAPE: Yes
NOTES: Killed women. Possibly killed six to eight more.

Wesley, Dameon Lareese
(1973 -)
YEARS ACTIVE: 1994, 2013
VICTIMS: 2-3
RACE OF VICTIMS: Black
AREA: Dayton, OH
KILL METHODS: Shooting
RAPE: Yes
NOTES: Killed a friend in 1994, served 19 years. Not long after release he raped and murdered his girlfriend's 13 year old cousin, and shot his girlfriend. He's suspected in one additional murder.

Wesley, Terry Carnell
(1965 -)
YEARS ACTIVE: 1985
VICTIMS: 2
RACE OF VICTIMS: White
AREA: Florida
KILL METHODS: Shooting, Beating

RAPE: No
NOTES: Killed over a 4 month span, he stole the car of one. Serving life in prison.

West, Kenneth (1964 -)
YEARS ACTIVE: 1983-1987
VICTIMS: +
RACE OF VICTIMS: Varied
AREA: New York City, NY
KILL METHODS: Strangulation
RAPE: Yes
NOTES: Convicted of his final murder, DNA evidence tied him to two additional murders. Suspected in other murders

Weston, Linda Ann (1960 -)
YEARS ACTIVE: 1983-2011
VICTIMS: 3
RACE OF VICTIMS: Black
AREA: Philadelphia, PA
KILL METHODS: Starvation, hammer
RAPE: No
NOTES: Each of her victims were imprisoned in closets and starved to death. The first victim was beaten with a hammer, and bled slowly to death.

Wheatfield, Daryl Keith (1965 -)
YEARS ACTIVE: 1990
VICTIMS: 4
RACE OF VICTIMS: Black
AREA: Houston, TX
KILL METHODS: Shooting, stabbing
RAPE: No
NOTES: Killed one couple. Three days later, he killed one person and attempted two

other murders. He later stabbed another man.

White, John (1946 - 1994)
YEARS ACTIVE: 1986-1992
VICTIMS: 7-8
RACE OF VICTIMS: Varied
AREA: Buffalo, NY
KILL METHODS: Strangulation
RAPE: Yes
NOTES: Police are convinced that he is guilty but cannot prove it because he died right after questioning. All evidence points to his guilt.

White, Garcia Glen (1963 -)
YEARS ACTIVE: 1988-1989
VICTIMS: 5
RACE OF VICTIMS: Black
AREA: Houston, TX
KILL METHODS: Strangulation, stabbing
RAPE: Yes
NOTES: Victims were women and girls.

White, Victor Rashaad (1989 -)
YEARS ACTIVE: 2007-2008
VICTIMS: 2
RACE OF VICTIMS: Varied
AREA: Jacksonville, FL
KILL METHODS: Shooting
RAPE: No
NOTES: Convicted of killing two men. He might have additional murders.

White, Larry Lamont (1959 -)
YEARS ACTIVE: 1983
VICTIMS: 3
RACE OF VICTIMS: Black

AREA: Louisville, KY
KILL METHODS: Shooting
RAPE: Yes
NOTES: Killed women. Had the
death penalty thrown out
because of a technicality and
was expected to be paroled,
but a DNA connection to
another murder in 2008 sealed
his fate to life in prison.

White, Nathaniel (1960 -)
YEARS ACTIVE: 1991-1992
VICTIMS: 6
RACE OF VICTIMS: Black
AREA: New York
KILL METHODS: Beating
RAPE: Yes
NOTES: Victims were women.

Whitelow, J. B. (1982 -)
YEARS ACTIVE: 2007-2008
VICTIMS: 3
RACE OF VICTIMS: Varied
AREA: Hammond, IN
KILL METHODS: Shooting
RAPE: No
NOTES: One victim was a
longtime friend. The others
were men he did not know.

Whitmore, George (1945 -)
YEARS ACTIVE: 1964
VICTIMS: 3
RACE OF VICTIMS: White
AREA: New York City, NY
KILL METHODS: Stabbing
RAPE: Yes
NOTES: Happened over a one-
month period. He also had one
rape and attempted murder.

Wilcox, Darius (1977 -)

YEARS ACTIVE: 1992, 2008
VICTIMS: 2
RACE OF VICTIMS: White
AREA: Fort Lauderdale, FL
KILL METHODS: Shooting
RAPE: No
NOTES: A repeat offender.

Wiley, Nicholas Lee (1962 -)
YEARS ACTIVE: 2003-2004
VICTIMS: 7
RACE OF VICTIMS: Varied
AREA: Syracuse, NY
KILL METHODS: Strangulation
RAPE: Yes
NOTES: He was only suspected in
the murders of two women, but he
surprised police by confessing to a
total of seven.

Wilkins, Carol L (1971 -)
YEARS ACTIVE: 1992, 2008
VICTIMS: 2
RACE OF VICTIMS: Varied
AREA: KS, NB
KILL METHODS: Shooting,
stabbing
RAPE: No
NOTES: Killed her Kenyan boyfriend
first. After release, she sliced the
throat of another man.

Wilkins, Jr., Edward Charles
(1974 -)
YEARS ACTIVE: 1999-2000
VICTIMS: 3
RACE OF VICTIMS: Black
AREA: Savannah, GA
KILL METHODS: Shooting
RAPE: Yes
NOTES: Victims were women.

Williams, Anthony Louis

(1968 -)
YEARS ACTIVE: 1995, 2000
VICTIMS: 4+
RACE OF VICTIMS: White
AREA: FL, NJ
KILL METHODS: Shooting
RAPE: No
NOTES: Called police about a body wrapped in plastic in a building near his house. He was arrested three days later in connection with the murder, and he confessed his role. He later murdered another inmate. He has at least two murders in NJ.

Williams, Connie J. (1951 -)
YEARS ACTIVE: 1974, 1999
VICTIMS: 2
RACE OF VICTIMS: Varied
AREA: Philadelphia, PA
KILL METHODS: Stabbing
RAPE: No
NOTES: Killed his landlord and later his wife. Stored landlord's body under his bed for a month. After parole, he butchered his wife and dumped her body parts in different locations.

Williams, Darnell (1987 -)
YEARS ACTIVE: 2013
VICTIMS: 2-3
RACE OF VICTIMS: Black
AREA: Alameda County, CA
KILL METHODS: Shooting
RAPE: No
NOTES: Youngest victim was 8 all were in a 4 month span. Police think he is connected to additional murders.

Williams, Donald (1977 -)
YEARS ACTIVE: 1994, 2013
VICTIMS: 2
RACE OF VICTIMS: Varied
AREA: Philadelphia, PA
KILL METHODS: Stabbing, Shooting, Burning
RAPE: No
NOTES: Served 15 years for murdering a man in 1994. One month after release he stabbed his girlfriend with a screwdriver, and then set her on fire while alive. She died 43 days later.

Williams, Dorothy (1954 -)
YEARS ACTIVE: 1987-1989
VICTIMS: 3
RACE OF VICTIMS: Black
AREA: Chicago, IL
KILL METHODS: Strangulation, Stabbing
RAPE: No
NOTES: Killed elderly women.

Williams, Frank Charles (1942 -)
YEARS ACTIVE: 1962-1964
VICTIMS: 2+
RACE OF VICTIMS: White
AREA: New Orleans, LA
KILL METHODS: Strangulation
RAPE: Yes
NOTES: After committing his second brutal murder, he confessed to one more.

Williams, George Travis (1962 -)
YEARS ACTIVE: 1988-1990
VICTIMS: 3-4
RACE OF VICTIMS: Black
AREA: Atlanta, GA

KILL METHODS: Shooting
RAPE: No
NOTES: An Atlanta drug dealer
who killed his competition.

Williams, Harry (1931 - 1952)
YEARS ACTIVE: 1950
VICTIMS: 2
RACE OF VICTIMS: Varied
AREA: Chicago, IL
KILL METHODS: Beating
RAPE: No
NOTES: Killed one black
woman and one prison guard.
Executed.

Williams, Jerry Lee (1982 -)
YEARS ACTIVE: 2004-2008
VICTIMS: 2-3
RACE OF VICTIMS: White
AREA: Orlando, FL
KILL METHODS:
Strangulation, suffocation
RAPE: Yes
NOTES: After being sent to
prison for one murder, DNA
pointed to him in at least one
other murder and another rape.
Police now suspect him in a
third murder.

Williams, John (1973 -)
YEARS ACTIVE: 2000
VICTIMS: 2
RACE OF VICTIMS: Black
AREA: Rochester, NY
KILL METHODS: Shooting
RAPE: No
NOTES: At least two homicides,
3 months apart. Arrested in
2015

Williams, Jr., John (1962 -)

YEARS ACTIVE: 1996-1997
VICTIMS: 5-6
RACE OF VICTIMS: Black
AREA: Raleigh, NC
KILL METHODS: Strangulation
RAPE: Yes
NOTES: Preyed on drug-addicted
prostitutes.

Williams, Joseph (1973 -)
YEARS ACTIVE: 1999-2003
VICTIMS: 3
RACE OF VICTIMS: Unknown
AREA: Georgia
KILL METHODS: Strangulation
RAPE: No
NOTES: Was already convicted on
two murder counts. Strangled
another inmate in prison and tried
to make it look like a suicide.

Williams, Kenneth (1959 -)
YEARS ACTIVE: 2000
VICTIMS: 2
RACE OF VICTIMS: White
AREA: Orlando, FL
KILL METHODS: Strangulation
RAPE: No
NOTES: Three attempted.

Williams, Kenneth (1961 -)
NICKNAME: Boobie
YEARS ACTIVE: 1990-1999
VICTIMS: 35-120
RACE OF VICTIMS: Varied
AREA: Florida and the South
KILL METHODS: Shooting
RAPE: No
NOTES: Was the leader of a gang
called the Boobie Boys. Police tied
him to fourteen murders in Miami
and at least thirty-five in Florida
where he either pulled the trigger or

participated in the murder. His drug ring extended into several Southern States and is suspected in up to 120 murders.

Williams, Laron Ronald (1949 - 1984)
YEARS ACTIVE: 1985-1987
VICTIMS: 3
RACE OF VICTIMS: Varied
AREA: Tennessee
KILL METHODS: Shooting
RAPE: Yes
NOTES: Died in prison.

Williams, Larry Lester (1949 -)
YEARS ACTIVE: 1980, 2004
VICTIMS: 2
RACE OF VICTIMS: Black
AREA: West Palm Beach, FL
KILL METHODS: Shooting
RAPE: No
NOTES: A repeat offender.

Williams, Marvin Hansel (1977 -)
YEARS ACTIVE: 1994
VICTIMS: 2
RACE OF VICTIMS: White
AREA: Orlando, FL
KILL METHODS: Shooting
RAPE: No
NOTES: Killed during robberies.

Williams, Robert E. (1957 - 1997)
YEARS ACTIVE: 1977
VICTIMS: 3
RACE OF VICTIMS: White
AREA: NE, IA

KILL METHODS: Strangulation, Stabbing
RAPE: Yes
NOTES: All victims were women. Had one additional rape. Executed.

Williams, Ronnie Keith (1962 -)
YEARS ACTIVE: 1984-1993
VICTIMS: 2-3
RACE OF VICTIMS: Black
AREA: Ft. Lauderdale, FL
KILL METHODS: Stabbing
RAPE: Yes
NOTES: A repeat offender.

Williams, Roy L (1964 -)
YEARS ACTIVE: 1988
VICTIMS: 2-3
RACE OF VICTIMS: White
AREA: MA, PA
KILL METHODS: Shooting
RAPE: No
NOTES: Said he was going to kill whites.

Williams III, Stanley Tookie (1953 - 2005)
YEARS ACTIVE: 1979
VICTIMS: 4-11
RACE OF VICTIMS: Varied
AREA: Los Angeles, CA
KILL METHODS: Shooting
RAPE: No
NOTES: Killed one white and three Asians. Executed.

Williams, Tom (1911 -)
YEARS ACTIVE: 1940, 1954
VICTIMS: 4-5
RACE OF VICTIMS: White
AREA: Georgia
KILL METHODS: Beating, knife

RAPE: No
NOTES: Was the subject of a huge manhunt that went into the swamps. After eluding police for a few days, he was caught and later confessed his crimes.

Williams, Wayne Bertram (1958 -)
NICKNAME: Atlanta Child Murderer
YEARS ACTIVE: 1979-1981
VICTIMS: 25-31
RACE OF VICTIMS: Black
AREA: Atlanta, GA
KILL METHODS: Strangulation
RAPE: Yes
NOTES: Killed two men and twenty-three to twenty-nine boys. Maintains his innocence despite physical and DNA evidence against him. (see index for more info).

Willis, Fred (1951 -)
YEARS ACTIVE: 1984-1997
VICTIMS: 2
RACE OF VICTIMS: Black
AREA: NV/CA
KILL METHODS: Strangling
RAPE: Yes
NOTES: Victims were women.

Wilson, Carl W. (1956 -)
YEARS ACTIVE: 1975-2004
VICTIMS: 2
RACE OF VICTIMS: Black
AREA: East St. Louis, IL
KILL METHODS: Shooting
RAPE: No

NOTES: Served time for first murder, murdered again after release.

Wilson, Daniel (1977 -)
YEARS ACTIVE: 1998-2000
VICTIMS: 2-5
RACE OF VICTIMS: Varied
AREA: Washington, DC
KILL METHODS: Shooting
RAPE: No
NOTES: Was the hit man for the Congress Park Gang.

Wilson, Herbert Titus (1975 -)
YEARS ACTIVE: 2000, 2003
VICTIMS: 2-3
RACE OF VICTIMS: White
AREA: Miami, FL
KILL METHODS: Shooting
RAPE: No
NOTES: Victims of robbery.

Wimberly, Anthony (1962 -)
YEARS ACTIVE: 1984-1985
VICTIMS: 3
RACE OF VICTIMS: White
AREA: Oakland, CA
KILL METHODS: Shooting
RAPE: Yes
NOTES: Killed women.

Winfield, Christina (1965 -)
YEARS ACTIVE: 1982, 2000
VICTIMS: 2
RACE OF VICTIMS: Black
AREA: Orlando, FL
KILL METHODS: Stabbing, Shooting
RAPE: No
NOTES: Both murders were boyfriends. She served four years, was released and attempted another murder before killing again.

Wise, Jesse Lee (1953 - 1999)
YEARS ACTIVE: 1971, 1984
VICTIMS: 2
RACE OF VICTIMS: White
AREA: Missouri
KILL METHODS: Beating
RAPE: No
NOTES: Executed

Womack, Shawn (1985 -)
YEARS ACTIVE: 2006
VICTIMS: 3
RACE OF VICTIMS: Varied
AREA: Portland, OR
KILL METHODS: Shooting
RAPE: No
NOTES: Two were male victims of carjackings. The third was a female friend he was afraid would go to police.

Woodward, Mario Dion (1973-)
YEARS ACTIVE: 1994, 2005
VICTIMS: 2
RACE OF VICTIMS: White
AREA: GA, AL
KILL METHODS: Shooting
RAPE: No
NOTES: After release for his first murder, he murdered a police officer during a routine traffic stop.

Wright, Dewayne Allen
(1972 - 1998)
YEARS ACTIVE: 1989
VICTIMS: 3
RACE OF VICTIMS: Black
AREA: MD, DC, VA
KILL METHODS: Shooting
RAPE: No

NOTES: Killed over a two-week period when he was seventeen. He was later executed.

Wright, George (1943 -)
YEARS ACTIVE: 1962
VICTIMS: 2
RACE OF VICTIMS: White
AREA: New Jersey
KILL METHODS: Shooting
RAPE: No
NOTES: Recently apprehended for a pair of murders in 1962 while a member of the Black Liberation Army. He had escaped in 1972 while dressed as a priest and helped other friends hijack a plane bound for Miami, FL. After receiving a one-million-dollar ransom, they set the passengers free and made for Algeria. He was caught in Portugal.

Wright, Michael (1976 -)
YEARS ACTIVE: 2012-2013
VICTIMS: 2
RACE OF VICTIMS: Black
AREA: Utica, NY
KILL METHODS: Shooting
RAPE: Yes
NOTES: He also kidnapped one person for over one month.

Wright, Jonas (1890 -)
YEARS ACTIVE: 1910-1915
VICTIMS: 2+
RACE OF VICTIMS: Unknown
AREA: Louisiana
KILL METHODS: Unknown
RAPE: No
NOTES: Found in Lousisana prison records. Possibly committed other murders.

York, Moses (? - 1900)

YEARS ACTIVE: 1890s
VICTIMS: 2
RACE OF VICTIMS: White
AREA: AR, MS
KILL METHODS: Unknown
RAPE: No
NOTES: Lynched.

Young, George 19X (1944 -)
NICKNAME: Carbine Murderer
YEARS ACTIVE: 1968
VICTIMS: 4
RACE OF VICTIMS: Varied
AREA: Jacksonville, FL
KILL METHODS: Shooting
RAPE: No
NOTES: Was a popular Muslim
  activist who spoke often of his
  hatred for the white race. In
  1968, he killed two whites
  during different burglaries. In a
  third, he killed a black man,
  which he later claimed was an
  accident.

Youngblood, Herbert
(1899 - 1934)
YEARS ACTIVE: 1933-1934
VICTIMS: 2
RACE OF VICTIMS: White
AREA: IL, UT
KILL METHODS: Shooting
RAPE: No
NOTES: Helped Dillinger escape
  from prison, and was later
  killed.

Youngblood, Kendrick
(1971 -)
YEARS ACTIVE: 1988-1989
VICTIMS: 6+
RACE OF VICTIMS: Varied
AREA: Detroit, MI

KILL METHODS: Shooting
RAPE: No
NOTES: A hit man for the Chambers
  Drug Gang. He is suspected in
  more hits.

Younge, Jr., Donald E.
(1967 -)
YEARS ACTIVE: 1999, 2008
VICTIMS: 4-6
RACE OF VICTIMS: Varied
AREA: IL, UT
KILL METHODS: Strangulation
RAPE: Yes
NOTES: Three rapes in Utah.

Chapter 8

Suspected and Unidentified Killers

Suspected

Franklin, Robert
YEARS ACTIVE: 1992-1999
VICTIMS: 10-12
RACE OF VICTIMS: Varied
AREA: Raymond, MS
KILL METHODS: Strangulation
RAPE: Yes
NOTES: Known as the
  "Vampire," Franklin has been
  caught and convicted of rape
  on two different occasions. He
  has been connected to
  numerous other rapes and
  assaults, and in many of the
  rapes he is reported to have
  drunk blood from their neck in
  classic vampire style. Police
  are positive that he is guilty of
  the murders around the area of
  women fitting the description
  of those he raped. He was
  brought to trial on three
  different occasions for the
  murders, but in each instance a
  mistrial was called because of
  a problem with the evidence or
  a technicality. One thing they
  noted was that whenever

Franklin was not in jail, women
were raped and killed.

Howell, Brandon B (1980 -)
YEARS ACTIVE: 1998, 2014
VICTIMS: 7
RACE OF VICTIMS: White
AREA: Kansas City, KS
KILL METHODS: Shooting
RAPE: No
NOTES: Despite overwhelming
  evidence, and eye witness accounts
  a jury acquitted Brandon of a
  double homicide in 1998. After
  serving time for another crime
  involving assault, kidnapping, and
  animal cruelty he was released in
  2011.In 2014 he went on a crime
  spree and murdered five people in a
  quiet neighborhood. Police
  apprehended him with a weapon,
  and blood on his clothes.

King, Robert Lee
YEARS ACTIVE: 2005-2009
VICTIMS: 3
RACE OF VICTIMS: Black
AREA: TN, MS
KILL METHODS: Unknown
RAPE: No

NOTES: Robert killed his girlfriend and then fled the scene. Soon afterward, he turned up in Sharkey County, Mississippi, according to witnesses who saw his story on *America's Most Wanted*. In 2009, a young woman and her three-year-old son were killed; police suspect him in the murder. He is currently at large and rumored to be in Illinois or Florida.

Unidentified

Atlanta's Jack the Ripper
YEARS ACTIVE: 1911-1915
VICTIMS: 20-24
RACE OF VICTIMS: Black
AREA: Atlanta, GA
KILL METHODS: Stabbing, axe
RAPE: No
NOTES: Several people were maimed for life but survived. They each identified a large black man, but no one was ever caught, leading police to think that the killer may have died.

Atlanta Lust Killer
YEARS ACTIVE: 1980-1982
VICTIMS: 7-11
RACE OF VICTIMS: Black
AREA: Atlanta, GA
KILL METHODS: Stabbing
RAPE: Yes
NOTES: While Wayne Williams was committing the Atlanta Child Murders, there was another serial killer lurking behind the scenes. While Williams killed men and boys, this killer preyed on young female prostitutes. After Williams was apprehended, this killer murdered at least two more victims but then suddenly stopped. Police are unsure if he moved on, died, or was arrested on another charge. Eyewitness reports put the last known person in contact with each woman as an attractive, nicely-dressed black man, fitting the same description.

Atlanta's Phantom Gunman
YEARS ACTIVE: 1977
VICTIMS: 3
RACE OF VICTIMS: Black
AREA: Atlanta, GA
KILL METHODS: Shooting
RAPE: No
NOTES: Police were baffled by the sudden appearance and disappearance of this killer. Police interviewed several leading suspects but no arrests were ever made. All evidence and eyewitness accounts identify a black male.

Baton Rouge Killings
YEARS ACTIVE: 1999-2000
VICTIMS: 5
RACE OF VICTIMS: Black
AREA: Baton Rouge, LA
KILL METHODS: Shooting
RAPE: Yes
NOTES: This killer was killing in the same area as Derrick Todd Lee. But while Lee focused primarily on white victims (he had only one black), his MO was to beat and strangle his victims. This killer raped and shot his

victims. Unlike Lee, whose victims were students or career women, this killer focused on prostitutes. Police so far have not made any solid connections, but they are positive the killer is black.

Bigfoot Killer
YEARS ACTIVE: 1975
VICTIMS: 7
RACE OF VICTIMS: Black
AREA: Detroit, MI
KILL METHODS: Strangulation, shooting
RAPE: Yes
NOTES: In the summer of 1975, a killer stalked the Cass Corridor of Detroit, which was one of the roughest areas and later the stomping ground of another large-framed serial killer, Shelly Brooks. This killer left a size-15 boot-print at the scene of every murder. There were so many gangs and drug organizations running the streets during this time that police are unsure if this killer was a part of one of those groups or killing on his own. Witnesses reported seeing a large black man near the scene of each murder, but were unwilling to identify him out of fear. It is thought that the killer either was arrested on another charge or was killed.

Chicago Slayings
YEARS ACTIVE: 1971-1972
VICTIMS: 6-8
RACE OF VICTIMS: Black

AREA: Chicago, IL
KILL METHODS: Shooting
RAPE: No
NOTES: Over a one-year period, this killer shot six to eight black men in the face, killing them during robberies. Police were given testimony from witnesses who gave the description of a black male, but no one was ever arrested. It is unknown if the killer was part of a violent gang or acted as an individual.

Columbus Killings
YEARS ACTIVE: 1991-1999
VICTIMS: 13+
RACE OF VICTIMS: Varied
AREA: Columbus, OH
KILL METHODS: Shooting
RAPE: No
NOTES: This killer shot sixteen people, thirteen of whom died. The same gun was used in each of the murders, and police are still looking for the killer. Descriptions given were of a black male in his early thirties.

Flint Serial Killer
YEARS ACTIVE: 1993-1994
VICTIMS: 6-7
RACE OF VICTIMS: Varied
AREA: Flint, MI
KILL METHODS: Shooting, strangulation
RAPE: Yes
NOTES: A black male was stalking the streets of Flint killing prostitutes over a one-year period. Then, as quickly as he started, he was finished and left no trace of his identity. Police have linked these

murders via DNA to each other, but thus far have not connected the DNA to any suspect.

Lake Erie Killer
YEARS ACTIVE: 1981-1999
VICTIMS: 21-27
RACE OF VICTIMS: Varied
AREA: OH, PA
KILL METHODS: Strangulation, stabbing
RAPE: Yes
NOTES: Police are unsure if these deaths are the result of a single serial killer or more than one. They are positive that at least one killer seems to be responsible for twenty-one murders in Geauga County, Ohio, and the dumping of a few of the bodies in nearby Crawford County, Pennsylvania. The victims all died in a similar manner and were all female prostitutes about the same age. There were six additional murders that police think might be tied, but they could be as the result of another killer. There is some corroborating DNA evidence on some of the twenty-one murders, but police have not been able to locate a killer. Eyewitness reports from other prostitutes claim that the last customer each of the ladies had was a black male 25-35 years old.

Memphis Cemetery Killer
YEARS ACTIVE: 2011

VICTIMS: 4
RACE OF VICTIMS: Varied
AREA: Memphis, TN
KILL METHODS: Shooting
RAPE: Yes
NOTES: Killed prostitutes. One attempted murder. Police have a composite sketch of the suspect who dumped the bodies over a four-month period in a cemetery. This case made *America's Most Wanted*.

Missouri River Killer
Independence Avenue Killer
YEARS ACTIVE: 1982-1999
VICTIMS: 10-11
RACE OF VICTIMS: Varied
AREA: Kansas City, MO
KILL METHODS: Strangulation, mutilation
RAPE: Yes
NOTES: When the bodies of prostitutes began appearing in the murky Missouri River, police noticed many similarities. Most had their legs severed, and all died as a result of strangulation. After investigating, they arrested a white male and accused him in one of the murders. The case fell apart as the evidence used was not conclusive, and he went to jail for counterfeit checks. Most of the Kansas City media was convinced that he was the killer, but no evidence tied him to the crimes. Eyewitnesses claim that the killer was a black male and not white.

Miami Prostitute Killings
YEARS ACTIVE: 1986-1995
VICTIMS: 17-26

RACE OF VICTIMS: Black
AREA: Miami, FL
KILL METHODS: Shooting, stabbing, strangulation
RAPE: Yes
NOTES: Over a nine-year period, prostitutes in Miami lived in fear. Someone was soliciting their service and later leaving them for dead. Police have no leads, but other prostitutes and witnesses gave a description of the black male in connection to each of the deceased women. As with other murders in the black community, police feel there are witnesses who know his identity but are scared to come forward.

New Haven Murders
YEARS ACTIVE: 1976-1978
VICTIMS: 6-7
RACE OF VICTIMS: Black
AREA: New Haven, CT
KILL METHODS: Beating, strangulation
RAPE: Yes
NOTES: The victims were all black prostitutes. They were all beaten and strangled to death. Police scoured the city looking for a black male tied to the crimes, but never arrested anyone in connection to the murders.

New Jersey Killer
YEARS ACTIVE: 1988-1992
VICTIMS: 8
RACE OF VICTIMS: Black
AREA: Union County, NJ

KILL METHODS: Stabbing
RAPE: Yes
NOTES: Police are positive that they have a serial killer on their hands. In a four-year period, eight black prostitutes were found dead, all stabbed in a similar manner. Thus far the only lead they have is that the murderer was a black male in his twenties or thirties.

Newark Prostitute Slayings
YEARS ACTIVE: 1994-1997
VICTIMS: 14-19
RACE OF VICTIMS: Varied
AREA: Newark, NJ
KILL METHODS: Shooting
RAPE: Yes
NOTES: Police in Essex County, New Jersey, have fourteen connected homicides on their hands. The victims are all prostitutes ages 19-37. After noticing the connection, investigators from neighboring East Orange County noted that the murders of five prostitutes in their area during this same time period appeared to be committed by the same killer. The standard MO was a gunshot to the head, neck, or chest, and leaving the victim in an empty lot. Witnesses reported a black male harassing many of the victims and soliciting their services. The killings ceased as quickly as they had started, leaving police baffled as to the murderer's identity.

Peoria Hooker Murders
YEARS ACTIVE: 2001-2010
VICTIMS: 6

RACE OF VICTIMS: Black
AREA: Peoria, IL
KILL METHODS: Strangulation
RAPE: Yes
NOTES: Police in Peoria are
  positive that they have a serial
  killer in their midst. The
  killings started in 2001 and the
  last one recorded was in 2010.
  They do not know if the killer
  is hanging low or is no longer
  in the area. All witnesses
  describe a black male in his
  mid-thirties.

Potomac River Killer
YEARS ACTIVE: 1991-1998
VICTIMS: 3-4
RACE OF VICTIMS: White
AREA: MD, DC
KILL METHODS:
RAPE: Yes
NOTES: Police interviewed
  several potential suspects who
  fit the description given by
  survivors of this killer, but no
  arrests were ever made. Efforts
  were recently made to reopen
  the cases.

Suitland Slayer
YEARS ACTIVE: 1983-1986
VICTIMS: 8-9
RACE OF VICTIMS: Black
AREA: Suitland, MD
KILL METHODS: Stabbing,
strangulation
RAPE: Yes
NOTES: The Suitland Slayer is
  one who has bugged police for
  almost two decades. After the
  deaths of five women, they
  arrested Alton Alonso Best in

connection with a murder that was
grouped with these murders. He
gave a full confession of the
murder but denied any involvement
in the other murders. Police were
not sure if he was a suspect in the
other murders or not, but they soon
cleared him after the Suitland
Slayer resumed killing. All the
victims were black prostitutes, and
witnesses gave a description of a
black male in connection with each
of the deaths.

Chapter 9

Black Serial Killing Duos

There are at least two instances not listed here in which individual black serial killers teamed up with another black serial killer to commit a murder together. In both cases most of their murders were committed as individuals, so they can be found in the individuals list.

Baltimore Duo
Williams, Jerry Antonio "Black Jerry" (1977 -)
Jones, Anthony Ayeni (1973 -)
YEARS ACTIVE: 1994-1997
VICTIMS: 12-15
RACE OF VICTIMS: Varied
AREA: Baltimore, MD
KILL METHODS: Shooting
RAPE: No
NOTES: This group used fear to run their drug enterprise, killing competitors or those who could not pay their debts. Police speculate that they might be responsible for more murders.

Beltway Snipers
Muhammad, John Allen (1960-2009)
Malvo, Lee Boyd (1985 -)
YEARS ACTIVE: 2002
VICTIMS: 16
RACE OF VICTIMS: Varied
AREA: DC area and the South
KILL METHODS: Shooting
RAPE: No
NOTES: Ten killed in the DC area, three wounded, and at least six others killed in Alabama and Mississippi. There is speculation that Muhammad might have made his first kill in Seattle, WA, his hometown, but thus far there is no conclusive evidence. Muhammad was executed. Malvo received life in prison.

Bronx Assassins
Wright, Blanche (1959 -)
Young, Robert (1946-1980)
YEARS ACTIVE: 1974-1980
VICTIMS: 4-6
RACE OF VICTIMS: Black
AREA: Bronx, NY
KILL METHODS: Shooting
RAPE: No

NOTES: Hired assassins who killed for $10,000 per hit. Robert died in a shootout with police.

Brooklyn Murders
Gist, Cory (? -)
Fleming, Lamont (1972 -)
YEARS ACTIVE: 1995
VICTIMS: 4-5
RACE OF VICTIMS: Black
AREA: Brooklyn, NY
KILL METHODS: Shooting
RAPE: No
NOTES: As part of a drug dealer organization, they eliminated rivals and those who did not pay their bills.

Brown/Coleman
Coleman, Alton (1955-2002)
Brown, Debra Denise (1962 -)
YEARS ACTIVE: 1984
VICTIMS: 8
RACE OF VICTIMS: Varied
AREA: OH, WI, IN, IL
KILL METHODS: Stabbing. strangulation
RAPE: Yes
NOTES: Coleman had Debra Brown, who thought she was his slave, assist with the few murders. The murders happened over an eight-month span. Aside from this, they committed burglaries, rapes, and assaults.

Buffalo Killers
Jones, Milton E. (1970 -)
Simmons, Theodore (1969 -)
YEARS ACTIVE: 1987
VICTIMS: 2

RACE OF VICTIMS: White
AREA: Buffalo, NY
KILL METHODS: Shooting
RAPE: No
NOTES: Both victims were Roman Catholic priests.

Congress Park Crew
Ball, Antwuan (1961 -)
Wilson, David (1990 -)
YEARS ACTIVE: 1996-2004
VICTIMS: 5+
RACE OF VICTIMS: Black
AREA: Washington D.C.
KILL METHODS: Shooting
RAPE: No
NOTES: Together they were found guilty of five murders together, and are linked to possible others. A judge later dismissed the charges, because he felt the related drug charges were enough to keep them off the street for awhile.

Cook Brothers
Cook, Anthony H (1949 -)
Cook, Nathaniel (1958 -)
YEARS ACTIVE: 1973-1981
VICTIMS: 10
RACE OF VICTIMS: White
AREA: Toledo, OH
KILL METHODS: Shooting, stabbing, strangulation
RAPE: Yes
NOTES: Originally convicted of one murder, the pair was tied to other murders in 1997 after DNA confirmed their tie to the earlier murders. Their typical MO was surprising couples in their car, then having the man drive to a remote location. After killing the male,

they would take turns raping the female before killing her.

Crack Dealers
Carrington, Arleigh (1968 -)
Chatfield, Tony (1967 -)
YEARS ACTIVE: 1990-1992
VICTIMS: 2-5
RACE OF VICTIMS: Black
AREA: Macon, GA
KILL METHODS: Shooting
RAPE: No
NOTES: The pair decided that the best way to prosper their drug business was to eliminate competition.

Drug Murders
Johnson, Shaheem (1972 -)
Johnson, Raheem (1972 -)
YEARS ACTIVE: 1995-1997
VICTIMS: 5
RACE OF VICTIMS: Black
AREA: VA, PA, MD, NY
KILL METHODS: Shooting
RAPE: No
NOTES: Twin brothers who enjoyed killing together. They are connected to five murders in four states and might be connected to others. Drugs were the motivating factor in their murders.

Haley Brothers
Haley, Reginald (1960 -)
Haley, Kevin (1964 -)
YEARS ACTIVE: 1979-1984
VICTIMS: 8
RACE OF VICTIMS: White
AREA: Los Angeles, CA
KILL METHODS: Shooting, beating, burning

RAPE: Yes
NOTES: The brothers were inseparable and committed all of their crimes together. They are responsible for over 500 burglaries and at least 60 rapes in addition to their murders. Rarely for serial killers, both openly confessed their crimes, giving investigators graphic details of how they enjoyed team-raping elderly women.

Hooker Murders
Wright-Ford, Angel (1978 -)
Peoples, Caroline (1977 -)
YEARS ACTIVE: 2004
VICTIMS: 4
RACE OF VICTIMS: Black
AREA: Chicago, IL
KILL METHODS: Shooting
RAPE: No
NOTES: In an usual twist, the killers posed as prostitutes, then killed and robbed their victims.

Indy Drug Killings
Brown, Jarvis (1981 -)
Jordan, Gabriel (1981 -)
YEARS ACTIVE: 2005
VICTIMS: 4
RACE OF VICTIMS: Black
AREA: Indianapolis, IN
KILL METHODS: Shooting
RAPE: No
NOTES: Murdered for drugs and attempted at least eight additional murders.

Jones and Reardon
Jones, Tom (? – 1879)
Reardon, Bill (? – 1879)
YEARS ACTIVE: 1870-1879
VICTIMS: 5-7

RACE OF VICTIMS: White
AREA: TN
KILL METHODS: Bludgeoning
RAPE: No
NOTES: After getting caught trying to sell the cuff links from their last victim, they were arrested. They confessed their crimes in full, but while awaiting trial, they were hanged by an angry mob of black and white townsfolk from a railroad trestle.

Louisville Dou
Garrett, Jerald (1981 -)
Richardson, Billy (1990 -)
YEARS ACTIVE: 2012
VICTIMS: 2-3
RACE OF VICTIMS: White
AREA: Louisville, KY
KILL METHODS: Shooting
RAPE: Yes
NOTES: Committed two murders in 2012, and possible others.

Nashville Murders
Berry, Gdongalay (1976 -)
Davis, Christopher (1976 -)
YEARS ACTIVE: 1995-1996
VICTIMS: 3
RACE OF VICTIMS: Black
AREA: Nashville, TN
KILL METHODS: Shooting
RAPE: No
NOTES: They were awaiting trial for a double murder when the both raped and then killed a twelve-year-old girl.

New Haven Murders
Bradley, Robert (1910 – 1948)

Lisenby, William (1912 -)
YEARS ACTIVE: 1946
VICTIMS: 3
RACE OF VICTIMS: Black
AREA: New Haven, CT
KILL METHODS: Axe, shovel
RAPE: No
NOTES: Lured three black men with the promise that they could have sex with pretty white women. Once they led them to a spot in the woods, they forced them to dig their own graves, killed them, and buried them. Bradley was the leader and was later executed, while Lisenby received life in prison.

New Orleans Drug Murders
Benjamin, Terrance (1979-)
Gilmore, Winston (1972 -)
YEARS ACTIVE: 2000-2003
VICTIMS: 3-4
AREA: New Orleans, LA
RACE OF VICTIMS: Varied
KILL METHODS: Shooting
RAPE: No
NOTES: They robbed victims of their drugs and killed other drug dealers in a brutal campaign.

Palmetto Duo
Houston, Jr., Earnest J (1948-2004)
Shoates, Charles Edward (1951-)
YEARS ACTIVE: 1970
VICTIMS: 4
RACE OF VICTIMS: White
AREA: Palmetto, FL
KILL METHODS: Shooting
RAPE: No
NOTES: All victims were in robberies. Houston died in prison.

Penn Brothers
Penn, William (1941-)
Penn, Thomas Lee (1948-)
YEARS ACTIVE: 1966
VICTIMS: 6
RACE OF VICTIMS: White
AREA: Richmond, VA
KILL METHODS: Shooting
RAPE: Yes
NOTES: All victims were elderly
  people whom they robbed.

Pettis Drug Organization
Pride, Tabius D. (1982 -)
Lewis, Martin (1978 -)
YEARS ACTIVE: 2000-2005
VICTIMS: 6-9
RACE OF VICTIMS: Black,
AREA: Memphis, TN
KILL METHODS: Shooting
RAPE: No
NOTES: As the hit men of a
  large drug ring, they took out
  snitches, non-paying
  customers, and rivals. Pride is
  connected to three to five
  murders, while Lewis is
  connected to three to four, in
  addition to (at least) one which
  they committed together. They
  possibly are connected to
  murders in other states and in
  Mexico for the drug ring.

Revenge Murders
Owens, Sir Mario (1984 -)
Ray, Robert K. (1985 -)
YEARS ACTIVE: 2004-2005
VICTIMS: 3
RACE OF VICTIMS: Black
AREA: Arapahoe County, CO
KILL METHODS: Shooting
RAPE: No

NOTES: Victims were two men and
one woman on separate occasions.

Richmond Spree Killings
Dandridge, Ray Joseph (1979 -)
Gray, Ricky Jovan (1979 -)
YEARS ACTIVE: 2006
VICTIMS: 9
RACE OF VICTIMS: Varied
AREA: Richmond, VA
KILL METHODS: Beating,
suffocation, strangulation, shooting
RAPE: Yes
NOTES: Committed numerous
  robberies and killed a family of
  four in one of the attacks.

St. Aubin Street Massacre
Biggs, Jamal Latiff (1971 -)
Bell, Mark Lamont (1969 -)
YEARS ACTIVE: 1988-1990
VICTIMS: 8
RACE OF VICTIMS: Black
AREA: Detroit, MI
KILL METHODS: Shooting
RAPE: No
NOTES: First murder was the
  execution of six people in a crack
  house, while the second was the
  execution of two people. Both are
  suspected in other murders.

Virginia Killings
Andrews, Joshua Wayne (1982 -)
Crawford, Jamel Saleks (1979 -)
YEARS ACTIVE: 2001-2002
VICTIMS: 3
RACE OF VICTIMS: Varied
AREA: VA
KILL METHODS: Shooting
RAPE: No
NOTES: Shot two more that
survived, they were apprehended in

New York City. The shootings
were all in conjunction with
robberies over a two month span.

Wichita Massacre
Carr, Reginald Dexter (1977 -)
Carr, Jonathan Daniel (1980 -)
YEARS ACTIVE: 2000
VICTIMS: 5
RACE OF VICTIMS: White
AREA: Wichita, KS
KILL METHODS: Shooting
RAPE: Yes
NOTES: Called one of the most
   heinous crimes in Wichita
   history. See page 154-157 for
   more details.

Chapter 10

Black Serial Killer Groups

       In some cases the difference between a group and a street gang is indistinguishable. Therefore, in an attempt to keep things easier to sort, the following are groups that funtioned as a group and less like a street gang. There are some instances in which some of the individual group members might have ties to a street gang or even to the entire group. However, in cases such as the Best Friends Gang, they were a local group that functioned at times like a street gang, and at most other times like an organization. Thus in their case, they fit the description of a group most of the time, leading to their inclusion in this list. For more information on the specifics of their crimes, see the brief descriptions on pages 123-129.

Alabama Axe Murders
Glover, Frank (? -)
Jackson, O'Delle (? -)
Jackson, Pearl (? -)
Johnson, Peyton (? -)
Reed, John (? -)
YEARS ACTIVE: 1919-1923
VICTIMS: 36
RACE OF VICTIMS: Varied
AREA: AL
KILL METHODS: Axe
RAPE: No

Armed Truck
Colston, Roshone (1970 -)
Loot, Kendrick (1972 -)
Millsap, Bruce (1967 -)
YEARS ACTIVE: 1995-1996
VICTIMS: Colston 4, Loot 4,
Millsap 8
RACE OF VICTIMS: White
AREA: Los Angeles, CA

KILL METHODS: Shooting
RAPE: No

Black Mafia
Harvey, Ronald (1940 - 1977)
Barnes, Russell (1949 - 1986)
Christian, Samuel (1940 -)
Rhone, Joseph "JoJo" (1948 -)
YEARS ACTIVE: 1973-1974
VICTIMS: Harvey 9-12, Barnes 3-6,
Christian 3-6, Rhone 2-3
RACE OF VICTIMS: Black
AREA: DC, NJ, PA
KILL METHODS: Shooting
RAPE: No

Best Friends Gang
Brown, Reginald
aka Rockin' Reggie (1966 -)
Brown, Terrance
aka Boogaloo (1969 - 1993)
Brown, Gregory

aka Ghost (1951 - 1986)
Brown, Ezra
aka Wizard (1962 - 1986)
Craft, Nate Boone
aka Grim Reaper (1957 -)
Culbert, Stacey
aka Killing Machine (1969 -)
O'Bryant, Lonnie (? -)
Wilkes, Charles 'Do' (? -)
Williams, Michael (? -)
Hardy, Darryl (?-1986)
Jackson, Patrick
aka Lunchmeat (?-1987)
YEARS ACTIVE: 1980s
VICTIMS: Rockin Reggie 5-7,
Boogaloo 3-11, Ghost 2-10,
Wizard 2-9, Grim Reaper 20-30,
Killing Machine 5-8, O'Bryant
6-9, Wilkes 10-11, Williams 2-6,
Hardy 2-10, Lunchmeat 3-6.
RACE OF VICTIMS: Black
AREA: Detroit, MI
KILL METHODS: Shooting
RAPE: No

Briley Gang
Briley, Linwood E (1955 - 1984)
Briley, James D (1957 - 1984)
Briley, Anthony R (1959 -)
YEARS ACTIVE: 1979
VICTIMS: 12
RACE OF VICTIMS: White
AREA: Richmond, VA
KILL METHODS: Shooting
RAPE: Yes

Bronx Group
McFarlane, Michael (1959 -)
Aikens, Thomas (1960 -)
Jackson, William (1960 -)
YEARS ACTIVE: 1980
VICTIMS: 11
RACE OF VICTIMS: Varied

AREA: Bronx, NY
KILL METHODS: Shooting
RAPE: No

Clifford Jones Drug Organization
YEARS ACTIVE: 1983-1992
VICTIMS: 50-130
RACE OF VICTIMS: Varied
AREA: Detroit, MI
KILL METHODS: Shooting
RAPE: No

DC Hitmen
Perry, Wayne Anthony
aka Silk (1962 -)
Jackson, Michael Anthony (1958 -)
Price, Tyrone LaSalle (1955 -)
YEARS ACTIVE: 1984-1993
VICTIMS: 30-120
RACE OF VICTIMS: Varied
AREA: Washington, DC
KILL METHODS: Shooting
RAPE: No

de Mau Mau Gang
Burse, Nathaniel (1955 - 1979)
Clark, Michael (1957 -)
Jackson, Garland (1956 -)
Moran, Edward (1955 - 1979)
Patry, Darrell (1958 -)
Taylor, Reuben (1956 -)
Taylor, Donald (1957 -)
Wilson, Robert (1960 -)
YEARS ACTIVE: 1978
VICTIMS: 12
RACE OF VICTIMS: White
AREA: Chicago, IL, NB
KILL METHODS: Shooting
RAPE: No

El Rukn
Hawkins, Earl (1955 -)

Bey, Charles E. (1944 - 2011)
Kees, Derrick (1957 -)
YEARS ACTIVE: 1974-1987
VICTIMS: Hawkins 10-15, Bey
4-11, Kees 5-10
RACE OF VICTIMS: Varied
AREA: Chicago, IL
KILL METHODS: Shooting
RAPE: No

Human Five Cult
aka Church of Sacrifice
aka Hand of Five
Barnabet, Clementine (1893 -)
Possible Members:
Barnabet, Tatite (? -)
Wilkins, J.W. (? -)
Harrison, King (? -)
YEARS ACTIVE: 1911-1912
VICTIMS: 49 total for group,
Clementine confessed to killing
19 and being present at 35
murders total. The court
convicting Clementine concluded
the group was responsible for up
to 300 murders over a six year
span.
RACE OF VICTIMS: Black
AREA: LA, TX
KILL METHODS: Axe
RAPE: No

Mall Murders
Hubbard, Vincent (1965 -)
Huber, Marie Eileen (1971 -)
Lewis III, John Irvin (1970 -)
Machua, Robbin M. (1966 -)
YEARS ACTIVE: 1991
VICTIMS: 5
RACE OF VICTIMS: Varied
AREA: Los Angeles, CA
KILL METHODS: Shooting
RAPE: No

Murder, Inc
Gray, Kevin (1971-)
Moore, Rodney L. (1965 -)
YEARS ACTIVE: 1990-1999
VICTIMS: Gray 19-22, Moore 10-12
RACE OF VICTIMS: Varied
AREA: Washington, DC
KILL METHODS: Shooting
RAPE: No

Preacher Crew
Heatley, Clarence
aka Black Hand of Death (1953-)
Cuff, John (1961 -)
YEARS ACTIVE: 1983-1995
VICTIMS: Heatley 3-6, Cuff 10
RACE OF VICTIMS: Black
AREA: New York City, NY
KILL METHODS: Unknown
RAPE: No

Racist Killings
Chaney, Ben (1953 -)
Rutrell, Martin (1955 -)
YEARS ACTIVE: 1970
VICTIMS: 4-5
RACE OF VICTIMS: White
AREA: SC, FL
KILL METHODS: Shooting
RAPE: No

Shakedown Entertainment
Gardner, Shawn Earl (1978 -)
Harris, Shelton Lee "Rock" (1982-)
Martin, Shelly Wayne Weazy (1978-)
Mitchell, Willie Edward (1979-)
YEARS ACTIVE: 2002
VICTIMS: 5
RACE OF VICTIMS: Black
AREA: Baltimore, MD
KILL METHODS: Shooting
RAPE: No

Yahweh Cult
YEARS ACTIVE: 1980-1991
VICTIMS: 23-27
RACE OF VICTIMS: 23 white,
4 black
AREA: Miami, FL
KILL METHODS: Machete,
bludgeoning, stabbing, shooting.
RAPE: No

Zebra Killers
A.K.A. Angel of Death Cult
Cooks, Jesse Lee (1945 -)
Green, Larry Craig (1952 -)
Harris, Anthony (1946 -)
Moore, Manuel L. (1944 -)
Simon, J.C.X. (1946 - 2015)
YEARS ACTIVE: 1973-1974
VICTIMS: 23-270
RACE OF VICTIMS: White
AREA: San Francisco, CA
KILL METHODS: Shooting,
machete
RAPE: No

Chapter 11

Black Serial Kiling Gangs

Each of these groups functioned primarily as a street gang. Many were members of the national gangs like the Bloods or the Crips, but some were locally grown. For a full description of their crimes, refer to pages 133-138.

89 Family Bloods
Johnson, Cleamon Demone
aka Big Evil (1967 -),
Allen, Michael
aka Fat Rat (? -)
Johnson, Timothy
aka Sinister (? - 2007)
YEARS ACTIVE: 1990-1996
VICTIMS: Big Evil 13-20, Fat
Rat 3-20, Sinister 4-20.
RACE OF VICTIMS: Black
AREA: Los Angeles, CA
KILL METHODS: Shooting
RAPE: Yes

Boyle Street Boys
Williams, Vincent (1979 -)
Cooper, Andre (1980 -)
YEARS ACTIVE: 2000-2001
VICTIMS: 3-4
RACE OF VICTIMS: Black
AREA: Chester, PA
KILL METHODS: Shooting
RAPE: No

Cash Money Brothers
Moore, Eric (1974 -)
Hardy, Damion (1974 -)

Meyers, Dwayne (1969 -)
Raheem, Abubakr Abdur (1960 -)
YEARS ACTIVE: 2000-2003
VICTIMS: 4-5
RACE OF VICTIMS: Varied
AREA: Brooklyn, NY
KILL METHODS: Shooting
RAPE: No

Chapel Hill Hoover 5 Deuce Crips
Meekins, Cornet Pokey (1978 -)
Warren, Jamarcus D (1976 -)
YEARS ACTIVE: 2003-2004
VICTIMS: 3-4
RACE OF VICTIMS: Black
AREA: Chapel Hill, TX
KILL METHODS: Shooting
RAPE: No

Small Crips Set
Tatum, Kenneth A (1980 -)
Smith, Damon (1980 -)
YEARS ACTIVE: 1998
VICTIMS: 3
RACE OF VICTIMS: White
AREA: Houston, TX
KILL METHODS: Shooting
RAPE: No

Down Below Gang
Diaz, Edgar (1985 -)
Calloway, Robert (1982 -)
Fort, Emile (1982 -)
Johnson, Don (1986 -)
Rollins, Ricky (1986 -)
YEARS ACTIVE: 2003-2004
VICTIMS: 9-12
RACE OF VICTIMS: Varied
AREA: San Francisco, CA
KILL METHODS: Shooting
RAPE: No

International Robbing Crew
Morris, Edward (1979 -)
Drennon, Carlos Kelsey (1978 -)
Hargrove, Maurice K (1982 -)
Stevens, DaQuan L (1984 -)
YEARS ACTIVE: 2005-2006
VICTIMS: 9-30
RACE OF VICTIMS: Varied
AREA: Atlanta, GA
KILL METHODS: Shooting
RAPE: No

John Doe Gang
Smith, Corey (1972 -)
Stevens, Julius (1974 -)
YEARS ACTIVE: 1995-1998
VICTIMS: Smith 6, Stevens 2-3
RACE OF VICTIMS: Varied
AREA: Miami, FL
KILL METHODS: Shooting
RAPE: No

LA Boys
Johnson, Daryl Reese (? -)
Green, Donald Sly (? -)
YEARS ACTIVE: 1990-1992
VICTIMS: Johnson 7-8, Green 2-3
RACE OF VICTIMS: Black
AREA: Buffalo, NY

KILL METHODS: Shooting
RAPE: No

Lexington Terrace Boys
Moses, Keon (1983 -)
Taylor, Michael Lafayette (1984 -)
YEARS ACTIVE: 1998-2002
VICTIMS: 9-40
RACE OF VICTIMS: Black
AREA: Baltimore, MD
KILL METHODS: Shooting
RAPE: No

M Street Crew
Dorsey, Tommie (1981 -)
Gooch, Larry (1980 -)
Robinson, Jonte (1982 -)
YEARS ACTIVE: 2000-2003
VICTIMS: Dorsey 2-3, Gooch 5-6, Robinson 2-3.
RACE OF VICTIMS: Black
AREA: Washington, DC
KILL METHODS: Shooting
RAPE: No

Newton Street Crew
McCollough, John Warren (1967 -)
Goldston, Anthony M (1963 -)
Hoyle, Mark Derrand (1968 -)
Harris, Mario (? -)
YEARS ACTIVE: 1988-1990
VICTIMS: 8-10
RACE OF VICTIMS: Varied
AREA: Washington, DC
KILL METHODS: Shooting
RAPE: No

Newtowne Gang
Johnson, Cory (1969 -)
Roane, Jr., James H (1966 -)
Tipton, Richard (1970 -)
YEARS ACTIVE: 1992
VICTIMS: 11

RACE OF VICTIMS: Varied
AREA: Richmond, VA
KILL METHODS: Shooting
RAPE: No

Poison Clan
Beckford, Devon Dale (1963 -)
Beckford, Dean Anthony (1967-)
Cazaco, Leonel Romeo (1973 -)
Dennis, Claude Gerald (1967 -)
Thomas, Richard A. (1974 -)
YEARS ACTIVE: 1988-1994
VICTIMS: 6-8
RACE OF VICTIMS: Black
AREA: Richmond, VA
KILL METHODS: Shooting
RAPE: No

Rollin 90's Crips
Payne, Eben (1979 -)
Shakir, Jamal (1973 -)
YEARS ACTIVE: 1994-1997
VICTIMS: 8-13
RACE OF VICTIMS: Varied
AREA: CA, OK, TN
KILL METHODS: Shooting
RAPE: No

Savage Drug Ring
Savage, Kaboni (1975 -)
Northington, Steven (1975 -)
Lewis, Lamont (1977 -)
Merrit, Robert (? -)
YEARS ACTIVE: 1998-2007
VICTIMS: 12-43
RACE OF VICTIMS: Black
AREA: Philadelphia, PA
KILL METHODS: Shooting,
arson
RAPE: No

Terrorist Boyz
Cadet, Benson (1986 -)
Charles, Johnny (1983 -)
Daniel, Max (1987 -)
Flowers, Walkens (1981 -)
Jean-Marie, Frantzy (1982 -)
YEARS ACTIVE: 2002-2003
VICTIMS: 12-15
RACE OF VICTIMS: Varied
AREA: Miami, FL
KILL METHODS: Shooting
RAPE: No

Young Boys, Inc
Jones, Milton David (1956 -)
Butler, James Earl (1962 -)
Canty, Raymond (1972 -)
Holloway, Spencer Tracy (1964 -)
Mallory, Farod (1966 -)
Mitchell, Eugene (1972 -)
Napier, Curtis Kirk McGurk (1965 -)
Obey, Charles Victor (1966 -)
Young, George (1959 -)
YEARS ACTIVE: 1980-1997
VICTIMS: Jones 6-10, Butler 3-5,
Canty 3-6, Holloway 2-4, Mallory 3-
4, Mitchell 5-12, Napier 3-6, Obey 2-
6, Young 3-5
RACE OF VICTIMS: Varied
AREA: Detroit, MI
KILL METHODS: Shooting
RAPE: No

Appendix I

U.S. Serial Killer Rate

As mentioned in Chapter 3, the rate of serial killers in America is relatively low, with only 1 in 1,155,638 people from 1860 to 2000. This can be represented also as 0.000087% of the population. To find these numbers, I first had to make a chart listing the overall number of serial killers for each decade in one column, with the total US population for that decade in the next column. Next, to find the percentage of people who were serial killers, I took the overall number of serial killers for each decade and divided this number by the US population for that decade. To find the rate, I did the exact opposite, dividing the US population for each decade by the number of serial killers.

This corresponds to what the FBI reports tell us, that there are at any given time approximately 50-75 serial killers roaming around, or approximately 200-300 who start each decade. But as with all statistics, these are based off of the available data. As cold cases are solved, and new serial killers appear the data will change. For now this is the best that can be done.

Overall Serial Killer Rates

DECADE	Serial Killers	US Population	Percent	Rate
1860	2	31,443,321	0.000006%	15,721,661
1870	10	38,558,371	0.000026%	3,855,837
1880	9	49,371,340	0.000018%	5,485,704
1890	18	62,979,766	0.000029%	3,498,876
1900	21	76,212,168	0.000028%	3,629,151
1910	25	92,228,496	0.000027%	3,689,140
1920	16	106,021,537	0.000015%	6,626,346
1930	32	123,202,624	0.000026%	3,850,082
1940	32	132,164,569	0.000024%	4,130,143
1950	43	151,325,798	0.000028%	3,519,205
1960	120	179,323,175	0.000067%	1,494,360
1970	385	203,211,926	0.000189%	527,823
1980	491	226,545,805	0.000217%	461,397
1990	420	248,709,873	0.000169%	592,166
2000	236	281,421,906	0.000084%	1,192,466
TOTAL	**1,860**	**2,002,720,675**	**0.000093%**	**1,076,732**

Appendix II

Top Black Serial Killer Cities

Most people assume that the Pacific Northwest is the primary breeding ground for serial killers, but despite this ominous designation, that simply is not true. While the area does have its share, cities with larger metropolitan areas than Seattle and Portland have spawned more serial killers. When discussing black serial killers, this trend holds true as well. Specifically, the large cities with the highest percentage of black populations tend to have the highest number of black serial killers. This stands to reason, because Seattle is largely white and has almost three times as many white serial killers as black. Therefore, to see a predominantly black city like Detroit at the top of the list for black serial killers should be no surprise.

The following list is for serial killers who killed within the metropolitan area of the city listed. For instance, John Floyd Thomas killed in Inglewood, Hollywood, and Pomona, which are all suburbs of Los Angeles. Thus the city name listed represents what is considered as the metropolitan area of that city and is not meant to convey that the murders happened strictly within the city limits. The one exception is with Washington, D.C.: all murders attributed to its tally were within its borders.

Another thing to consider is that the following totals include only killers who murdered just within that metropolitan area, and not those who killed in numerous areas. For instance, Eugene Carl Watts killed in Detroit and Houston and was excluded from the tallies of both cities. Likewise, there are some killers who were active in Washington, D.C., and New York City; they were excluded from both as well.

Here are the top ten cities with the highest number of black serial killers. Others that almost made the cut were New Orleans, LA, Jacksonville, FL, Dallas, TX, and Baltimore, MD.

1. Detroit, MI - 47
2. Los Angeles, CA - 41
3. Chicago, IL - 35
4. Miami, FL - 34
5. Washington, D.C. - 34
6. New York City, NY - 32
7. Atlanta, GA - 28
8. Philadelphia, PA - 25
9. Richmond, VA - 21
10. Houston, TX - 17

For those who are curious, the following states have the highest number of black serial killers who stayed within their borders. Like the last list, if they killed in more than one state, the killers were excluded from the list. The states are listed from highest frequency to lowest.

1. California
2. Florida
3. New York
4. Michigan
5. Texas
6. Illinois
7. Georgia
8. Pennsylvania
9. Virginia
10. Ohio

BIBLIOGRAPHY

Aamodt, Mike, *Serial Killer IQ*, Radford University.
http://maamodt.asp.radford.edu/Serial%20Killer%20Information%20Center/Serial%
20Killer%20IQ.htm

Armstrong, S, *Freud's Hannibal: New Light on Freud's Moses*, Psychoanalytic
Review, 2008, 95:231-257.

Askari, Emilia & Schaefeer, Jim, *Suspect Charged with 2 Slayings- Police say man
Kept Bodies in His Basement, Detroit Free Press*, January 17, 2002.

Associated Press *Axe-Swinging Jake Bird Admits 44 Murders—Police Confirm 11*,
Eugene Register-Guard, January 15, 1948.

— *Bird Rapped by Attorney*, Tri-City Herald, December 8, 1947.

— *Blacks Re-enact Selma-Montgomery Rights March*, Record Journal, April 6,
1981.

— *Dahmer Case Raises Racism Complaints*, Times-Union, February 1, 1992.

— *Dahmer Victim's Family Sues City, Citing Racism*, Star News, September 21,
1991.

— *Davis Charged in Spiller's Slaying*, The Albany Herald, May 5, 1987.

— *Defense Lawyers Claim Racial Bias*, Toledo Blade, April 17, 2002.

— *DNA Tests Could Solve 15 Slayings*, Fort Worth Star-Telegram, May 27, 2005.

— *Family Urges jury to Spare Prince's Life*, times Daily, August 6, 1993.

— *Indiana Man Sentenced to 245 Years in Prison for murders of 3 Women, Rape*,
Fox News, November 4, 2006.

— *Internet Used to Find Man Who is Charged in 2 of 10 Killings*, New York
Times, June 11, 2002.

— *Investigator: Prayer Led to Wallace Confession*, Charlotte Observer, April 4, 1995

— *LA Jury Recommends Death for Twice-Convicted Killer*, USA Today, October 14, 2004.

— *Lawyer Uses Slave Syndrome Defense*, Moscow-Pullman Daily News, May 31, 2004.

— *Leader of Black Yahweh Sect Charged in Murder, Extortion*, Pittsburgh Post-Gazette, November 8, 1990.

— *Lemuel Smith resentences 25-to-Life for Payant Murder*, Schenectady Gazette, March 27, 1985.

— *Mother of Suspect, "Society" Blamed*, Spokane Daily Chronicle, January 11, 1973.

— *Murder Spree Called 'Racist'*, Gadsden Times, July 24, 1991.

— *Residents Arm Themselves as Police Search for Widow Slayer, Kentucky* New Era, April 8, 1987.

— *Ridge Signs Death Warrant*, Pittsburgh Post-Gazette, March 21, 1997.

— *Seattle Woman is Stabbed*, Lewiston Evening Journal, August 14, 1973.

— *Serial Killer's Case Splits Milwaukee*, New Straits Times, August 5, 1991.

— *Sniper's Room Filled with Anger*, Milwaukee Sentinel, January 13, 1973.

— *Sniper Spree is Reminder of Milton Johnson*, The Herald News- Joliet, IL, October 187, 2002

— *Stocking Killer Suspect Lashes Out at Judge*, Waycross Journal Herald, July 29, 1986.
— *Taxi Cab Driver Charged in Serial Killings*, Sarasota Herald-Tribune, June 17, 2003.

— *Three Deaths Were Work of Serial Killer*, Moscow-Pullman Daily News, March 5, 1991.

— *Town Questions Celebrities' Interest in Dragging Death*, Victoria Advocate, June 21, 1998.

— *Williams Appeal Heard*, The Albany Herald, February 11, 1985.

— *Witness: Suspect Doesn't Fit Profile*, Morning Star, December 14, 1996. p. 8b.

— *Yahweh was Former Cult Leader Linked to 23 Killings*, Milwaukee Journal Sentinel, May 11, 2007, page 4.

Atassi, Leila, *Serial Killer Anthony Sowell Requests New Trial*, Argues Juror was Biased from the Start, The Plain Dealer, August 15, 2011.

Bakersfield Californian, *Stanley Williams Deserves to Die for 1979 Murders*, Bakersfield Californian, December 7, 2005.

Berry, Brewton, *Race and Ethnic Relations*, Houghton Mifflin Company, 1951.

Bradley, Alan, *The Benjamin Atkins Story: America's Most Prolific Serial Killer*, Kindle Edition, 2013, 27 pages.

Braun, Bill, *Jury Hears of Suspect's Confession*, Tulsa Word, October 23, 2008.

Britt, Donna, *Racial Naiveté Emerges Amid Attacks*, The Spokesman Review, October, 25, 2002.

Caruso, David B., *Citing Court Ruling, Retarded Man Being Taken Off Death Row*, Beaver County Times, July 4, 2002.

Celona, Larry, *Brooklyn Strangler Admits Killing 5*, New York Post, August 6, 2000.

Chapman, Steve, *Race and the 'Flash Mob' Attacks*, Chicago Tribune, June 8, 2011
Charles, N., *Black serial killers: A rare breed*. Harlem Times, p. 1., November 2, 2002.

Clouse, Thomas and Cuniff, Meghann, *White Supremacist Arrested in MLK Bomb Plot*, Spokesman-Review, March 10, 2011.

Cropper, Carol Marie, Town *Expresses Sadness and Horror Over Slaying*, New York Times, June 11, 1998.

Crook, John, *Showtime Bungles Tense Tale of Atlanta Child Murders*, Times-Union, July 15, 2000.

DeLauter, Lori, *A KILLER CONFESSES: Edward Surratt Admits Quilt in Six Area Slayings*, Beaver County Times, February 24, 2007.

Dennis, Jan, *Accused Serial Killer Gets life in Prison*, Associated Press, Mary 30, 2006.

DuBois, W.E.Burghardt, *The Philadelphia Negro: A Social Study*, University of Philadelphia, 1899.

Ensslin, John C., *Crimes Go To Grave With Dead Murderer*, Rocky Mountain News, November 4, 1996.

Falk, Gerhard, Murder, *An Analysis of It's Forms, Conditions, and Causes*, McFarland & Company, 1990.

Farr, William, *Greenwood Gets 9 Life Terms in Slasher Slayings*, Los Angeles Times, January 19, 1977.

Federal Bureau of Investigation, *Serial Murder: Multi-Disciplinary Perspectives for Investigators*- Produced by the FBI in July 2008.

Firestone, David, *Speakers Stress Healing at Service for Dragging Victim*, New York Times, June 14, 1998.

Fleming, Walter Lynwood, *Civil War and Reconstruction in Alabama*, MacMillan Company, 1905.

Foley Davis, *Lemuel Smith and the Compulsion to Kill: The Forensic Story of a Multiple Personality Serial Killer*, New Leitrim House Publishing, 2003.

Friedberg, Ardy and McMahon Paula, *Murder Suspect Unfit for Trial Psychologist Says*, Sun Sentinel, November 17, 2001.

Foreman, Laura & Mack, Darrell, *The Private War of Mark Essex: How He Killed 7 in Hate Orgy*, Pittsburgh Press, January 14, 1973.

Fox, James Alan; Jack Levin . *Extreme Killing: Understanding Serial and Mass Murder,* Sage Publishers, 2005.

Frosch, Dan, *Colorado Police Link Rise in Violence to Music*, New York Times, September 3, 2007.

Freifeld, Karen, *Tale of Death Suspect says `Robocop' sparked spree,* Newsday, August 6, 1992.

Gado, Mark, *Nightcrawler,* Rosetta Books, 2011, Chapter Four.

Gemperlein, Joyce, *Surratt Gets 200 Years and Life*, Pittsburgh Post-Gazette, October 28, 1978.

Glod, Maria, Va. *Attacks May be Linked to Serial Killer*, The Washington Post, August 9, 2010.

Graman, Kevin, Jesse Jackson: *MLK Bomb Planter 'More Sick than Mean'*, Spokesman Review, February 7, 2011.

Graman, Kevin, *NAACP Leader Coming to Spokane*, Spokesman Review, March 28, 2011.

Guitierrez, Hector, *Groves Gets life in Slaying*, Rocky Mountain News, May 26, 1990.

Hansen, Ronald, J, *Man Charged in 7 Prostitute Deaths—Prosecutor says Suspect in String of Slayings Projected Anger Toward Mom onto His Victims*, The Detroit News, August 40, 2006.

Hare, Robert D., *Without Conscience: The Disturbing Word of the Psychopaths Among Us*, Guilford Press, 1999.

Herbert, Bob, *In America; Judicial Coin Toss*, New York Times, April 3, 1994.

Herrnstein, Richard J., and Murray, Charles, *The Bell Curve*, Simon and Schuster, 1994.

Hickey, Edward, *Serial Murderers and Their Victims*, Wadsworth, 2009.
Hillard, Terry G, & Jurkanin, Thomas Joseph, *Chicago Police: An Inside View-The Story of Superintendent Terry G. Hillard*, Charles C. Thomas Pub., 2005.

Ho, Vanessa, *Northwest No Breeding Ground for Serial Killers, Writer Says*, Seattle-Post, November 6, 2003.

Hoffman, Frederick, *Race Traits and Tendencies of the American Negro*, MacMillan Company, 1896.

Holloway, *Lynette, Of Course There Are Black Serial Killers, The Root*, July 16, 2010

Holmes Ronald M., *Mass Murder in the United States*, Prentice Hall, 2000.

Holmes Ronald M., Holmes Stephen T., *Serial Murder*, Sage Publications, 2009.

Holmes, Steven A., *The Hunt for a Sniper: An Assumption Undone; Many Voice Surprise Arrested Men Are Black*, New York Times, October 25, 2002.

Horowitz, David, *Black Racism: The Hate Crime That Dare not Speak It's Name*, July 16, 2002.

Howard, Amanda; Martin Smith, *River of Blood: Serial Killers and Their Victims*, Universal Publishers, 2004.

Howard, Clark, *Zebra- The True Account of the 179 Days of Terror in San Francisco*, Richard Marck Publishers, 1979.

Innes, Brian, *Serial Killers*, London: Quercus Publishing Plc, 2007.

Isaad, Virginia, *It Happened this Week in L.A. History: The Skid Row Slasher Strikes*, LA Magazine, November 30, 2012.

Jenkins, P. African Americans and serial homicide. In R. Holmes & S. Holmes (Eds.),*Contemporary perspectives on serial murder*, Sage Publications, 1998.

Johnson, Emory R., *The Negro's Progress in Fifty Years*, American Academy of Political and Social Science Vol. XLIX, American Academy of Political and Social Science, 1913.

Johnson, Mary A., *Crime: New Frontier - Jesse Jackson Calls It Top Civil-Rights Issue*, Chicago Sun-Times November 29, 1993.

Kaganski, Serge, *Alfred Hitchcock*. Hazan. 1997.

Kelleher, Michael D., Kelleher C.L. *Murder Most Rare: The Female Serial Killer*, Praeger Press, 1998.

Kiefer, Michael, *Baseline Killer Sentenced to Death*, the Arizona Republic, November 30, 2011.

Kimberley,M., *John Ashcroft and the bloodthirsty actions of a bible quoting prosecutor*. Black Commentator, November 20, 2003.

King, Jonathan, *Remembering the Dead; Obsessed with Justice*, Broward Bulldog, November 20, 2009.

King, Jonathon, *The 15-Year Hunt for a Serial Killer*, South Florida Sun, October 30, 1988.

Kleinfield, N.R., Goode, Erica, *Retracing a Trail: The Sniper Suspects; Serial Killing's Squarest Pegs: Not Solo, White, Psychosexual or Picky*, New York Times, October 28, 2002.

Kotz, Pete, *Why the Media Loves Missing White Women (Hint It's Not Just Due to Race)*, True Crime Report, October 25, 2009.

LaFree, Gary, *Race and Crime trends in the United States 1946-1990*, in *Ethnicity, Race, and Crime* edited by Darnell F. Hawkins, New York Press, 1995, p. 170.

Lambe, Joe, *Lawyers Sum Up Gilyard Case, After Closing Arguments, Judge Says He Will Return Verdicts Thursday in Seven Slayings*, Kansas City Star, March 14, 2007.

Lang, Denise, *A Call to Justice: A New England Town's Fight to Keep a Stone Cold Killer in Jail*, Avon Publishers, 2000.

Lighty, Todd and Kiernan, Louis, *South Side Slayings Defy Myths About Serial Killers*, Chicago Tribune, August 10, 1999.

Malkin, Michelle, *Winona and the Wichita Massacre*, retrieved from www.TownHall.com.

Mansfield, Duncan, *Critics Say Media Ignoring Slaying of Knoxville Couple*, The *Tuscaloosa News*, May 20, 2007.

Mather, Kate and Blankstein, Andrew, *LAPD to Post 'Grim Sleeper' suspect's photos on Facebook and Twitter*, Los Angeles Times, October 18, 2012.

McFadden, Robert, *Ex-Convict Gives Details of Seven West Side Murders*, New York Times, September 15, 1974.

Mcgreal, Chris, *Israelis Elias Abuelazam Appears in US Court Accused of Racist Murders*, The Guardian, August 13, 2010.

Miami Herald, *Townsend Set Free After 22 Years*, The Miami Herald, June 16, 2001.

Milwaukee Journal, *Coalition of Black Elected Officials Calls for Federal-Level Investigation*, Milwaukee Journal, July 30, 1991.

Mitchell, Corey, *Evil Eyes: The Most Insatiable Serial Killer Ever*, Kensington Publishing Corp, 2006.

Mitchell, Kirk, Deceased Serial Killer Linked to Murders of 4 Colorado Women, Denver Post, March 7, 2012.

Moreno, Sylvia, *Stakes High in Murder by Rap Fan*, Dallas Morning News, June 21, 1993.

Morton, RJ, *Serial Murder: Multi-Disciplinary Perspectives for Investigators-*Produced by the FBI in July 2008.

Musick, Phil, 'Atlanta *Child Murders' a Frightening Poor Effort*, Pittsburgh press, February 12, 1985.

Musta Susan D. and Clayton, Tony, I've Been Watching You: The South Louisiana Serial Killer, AuthorHouse, 2006.

Newton, Michael, *Serial Slaughter: What's Behind America's Murder Epidemic?*, Indiana University, 1992.

— *The Encyclopedia of Serial Killers*, Second Edition, Facts on File, 2006.

— *Criminal Investigations: Serial Killers*, Chelsea House, 2008.

Olsen, Jack, *Charmer: The True Story of a Ladies' Man and His Victims*, Avon Books, 1995.

Otken, Charles, *Ills of the South*, G. P. Putnam's Sons, 1894.

O'Boye, McMahon, & Friedberg, *Death Row Prisoner Dies; Now, DNA Test Clears Him*, South Florida Sun, December 15, 2000.

Patel, Tina, Tyrer David, *Race, Crime and Resistance*, SAGE Publications, 2011.

Patrick, Christopher J, *Handbook of Psychopathy*, Guilford Press, 2007.

Peabody, Zanto, *Stories Emerge on Suspect in LA. Serial Killings*, Record-Journal, June 1, 2003.

Port Arthur News, *Sinegal Sentenced to Life in Prison*, Port Arthur News, April 9, 2007.

Prince, Stephen, *Classical Film Violence: Designing and Regulating Brutality in Hollywood*, Rutgers University Press, 2003.

Ressler, Robert K., Douglas, John E., Burgess, Ann W., & Burgess, Allen G., *Crime Classification Manual: A Standard System for Investigating and Classifying Violent Crimes*, Wiley, John & Sons, 2011.

Ressler, Robert K.; Thomas Schachtman, *Whoever Fights Monsters: My Twenty Years Tracking Serial Killers for the FBI*, Macmillan/St. Martin's, 1993.

Romell, Rick, 2 Black Officials Call Dahmer Killings Racist, Milwaukee Sentinel, February 7, 1992.

Rosen, Fred, *Body Dump*, Pinnacle Books, 2002.

Rothrock, Millicent, *Serial Killer Admits to Two More Killings, News & Record*, Greensboro, NC, September 4, 1998.

Rowan, Carl, *Racial Fear Compounds The Horror in Atlanta*, Miami News, March 4,1981.

Schaefer, Jim, *Victim's Kin Upset as Killer Skips Sentencing*, Detroit Free Press, September 24, 2002.

Schechter, Harold, *The Serial Killer Files: The Who, What, Where, How and Why of the World's Most Terrifying Murders*, Random House Publishing, 2003.

Seewer, John, *Jury Recommends death for Ohio Killer*, Boston Globe, August 11, 2011.

Shephard, Joseph, *Stolen Trinkets Led to Catoe's Undoing*, Afro-American Newspaper, September 6, 1941, p. 8.

Siemaszko, Corky, *Death for Drag Suspects? Texas Cops Mull Deal in Probe of Horror Slaying*, New York Daily News, June 11, 1998.

Smith, Leef, *Man Executed by Virginia for 1988 Dale City Slaying*, Washington Post, November 14, 1997.

Spano, John, *Killer is Sentenced to Death*, Los Angeles Times, July 11, 2007.

Spencer, Buffy, *Convicted Serial Killer, Alfred Gaynor, Admits Killing Another Springfield Woman and Leaving her Infant Daughter to Die*, The Republican, December 2, 2008.

Steffgen, Kent H., *The Bondage of the Free*, Vanguard Books, 1966.
Swickard, Joe, *Serial Killer Dies 4 years into 11 Life Sentences*, Detroit Free Press, October 11, 1997

Swint, Jack, *Who Killed...?* Pittsburgh, PA, Rooftop Publishers, 2007
Stone, Alfred Holt, *Studies in the American Race Problem*, Doubleday, Page & Company, 1908.

Sykes, Leonard, *Black Officers Had Warned of Racial Strife at Academy*, The Milwaukee Journal, August 16, 1991.

Time-Life. *Mass Murderers*, Time-Life Books, 1993.

Tithecott, R. *Of men and monsters: Jeffrey Dahmer and the construction of the serial killer.*, The University of Wisconsin Press, 1997.

U.S. Department of Justice, *Capital Punishment, 2010 Statistical Tables, 1977-2010*, page 13. Published December 2011.

— *Homicide Trends in the United States, 1980-2008*, page 13. Published November 2011.

Urbina, Ian and Maag, Christopher, *After Gruesome Find, Anger at Cleveland Police*, New York Times, November 5, 2009.

Veale, Jennifer, *A Family's Shame in Korea*. Time Magazine. April 22, 2007. Retrieved September 16, 2008.

Vogell, Heather and Rankin, Bill, *A Death Case Derailed, Atlanta Journal-Constitution*, September 25, 2007.

Vronsky, Peter, *Serial Killers: The Method and Madness of Monsters*, Berkley Publishing Group, 2004.

Vronsky, Peter, *Female Serial Killers: How and Why Women Become Monsters*, Berkley Publishing Group, 2007.

Wagner, Dennis, *Man Who Confessed to Phoenix Killings Suspect in Oklahoma*, Tucson Citizen, April 15, 2003.

Walsh, Anthony (2005). *African Americans and serial killing in the media: The myth and the reality*. Homicide Studies 9:282.

Walsh, Edward, *Cannibal Killer Beaten in Prison*, Ocala Star Banner, November 29, 1994. First printed in the Washington Post.

Warren, Jenifer and Dolan, Maura, *Death Watch at San Quentin*, Los Angele Times, December 13, 2005.

Warrick, Joe, *Gruesome Crimes Dog City of Brotherly 'Love'*, Schenectady Gazette, August 15, 1987.

Washington, Booker T., *The Story of the Negro: the Rise of the Race From Slavery, Volume 2*, Association Press, 1909.

Wattley, Phillip, *How Red Tape Tied Law's Hands, Freed Harrison*, Chicago Tribune, August 19, 1973.

Weirich, Charles, *Society not to Blame for Death of Essex*, Observer-Reporter, January 18, 1973.

White, T.,Willis, L.,& Smith, L. (). *African Americans grapple with race of sniper suspects: Relief at capture, worry about repercussions*, Baltimore Sun, October 25, 2002.

Wilkinson, Howard, *Alton Coleman Finally Faces Justice*, Cincinnati Enquirer. April 24, 2002.

Williams, A. (2002, October 23). *Hate crime reversed*. www.TownHall.com

Williams, Chuck, *Muscogee County Jail Records Offer Insight into Carlton Gary*. Ledger Enquirer, December 15, 2009.

Williams, Walter E., *Double Standards Fomented by Hypocrisy*, Reading Eagle, January 7, 1990.

Wolcott, Martin Gilman, *The Evil 100*, Kensington Publishing Corp, 2002.

Woodford, Carol, *Showtime Movie Renews Case of Atlanta Child Murders*, Ocala Star-Banner, July 16, 2000.

Index

About the Author

I grew up in the plains of Oklahoma, watching red-tinted dust-devils swirl up into blue skies while listening to the old-timers tell the outlaw tales of old. Partially due to the rich stories of which I was fond, and partially due to my innate curiosity, I have never been able to stop digging up stories and learning about history. This journey has taken me to explore the interconnected paths of history, science, and true crime. The journey has been a rich one, full of surprises around every corner. But whenever I think that I have scaled the peaks of understanding, I realize my journey has just begun.

I have had many people ask what my qualifications are, so, in short, here they are. As for formal university training, I have little to none. As a man who was blessed with a family at a young age, higher education was not a path before me; instead, I was on one to provide for my family. This did not discourage me from learning or from schooling myself (though some may ask if that is even legal!). As a result, I have been collecting college-level textbooks for nearly two decades—from basic ones to upper-level Ph.D. courses, on all topics, including a healthy selection of historical and scientific books. But not wanting to have a cookie-cutter knowledge base that most universities punch out, the bibliophile in me has taken to collect a wealth of books, some new, some ancient, to give me a proper understanding of the subjects that interest me. This has allowed me to paint a much more detailed picture of history, one that does not merely put together random bits and pieces, but rather gives a complete view of all history—not only my own race's history, but the history of all races and cultures.

When exploring the history of the world, it did not take long before my interest in crime transformed from a minor curiosity to a significant part of my studies. The one thing that helped fuel this desire was the steady increase in crime over the past two hundred years in America. At first, I was interested in the causation and in trying to find possible solutions. This soon led me to track trends across different demographics without fear of what politically incorrect implications that might produce. Along the trail, someone asked me why serial killers were always white. This opened up another trail, which eventually led to the publication of this book.

Printed in Great Britain
by Amazon